A RIGHTEOUS SMOKESCREEN

A RIGHTEOUS SMOKESCREEN

POSTWAR AMERICA AND THE POLITICS OF CULTURAL GLOBALIZATION

Sam Lebovic

The University of Chicago Press *Chicago and London*

Publication of this book has been aided by a grant
from the Meijer Foundation Fund.

The University of Chicago Press, Chicago 60637
The University of Chicago Press, Ltd., London

For more information, contact the University of Chicago Press,
1427 E. 60th St., Chicago, IL 60637.
Published 2022
Printed in the United States of America

31 30 29 28 27 26 25 24 23 22   1 2 3 4 5

ISBN-13: 978-0-226-81608-1 (cloth)
ISBN-13: 978-0-226-81609-8 (e-book)
DOI: https://doi.org/10.7208/chicago/9780226816098.001.0001

Library of Congress Cataloging-in-Publication Data

Names: Lebovic, Sam, 1981– author.
Title: A righteous smokescreen : postwar America and the politics of
cultural globalization / Sam Lebovic.
Other titles: Postwar America and the politics of cultural globalization
Description: Chicago : The University of Chicago Press, 2022. |
Includes bibliographical references and index.
Identifiers: LCCN 2021035772 | ISBN 9780226816081 (cloth) |
ISBN 9780226816098 (ebook)
Subjects: LCSH: International travel—Political aspects—United States. |
International travel regulations—Political aspects—United States. |
Reconstruction (1939–1951) | Globalization—History—20th century. |
United States—Relations. | United States—Cultural policy. | United States—
Foreign relations. | United States—History—1945–
Classification: LCC E744.5 .L33 2022 | DDC 327.73—dc23
LC record available at https://lccn.loc.gov/2021035772

♾ This paper meets the requirements of ANSI/NISO Z39.48-1992
(Permanence of Paper).

For Em

CONTENTS

INTRODUCTION

As World War II entered its final months, Archibald MacLeish was contemplating the postwar order. MacLeish was known colloquially as Franklin Delano Roosevelt's "minister for culture," and the erstwhile journalist, poet, and lawyer had recently taken up a new post as US assistant secretary of state. So he was privy to the administration's frenzied planning for the peace, and he was confident that the United States would "have an opportunity at this war's end to build the world we want." But he remained worried that the world had already been transformed by "instantaneous communication and rapid transport," that it had become a "world shrunk and shriveled in size, a smaller world." And so, MacLeish explained to readers of the *New York Times*, "the principal question in the field of foreign relations in our time is this: what will we do with that world? How will we live in it? How will we prevent war and preserve peace?" The title of MacLeish's article revealed his answer: "People Must Speak to People." The "best hope . . . of preparing the climate of understanding in which peace can breathe," MacLeish concluded, was to increase "freedom of communication [and] freedom of exchange of information."[1]

The war had upended the flow of culture around the globe and raised new questions about the ways that citizens of the world would relate to one another in the future. Over the following few years, a wide variety of diplomats, politicians, intellectuals, bureaucrats, lawyers, and journalists would, like MacLeish, place their political hopes in the seemingly mundane exchange of information among people. In the emerging institutions of the young United Nations, they debated the regulation of international air travel and the visa and passport policies that allowed travelers to cross international borders. They wondered about the best ways to reform and improve educational systems that had been destroyed by war or neglected by colonial occupiers. They suggested new ways to encourage the exchange of art and science and culture between nation-states and argued about whether it was possible to improve the quality and quantity of news and information that flowed around the world. Some of these debates produced little more than anger and acrimony; others produced new international institutions. In either case, their discussions had important consequences for the ways in which culture would circulate throughout the postwar world. And when taken together, they reveal that the structures of international communication and connection were being reimagined and remade in the 1940s.

This book is a study of the importance of this neglected juncture. By focusing on the politics of information, it provides a new account of the nature of the postwar order, of the relationship of the United States to the world, and of the trajectory of cultural globalization. These subjects are of more than antiquarian interest. At a moment when pundits ponder the end of "liberal internationalism" and worry about the decline of globalism in an era of rising nationalism and isolationism, it is important to ask how "global" earlier versions of international engagement truly were and how "liberal" or "internationalist" the postwar order actually was.[2] To better understand the present, we can return to another moment when Americans were worried about the political impact of new forms of communication, when they feared the impact of foreign propaganda on their political culture, and when relationships with international institutions were fraught and contentious.

Historians, political scientists, and international relations theorists have long debated what sort of international order the US constructed after World War II and how best to characterize America's role as a global superpower. Was it a grasping empire, a liberal hegemon, a reluctant champion of beleaguered democracy?[3] Whereas most scholars focus on grand problems of geopolitics and international finance to explore these questions, this book focuses instead on visa and passport regulations, the funding for educational exchange and school construction, the purchase of land for embassies, civil aviation agreements, the rights of international correspondents, and other equally pragmatic and practical problems of international relations. Focusing on such quotidian world-ordering clarifies America's vision of world order better than studying institutions such as the UN Security Council, the International Monetary Fund, or the Cold War security apparatus. Those more famous and familiar institutions existed to *repair* problems in the world order. Expanding the exchange of culture and information, however, was intended to create the positive substance of world peace, to produce an international climate that would never descend into crisis. Detailing how cultural globalization was meant to work in practice therefore reveals a great deal about how the postwar order was actually supposed to operate. The mundane politics of information turn out to be deeply intertwined with, and revelatory of, the most consequential problems of international security and economics.

If you asked American politicians what sort of world they were creating in the 1940s, you would have received a simple answer: a liberal order that was defined in large part by a commitment to the free flow of culture around the world. In 1944, both Republicans and Democrats had included calls for global freedom of information in their electoral platforms, and Congress had unanimously expressed its commitment to increasing the international exchange of ideas. "The U.S. believes a concerted effort must be made to break down the barriers to a free flow of information among the nations of the world," Harry Truman announced to the opening session of the UN General Assembly in 1946, "the U.S. therefore attaches great importance to all activities designed to break down barriers to mutual understanding to wider tolerance." Even conservative Cold Warrior John Foster Dulles agreed, confessing, "If I were to be granted one point of foreign policy and no other, I would make it the free flow of information."[4] If ever there was a liberal consensus in postwar American politics, this was probably it.

But what did this abstract commitment to the "free flow of information" mean in practical terms? It soon became apparent that the US was primarily interested in the export of its culture to the world; it was far less interested in importing ideas and culture or in acceding to the limitations of international agreements. When it thought that international institutions and agreements would help open the world to its culture, the United States was willing to work with them—for this reason, it played a role in the creation of a United Nations Educational, Scientific and Cultural Organization in 1945, established programs of educational exchange, and helped draft international treaties on civil aviation, visa and passport policy, and the global exchange of news. But the US remained leery of any interference with its own cultural autonomy. When foreign nations insisted on cultural reciprocity—when they asked that America open up to their travelers, their news, and their airlines, when they suggested that globalization would require some redistribution of resources from the United States to the less wealthy—the US lost interest in multilateralism. Rather, it worked to ensure that international institutions were stillborn or granted only limited powers. And it turned instead to other means to increase the international flow of its culture, such as bilateral negotiations, in which it could bring to bear the full weight of its economic and military might, or unilateral action, such as the creation of a vast propaganda program to pump its culture into the world.

American promotion of the "free flow of information" was guided less by liberal principle than by realist calculations of power—that is, less by benevolent multilateralism than by the canny assessment of cost and benefit and the calculated deployment of the incomparable wealth and strength of the United States in the 1940s. Americans might have called their attitude to global culture "liberal," but they acted like mercantilists—they sought to protect their home market and to expand their international control. They did so for a variety of reasons; policy in the field of international culture emerged, as does all policy, from the intersection of competing interests and impulses. Some who spoke the language of international exchange simply assumed that the United States was the rightful center of the world—as did J. William Fulbright, who imagined that his educational exchange program would cultivate a global cultural elite attuned to US world leadership. Other liberal internationalists found themselves thwarted by political opponents with more nationalistic philosophies. Commitments to international organizations, for instance, were policed by a powerful conservative bloc in Congress, keen to protect both their racial hierarchies and their anti-Communist politics. Hawkish bureaucrats in the visa and passport offices carefully monitored US borders, ensuring that subversive foreigners could not get in and that dissident Americans could not get out. Economic power also structured the politics of cultural exchange. Dominant companies in the culture industries worked with diplomatic and propaganda agencies to improve their export markets; they cared little for the import of foreign content. Obscure bureaucrats in the State Department found ways to sell surplus military equipment to fund new networks of US cultural expansion: the Fulbright educational exchange program, a chain of glittering new embassy buildings scattered across the globe, and a commercial aviation network open to US airlines. Such stories remind us that there was nothing exceptionally liberal about US foreign policy in the 1940s—even in the field of cultural exchange, where we might most expect liberal idealism to shine through, it was deeply shaped by the pursuit of self-interest and structured by the nation's disproportionate power.

The result was a lopsided flow of culture in which the United States disproportionately exported culture to the world. Americanization and globalization became major topics in both academia and the polity—from foreign attacks on "Yankee cultural imperialism" to triumphant embraces of American "soft power" to detailed ethnographies of the ways that American mass culture has been appropriated and remade in foreign contexts. Yet less attention has been paid to the surprising insularity of American culture in the postwar years. In the 1950s, the United States was importing very little culture, and a conservative national security regime was deeply suspicious of international institutions and networks and keen to protect American citizens from "un-American" ideas. The United States had isolated itself from significant forms of international connection at the moment of its rise as a global superpower.

Recognizing these contradictions helps us to appreciate the peculiarities of globalization in the second half of the twentieth century. In the postwar years, Americans tended to presume that the US represented the center of the world, that American values were universal, and that what was good for the United States was good for the world.[5] But Americanization and globalization are not synonymous, and the US was not the only advocate of globalization in the postwar years. In fact, the most robust champions of cultural globalization came from the Global South. At international conferences, representatives from the decolonizing world argued that globalization would require the creation of new networks of exchange—thicker, more varied, and more reciprocal than those contemplated by American champions of "freedom of information."[6] And as civil libertarians and political radicals within the United States challenged McCarthy-era restrictions and sought connections with international movements, they, too, expressed an interest in more reciprocal exchanges. In important ways, US cultural policies were shaped by opposition to these alternative visions of globalization: when US-based radicals sought to create transnational networks in what they called the "Second World" and "Third World," the US state sought to police international travel and exchange; when poorer nations proposed vigorous international institutions that could redistribute cultural flows, the US opposed them. Neither official US cultural policy nor the actually existing institutions of the UN system were the natural endpoints of a teleological drive to cultural globalization; rather, they were the outcome of deeply politicized clashes. By the 1950s, the United States had moved far away from any effort to construct genuinely global flows of information between its citizens and the decolonizing world. Instead, it was constructing what the radical, Black American journalist William Worthy called "righteous smokescreens"—it was pumping propaganda to the world and trying to prevent its citizens from gaining firsthand knowledge of many of the most important parts of the world.[7]

This book puts formal, institutional politics at the center of the story of cultural globalization. In so doing, it is a departure from much of the existing literature on the subject. Broadly speaking, early approaches to the history of global culture centered on the concept of "media imperialism," in which autonomous national cultures were obliterated by the commercial juggernaut of American media industries. This turned out to be an inadequate theory for a number of interrelated reasons: it incorrectly presumed that there existed homogenous, pristine national cultures that could be "invaded" by foreign media; it focused on the political-economic and technological structure of the media industries to the near total exclusion of the lived experience of cultural meaning; and it underemphasized both the diverse ways in which culture is actively interpreted and the importance of creolized, hybrid cultures.[8] For understandable reasons, much recent work has turned toward locally situated studies of particular places, networks, and cultural forms. That is the only way to make sense of the complex and highly variable *impact* of internationally circulating forms of American culture, let alone modern mass culture, and such work has revealed much about how particular cultural formations have been intertwined with structures of power. But zooming in on particular cultural formations has made it harder to grasp some of the broader patterns of globalization, such as the avenues and obstacles to exchange built by legal and political institutions, the uneven opportunities created by the inequalities of political economy, and the surprising insularity of the postwar United States.[9] To better appreciate the political history of particular instances of cultural exchange—to understand why some representations of global culture had such hegemonic power and to understand why dissident groups invested so much in building counterhegemonic networks—it is important to contextualize them within the broader arc of US engagement with the politics of cultural globalization. Thus, this book seeks to both document the uneven landscape of cultural exchanges in the postwar world and show that that landscape was not an inevitable consequence of technologically driven cultural convergence, nor a natural process determined by "free flows of information."[10] Rather, the patterns of cultural globalization were made politically and subject to political contestation.[11]

Understanding the history of that contestation involves focusing on the institutions of diplomacy and policy and law. The action and drama of this book take place almost exclusively within committee meetings and policy working groups nestled in the gray heart of the federal bureaucracy and the beige corridors of international agencies. Uncovering these stories has required fairly old-fashioned research in the archives of these organizations. I have approached the subject in this way out of a conviction that the otherwise obscure decisions of bureaucrats and diplomats, both major and minor, mattered. In the 1940s, as liberal internationalists like Archibald MacLeish contemplated a new world of freely moving information and people, they imagined that they were responding to pressing social problems, that they were acting in the interests of the great mass of humanity to produce a more just and egalitarian world. Yet it is clear that their decisions had real consequences for the people who did not sit—who had never been asked to sit—on their committees. The pressing need to remake a world ravaged by depression, colonialism, and war provided the reasons that those committees existed, as well as the moral stakes against which their actions should be judged.

CHAPTER ONE

THE BIRTH OF UNESCO AND THE LIMITS OF POSTWAR CULTURAL RECONSTRUCTION

World War II devastated schools and universities. Across the conflict's many fronts, teachers were killed and books were burned. Buildings were bombed, occupied, and stripped of resources. In Greece alone, occupying soldiers burned 320,000 school desks for firewood. The University of Naples in Italy was devastated by Allied troops who looted educational material with cavalier abandon: from optical instruments, they took the lenses so they could more easily read the tiny print on wartime airgraph letters; and from the "extensive zoological collection," they took "valuable specimens" that they attached to the hoods of trucks as garish mascots. Meanwhile, entire educational systems were disrupted: the Nazis closed two-thirds of the schools in Czechoslovakia; and in China, whole universities were uprooted and moved inland to avoid Japanese attacks, with students and professors carrying books and equipment on foot.[1]

By the time peace came, the scale of the destruction was overwhelming. In Greece, some 91 percent of the nation's 8,390 schools had been seriously damaged or destroyed. One international observer thought it was "impossible to exaggerate the educational losses." In the Philippines, the losses were larger still, with 8,380 schools totally destroyed and another 3,900 "partially destroyed." Ninety-five percent of the educational infrastructure had disappeared; and damages to schools were estimated to be $113 million (which excluded the forty-eight universities that were destroyed and the eradication of almost all the nation's library holdings). Elsewhere, the same grim statistics piled up: Poland had lost 60 percent of its educational resources; China had suffered damages estimated at $966 million; four out of every five schools in Yugoslavia were damaged or destroyed; Burma had suffered "an almost total loss of books and equipment."[2]

Reconstructing the world's schools was a pressing social problem in the aftermath of the war—one pedagogical pamphlet from the period was entitled, heartbreakingly, "Physical Exercises for Undernourished Children in Cold Classrooms." But it was also a political problem; and the reconstruction of the world's schools could not be disentangled from the reconstruction of the international order. Those concerned with rebuilding bombed-out university buildings or providing students with pencils and paper soon found themselves arguing about much more abstract issues: international governance, global inequality, North-South relations, the future of liberalism. The problem of educational reconstruction thus laid the groundwork for the creation of a new international body dedicated to educational and cultural affairs.[3]

Ultimately this body would be known as the United Nations Educational, Scientific and Cultural Organization (UNESCO). In earlier drafts, however, it had been dubbed the United Nations Educational and Cultural Reconstruction Organization and it had been expected to play a central role in funding and administering the rebuilding and restocking of the world's classrooms. Under US influence, the scope and ambition of the organization changed, and UNESCO emerged as heir to the long-standing efforts to promote the international exchange of culture and information—efforts that had been given new urgency by the traumas of the 1940s. "Since wars begin in the minds of men," declared the new organization's constitution, "it is in the minds of men that the defenses of peace must be constructed." UNESCO thus sought to advance "the mutual knowledge and understanding of peoples," to "promote the free flow of ideas," and to "give fresh impulse to popular education and . . . the spread of culture."[4] For this reason, the birth of UNESCO is normally treated as an expression of the rising tide of global consciousness. And the central role that the United States played in its creation is seen as evidence of its quintessentially liberal and benevolent streak.[5]

However, recalling the origins of UNESCO in the problems of educational reconstruction reveals a more complicated story. As the ambitions of the new organization expanded, the United States insisted that the commitment to a practical program of educational reconstruction should be dropped. This development captured a deeper truth: despite its global ambitions, UNESCO was a weak and resource-poor institution with little capacity to deal with practical problems like war devastation. UNESCO's efforts to promote international understanding thus tended toward abstract idealism.

The establishment of UNESCO in 1945 could have been a significant moment in the history of cultural globalization. Many nations, particularly those devastated by war and colonialism, wanted to create a robust organization with considerable capacity for handling problems like educational rebuilding as well as for engaging in a more fundamental reconstruction of postwar global culture. But the US, in particular, opposed the creation of an organization with the capacity and financial means to redistribute resources. Its attitudes toward UNESCO were ambivalent and parsimonious and led to a weak organization that had to rely on preexisting institutions and networks to promote the flow of information around the world. As a result, UNESCO could not meaningfully challenge the inequalities of global culture. What it produced instead was an uneasy and contradictory form of international order: expressed in powerful, liberal rhetoric but instantiated by thin institutions with limited resources; idealist and universalist in theory but uneven and partial in practice; and multilateral in conception but disproportionately shaped by unilateral American power.

The political history of educational reconstruction and the institutional history of UNESCO began at the same moment. In October 1942, Richard Butler, president of the British Board of Education, and Malcolm Robertson, chairman of the British Council, proposed a meeting of educational ministers from France, Greece, Netherlands, Norway, Poland, and Yugoslavia, all of whom were living in exile in England. In November, they gathered informally to discuss common problems and to make plans for postwar educational programs. Very quickly, the meetings took on a surprisingly formal nature. By the time of their second meeting in January 1943, they were calling themselves the Conference of Allied Ministers of Education (CAME). By the middle of 1943, Australia, Canada, India, Luxembourg, New Zealand, and South Africa had joined the conference, and the United States, China, and the USSR had sent observers.[6]

In its lifetime, CAME focused primarily on the challenges posed by rehabilitating war-ravaged educational systems. Richard Butler, presiding over the first meeting, declared that it would be best to "concentrate on specific and perhaps modest practical issues, rather than to enter on wider discussion of nebulous and ambitious plans which might later prove impracticable"; and in the various commissions and subcommissions that it created, CAME followed through on that suggestion. Surveying foreign governments, it drew up detailed lists of the materials that would be required when peace came. The Basic Scholastic Equipment Commission, for example, developed an inventory of the "standard" requirements needed to educate twenty-five students: 150 pencils; 12 rulers; 5 erasers; 2 boxes of chalk; 100 packets of toilet paper; between 5,000 and 10,000 loose sheets of paper (on this there was disagreement); schools for boys needed a football and a softball; schools for girls could do without the balls but required 10 pairs of knitting needles. Similarly, in sixty-one painstakingly detailed pages, CAME outlined the "first re-equipment needs for one medical school in Czechoslovakia": 25 pounds of asbestos cloth; 367 camel-hair brushes; 264 Bunsen burners; 177 teaching microscopes; 27 dissecting microscopes; 15 research microscopes; and 6,500 light bulbs. Later, some observers would question the accuracy of these catalogs; and there was no doubt that the process, dependent on self-reported "needs" by governments amid the confusion of war, was open to abuse, error, and manipulation. Still, CAME's early inventories shaped expectations and provided the start for UNESCO's postwar *The Book of Needs*, which documented educational shortages around the world. And most importantly, in the slightly surrealist specificity of its inventories, CAME displayed its interest in practical and material problems.[7]

CAME's operational programs likewise revealed a preoccupation with problems of material relief. A Commission on Special Educational Problems in the Liberated Countries was concerned with improvising basic pedagogical strategies amid the shortages and with providing simple pedagogical aids. Maps, for instance, were in incredibly short supply—apparently, they had been a favored target of Axis occupiers—and CAME reached out to Dunlop Tyres to see if it could produce cheap rubber globes for classrooms. (Dunlop could not, perhaps due to rubber shortages.) In the absence of materials, plans were made to improvise: maps could be stitched onto stuffed cloth globes or traced into sandboxes; and lamp black, candle wax, and paraffin could be mixed into a chalk substitute that could be used on glass surfaces. Meanwhile, the Audiovisual Aids Commission screened educational films, negotiated with public broadcasters for rights to educational radio programs, and looked for cheap radios, film projectors, episcopes, and epidiascopes to donate to European classrooms. In September 1944, the Books and Periodicals Commission established the Inter-Allied Book Centre in London's Salisbury Square, which would send donated volumes to liberated nations for restocking their libraries. In its first year, the Centre shipped some 36,395 volumes, received 345,000, and had been pledged many more (wartime transportation shortages were gumming up the works).[8]

In this context, CAME participants expressed repeated hopes that surplus war stock, ranging from surplus scientific equipment to more basic supplies, would provide material support for reconstruction. The politics of war surplus disposal would become a potent symbol of plans for the global reconstruction of culture in the 1940s. CAME's plans were to use the surplus as a central fund for charitable donation, allocating material from a common pool to aid reconstruction on the basis of need.[9]

Despite the practical nature of this program, it was not motivated purely by altruism. CAME members argued explicitly that they were seeking to displace "German domination" of European educational and cultural life—an understandable impulse given the experience of Nazism. But something would have to fill the void, and therein lay an opportunity. British officials apparently imagined that London would become the center of continental culture. The first meeting of CAME saw the British Council extend offers of British aid to the Europeans, as well as access to British schools where they could find models for postwar schooling. This mingling of altruism, anti-Fascism, and opportunism was made most explicit in plans to dislodge German domination of the European market in basic scientific equipment, such as beakers, optical glass, and laboratory porcelain. "It is essential," argued a British representative, "that the countries of Europe should be saved from dependence on German scientific supplies as a way of evading German and possibly Nazi ideas." British manufacturers of scientific equipment agreed. They told CAME that blocking German exports of scientific apparatus was of the "utmost importance in the disarmament of Germany." They were pleased when the British Ministry of Supply and the US State Department organized an Anglo-American Commission to tour the continent, surveying scientific needs and building contacts between European customers and manufacturers back home.[10]

CAME's focus on material relief to the continent was also political and self-interested in another sense: the organization was resolutely Eurocentric in its planning, and the problems of reconstruction in Africa, Asia, and the Middle East went almost entirely undiscussed. On the rare occasion that the latter subject surfaced, CAME participants seem to have imagined that the colonial powers would be responsible for reconstructing the educational systems of their holdings. For example, it was expected that France would fulfill the need for printing machinery in Algiers and that Indonesia would be resupplied by the Dutch. In 1943, a request for assistance from the University of Rangoon, which the Japanese had dynamited and set on fire, was met with a consensus that Rangoon was outside CAME's scope and that its problems should be taken up with the High Commissioner for India. In 1946, while the Anglo-American Commission was already busy reestablishing the European scientific equipment market, W. E. Dyer of Raffles College in Singapore asked CAME for assistance in restocking its "entirely vanished" physics and chemistry labs, but he only received an indifferent shrug. There were shortages, Dyer was informed, everywhere.[11]

Most significantly, this indifference meant that while CAME was developing its detailed accounting of needs and damages, it simply did not conduct surveys in much of the world. Not until 1947 and 1948 were the first surveys of war damage to schools in the Philippines, Burma, or China undertaken. And even then, they were shockingly brief; UNESCO sought to survey the vastness of China in six weeks. As a result, in its first publication of *The Book of Needs* in 1947, UNESCO called its knowledge of needs in the Far East "admittedly inadequate." Although it devoted ten pages to problems in Czechoslovakia, five pages to France, and fifteen pages to Poland, it devoted only one page to the Philippines and two to Burma. And whereas the non-European entries were impressionistic and vague, the sections on Europe, building on earlier CAME studies, were impossibly precise: Yugoslavia needed 14 million pen nibs and 8 million pencils; Italy needed 20 million pieces of chalk; Poland needed 4 million pencils and 6.5 million exercise books.[12]

Despite its disinterest in reconstructing the war-ravaged schools in the Global South, CAME was interested in some broader programs of international cultural and educational cooperation. This was unsurprising, as CAME was the obvious heir to the various programs for international understanding that had emerged between the late nineteenth century and the interwar years, all of which had taken on increased urgency after the rise of Fascism and the outbreak of World War II. Like earlier cultural internationalists, individuals associated with CAME imagined creating global bibliographies and indexes; flirted with the idea of revising history textbooks (or writing new ones) to promote world peace; and hoped that programs to circulate liberal cinema (preferred films: *Bambi* and *Goodbye, Mr. Chips*) would "combat prejudice" in students who had been educated by the Nazis.[13]

Most significant was the proliferation of calls to create a robust successor to the International Bureau of Education, founded in Geneva in 1925 as a private institution, that had remained small, underfunded, and rather marginal even after its transformation into an intergovernmental organization in 1929. In early 1944, CAME appointed a subcommittee to analyze the various plans for a postwar international educational organization that had already been proposed, on both sides of the Atlantic, by a mushrooming of umbrella groups, such as the US Committee on Education Reconstruction; a joint commission of the London International Assembly and the Council on Education in World Citizenship; and an International Education Assembly. In its review, CAME concluded that their "striking resemblances manifest[ed] a remarkable conformity of opinions already formed on the problem under review." The zeitgeist was clearly encouraging CAME to evolve into a permanent and far-reaching educational organization.[14]

Still, despite the increasingly universal and idealistic projects that CAME flirted with in its early years, it always imagined that the first order of business was the grubby problem of postwar reconstruction. Indeed, it is striking that even the most far-reaching proposals for a permanent international educational organization always anticipated that reconstruction would be, at least initially, its primary concern. In April and May 1943, the US Committee on Education Reconstruction, whose name alone revealed its priorities, held conferences to plan both the founding of an international organization to promote the exchange of ideas and teachers, and the provision of facilities, programs, and machinery for educational reconstruction. Also in April, Stanford education professor Grayson Kefauver wrote to Sumner Welles in the State Department to announce that his Liaison Committee for International Education had passed resolutions calling for the creation of an international agency for education, as well as to emphasize the "urgent importance of immediate aid and cooperation for the restoration of educational equipment, facilities and services" in occupied countries. Given the focus on material reconstruction, it was appropriate that in May 1944, after eighteen months of operations, CAME thought it was developing "into something parallel with UNRRA," the United Nations Relief and Rehabilitation Administration.[15]

It was in this context that, in April 1944, the United States came to CAME (the *New York Times* reported that this augured the "creation of UNRRA for Culture"). Throughout 1943, embassy observers had been keeping an eye on CAME's developments, forwarding its minutes back to Washington; in May, the State Department had sent formal observers. By September, when Secretary of State Cordell Hull asked Ambassador John Gilbert Winant what CAME was all about, the response made it clear that to be involved in the organization was to be involved in reconstruction work. "American representation in the conference," Winant reported, "would involve a moral commitment to assist financially in providing books, laboratory and other educational equipment in allied countries which have suffered from enemy action."[16]

But American observers also sensed an important opportunity to make the new organization more globalist—and to wrest control from the Europeans. In October, Harry Gideonse, president of Brooklyn College, had been in London speaking with people interested in international education. "My impression," he reported to the State Department upon his return to the United States, "was emphatically that our contribution in the formative stages was needed in a very urgent way. There was a continental parochialism in the atmosphere that was depressing." A strong American presence, on the other hand, could "widen [the] perspective." Other nations, such as China, Canada, and Australia, began approaching the United States to express dissatisfaction with British dominance and Eurocentrism; planners in the State Department began imagining it could leverage that dissatisfaction to position the United States at the head of a more global organization.[17] As 1943 turned into 1944, American observers in London were putting the point more urgently, writing, "We should enter the conference as quickly as possible if we are to affiliate with it at all, because the longer we stay out the less fluid it will become and the more difficult it will be to secure modifications in its organization or objectives."[18]

A decision was thus made to join CAME and to take the lead in rebuilding the educational and cultural capacities of war-damaged nations. In March, a formal US delegation to CAME was named. It was headed by J. William Fulbright, then serving his first term as a congressman from Arkansas, who had shot to prominence as a leading advocate of internationalism. Fulbright was joined by Ralph Turner of the State Department, who had been observing CAME meetings, and Grayson Kefauver, the Stanford dean who had played such a central role in lobbying for an international educational organization, as well as John Studebaker (US Commissioner of Education) and C. Mildred Thompson (dean of Vassar College). Archibald MacLeish rounded out the delegation. As the delegation was leaving for London, the State Department issued a public statement committing the United States to participation in "an international program for the rebuilding of essential educational and cultural facilities of the war-torn countries in the period immediately following hostilities."[19]

The United States came to London with a missionary zeal to turn what had been a Eurocentric organization into an international one, with the US, of course, in a leadership role. In meetings between the US delegates and CAME officials in April, a constitution was drafted for a United Nations Educational and Cultural Reconstruction Organization.[20]

Afterward, Fulbright cabled the secretary of state to announce that "excellent progress" had been made, that CAME had agreed to the US plans, and that the constitution of the new organization reflected the "main principles of the Department's declaration of policy on educational reconstruction." Kefauver, too, wrote to State Department planners about the surprising extent of the agreement at London, observing that the new draft constitution "was very much along the line of our discussions in Washington." CAME members had agreed to the US plans because, in truth, those plans very much aligned with their own. For CAME members, the key issue was that funds should be forthcoming for reconstruction. If that happened, they could live with the more grandiose American pronouncements about global liberal culture. As Julius Hoste, Belgian undersecretary for education, put it, "We must not only talk things over, but try to come to practical results, and these practical results would have in the world a great appeal for the realisation of the moral proposals as defined by our American friends." Hoste would have been calmed by Ralph Turner's assurances that "there can be no question about the desire of the American government to collaborate in those activities which the conference has initiated, looking forward to providing any aid and assistance which is necessary for the rehabilitation of educational processes in the countries when they are liberated." And he would have been thrilled that the plans for the new UN body included an emergency rehabilitation fund that would be paid into by members and apportioned by a central committee on the basis of need. The idea of the fund had not emerged with the United States, but, as Kefauver explained, the US was happy with it because it would be under the "control of a small committee with large representation by the principal contributor nations." In other words, the committee achieved the US goal of dislodging the European nations from monopolizing the reconstruction program and elevating its own role. (The United States also succeeded in keeping the question of reconstructing enemy education systems off the CAME agenda; it wanted to handle that problem unilaterally.) The Europeans, meanwhile, were happy to bind the US to a program of reconstruction.[21]

So, on April 17, when Fulbright cabled the secretary of state, he was optimistic that all would soon agree to it, and when twenty nations had agreed to it, the UN Educational and Cultural Reconstruction Organization would come into existence. Only twelve hours later, Secretary Hull cabled back to ask Fulbright to slow down. Hull wanted to discuss the plan informally with Congress before it was formally submitted to the United States. Fulbright was instructed to ask that the agreement be circulated to interested governments for preliminary comment before it was sent out for formal approval. Fulbright did so dutifully, although when the Fulbright delegation returned to the US, it urged the State Department to "act immediately" to approve the draft constitution and to request appropriations from Congress for rehabilitation costs.[22]

Hull's stalling tactics reflected deeper ambivalence within the State Department about the proposed organization. In early 1944, the main game was planning for the broader United Nations organization, which was then conceived of as little more than a security council of the great powers. Within the foreign affairs offices of the United Kingdom, the United States, and the Soviet Union, there was no expectation that the United Nations would ultimately feature an array of organizations committed to human rights, culture, and economic and social affairs. In fact, there was considerable hostility to the idea, out of fears that such institutions could both distract from security concerns and undermine state sovereignty. (Franklin Delano Roosevelt, for instance, was focused on the importance of great power policing by the Big Four; even the General Assembly, which he thought would meet maybe once a year to let the smaller nations "blow off steam," was an irrelevancy. The organization wouldn't even need a permanent headquarters, FDR thought, only a "storage warehouse for records—most of them obsolete.") As preparations were made for the Dumbarton Oaks discussions with the United Kingdom, the Soviet Union, and China, the Division of International Security and Organization "applied the brake" to planning for any kind of cultural organization, lest it interfere; a cultural organization could, if needed, be planned after the security organization was established.[23]

Even among the cultural divisions of the State Department there was surprising uncertainty about the educational reconstruction organization. They were worried that it would be hard to get congressional approval for funding. Providing money for multilateral reconstruction had already become controversial. Congressional conservatives were loudly complaining that the UN Relief and Rehabilitation Administration was corrupt, wasteful, and using US dollars to prop up Communist regimes. They were outraged that the United States was providing some two-thirds of the organization's budget. (The reason was simple and had little to do with charity: UNRRA was funded by a 1 percent donation of national income from each nation, and the US income dwarfed that of the other members.) In this context, even those committed to cultural internationalism worried about the politics of a multilateral reconstruction fund. They wanted to wait until Congress had provided funds for a permanent US cultural relations program before going back, cap in hand, to ask for more.[24]

As a result, planning for the UN Educational and Cultural Reconstruction Organization stalled during 1944. The State Department confessed that it "never fully defined its policy with regard to the draft constitution developed in London." For a time, it flirted with dropping plans for a permanent organization in favor of establishing a short-term reconstruction organization, but by September 1944, it became clear to the British that "no formal action regarding the draft constitution can be expected" by the United States, which the British knew was "determined entirely by domestic politics" in the United States. The British, too, dragged their heels, as messages from the United States probing possible revisions to the constitution went unanswered for months, lost in a limbo between the Ministry of Education (which remained keen to pursue matters) and the Foreign Office (which was disinterested, preferring bilateral cultural relations agreements to any international organization).[25]

It was pressure from other, "smaller" powers that put a cultural organization back on the international agenda. At Dumbarton Oaks, it was the Chinese who insisted that the proposed United Nations should promote cultural and educational cooperation. During the first phase of those negotiations, from which China had been excluded, the United States, the United Kingdom, and the USSR focused on the politics of the Security Council and paid little attention to human rights and economic and social issues, let alone questions of culture. But when China joined, they proposed a much more robust United Nations: they were willing to "cede as much of [their] sovereign power as may be required" to protect human rights, they wanted to strengthen international law, and they asked for a statement on the principle of equality of all states and all races. The Big Three were unwilling to concede much to the Chinese—the Soviets refused to even meet with them; Winston Churchill was upset that the Chinese were at the table at all, dismissing them as a "faggot vote on the side of the U.S."; and none of the three wanted to unsettle the fragile agreement they had reached on security by opening discussion on what the chairman of the US delegation, Edward Stettinius, dismissed as the "extremely idealistic" proposals of the Chinese. In the end, the Chinese dropped most of their proposals, settling for adding the promotion of cultural cooperation to the mission of the future United Nations, as well as some loose verbiage about the importance of international law. Gladwyn Jebb of the British Foreign Office thought the concessions "quite harmless."[26]

But by the time of the San Francisco conference, it had become clear that the Big Three could not contain broader demands to turn the United Nations into a more idealistic organization, committed to human rights, racial equality, and the mitigation of economic and social problems. It was pressure from delegates from such nations as Haiti, Egypt, Mexico, Guatemala, India, New Zealand, and Cuba, as well as from the assorted representatives of nongovernment organizations, that expanded the role of the Economic and Social Council (ECOSOC), that ensured the establishment of a Human Rights Commission, and that committed the United Nations, in theory at least, to a program of universal rights enforcement on the basis of racial equality.[27]

A renewed emphasis on culture and education was part of this broader trend, with cultural and educational rights intertwined with demands for independence, self-determination, and equality. In 1943, for instance, a delegation of African newspaper editors, inspired by the Atlantic Charter, called for Africanization of the civil service, a fixed timeline for independence, and reforms to education, health, and social welfare—including the award of four hundred university scholarships annually. When, at San Francisco, the West Indies proposed a new federated state, they asked for a British-American fund to pay for social, educational, and economic development. Amy Jacques Garvey and the United Negro Improvement Association likewise asked the San Francisco conference to issue an African Freedom Charter that would ensure educational, social, spiritual, and moral progress alongside economic and political progress. Meanwhile, an anticolonial meeting in Harlem demanded that all people be guaranteed "the same economic, social, cultural, legal and political rights," and a Pan-African Congress meeting in Manchester called for the "right to education, the right to earn a decent living; the right to express our thoughts and emotions, to adopt and create forms of beauty."[28]

In general, the US delegation was worried about the threat that this more robust agenda posed to US sovereignty and thus worked to insulate the United States from the emerging international rights regime. To limit the scope of any universal guarantee of rights, US delegate John Foster Dulles produced what he called a compromise. Rights could be guaranteed without respect to race, gender, or religion, but only if a clause was added to the United Nations charter that clarified that the new organization had no authority to intervene in domestic matters. If that clause were rejected, threatened Dulles, "we shall be forced to reexamine our attitude toward increases in the economic and social activities of this organization."[29]

This desire to protect domestic prerogatives was particularly pronounced when it came to educational and cultural matters, for any international guarantees on these fronts would provide avenues for international regulation on the most intimate of terrain. When Cuba and Ecuador proposed the creation of a UN Cultural Relations Council with the same standing as ECOSOC, the United States opposed them because such a council would have "authority over educational and cultural matters which would prove unacceptable to this country." US delegate Arthur Vandenberg, for instance, was worried that an international educational organization would provide the Soviets a tool to insert Communist propaganda into American schools. Senator Tom Connally, vice chairman of the delegation, was "opposed to any plan to provide education irrespective of race." Hailing from a segregated and solidly Democratic Texas, Connally was head of the Senate Foreign Relations Committee and thus one of many Southerners to rise to senior committee roles by virtue of the disenfranchisement of Black voters in his electorate. A committed Wilsonian internationalist, Connally was equally committed to preserving racial inequalities at home—he had had a long Senate career blocking antilynching and civil rights bills. Any international expenditure on educational reconstruction, he feared, would undermine the principle that education was a local matter, thus opening the door to both international and, perhaps more worryingly, *federal* intervention in the schools of the Jim Crow South. So although these conservative Americans were willing to give some ground to the Global South and the nongovernmental organizations by conceding that the United Nations could be charged with promoting "solutions to economic, social, health and other problems, including full employment," they drew the line at the idea that there could be any "solutions" to educational and cultural matters. Instead, they only allowed the United Nations to "promote cultural and educational cooperation"—a weaker promise and one safely contained in the realm of international collaboration. To ensure congressional ratification—everyone remembered that the Senate had rejected the League of Nations—those hoping for a more robust organization went along with them.[30]

In this precarious political environment, the State Department decided to revise the draft constitution for the UN Educational and Cultural Reconstruction Organization. "After taking the temperature of Congress," MacLeish explained to the British, it was thought best to remove the emphasis on reconstruction. Tellingly, the word *Reconstruction* was dropped from the title of the new UN Educational and Cultural Organization that was proposed in the spring of 1945. The mission of the organization, too, had changed. The preamble to the 1944 constitution had spoken of the "cold-blooded and considered destruction by the fascist governments of the cultural resources of great parts of the continents of Europe and Asia." The 1945 preamble, by contrast, spoke more abstractly of "advancing the welfare of the peoples of the world, recognizing that cooperation in education, science and scholarship and the furtherance of cultural interchange among the peoples of the world will promote the freedom, the dignity and the well-being of all and therefore assist in the attainment of security and peace." Similarly, whereas five of the six proposed functions of the 1944 organization had been concerned with reconstruction, the six functions of the 1945 constitution made no reference to war damage. They spoke only of abstract liberal goals: "to assist the free flow of ideas and information"; "to encourage . . . the growth of education and culture which give support to international peace and security" and so forth.[31]

In principle, there was nothing objectionable in removing the emphasis on reconstruction. The International Labour Organization actually suggested the same thing to the British, arguing that the old draft was written with 1945 in mind, when it needed to be written for 1960 or 1970. And CAME thought that a more expansive vision of the organization was perfectly in keeping with its priorities. When it circulated the new draft to member states in May 1945, CAME explained that "problems of reconstruction in the educational and cultural field which grow out of the war will naturally be among the chief concerns of this international organization during the first years of its existence" and had "not been specifically referred to in the constitution partly because of the permanent character of the organization which is contemplated, and partly because of uncertainty at this time as to the methods which will be used in the broad field of economic and social reconstruction."[32]

The State Department, however, didn't simply want to remove the emphasis on reconstruction from the constitution. It was now opposed to the very existence of a fund for reconstruction because it thought that it was a "practical certainty that the American Congress would refuse to participate in such a plan." Not only was there the problem that funding for education was controversial in a Congress controlled by Jim Crow Democrats. (Privately, MacLeish worried that Congress would kill the organization, unless it was made very clear that UNESCO was barred from saying that "Mississippi [should] be brought higher in the educational scale.") It was also becoming clear that nations like France and the Netherlands would be able to pay for much of their own reconstruction, and Congress was disinclined to support those nations that still needed reconstruction help, such as Poland or Yugoslavia, because they had "uncertain political futures." Between these intersecting pressures, plans for a robust program for spending had to give way. When the new organization was presented to Congress, State Department representatives emphasized that it had been "completely separated" from any question of expenditure on reconstruction and that it was blocked from acting on domestic matters or interfering with the local autonomy of schools. In such ways did the conservative priorities of US senators ripple up to delimit the growth of a robust international institution.[33]

Other nations reacted to the new American plans with fatalistic resignation. "I do not feel optimistic about our chances of persuading either the Treasury or the US government to put any substantial funds at our disposal for educational rehabilitation," confessed W. R. Richardson of the British Ministry of Education as he got wind of shifting American priorities. He continued, "I am not hopeful that the emergency rehabilitation fund will ever amount to much. In these circumstances, all that we can do, perhaps, is to turn our minds to those things which an international educational organisation could accomplish without large funds." The next month, Brazil, China, and Egypt sent notice that they intended to sign the April 1944 constitution, which would have provided the requisite quorum to bring the UN Educational and Cultural Reconstruction Organization into existence. But with the new US-written constitution, that organization was no longer a live proposition. (The British Foreign Office observed that the discarding of the old draft was "disturbing after all the work which has been put in. . . . I do not envy the U.S. delegate who is coming to tell the United Nations that they can rub out their work and begin all over again.") It was soon decided to hold a new international conference in London in November, where the details for the new UN Educational and Cultural Organization (UNECO) could be finalized. Plans for multilateral reconstruction began to fall by the wayside, as the United States declared its "conviction that aid can best be given by this country by direct assistance rather than by participating in an international fund."[34]

So as the war came to a close in the summer of 1945, CAME's planning for reconstruction was replaced by preparations for the new permanent organization. Important decisions were made—most significantly, UNECO became UNESCO when *Science* was included in its ambit—and administrative details about voting, representation, staffing, and the physical location of the organization were contested (particularly by the French, who were reinvigorated after liberation and seeking to secure a stronger role for their vision of intellectual internationalism; their only real victory was the decision to locate UNESCO's permanent headquarters in Paris). But nothing was done in the field to relieve postwar conditions. On September 12, 1945, Eastern European representatives passed a motion "to place on record afresh . . . [our] serious concern over the slow progress of education reconstruction in the liberated countries."[35]

By the time that delegates from forty-four nations gathered in London in November to formally draft and adopt a UNESCO constitution, there was basic unanimity about almost all of the administrative details. "The only substantial question on which there was a fundamental difference of opinion," reported MacLeish, head of the US delegation, "was the question of the relation of the proposed organization to the work of educational and cultural rehabilitation in countries ravaged by the war." Disputes over the program of rehabilitation were entirely predictable and had been anticipated by the State Department. In September and October, Kefauver had cabled Washington to report that CAME delegates still wanted UNESCO to handle reconstruction. Per his instructions, Kefauver was stonewalling and trying to keep such a program off the agenda for the November conference. But, he argued reasonably, if the United States were going to continue opposing the educational rehabilitation fund, the "importance of some significant action by us in giving direct assistance becomes more pressing, both in meeting the important needs of devastated countries and in avoiding embarrassment of the American position."[36]

But the State Department had developed no such policy by the time of the London conference. Instead, the thirty-person US delegation was briefed that although "every effort has been made by the department to exclude the problem of reconstruction, so far as it might involve large-scale financial assistance, from the agenda . . . the situation is so critical in some countries that . . . it will be impossible to prevent discussion of the reconstruction problem." This position placed the United States, as the "only great power whose educational and cultural facilities were not physically injured by the war," in a tricky position: it could not "well refuse to discuss the problem altogether," but there were no "funds at the disposition of the US government for the rehabilitation of educational and scientific facilities destroyed by the war."[37]

In London, the obvious limitations of this position came to light when representatives from war-devastated nations began calling for reconstruction funds. The setting for the dispute was the Fifth Commission of the Conference, which was devoted to planning the composition, functions, and budget of the interim organization that would operate between the London conference and the formal creation of UNESCO, slated to occur whenever enough nations had ratified its constitution. (The somewhat obscure location of the debate about reconstruction was itself a product of earlier efforts by the United States to sideline the subject.) Now the issue was whether the Interim Commission would devote itself purely to preparatory work for the future operations of UNESCO or whether it would have any institutional capacity to do relief work.

On November 8, Belgian, Chinese, Dutch, Yugoslav, Greek, Czech, and Polish delegates spoke of their urgent needs for relief and argued that these could not wait until UNESCO came into formal existence. Delegates from India and South Africa again raised hopes that war surplus could be used to aid with reconstruction, proposing a common fund in UNESCO that could purchase things like army huts from disposal boards. Dean Thompson of Vassar College, the US delegate to the Fifth Commission, reported to her colleagues that "the emotion in favor of doing something was strong and intense." (After the meeting, Thompson had been approached by the commission's Greek representative, Professor Alex Photiades of CAME, who had said, simply, "you must help.")[38]

Appearing before the Fifth Commission the next day, MacLeish tried to defend the US position, arguing that any interim organization should not be responsible for distributing funds or making loans. But he struggled to explain how reconstruction needs would be met, offering only that educational reconstruction loans could be made under the Bretton Woods Agreement or through the US Export and Import Bank and explaining that the United States preferred to provide aid through UNRRA rather than UNESCO. In fact, the World Bank wouldn't loan a single dollar for educational projects until the 1960s. And the invocation of UNRRA was disingenuous: the US delegation had been briefed that UNRRA had little capacity to do educational work; and out of the same desire to protect local control of education, Congress had specifically prevented UNRRA from expending any American money on educational work. And UNRRA had repeatedly communicated to both CAME and the State Department that its "relationship to educational activities will be indirect and very limited in scope": schools might benefit from general reconstruction programs, but they would not be directly aided; and UNRRA would assist private charities in ordering and distributing educational materials, but it could not pay for them. In fact, a UNRRA representative reiterated this point to the Fifth Commission immediately following MacLeish's speech.[39]

So it was little wonder, as the *New York Times* reported, that MacLeish's explanation "did not entirely satisfy many of the delegates from the formerly Axis-occupied lands." Photiades spoke of the promises of reconstruction funds that Fulbright and the United States had made in 1944 and wondered sarcastically if the US had changed its position. The delegate from the Philippines "gave graphic figures of the educational havoc wrought in the Philippines by the occupation and the battle for the liberation. Manila had been levelled to the ground, the majority of school buildings and libraries destroyed, thousands of teachers killed. The basic material needs were enormous." Thompson, put back on the spot, could only suggest that voluntary organizations would meet these needs, even though US delegates privately confessed that the problem was "too big" for private measures.[40]

The next day, matters reached a head when the Fifth Commission proposed that the Interim Commission should be endowed with the capacity to administer funds for the "realization of immediate tasks of educational reconstruction." The US delegation split on the proposal. Some of the delegates, particularly Thompson and Alexander Meiklejohn, thought that such a fund was appropriate and that the United States "did not have a free field" to determine international policy on the reconstruction of war-damaged nations. Senator James Murray had earlier confessed that "he didn't see how we could stand before the world and defend ourselves if we do nothing"; now he favored the idea of expanding UNRRA's mission into educational work. And George C. Stoddard, commissioner of education for New York, argued that surplus war property could be disposed of to aid reconstruction. If the war had gone on another few months, he pointed out, it would have cost ten times more than this proposed fund.[41]

But MacLeish remained resolutely opposed to any such fund, fearing that it would put congressional approval of UNESCO at risk and "side-track" UNESCO from "its real purpose." (He had a point in that Representative Chester Merrow was on the delegation and shuddered at the proposition that UNRRA's role could be expanded. UNRRA was "doing policy things which he feared.") MacLeish thought of UNESCO's real purpose as a broad commitment to international understanding; he had written the preamble to the new constitution that, in the words of the State Department, "insisted upon the objective of international understanding as the central purpose of the organization and the basic reason for its existence." For MacLeish, the abstraction of these aims only underlined their world-historical significance, and he had opened the first meeting of the US delegation by emphasizing the "crucial importance of [UNESCO's] success if the civilization of our time is to be saved from annihilation." With such convictions, MacLeish was dismissive of the more immediate and practical concerns of war-devastated nations. When Photiades had called out the United States for its retreat from earlier promises of aid, MacLeish had privately fumed that "the Greek" should "grow up": "the matter had gone to a much higher level—a permanent organization to get understanding between nations—the schools of Greece were relatively unimportant."[42]

That night, MacLeish telegrammed Dean Acheson: "Urgently (repeat urgently) need your advice on following development. Strongest appeal has been made by Greece and other war-devastated countries for money aid from or through preparatory commission." Acheson advised MacLeish to stay the course, as the Interim Commission was to be a Preparatory Commission only, and it should not handle funds. If it was necessary to deal with reconstruction, perhaps the Preparatory Commission could serve as an intermediary, providing information on needs to suitable relief organizations "without assuming heavy administrative duties." Although the United States would not provide funds for educational aid, Acheson was, of course, "willing for other people to give their money to UNRRA for distribution for educational relief purposes."[43]

Over the next two days, the Americans met privately with the other delegations to convince them to drop plans for a reconstruction fund. On

November 12, MacLeish reported back to the State Department that these meetings had been successful and that the "U.S. won complete victory on its position with respect to educational and cultural reconstruction." No apparent record of these meetings was kept, so we can't know exactly how the US delegation accomplished this task; but it seems likely that MacLeish argued that any expansive reconstruction program would require clearing the Interim Commission through Congress, which would, at the very least, delay relief action. That, in any case, is what a Polish representative claimed three months later: "We were terrified then because we thought that if nothing was done for six months for certain countries, like Poland for example, it would be a tragic situation."[44]

However it happened, the final instrument establishing the Preparatory Commission reflected US desires. The change of its name from an "Interim" to a "Preparatory" Commission itself emphasized that it was to do little but prepare for the creation of UNESCO.[45] Although the Polish delegation had managed to insist that the Preparatory Commission would "provide without delay for immediate action on urgent needs of educational, scientific, and cultural reconstruction in devastated countries," it was a hollow commitment. Reconstruction was relegated to a technical subcommittee of the new organization; the "action" that the subcommittee was to take was limited to reporting on needs to the Preparatory Commission, which would, if it saw fit, take steps only to report those needs to other "governments, organizations and persons." As the State Department explained, this policy meant that the Preparatory Commission "should not assume relief functions which it could hardly perform without being diverted from its chief business."[46]

On November 16, 1945, exactly three years after the first CAME meeting to consider postwar education problems, delegates to the London conference approved the UNESCO constitution and signed a separate document establishing the Preparatory Commission. To protest the inadequacy of the plans for reconstruction, Poland abstained from signing the instrument establishing the Preparatory Commission, and delegate Bernard Drzewieski delivered what even MacLeish conceded was a "very moving plea" for aid. But, in all, the State Department was pleased with its work. The constitution did not differ from the US draft "in any important principle." And despite "considerable controversy" and the insistence of many other nations, there was no reconstruction fund. "It is probably not too much to say," the State Department concluded, "that it was only the refusal of the Delegation of the United States to accept this view that kept it from being adopted."[47]

After London, the Preparatory Commission lacked the capacity to begin the vast task of reconstruction. It continued the studies of needs, pedagogy, and pedagogical aids begun by CAME, and helped with the distribution of tiny amounts of material donated to help rebuild schools, but it could do little to address the scale of the problems.

At the same time that the Preparatory Commission struggled to scratch together resources, accelerating demobilization was producing an abundance of surplus materials. On July 26, scientist Joseph Needham asked the commission to discuss what he thought of as a "most urgent problem": "every day[,] quantities of scientific material and equipment are being destroyed by being blown up or thrown into the sea, or left rusting in the rain and lost to humanity." The day before, Needham had seen a newspaper report that ten million radio valves were being destroyed in Britain because the market was flooded, and manufacturers would have been forced to close for a year—a phenomenon that also applied to "all kinds of optical, electrical, physical and chemical apparatus, prisms and lenses, radio valves, ammeters, voltmeters, wheatstone bridges, post office boxes" and more. Needham had recently returned from China where, at the National Northwestern University at Chengku, he had witnessed scientists break down war surplus into component parts to rebuild their laboratories. Now he proposed that UNESCO should purchase this material that was otherwise being wasted and ship it to southeastern European countries, China, or other places that were struggling to reconstruct their educational and scientific apparatus.[48]

Needham had a distinctive vision of the politics of educational reconstruction. CAME had wanted a multilateral program of quite material reconstruction, but its vision had been highly Eurocentric. The United States, by contrast, had favored a more universal, global UNESCO, but one that lacked the means to centrally manage reconstruction. Needham now argued that there was a need for a UNESCO with broad ambitions and deep capacity; it should work globally to reconstruct educational capacity.

Needham spoke with considerable authority, for he was the man who had literally put the "S" in UNESCO the previous spring. He had made his name as a biochemist, and by World War II, when he was only forty-one, Needham had collected the academic laurels of a much-older scholar: he had published two widely respected multivolume works on embryology and morphogenesis; earned a lifetime post at Cambridge University; and had been elected as a fellow of the Royal Society. Despite the donnish achievements, Needham was also something of a free spirit—he was a nudist, a socialist, a civil libertarian, a womanizer (and a Morris dancer, a chain-smoker, and much else besides). In 1937, Needham's intellectual and romantic curiosities had been piqued by the arrival at Cambridge of a young Chinese scientist, Lu Gwei-djen, with whom he had soon begun a lifelong affair. (From 1946 to 1957, it was a long-distance affair, because Lu worked for UNESCO in Paris; when Needham's first wife passed away in 1987, he and Lu married.) The affair changed the trajectory of Needham's life. He learned Chinese and became intrigued by the scientific history of China. In 1942, when the British government decided to send aid to Chinese scientists to develop cultural relations and build morale, they chose Needham to head the newly created Sino-British Science Cooperation Office. He spent the next three years in China, traveling thirty thousand miles around the country and arranging for the arrival of scientific supplies cut off by the Japanese blockade: seven tons of scientific apparatus, microfilm copies of British journals, and three thousand books. He also arranged for Chinese scientists to publish one hundred papers in Western journals, assisted in the selection of fellows to study in Britain, and established connections between Chinese and Indian scientists.[49]

Those wartime experiences led Needham to a lifelong interest in the problems of international scientific exchange. His discovery of China's rich scientific legacy, until then unknown in the Anglosphere, led him to ask what has become known as the "Needham question": why had China lost its head start in scientific invention and fallen behind the West after the fifteenth century? And it led him to try to answer that question in the vast *Science and Civilization in China*, the twenty-five-volume, fifteen-thousand-page work that would consume the final fifty years of his life.

In the short term, Needham's experiences shaped his attitudes to UNESCO. In March 1945, in papers that convinced the British and US governments to include science in the mission of the new organization, Needham outlined his vision of a newly reconstructed world of international exchange. The war had revealed the efficiencies of scientific cooperation among the allies, who had shared scientific and technical information for military purposes. The challenge now was to extend such cooperation into peacetime. But doing so would require active promotion and regulation on a global scale. To simply promote the laissez-faire transit of information would not build new networks of exchange; it would limit networks to what Needham called the "bright zone" of Western Europe and the United States, areas that were already dense with exchange possibilities. "It would obviously be absurd," he argued, "for any international funds to be spent encouraging communication between people in the UK and the US, for example, who are quite well able to communicate with each other." Rather than this "parochial theory," Needham wanted to foster exchanges between "scientific men isolated around the periphery"—he wanted, for instance, to help a Venezuelan entomologist communicate with a Chinese entomologist.[50]

His vision of the use of war surplus reflected these priorities. Needham wanted a more rationalized world of exchange, a more globalized scientific community, and he realized that to do so would require redistributing resources from the imperial center to the colonial periphery. At his urging, the Preparatory Commission passed a motion in July 1946 registering its "shock and concern" at the destruction of war surplus that could be used for reconstruction and urging "immediate steps" to rectify the situation. But preliminary efforts to reach out to surplus disposal authorities accomplished little. As we will see, the United States had decided to sell its surplus material, leading to a chaotic period of sales according to the logic of the market, not need. Without coordination by an organization like UNESCO or UNRRA, a French delegate observed ruefully, richer nations "may snap up everything while those who lack the money arrive late and come away empty handed."[51] Amid ongoing shortages, such waste of surplus materials continued to mock those committed to centrally coordinated reconstruction efforts.

Meanwhile, the Preparatory Commission plowed ahead with ever-grander planning for UNESCO. By February 1946, it had already received fifty-three suggestions for potential UNESCO projects: the Danes suggested an international center for the exchange of books; the British Drama League suggested a theatre section to hold annual conferences; the Belgians proposed an international organization for microfilm documentation; Mexico called for an international campaign against illiteracy as well as a textbook on world history to replace Eurocentric texts that "strongly encourage an imperialistic and racial outlook." The proposed UNESCO program, increasingly universal, was stretching and fragmenting. And as the scope of the potential activity increased, the substance of many of the proposals became harder to discern. The program proposed by the United States represented perhaps the most extreme form of this abstract and dematerialized liberalism. It wanted UNESCO to produce an international yearbook on educational subjects; develop bibliographies on education; study educational problems, including "consideration" of illiteracy; promote educational exchange; and, in a vague mouthful of collapsing platitudes, "assume responsibility for promoting international cooperation in order to advance education for international understanding."[52]

All of these projects were clearly worthy in some sense, none were necessarily objectionable, and some, such as the literacy plans, were of considerable importance (in 1948, UNESCO estimated that 60 percent of the world's population was illiterate). But it was becoming hard to see where the funding was going to come from or how UNESCO was going to prioritize its course of action. The Preparatory Commission was simply piling up the proposals to hand off to the First UNESCO General Conference, to be held in Paris in November 1946. By July, when the Preparatory Commission had endorsed 150 different specific projects—making no claims as to whether they were "expedient or practically realizable"—Julian Huxley, its head, was already feeling overwhelmed by the dizzying diversity: "I must confess, it has been rather bewildering, especially for the deputies and myself, who find ourselves jumping from the fine arts to applied science, from social science to architecture, from architecture to rural education, from rural education to literature and philosophy—all in the space of a few hours."[53]

Delegates from war-devastated nations, meanwhile, were becoming increasingly agitated by the lack of relief activity. "We have now been working for two months," complained a Belgian delegate in February, "without accomplishing very much. In my country we have a proverb which says: 'while the corn is growing the horse dies.'" Mr. Protitch from Yugoslavia agreed: "It is three months since we started work and we have seen no results. Reports have been drawn up . . . and I think it is time we get results." Likewise, Dr. Jastroch from Poland agreed: "We are about at the end of three months and we have not moved. I do not want to be a bore, and I do not want to be a modern Jeremiah, but I want to say to you that there are schools in Poland where there are no pencils, no copybooks, no books at all. . . . Could I have an answer to the question how soon will this committee probably begin to work in a tangible way?" Alonzo Myers, who had led calls for a UN educational body when he was head of the US Committee for Educational Reconstruction, was worried that UNESCO was turning into "just another international debating society."[54]

At the end of 1946, UNESCO's first general conference adopted a program that seemed to confirm these fears. It simply approved all of the Preparatory Commission's recommendations, including the development of a UN radio network and the promotion of public libraries; programs to eradicate illiteracy and promote global cultural equality; bibliographic aids and translations of great works; international conferences on pedagogy; the writing of world history; and scientific studies of tropical areas and sociological studies of political tensions and philosophical studies of cultural universalism.

But if the ambitions of UNESCO's planners were apparently limitless, the organization's budget was not. To minimize potential congressional opposition, the United States insisted on miniscule budgets of less than $8 million per year in the 1940s. (In 1947, by contrast, the United States was spending $30 million on unilateral cultural programs, and the United Kingdom was spending $42.5 million.) Divided over so many projects, there simply was not enough money for UNESCO to accomplish a great deal in any one area. It therefore tended to emphasize minimalist, supervisory projects that could piggyback on already existing activities. Although early advocates proclaimed this diversity as evidence of the organization's liberal pluralism, there would soon be a widespread sense of frustration with UNESCO's eclecticism and ineffectiveness. The overall result was that UNESCO played a minor role in the postwar reconstruction of culture.[55]

Take, for instance, the question of educational reconstruction. Given the origins of UNESCO in planning for this work, it is remarkable how little the organization did in the field. At the insistence of representatives from war-ravaged nations, UNESCO did create a small reconstruction program, which spent $883,381 in direct aid between 1947 and 1949. The United States had insisted that the funds for the program remain "limited," which meant, as the Polish head of the program Bernard Drzewieski readily admitted, that it could only make "token" efforts. From surplus war stock, it purchased equipment for fifty workshops that it sent to China, Poland, Czechoslovakia, Greece, and the Philippines; it also bought and redistributed $45,000 worth of 16-millimeter sound projectors, $4,500 worth of microfilm projectors, $90,000 worth of scientific equipment, and $4,500 worth of typewriters. Still, Drzewieski, who had spoken so movingly of the need for material aid at the London conference, thought that even this small amount of activity provided "an answer to the persistent criticism that UNESCO is completely engrossed in purely theoretical work. The emergency reconstruction materials provided by the organisation, tokens though they may be, are nevertheless strong persuasive manifestations of UNESCO's practical usefulness."[56]

Indeed, Drzewieski's reconstruction section spent a far greater portion of its time doing the same sort of indirect relief work that had occupied the Preparatory Commission: sharing information, publicizing relief needs, and stimulating and coordinating the aid work of voluntary organizations. It produced a newsletter on reconstruction, published a *Book of Needs*, and consulted with experts. Some of its work in facilitating private aid work was significant, such as its Book Coupon and Gift Coupon schemes, which created a mechanism to mitigate foreign exchange difficulties, allowing donors and beneficiaries to deal only in their own currencies, with UNESCO acting as intermediary. But in the main, UNESCO simply rode along with private sector activity, providing little effective guidance or structure. The centerpiece of UNESCO's effort to promote voluntary reconstruction activity was a short-lived Temporary International Council on Educational Reconstruction (TICER), whose sole role was to organize discussions and share information among twenty-nine member organizations, many of which were themselves simply loose federations of other organizations, most without much money. TICER accomplished very little: it put out a pamphlet, organized some meetings of experts, and provided advice to the handful of European youth work camps that had been founded by charity organizations to create little communities of international understanding through the inspirational labor of reconstruction. (In Belgium, for instance, young people from ten nations were spending their days leveling a slag heap to turn it into a school playground.) At the end of 1949, in response to severe criticism, TICER created a fact-finding committee to explore its effectiveness. Although the committee conceded that it had "not achieved many concrete results," it concluded that TICER meetings had been worthwhile because they "helped to create the moral atmosphere necessary for the coordination of efforts in the field of international understanding and solidarity" and "provided a platform for the exchange of ideas." That summed up the logic of UNESCO's early years: as efforts to grapple with material problems faltered, the organization doubled down on the lofty idealism of mutual understanding.[57]

The same dynamics were at work in UNESCO's tentative efforts to directly address the inadequacy of educational infrastructure in poorer nations. A more interventionist, redistributionist vision of UNESCO was never jettisoned; too many delegates from the Global South remained convinced of its importance. In 1948, Jaime Torres Bodet became the organization's second director and was committed to raising global educational capacity—he had cut his teeth on a massive literacy campaign in Mexico that taught one million people to read and write. At the London conference in 1945, Bodet had asked whether wealthier nations would help raise the educational levels of the world; now he complained, "The world is waiting while we carry on our discussions. . . . What the masses hope from UNESCO is not fair promises . . . but tangible immediate undertakings which are directly related to the wishes of mankind in general." He was particularly interested in UNESCO's program in Fundamental Education, which he had developed on the Preparatory Commission with China's Kuo Yu-Shuo. The idea was to teach basic literacy in conjunction with agricultural, public health, and economic development initiatives, thus uplifting a community as a whole. Pilot programs were soon proposed for Haiti, China, and East Africa. Nothing ever came of the Chinese or African plans; but in Haiti, a literacy program was launched in the isolated

Marbial Valley, where one in five children died as infants, the soil was badly eroded, and only 15 percent of its thirty-thousand inhabitants were literate. Expectations for the program had been raised by a great deal of publicity, but it soon ran into deep problems. The most important of these was a lack of funding, as the project was supposed to run on only $60,000. Of this miniscule amount, UNESCO had pledged only $13,200; the Haitian government was to match those funds; and the remainder was to be raised via charities like the Rockefeller Foundation. After five years of ongoing difficulties—conditions were much tougher than expected and aid much harder to come by—UNESCO washed its hands of the project, turning it over to the Haitian government. In 1956, anthropologist Alfred Metraux concluded that the program had "had virtually no effect. The conditions of life of the Valley have hardly altered."[58]

The experience had soured UNESCO on field operations, but the desire to do something about educational inequality remained—in 1951, UNESCO decided to refocus on training individuals to run their own programs on the dime of their own organizations. UNESCO proposed establishing six global training centers, hoping that the lion's share of the $20 million needed would be covered by member nations and private foundations. The money never arrived, however, and only two centers were ever created (and they trained not thirty-five hundred individuals, but six hundred). UNESCO abandoned fundamental education as a program in 1958. The next year, when Vittorino Veronese, the director-general, was asked what UNESCO could do to aid educational development in Africa, he could only suggest that African governments send delegates to a conference on adult education being held in Canada.[59]

In contrast to the sputtering, tiny programs of educational aid that UNESCO conducted, unilateral US activity in the field blossomed. American charities played a central role, particularly after a loose affiliation of 160 of them established a Commission for International Educational Reconstruction (CIER) in 1946. By the time it folded in 1949, the commission had spent around $215 million to help rebuild war-devastated schools. The overall figure represents an incredible outpouring of American charitable giving, but one that was made up of countless decisions based on idiosyncratic and highly localized impulses: one Rotary district sent books to Europe, another sent toys to Bavaria; the Northwest region of the American Federation of Soroptimist Clubs raised funds for a scholarship for a Filipino student to study audiovisual aids, while the South Atlantic region purchased a radio receiving set for India, and the Anacortes club placed a keg on a downtown corner to be filled with lead pencils for Greece.[60]

There was no coordination, no central planning, no rationalization of expenditure, no rationing of resources, and no standardized modes of reporting. As CIER itself confessed, it was therefore "difficult to evaluate" the efficacy of its expenditure; in fact, it couldn't even track where most of its money went. But it is clear that American private charity flowed disproportionately to Europe, particularly when compared with the scale of devastation in the non-European world. In 1949, of the $24 million that CIER could trace, 33 percent went to Europe (half of which was split among Greece, France, and Germany); 20 percent went to the Middle East ($5 million of the $5.3 million going to Israel); 20 percent went to Asia (the Philippines receiving only $264,000); and only 1.5 percent, a tiny $360,000, went to Africa. Similarly, Europe was crisscrossed with aid workers: there were 64 organizations working in France; 51 in the Netherlands; 45 in Czechoslovakia; 28 in Norway; and 41 each in Poland and Hungary. But there were only 26 organizations doing work in the Philippines; 6 in Burma; 3 in Indonesia; and 4 in Ethiopia.[61] And although there was an urgent need for scientific equipment and audiovisual aids, CIER had to admit its "dismay" in finding some of its lowest giving in these priority areas—less than 1 percent of the spending it could track. The problem was that this equipment was hard to source and did not "make convenient gift packages." As the head of CIER, Harold J. Snyder, understood very clearly, these were the sorts of "weaknesses inherent in a decentralized operation, dependent upon work by and through scores of organizations." As a result, there were "big gaps . . . [where] no organization can be found to render certain needed services or to aid particular neglected countries."[62]

Relying on private organizations for educational reconstruction inevitably meant abandoning any hopes for a rationalized distribution of resources. Americans understandably gave to causes to which they felt some connection, whether that was based on ethnic, religious, or political sympathies, their familiarity with parts of the world, or their more quotidian assumptions about foreign needs. It was easy, for instance, for Junior Red Cross to develop "quite a program for candy" alongside their educational aid; candy was easy to package, and kids liked to give it. And perhaps more familiar with Europe than Asia, American families sent French children thirty thousand packages of candy, Dutch children twenty-five thousand packages, but Filipino children only one thousand packages. It all depended entirely on a culture of charitable giving; it was always possible for individuals to simply decline to participate. (In 1947, Henry Luce rebuffed as too expensive a request that Time Life donate art reproductions to be used as audiovisual aids in postwar classrooms.) By the late 1940s, charitable giving began to dry up. As early as 1947, CIER was worried that "general postwar apathy" was interfering with its fund-raising efforts, and in the middle of 1949, it dissolved. At the same time, UNESCO's reconstruction section began to observe that although complete reconstruction of schools was still years away, it was having increased difficulties in raising funds. "To many people," it concluded, "the days of international relief were virtually past as soon as they stopped being excited about having won the war."[63]

Meanwhile, a more sustained and holistic program of educational reconstruction was being run in Germany and Japan, which were occupied by US military authorities. In the defeated Axis nations, the United States viewed educational reconstruction as essential to the broader goals of the occupations. "German education shall be so controlled as completely to eliminate Nazi and Militarist doctrines and to make possible the successful development of democratic ideas," announced the Potsdam Declaration. Added one journalist, "The goal, of course, is to rebuild the German educational system from the boiler room up." In Germany, the authorities worked rapidly to reopen schools. Nazi teachers were purged. In just two and a half months, five million new textbooks were printed, some of them based on old Weimar texts found in libraries in the United States and the United Kingdom. By October 1945, the schools were open, even in bombed Berlin, and the occupiers turned their minds to broader reforms. New textbooks were written—some six hundred new titles in Germany by 1949—and the training of teachers was reformed. And yet more ambitious plans were made to reorganize the entire educational systems of both countries along American lines; in Japan, for instance, reformers hoped to replace the character-based Kanji script with a phonetic system, Romaji, to make learning easier and to allow for the easier "transmission of knowledge and ideas in the interest of better world understanding." Even though these more wild-eyed plans ultimately sputtered out, the period of the occupation nevertheless saw a serious injection of US money in support of educational reconstruction. Students and teachers were brought to the United States on educational exchange, money from both the US government and the Ford Foundations helped support the new Free University in Berlin (est. 1948), and Douglas MacArthur helped raise private funds for a new International Christian University in Japan. At a time when the entire UNESCO budget was $8 million, General Lucius Clay was spending $16.5 million on German reeducation.[64]

It is impossible to know what the impact of a more robust and centralized program for global educational reconstruction might have been. Redirecting aid to all the places where it was urgently needed would have required a more centralized apparatus. Without that apparatus, the funding of educational reconstruction ended up blending back into a variety of discrete national projects of school building and international development, each dependent on local funding, each with their own politics and tempo.

The trajectory of educational reconstruction captured the marginalization of UNESCO from the main currents of cultural reconstruction, particularly when compared to the disproportionate role of unilateral US power. The same dynamics were at play in highly significant debates about the international circulation of scientific information. The big question in that field was the regulation of atomic information. As UNESCO was being created in London in the fall of 1945, the US polity was simultaneously debating how to regulate atomic energy. A first draft of an atomic energy bill, written by the War Department, had been introduced to Congress with the intent of maintaining both military control over, and high levels of secrecy around, the bomb. It was controversial—particularly among scientists—and was quickly replaced by a bill proposing the establishment of civilian control. But the new law retained the emphasis on maintaining unilateral US control over knowledge of atomic energy. Many scientists thought that it was more important to share such information with potential rivals overseas. Influenced by the long history of scientific internationalism, they favored "the full dissemination of fundamental information of science in all fields." They knew, too, that there was no real "secret" about the bomb to be kept; the science was common knowledge, and once the United States had demonstrated that atomic bombs were feasible, it was just a matter of throwing sufficient resources at engineering, logistics, and delivery problems until you could produce them. (In 1945, when the military thought that the United States could maintain an atomic monopoly for two decades, scientists accurately predicted that the Soviets were only three to five years away from developing a bomb.) Scientists therefore concluded that international acrimony was the only possible outcome of a quixotic desire to monopolize atomic information and so thought it better to try to reap the political benefits that might flow from sharing such information through the United Nations. As Katharine Way, who had worked on the Manhattan Project, put it in the title of a 1946 book on the subject, it was a choice between *One World or None.*[65]

Congressional representatives drafting the new Atomic Energy Act saw things differently. Amid fears of Soviet atomic espionage—the Ottawa spy ring became public in early 1946—they were insistent on keeping information about atomic energy within the bureaucracy of the US security state. "Complete secrecy should be maintained regarding the atomic bomb," proclaimed Tom Connally, who played a central role in drafting an act that ultimately declared that all information about atomic energy was to be classified and that made it treasonous, and punishable by death, to transfer atomic information abroad. Connally was joined by his fellow-delegate to the San Francisco conference, Arthur Vandenberg, who made plain the unilateral rejection of scientific internationalism that was involved; Vandenberg thought that "an 'exchange' of scientists and scientific information [w]as sheer appeasement." Watching this nationalist backlash against the international exchange of scientific information, MacLeish feared that Congress was "junking UNESCO before we have even joined it." By rights, he argued in an angry letter to Acheson at the end of 1945, UNESCO should be handling atomic information: "You can't divorce nuclear physics from the rest of science. Moreover, any attempt to do so would be understood as a vote of no confidence by our government in an organization which it has played an active part in creating." But it was to no avail. In May 1946, having been assured that UNESCO would "have nothing to do with the dissemination of knowledge in connection with atomic energy," Congress joined UNESCO only when it added a clause clarifying that doing so did not require or authorize the "disclosure of any information or knowledge" that was prohibited by law, such as the Atomic Energy Act it would pass two months later or the Export Control Act of 1949, which barred the exporting of technical data that might threaten US national security. Representative Edith Nourse Rogers of Massachusetts liked the clause because it "would prevent our scientific secrets from being given away."[66]

And so international flows of scientific information in the wake of World War II were determined much more by nationalist priorities than multilateral governance. In defeated Germany, for example, occupying governments raced to extract scientific and technical information as a form of intellectual war booty. On August 25, 1945, Harry Truman signed an executive order to obtain "scientific and industrial information" from the enemy. The Commerce Department and War Department sent thousands of scientists, industrialists, and engineers to Germany, where they took copies of drawings, patents, and plans from industrial firms and detained and interrogated Germans with specialized knowledge; as a draft press release put it in 1946, the US was using "vacuum cleaner methods to acquire all the technical and scientific information the Germans have." (Because the entire project was declared classified, the statement was never released.) Meanwhile, Operation Overcast and Project Paperclip recruited hundreds of German scientists to the United States, many of them ex-Nazis who should have been denied US visas but who were carefully shepherded through the obstacles posed by US immigration law. This was all a boon to postwar American science. Just the intellectual assets seized from the underground V-2 factory near Nordhausen, which was built and staffed by slave labor from the nearby Dora concentration camp, were by themselves conservatively estimated to be worth hundreds of millions of dollars. These projects included scientists who would go on to play a central role in building the rockets that would take the United States to space. Similarly, US occupation authorities in Japan provided members of Unit 731 of the Japanese Imperial Army immunity from war crimes prosecutions in exchange for access to the data they had gleaned from their ghastly and inhuman experiments, including vivisections given without anesthetic, deliberate exposure to the plague and other bacteriological weapons, and tests of the limits of human exposure to cold and tolerance of extreme variations in air pressure. As one official put it, the information was "of such importance to national security as to far outweigh the value accruing from 'war crimes' prosecution." Compared to such hard-nosed, well-funded, and secretive decisions to annex science to the national interest, UNESCO's bargain-basement scientific programs—the creation of Scientific Cooperation Centers in Jakarta, New Delhi, Cairo and Montevideo; the hosting of expert panels to help popularize science—were, whatever their merits, inconsequential to the flow of information in the Cold War and inadequate to the task of building a more peaceful world.[67]

The shortcomings of UNESCO's capacity to manage problems like scientific exchange or educational reconstruction did not undermine its ostensible universalism or idealism. In fact, the idealist universalism of UNESCO's early years was, in important ways, purchased at the cost of any practical capacity to take control of these issues. The history of UNESCO and educational reconstruction thus provides a useful vantage point from which to reconsider the politics of world-ordering in the 1940s, particularly the role of the United States in delimiting the scope of the period's new international institutions. The story illustrates the ways in which the US worked to marginalize more radical, redistributionist visions of global order. It did so by leveraging its economic and political clout to redirect the development of the new institutions. It did not have to publicly oppose redistributionist visions and it never purged them from the organization—rather, it undermined them behind closed doors, starved them of resources, and buried them amid a plurality of other programs. It then proceeded to act unilaterally to restructure the flow of international culture and information in ways more in keeping with US interests.

The US had nevertheless helped bring into being an organization at least nominally devoted to the global flow of information and so continued to assert that this was a liberal act of world-historical significance. When promoting the organization in 1946, the State Department reached for a celestial metaphor. "UNESCO is to be a star of first magnitude in the new world constellation of the United Nations," it claimed. "It will also be a sun around which a system of great world associations both public and private will cluster, shedding and receiving both light and warmth."[68] However unintentionally, the image captured an uncomfortable truth: UNESCO now belonged to the heavens, where it represented grand ideals and provided warmth and light to existing networks of power. It existed, as Needham had feared, in the "bright zone" of exchange. For most of the world, however, it was a distant star, little involved in concrete programs such as the difficult business of rebuilding war-ravaged schools.

CHAPTER TWO

AIRPLANES, EMBASSIES, AND EDUCATIONAL EXCHANGE (OR, THE FRUIT OF WAR JUNK)

In 1944, J. William Fulbright returned from the Conference of Allied Ministers of Education to run, successfully, for the US Senate. From his new perch, Fulbright continued to advocate a broadly internationalist vision. In "this modern world of instantaneous communication and swift transportation," he said, "isolation is a figment of the imagination." He was a committed free trader, helping to shepherd the Anglo-American Financial Agreement through the Senate (to the benefit of the many soy, poultry, and cotton exporters among his Arkansan constituents). He believed, too, that some measure of sovereignty had to be given up in favor of genuine international governance—he opposed the veto power held by members of the Security Council and favored the international control of atomic weapons. But despite his deep engagement with such geopolitical and economic issues, Fulbright continually returned to questions of education. The day-to-day politics of learning, he thought, was the true key to world peace. "I know people think of education as a dull subject," he explained in 1944: "It's got no glamour, on the surface at any rate . . . [, but] the world in 2,000 years has found no ways to prevent wars. I believe the real solution is education of the people. Let there be understanding between the nations of each other and each other's problems and the causes of quarrels disappear."[1]

The challenge was to find new ways to educate people. A month after the end of the war, Fulbright took the lead in creating an educational exchange scheme that would bring foreigners to the United States and allow American students to study abroad. Today, the Fulbright Program is perhaps the world's most famous international exchange program; it boasts more than 370,000 alumni, and "Fulbright" has entered the dictionary as a noun meaning educational exchange. Given the program's contemporary reputation, and because it was created by a leading liberal internationalist (now remembered particularly for his Vietnam-era dissent), it is tempting to think of the creation of the Fulbright Program as simple and powerful evidence of a benevolent streak in US postwar policy. Historian Arnold Toynbee, for instance, has described the program as "one of the really generous and imaginative things that have been done in the world since World War II."[2]

But a closer examination of the origins of the Fulbright Program reveals a more complex, and more interesting, story about the US vision of international order in the 1940s. That Senator Fulbright would be drawn to an international exchange program in the wake of World War II was unsurprising. He had recently returned from the Conference of Allied Ministers of Education (CAME), had served briefly as president of the University of Arkansas, and both his life and his internationalist philosophy had been shaped profoundly by a Rhodes Scholarship in his early twenties.[3]

More surprising, and more significant, was the specific plan Fulbright developed to fund the exchange program: it would be paid for by the sale of vast amounts of surplus US war materiel that had been left scattered around the world at the end of the conflict. More than $10 billion worth of all sorts of noncombat materiel—aspirin, typewriter ribbons, locomotives, lighter fluid, silica gel, canned food, portable bridges, ball bearings, candy, tents, trucks, and dentures—were lumped overseas, costing money to guard and deteriorating in the elements. Fulbright would transform this problematic material excess into an asset. The Fulbright Program, in other words, was less an act of simple generosity than, as one newspaper columnist put it in 1946, "an ingenious piece of higher mathematics . . . [that] found a way to finance out of the sale of war junk a world-wide system of American scholarships."[4]

In fact, the legislation that created the Fulbright Program did much more than that. The State Department used Fulbright's revisions to the Surplus Property Act to trade war surplus for a wide range of new benefits. As foreign nations hungrily purchased war surplus to alleviate postwar shortages, the State Department received in return promises that foreign nations would pay for educational exchanges with the United States, but also the purchase and construction of a new network of embassies. And the exchange of surplus airfields and air equipment also helped the United States negotiate agreements that facilitated the postwar hegemony of US commercial airlines. These new cultural networks each appeared, superficially, to represent a new commitment to US liberal internationalism; each favored the movement of culture, expressed through metaphors of transparency, circulation, and exchange. But the origins of these networks in the lumped mass of surplus war materiel reveals the disproportionate role that US power played in shaping them. Each sought, in their own ways, to constitute the United States as the center of the emerging international order; each was molded to facilitate US dominance; and each was geared more to the export of American culture than to genuine international exchange. The ability of the United States to accomplish all this was created by its uniquely powerful economic status, as manifested by the mass of surplus war materiel. Fulbright's bill provided the lever to convert that economic status into cultural power.

Exactly how and when Fulbright hit upon this idea remains something of a mystery. The standard account identifies the key moment as happening at a quintessentially Washington, DC, garden party on September 26, 1945, when Fulbright was hobnobbing with government officials and journalists and the subject of war surplus apparently came up.[5] The problem with this story is that Fulbright had announced the scheme four days earlier, at a planning conference for the United Nations Educational, Scientific, and Cultural Organization.[6] That connection to UNESCO is telling, for Fulbright must have heard the conversations swirling around CAME that imagined using surplus war materiel for educational reconstruction—it cannot be an accident that he continued to connect the question of surplus disposal to the politics of education upon his return to the United States.

In any event, the juxtaposition between CAME's imagined use of the surplus and the actual history of the surplus disposal is instructive. UNESCO planners had thought that part of the surplus could be redistributed multilaterally to reconstruct the world's schools. But the State Department exchanged the surplus much more strategically, creating a circuitry of global exchange centered on the US and new vectors for the expansion of American culture (as well as a not inconsiderable sum of money). It is one of the remarkable, forgotten stories of the postwar moment.

When the atomic bombings of Hiroshima and Nagasaki brought the war to a rapid conclusion in August 1945, it surprised even those responsible for managing the US military's formidable logistical networks. "The termination of the Japanese war," reflected Admiral Cotter, vice chief of the Materiel Division of the US Navy, "occurred at a time when the Navy was feverishly assembling logistical supplies in sizeable quantities for the impending invasion of the Japanese mainland." "The surrender hit us quickly," confessed one brigadier general in the Pacific theater, "and all plans had to be changed." Unsurprisingly, as the director of War Mobilization and Reconversion put it, "there was an inevitable period of confusion."[7]

It was as if the music had stopped in a globe-circling game of musical chairs. On August 15, all ships east of the Panama Canal turned around and brought their cargoes to the United States. All to the west continued on to their original destinations, piling their loads on top of the vast quantities of materiel that had already been assembled. The results were chaotic. Combat-worn materiel was mixed with new supplies; in Japan, a shipload of unnecessary materiel had to be unloaded to get to the theater's supply of dental equipment, stowed, unhelpfully, at the bottom of the hull. US military personnel in Africa, already hurriedly packing to speed their withdrawal, became so eager to return home that they cut even more corners—materiel was "crammed indifferently into crates . . . [and] stacked in complete confusion in the warehouse." Once the materiel was assembled in "huge solid piles of ill-assorted crates and cases," confessed the despondent colonel responsible for the mess, they had "no notion" of what they contained—there was no meaningful inventory. The situation was no better in Manila, where one administrator complained that the surplus was in "unsorted mounds indoors and out." During a fact-finding congressional tour in early 1946, Senator James Tunnell complained, "What is disturbing to me is that we can't get any idea what is here."[8]

If the particulars were murky, there was no missing the scale of the surplus. Everywhere, masses of materiel were creating problems. In India alone, more than half a billion dollars' worth of surplus was stored in the open: 1,700 mules and 1,400 horses were stuck outside New Delhi, eating more than their value in feed and dying off in the unfavorable climate; 5,500 Dodge trucks were still in their crates outside Calcutta. In Iran, 1,700 rail cars, several fleets of trucks, 20,000 car tires, and a quarter of a million dollars' worth of grain needed disposal. There were 300,000 tons of materiel in New Hebrides and the Solomon Islands; and the Chemical Warfare Technical Service on Saipan needed to dispose of 1.3 million eye shields, 6 million containers of decontaminating agent, and 100,000 tubes of protective ointment. The surplus was a most tangible expression of US economic abundance.[9]

But what to do with all of this materiel? Given the cross-cutting pressures at work, it was difficult to find an obvious solution. In late 1945 and early 1946, congressional representatives toured the surplus to see if building materials and automobiles could be brought home to ameliorate domestic shortages (they also took a very close look at what turned out to be false rumors that some materiel was being wantonly destroyed).

But bringing the materiel home made little practical sense, and domestic producers were not keen to see their markets flooded. Selling the materiel abroad seemed more logical, but that, too, was deeply complicated. Foreign nations, bankrupted by the war, had few US dollars, and given the consequences of the post–World War I debt deals, sales for credit or foreign currency were not considered particularly appealing. Finding foreign buyers, then, threatened to soak up the few dollars circulating in the global economy, thus harming US exports. (One frustrated disposal official in Thailand experienced firsthand how little currency there was when he was offered his own travelers' checks as payment for surplus material.) And while selling to American firms abroad made some sense to administrators, it was hard to find takers among American manufacturers—in New Caledonia, they tried to sell surplus cigarettes to their manufacturers so they could avoid flooding the market with old, potentially damaged products, but the companies weren't interested. Trying to work out the best way to help the US economy in the midst of all of this led one operative in Malaya to throw up his hands: "I realize," he concluded, "the difficulty of exactly defining 'national interest' and where it begins and ends."[10]

The longer the disposal dragged on, the worse things got. Efforts to sort the materiel to bring to the United States or to find foreign buyers slowed demobilization, and the cost of maintaining guards ate into any value to be realized from the surplus. "If we could get rid of our supplies tomorrow," complained Major General T. A. Terry in India, "the men could go." In Shanghai, "elaborate defense works" had to be constructed to secure the surplus—high walls, block houses, roving lights, and barbed wire barricades. Even so, there were "numerous exchanges of gunfire between guards and marauders." Desperate postwar conditions meant that much of the surplus war materiel ended up on the black market anyway. In the ravaged Philippines, storage facilities were repeatedly raided, women wore dresses made from stolen parachute silk, and stolen jeeps were repainted and resold.[11]

More troubling still were the impacts of time and environmental exposure. After monsoon season in India, canned goods began to bulge. Thousands of tons of surplus potatoes in New Zealand began to rot and were dumped at sea. Admiral Wellings thought that mechanical equipment on Pacific beaches was losing up to a quarter of its value each month as it sat on beaches and in jungles, exposed to heavy rains, salt spray, and high humidity. "Unless you are familiar with the jungle," he explained to a congressional committee, "words cannot express how rapidly this material deteriorates." Trucks and tents lasted only months on Pacific islands before they corroded or rotted, added his colleague General Marston: "You may have a box of shoes that you haven't even opened where the box appears solid, when you get in to take the shoes out and the shoes haven't been worn, you can pull the shoe to pieces in your fingers. . . . The mildew, the sun, the rain, the tropic rot, the corrosion and the rust from salt spray are enemies working all the time. They did not stop on V-J day."[12]

In October 1945, H. Wendell Endicott, responsible for surplus disposal in the Pacific, wrote to his boss in Washington to concede defeat. Looking over what he considered to be "perhaps one of the greatest aggregations of material ever assembled in any area for one purpose alone"—there were four million types of materiel in his theater, much of it "dumped on beaches"—he could see no way to sell it and no point in continuing to guard it. He had come to think that "it would be a pure matter of economic advantage to Uncle Sam to abandon it on the spot thus terminating any future expense."[13]

In Washington, Foreign Liquidation Commissioner Thomas B. McCabe, did not share his operative's pessimism. In December, he forwarded Endicott's report to Fulbright, who had proposed funding the Fulbright Program through surplus property sales only weeks before. "I do not entirely agree with [Endicott's] suggestion regarding the abandonment of property," McCabe explained in a cover note, "as I feel that we should fully explore the possibilities of using the unsalable military property in either the United States or other parts of the globe even at a loss to this Government."[14]

McCabe was at the head of a growing group of policy makers who had begun to realize that the surplus was more than a headache—it was also a strategic asset. When planning for disposal had begun in 1943, it had been assumed that the best possible return would be a high dollar price, for this would strengthen the US economy, aiding the transition to postwar abundance. But by early 1944, when a committee of representatives from the Foreign Economic Administration and the State, War, and Navy Departments took a deeper look, they began to realize that it was not simply a matter of short-term economic gain. It was deeply intertwined with broader questions of world politics. In early 1945, a joint Army-Navy Liquidation Commissioner was established to better manage the disposal. Explaining the setup to Congress, Assistant Secretary of State Clement C. Dunn observed that there was a "very close and important relationship between the developments in closing up shop out there, or settling things, and our diplomatic relationship and economic relationship with the area as we go forward." Three months later, Thomas McCabe took up the new position.[15]

McCabe was an ambitious man—he was on leave from positions as chairman of the Federal Reserve Bank of Philadelphia and the president of the Scott Paper Company, and he would later become the head of the US Federal Reserve. But he was frustrated by his lack of control over the surplus disposal—the Foreign Economic Administration retained control over the settlement of lend-lease surpluses, and there were eight different bureaucratic processes for agencies to transfer surplus property. McCabe began asking for a "clear-cut policy," and in an executive order in September, President Truman moved McCabe's organization into the State Department, renamed it the Office of the Foreign Liquidation Commissioner (OFLC), and gave McCabe complete control over the surplus disposal. The new arrangement was appropriate, McCabe thought, because "the problems involved in foreign disposal were so closely bound up with the international political and economic interests and activities of the United States under the State Department."[16]

In the middle of McCabe's efforts to secure this authority, Fulbright proposed that surplus sales could fund educational exchange; in fact, Fulbright introduced his bill to the Senate on the same day Truman issued the executive order transferring McCabe's organization to the State Department. Fulbright had first proposed amending the Surplus Property Act to allow the use of funds from the sale of war surplus "for the promotion of international good will through the exchange of students." But when McCabe and the State Department got wind of the proposal, they "saw tremendous possibilities for utilizing the same procedure for other objectives which would be in the interest of the United States." Fulbright's proposed bill was rewritten. It became simultaneously more technocratic and more expansive, allowing the secretary of state to exchange surplus property "for foreign currencies or credits, intangible rights or benefits, or the discharge of claims"—in short, it empowered the State Department to accept a whole range of payments for surplus property. Only at Fulbright's insistence did the final act specify that the funding of educational exchange was an acceptable form of payment. McCabe was more interested in the broader potential of the act, which, he said, created "a very real, and to me a very attractive, possibility of securing a substantial return to the United States by the use of surpluses to acquire property rights or concessions of direct value to the United States." He was particularly intrigued by the possibility of trading the surplus for "certain intangibles that will lead to trade developments and friendly relations with foreign countries."[17]

Fulbright's bill was quickly and surreptitiously passed through Congress, where it was presented as a way to salvage something—*anything*—out of surplus materiel. Although Fulbright continued to insist that educational exchange programs would "help break down mutual misunderstandings," he spent more time arguing that the bill would "strengthen the hand of the disposal authorities by giving them the necessary power to accept other types of benefits." He later confessed, "I decided not to take the risk of an open appeal to the idealism of my colleagues." Instead, advocates for the bill emphasized that, as Assistant Secretary of State William Benton put it, it was a "sound business procedure" to receive some return from surplus sales. And Fulbright tightly managed the passage of the bill through a Congress leery of international commitments and keen to balance the budget. Only Fulbright and his ally, Senator Joseph O'Mahoney of Wyoming, turned up to Senate Foreign Relations Committee hearings on the bill; only four people appeared before them. The bill slipped through the Senate late one day, when only a handful of senators were present, and passed as a routine measure without a roll call vote. (It was passed at a time, crucially, when Senator Kenneth McKellar, chair of the Senate Appropriations Committee, was absent; he opposed the bill's education provisions because it would be "dangerous . . . to send our fine young girls and boys abroad: they'll be infected with those foreign 'isms.'") As it passed through the House in just ten minutes, one advocate barely had time to clarify that there was no question of donation to foreign nations and to "hope that there will be no objection to this bill. It does not cost us a cent. It enables us to salvage something out of surplus property abroad which otherwise would be a total loss."[18]

In 1946, the Office of the Foreign Liquidation Commissioner began a brief and intensive period of surplus sales in which it took full advantage of its new powers. The United States began by setting a dollar value on the materiel—it took the original procurement cost and then relied on a complex and highly variable series of bureaucratic appraisals to factor in depreciation (for a time, it also *added* 25 percent to cover the costs it had accrued transporting the materiel to the war front). The dollar values that emerged were something of a fiction and often objectionable to purchasers. But it was a starting point, and the surplus sales were ultimately governed by wide-ranging, multifactored political negotiations, not the ordinary mechanisms of supply and demand. After a period of flirtation with small-scale auctions and sales by catalog, the OFLC came to prefer bulk sales—it simply lumped everything together and negotiated to sell it all at once to a foreign government.[19]

Selling in bulk was not only administratively efficient, it also helped the OFLC ensure that foreign governments would not "skim the cream" off the surplus, leaving it with a residue of worthless scrap. Although it was not possible to inspect the surplus before purchasing in such a bulk sale, and although inventories of the surplus were absurdly imprecise, all sales were final and included an "as is, where is" clause to try to prevent subsequent complaints. Even so, complaints were frequent, which was no surprise given the sorts of materiel that US administrators were passing on to customers. As one military official observed of the bulk sale to the Chinese, the entire operation proceeded from "the idea that you can use anything in China for something." As late as 1947, Army officials in Beijing were still trying to offload surplus candy that it described as having "a grayish color but is still edible and nutritious." (Another captain described it more plainly: it "had melted due to extreme heat of the Island and India and had then packed into one solid mass, in addition had turned white. All candy and nuts are stale and rancid.") It is unclear if the OFLC ever managed to offload that particular batch of candy, but in the Philippines, half of the six million Hershey bars sold to purchasers were unfit for consumption, and $1.4 million worth of batteries were dead upon receipt. In Samar, 18,000 tons of flour were declared "unfit for human consumption" by the navy after a weevil infestation but were nevertheless sold.[20]

Purchasers knew that they were paying a surcharge—and assuming a logistical headache—when they made bulk purchases, but they did so to get access to the valuable items among the dreck. Even so, US desire to offload materiel stretched the limits of good faith. When the United Nations Relief and Rehabilitation Administration (UNRRA) bought $100 million worth of materiel it knew it was taking good materiel along with bad; it even agreed that every shipment would be packed according to an odd formula—25 percent would be goods that UNRRA had publicly listed as necessary, 60 percent would be items that it had not requested but that the OFLC thought were adaptable for UNRRA's purposes, and the remaining 15 percent would be worthless. But within months, disagreements about these categories became so bad that the entire contract had to be renegotiated, and the OFLC had to extend a $4 million credit to UNRRA. Such tactics were nonetheless effective in moving all manner of deteriorating materiel. It was telling that the United States ended up abandoning only $400 million worth of surplus.[21]

In exchange for this materiel of uneven value, the OFLC received all sorts of benefits for the US. The full history of these complex negotiations, which were intricately intertwined with broader geopolitical and economic negotiations at the dawn of the postwar order, remains to be written. But the US emerged being owed hundreds of millions of dollars in credit arrangements that were negotiated alongside broader currency and foreign exchange rate agreements. It used surplus sales to repay wartime debts to allies and to pay off financial obligations to UNRRA (a distinct line of business from its bulk sales to UNRRA). It offered strategic allies, such as France and Greece, the opportunity to make selective purchases from surplus inventories. Before it made its bulk sale to the Philippines, for instance, delegations from French Indochina, Thailand, and the Dutch East Indies had toured the surplus to pick out desirable materiel. After them came a Uruguayan delegation, which wanted road-building equipment but complained that the best items of surplus had already been purchased, and only made a small purchase of $50,000. And then the United States transferred the remaining surplus to the Philippines to repay $32 million of wartime debt and to discharge obligations to provide $100 million in war rehabilitation, part of a series of economic agreements negotiated during the recent decolonization.[22]

In short, the US had proven effective in exploiting demand among a war-ravaged world to sell materiel it had considered almost worthless and that it could have easily written off as the cost of victory or as a charitable investment in the construction of a new world order. It was all very far removed from the kinds of humanitarian redistribution of wartime surplus that Joseph Needham and other UNESCO planners had imagined. (It does seem, though, that some nations did use the surplus they purchased to help rebuild schools. For example, Shantung University, in China, used surplus Quonset huts, some attached to the roofs of existing buildings, to create more classroom space.)[23]

And very little of the surplus was used to fund the sorts of cultural networks Fulbright had imagined. The Philippines surplus sale, for instance, set aside only $2 million for educational exchange. Similarly, when the Chinese purchased surplus valued at more than $800 million, they canceled $120 million of wartime debts that the United States owed and gave the United States $35 million for real estate purchases, but provided only $20 million for cultural and educational exchange.[24] In fact, the Fulbright bill had capped the amount each country could spend on educational exchange at $20 million and also limited annual expenditures to only $1 million. (Fulbright had originally proposed an annual cap of

$2.5 million, but a leery Congress reduced it yet further.) All told, only something like 5 percent of the value realized from the bulk sales went to funding educational and real estate purchases combined.[25] But so vast were the overall sums that even these relatively minor portions of the revenues would play a major role in reconfiguring the cultural circuits of the postwar world.

Despite their limited role in the surplus disposal, the educational exchanges nevertheless featured prominently in public commentary because of the promise that they would produce a more harmonious world. "Certainly the furtherance of international understanding which the Fulbright bill would encourage," noted the *Washington Post*, "is preferable to watching our property rust away and finally be abandoned." The *New York Times* agreed that the bill created a "good swap": it was "an excellent method of securing compensation for American property left from war's demands and promoting friendship among peoples." A newspaper in Toledo concluded: "In signing the Fulbright bill, President Truman has taken a long step toward creating the understanding of one another by the peoples of the world which is a requisite for world amity."[26]

Such hopes reflected a liberal faith that everyday cultural contacts between diverse peoples was the surest way to create the mutual understanding and global knowledge necessary for a functioning and stable world system. Fulbright promotional materials frequently cited a phrase attributed to Robert Oppenheimer: "perhaps the best way to send knowledge is to wrap it up in a person." It was the very granularity, the specificity of the individual experiences studying abroad, that made them appealing as a way to stabilize the world order. They only needed to be scaled up. "If 50,000 students from other countries could come here annually and 50,000 of our students go to other lands," opined the *New York Times*, "it would constitute a powerful lever toward the realization of mankind's greatest dream—a world at peace."[27]

Underpinning this valorization of everyday, interpersonal encounters was a critique of efforts to build intercultural understanding through books, films, or radio. These were assumed to be ephemeral, superficial, and fleeting. And as the example of Nazi propaganda proved to many commentators, mass-mediated forms of communication were also dangerously susceptible to appropriation and abuse by antidemocratic, warmongering minorities. By contrast, firsthand experiences living with foreigners, as Fulbright put it, provided "more solid background" and thus the basis for "truer understandings of other peoples." "Although the [Atlantic] Pact is important at the present," Fulbright concluded, "in the long run the movement of thousands of young men and women among the various nations under our government's student exchange program will give us a strong basis for true understanding and a lasting peace."[28]

There was nothing particularly novel about these ideas. Educational exchange had long been a favored technique for internationalists of various stripes. In 1901, the British Empire had created the Rhodes Scholarships to organize exchange within the empire as well as with the United States and Germany, because, as Cecil Rhodes put it, an "understanding between the three great powers will render war impossible [as] educational relations make the strongest tie." An international educational congress had been held at the 1876 World's Fair in Philadelphia, and a World Federation of Education Associations had been created in 1923, which considered proposals to organize an exchange of university professors and endorsed a "Plan to Develop International Friendship, Goodwill and Justice through Education." By 1925, 120 private organizations were already promoting international education in the United States; they included the Committee on Friendly Relations with Foreign Students (established in conjunction with the YWCA and YMCA in 1911) and the Institute for International Education, which was organized by Stephen Duggan, Nicholas Murray Butler, and Elihu Root to keep alive the hopes of disappointed internationalists after the Senate rejected the League of Nations. In 1928, private philanthropies established an International House in New York to provide accommodation and support for foreign students and aid the cause of international understanding. Similar houses were opened in Chicago, Paris, and Berkeley in subsequent years—although construction in Berkeley was nearly derailed when eight hundred Americans protested it, shouting angrily that they didn't want to be "overrun with blacks and Asians."[29]

By the 1940s, as the creation of UNESCO revealed, there was international consensus about the role that educational and cultural exchange could play in the creation of a peaceful world. Some even hoped that the United Nations would create an institutional infrastructure to facilitate such exchanges. China, for instance, had proposed that a UN university should be established on each continent and that an international exchange system of university teachers be set up between them. A small group of Italian, British, and American reformers in occupied Rome similarly proposed the creation of a university with four thousand to five thousand students that would bring individuals around the world to study together and then return home to become "opinion-influencing agents." (The group thought that the United Nations would pay for all these students, except those from the Axis countries, who would have to pay their own way;

each nation would also provide a "complete library covering the history and all the cultural aspects of its own civilization.") A lawyer from Chevy Chase, Maryland, proposed the creation of a UN University in Washington, DC; a lawyer from Detroit proposed the creation of such a university in Geneva, the Azores, or Panama, which would educate students from every country—one student per every five hundred thousand inhabitants—who would earn certificates naming them "citizens of the world" and who would swear allegiance "to all humanity." A French music professor similarly wrote to Truman to propose that a "temple of education" be erected in every community so that "man may develop the physico-psychic aspect of his nature rather than the materialistic side . . . thus eliminating the danger of his destroying himself with the atomic bomb."[30]

The Fulbright Program inherited these internationalist hopes and institutionalized them not via the United Nations, but as a state-based mechanism of US foreign policy. For advocates of the program, the status of the United States as a global superpower made it uniquely responsible for making older dreams of global peace more fully effective. John Temple Graves, for example, threw his support behind the Fulbright Program because "it is so logical, so inducive of good will among nations, and so related to the whole program of an America influencing the world to its way at a time when that way alone can save the world."[31] As Fulbright himself explained to an audience at the College of William & Mary:

> It is peculiarly the responsibility of Americans to take the lead in the creation of a peaceful world. Not only is it to our selfish material interest because we have more to lose by chaos than any other people, but it is also our moral duty to give direction and strength to the bewildered people of this earth who are groping helplessly for peace and a decent life. If for no other reason it is our duty because we are the favored heirs of western Christian civilization.[32]

As befitted such universal ambitions, the Fulbright was, as the *New York Times* put it, "the most comprehensive program of student exchange ever undertaken by any nation." "It is obvious," asserted an early promotional pamphlet for the program, "that the Fulbright Act makes possible a program of educational exchange on a scale without precedence in modern times." This was not simple hubris; earlier programs of exchange had been tiny. The much-ballyhooed Rhodes Scholarship, for instance, had brought only 2,900 men from seven countries to Oxford in its first fifty years; in 1943, amid the disruptions of war, only one scholarship had been awarded. The Fulbright Program, by contrast, funded 4,308 exchanges in its first three years; grantees went to fifteen countries. After that, it ballooned—by 1955, there had already been more than 21,000 Fulbright scholars. The sheer scale of the program has frequently moved commentators to hyperbole of a world-historical variety. Fulbright's old tutor at Oxford, R. B. McCallum, said that it was "the largest and most significant movement of scholars across the earth since the fall of Constantinople in 1453."[33]

Nevertheless, the geographical reach of the Fulbright Program was circumscribed by its curious source of funding: if a nation didn't purchase war surplus, it couldn't participate in educational exchange. And you could purchase war surplus only if war materiel had ended up in your neck of the woods at the end of the war. This meant that the geography of international understanding created by the program was shaped directly by the logistical networks of World War II. The twenty-seven nations that had established Fulbright exchanges by 1954 were therefore clustered in the areas of heaviest US military activity in the late stages of the war: twelve of them were in Western Europe (Austria, Belgium, Denmark, Finland, France, Germany, Greece, Italy, the Netherlands, Norway, Sweden, and the UK); seven were central sites in the Pacific theater (Australia, China, Japan, Korea, New Zealand, the Philippines, and Thailand). Burma, a site of vicious fighting throughout the war, had a program, as did India and Pakistan, which had been staging grounds for the supply of China "over-the-hump" and along the Stillwell Road. Only four (Turkey, Egypt, Iran, and Iraq) were in the Middle East—they had been logistical hubs, through which material was distributed to the USSR (by rail and the Aid-to-Russia Highway) and to the Pacific and India theaters (via the Suez Canal). South Africa had a Fulbright Program—it had received lend-lease shipments through the war, inherited some of the surplus, and established a tiny exchange program as part of a surplus settlement in 1952. But the rest of sub-Saharan Africa, still colonized, had no exchanges. Neither did the nations of Latin America, which had to wait until the late 1950s, and alternative sources of funding, to join the program.[34]

While military geography thus shaped the Fulbright Program deeply, the purchase of surplus only created the *possibility* for educational exchange. After that, Educational Exchange agreements had to be negotiated, and individuals and institutions had to choose to participate. At both of these levels, cultural and political factors shaped and exacerbated the geographical biases. In 1949, just as the Fulbright Program was beginning to expand, exchange with China (the second largest purchaser of surplus) was ended by the Chinese revolution. On top of such geopolitical pressures, the size of the program in each country was shaped by cultural preferences. The hard cap on the amount of money that could be set aside for educational exchange by each nation meant that the size of that nation's Fulbright Program was not determined by the size of the surplus sales. Norway, for instance, had almost double the exchange grants of India in 1950, despite purchasing much less surplus materiel. Such trends were created by the intangible decisions and assumptions of individual scholars, students, and schools as to what forms of exchange were most desirable, as well as which were the easiest to arrange.[35]

The overall result was a deeply Eurocentric program in the early years. Of the 4,300 awards made in the first three years, 1,172 were for exchanges with the UK (which had purchased the sixth largest amount of surplus); 960 were for exchanges with France (the largest purchaser); and a further 1,122 were devoted to exchanges with Greece and Italy. In the same period, the third largest buyer of surplus materiel, the Philippines, received only 155 grants.[36] And the absence of Fulbright agreements with vast portions of the world also meant that scholars working in the Global South were often channeled back to the metropole to continue their research. For instance, Donald W. Wyatt, assistant professor of sociology at Fisk University and erstwhile race relations advisor in the National Housing Agency, traveled to France to study "Race Composition and Assimilation among Arabs of Morocco." William E. H. Howard, who had been working in Ethiopia, similarly received a grant to the UK to study the influence of British Commonwealth politics on commerce and industry in Ethiopia.[37]

Whatever the curiosities and complexities of the global footprint of the Fulbright Program, the most significant feature of its geography was very straightforward. Because it was organized as a sequence of binational exchange programs, the Fulbright built a hub-and-spoke network. And the United States was the hub.

The rise of the US as a hub of global education in the 1940s marked a distinct break with the past. In the late nineteenth and early twentieth centuries, as international study began to emerge as a more regular practice, the educational world was multipolar, and the US was not one of the main poles. Germany was—its innovative research universities drew in people from around the world who were attracted to the latest and most rigorous scholarly practice. In 1904, when there were only 3,700 international students in the United States, there were 9,000 in Germany. France was also a major pole, having built close educational ties with Eastern European and Ottoman countries before World War I. And just as Britain (a third pole) drew in students from its empire throughout the interwar period, so did the French Empire. By 1931, France hosted about one-quarter of all international students, some 17,000, and almost twice as many as the US.[38]

The United States *was* trying to close the gap in these years. It had begun to develop educational networks that followed the contours of its emerging empire. In 1903, seeking to pacify the Philippines, it created the *pensionado* program, which brought about 300 students to the US mainland for education. Exchange networks emerged in its informal empire, too. In the late nineteenth century, missionaries started a program to bring young Chinese men to New England high schools and colleges; the program lasted eight years and educated about 120 individuals, some of whom went on to prestigious careers. A larger effort followed the Boxer Uprising in the early twentieth century, when about a quarter of the damages that the US claimed from China were placed in a fund that was used to educate some 2,000 Chinese students in the United States. (The Boxer Indemnity Fund was frequently invoked by advocates of the Fulbright Program in 1945 and 1946; they said that it had created a "river of good will that never dried up, and that watered the whole Orient.") And in 1938, the US State Department established a tiny program of educational exchange with nations in the Western Hemisphere. Involving just two students from each country, the program mainly reflected the ongoing status of the United States as a second-rate educational power—it had been conceived out of fears that German influence remained too strong in Latin America. As late as September 1942, the US ambassador to Chile was still worried about the limited influence of US education in the region. "We must," he pleaded, "sell the idea that the U.S. is now the world's most important intellectual center, and that Chileans must in future look to it rather than to Europe for educational and cultural opportunities."[39]

The second half of the 1940s witnessed a revolution in international education. There were only about 7,000 foreign students in the United States in the latter stages of the war. There were 17,000 by 1948 and twice that many five years later. The Fulbright alone was not responsible for the surge; about six in ten of the students funded their own way. Indeed, given the general economic prosperity of the United States and the particular prosperity of the university sector—growing fat on enrollment growth funded by the GI Bill, as well as Cold War research contracts—it was inevitable that the United States would emerge as the "educational capital of the world" (as the *Washington Star* put it in 1947). But the Fulbright Program helped accelerate the general trend. It was precisely the kind of networking within already "bright" zones of exchange that Joseph Needham had thought "obviously absurd." Using public funds (coming from foreign nations), the Fulbright helped consolidate the US as the new center of the educational world.[40]

The institutional logic of the early Fulbright Program similarly privileged US interests. Once a nation had set funds aside for educational exchange, the State Department worked to establish a binational educational exchange commission to administer the program there. In theory, the commissions represented a liberal commitment to shared governance of the program, but in practice, Americans held the reins. "We want to establish the fact that this entire program is a partnership," explained the State Department's chief of exchange programs in 1948. "[The commissions] are legal entities set up by the State Department, generally with 5 Americans and 3–5 representatives of the country concerned. In all cases the Americans will be in control." Control took a variety of forms. The State Department retained power to review the decisions and budget of all of these boards. Sometimes the Americans negotiated for a majority of seats on the board. Other times they conceded an equal number of votes to their partners but insisted that the chairman of the board, with the deciding vote, had to be American. In the Chinese case, the board was exclusively American, consisting of embassy and cultural relations staff, as well as representatives of the Rockefeller Foundation and the National City Bank of New York in Shanghai. The Chinese protested vigorously, understandably demanding some role in administering the funds they were providing. But they only succeeded in placing three advisors on the board. They thus had less control over the operation of this "binational" program of "mutual understanding" than they had over the Boxer Indemnity fund four decades earlier.[41]

Even under US control, the commissions became arenas for contestation over the purpose of the program. Under pressure from foreign members, many commissions requested that Fulbrights be granted to senior, eminent US scholars in scientific and engineering fields, who could act as technical advisors. They also emphasized sending their own experts to the United States to tap into the cutting edge of applied research—the Dutch, for instance, used the Fulbright to send established engineers and physicists to the US for further training and networking. American administrators complained that such requests were not giving due regard to "American interests." They expressed "serious reservations regarding the predominance of elderly men" in the program, because such eminent scholars lacked the "physical and intellectual vigor which should be a requisite for participation in the program." Instead, they explained, "the primary objective of the program must be to provide a maximum number of opportunities for participation in educational exchange activities to younger persons."[42]

The exchange revealed a key assumption: the ideal American "Fulbrighter" was not an eminent intellectual, but a more representative citizen. During the passage of the Fulbright bill through Congress, it was amended to ensure that "due consideration shall be given to applicants from all geographical areas of the United States." But in the first years of the program, something like half of all grants went to universities in five states: New York, Massachusetts, Illinois, California, and Pennsylvania. Fulbright complained to the Board of Foreign Scholarships (BFS), which administered the program, about the "undue emphasis on the purely academic aspects of the program," which "was exactly the opposite of the desirable one which is to disseminate the participants in this program as widely as possible through all of the states." The participation of "young people from all over the US," he concluded, "is probably more important to the advancement of our ultimate objective than the increase of knowledge per se." The BFS quickly implemented a "State Scholar Plan," guaranteeing two grants to each state. It made sense that Fulbright would seek such a geographical distribution. It was an easy form of constituent service for the Arkansan senator, and Fulbright had received his Rhodes Scholarship in large part because of just such a state quota scheme.[43] Nevertheless, the dynamic revealed that the American Fulbrighter was intended to be a representative, not an exceptional, American.

The emphasis on geographic distribution was also significant because it constructed the Fulbright as an opportunity that was owed to a wide swath of American citizens. A similar political logic was at work in the preference given to veterans—another adjustment made to the bill in Congress, which was seen by some as a study-abroad corollary to the GI Bill. In the first three years of the program, 46 percent of all grants were made to veterans. That skewed the distribution of awards away from women—only 39 of the 889 veteran Fulbrighters were women—and undermined what might have been a noteworthy, and sadly isolated, commitment to gender equality in the midcentury academy—the program was open to women from the start. (The Rhodes Scholarship, by contrast, was not open to women until 1977.) But because of the preference for veterans, women received only 30 percent of the grants made to Americans in the first years of the program. The BFS was, from its first meeting, conscious of this bias and surprisingly effective in achieving gender parity in its grants to nonveterans—women received 52 percent of them. But that could not overcome the gender inequalities built into the occupational and educational distribution of the 1940s. Of the 576 grants to women in these years, 199 were for primary and secondary school teachers, while a combined 44 went to research scholars and university lecturers. Women received 69 percent of the Fulbright grants made to teachers, but only 27 percent of grants to students; 12 percent of grants that went to researchers; and a miserable 9 percent of grants that went to lecturers.[44] Tellingly, 9 percent was also the percentage of female BFS members in the first three decades of the program—the commitment to gender equality had its limits.[45]

The early Fulbright Program was far less committed to racial equality. As the Fulbright bill was being debated, Senator O'Mahoney had actually proposed inserting an antidiscrimination clause. But Fulbright convinced him not to, arguing that it would be "exceedingly dangerous" to the political chances of the bill. The comingling of liberal internationalism with domestic racism was a central feature of Fulbright's political career. He consistently voted against civil rights legislation and signed the Southern Manifesto. In turn, his electoral security, and subsequent seniority in the Senate, were products of the solid South, providing him a safe platform for his liberal inclinations in foreign affairs. In 1964, for instance, Fulbright gave a long speech on the Senate floor in which he outlined the need for a relaxation of Cold War tensions and a more liberal foreign policy. Whatever its virtues as a policy speech, it mainly served a less admirable function—it was given to filibuster the Civil Rights Act.[46]

Once the program was up and running, Fulbright had less ability to scuttle antiracist efforts. Under pressure from the United Negro College Fund, Truman appointed Charles S. Johnson, president of Fisk University, to the first BFS in 1947. (Fulbright privately campaigned for the addition of another southerner to the board the next year, complaining that there "is no southerner on the board except the president of Fisk University who was selected, as you know, because of his race.") And at its first meeting, the BFS passed a motion to evaluate applications "without respect to race, color or creed." But what that meant in practice is hard to know, as the Fulbright Program did not begin keeping racial data on grantees until the 1990s—one legacy of the lack of a legislative mandate to racial equality, as well as a sign of general indifference to the subject. There is reason to believe that it meant little and that there were very few Black Fulbrighters. According to one 1950 report from the Institute of International Education, only ten of the 548 grants made to graduate students that year were given to Black Americans. In any event, without a conscious commitment to racial diversity, it was inevitable that the Fulbright Program would reflect the inequalities of the midcentury academy: as of 1950, only 1.9 percent of Black American males graduated from college, compared with 8.8 percent of white males.[47]

Still, however much it was circumscribed by the gender and racial biases of the 1940s, the granting of Fulbrights to American citizens revealed a desire to democratize the experience. That stood in stark contrast to the ideal *foreign* recipient of a Fulbright. "My original idea," Fulbright later explained, "was not a general education program for all needy people but a program designed to influence political matters through the intelligent leadership of the important countries." Across the life of the program, commentators and administrators would see foreigners coming to the United States as a future global elite, soon to be in charge in their home countries. One 1946 *Washington Post* article, approvingly noting that "the men and women of tomorrow . . . are now in this country's classrooms," pointed out that the Indian Fulbrighters "are expected to be leaders in the industrialization of their country." In 1961, the head of the BFS testified to Congress about the experiences of 350 Indian Fulbrighters, who were "leaders or the leaders to come in India, one of the critical areas of the world." In a revealing speech the next year, in which Fulbright offered a "progress report" on international education, he boasted that among the grantees, there was a "large percentage of men and women headed for positions of leadership and responsibility in their respective countries" and drew attention to many of the alumni of educational exchange who were already "active political leaders": Pierre Pflimlin and Felix Gaillard, former French prime ministers then serving in the De Gaulle cabinet; Constantine Karamanlis, prime minister of Greece; Manouchehr Eqbal, prime minister of Iran; Paolo Rossi, Italian minister of education; Phagna Bouasy, foreign minister of Laos; and Sir Leslie Munro, president of the UN General Assembly.[48]

This asymmetry between the assumed US and foreign recipients of a Fulbright—a broad swath of American citizens, on the one hand, and a hand-picked global elite on the other—reflected the underlying structures of the Fulbright as a network of exchange. Structuring a global exchange program as a series of binational partnerships, in which the United States was always one of the partners, simply gave the US a disproportionate presence in the program: 21,000 Americans had received a Fulbright by 1964, while the rest of the world combined had received 30,000. Such demographic dynamics democratized the opportunity for educational exchange for US citizens, elevating them, as citizens of a world superpower, to a position of functional equivalence to elite leaders in foreign nations.[49]

The asymmetry also reflected and reinforced a deeper set of assumptions about the contradictory way that educational exchange would work to spread culture. Today, whole teams of university administrators are devoted to the study and management of foreign exchange students—it is a tricky subject, and it is by no means obvious or predictable what the cultural consequences of educational exchange are. But when the Fulbright was created, that field of study was basically nonexistent, and early administrators developed their theories of acculturation based on little more than anecdote and inherited assumption. (In fact, the creation of the Fulbright Program was an important spur to the creation of the foreign student infrastructure. In 1948, a State Department–led conference established the National Association of Foreign Student Advisors, which aimed to "develop a dynamic international cultural relations program, particularly through student exchanges.") And although early Fulbright administrators said that both Americans and foreigners would be profoundly shaped by the experience of educational exchange, they believed that those experiences would be fundamentally different.[50]

Foreigners were expected to be converted to American political values by virtue of their experiences in the United States. Francis Colligan, acting chief of the State Department's Division of International Exchange, said that an expanding Fulbright Program would mean that there would be "a growing number of men and women educated in our institutions, with the result that the cause of democracy would be strengthened everywhere." Early administrators were so convinced that studying in the US would have a powerful effect on foreign students that they were primarily worried about the best way to harness the process. At its first meeting, the BFS had to decide whether Fulbright grants should be open to undergraduates or restricted to graduate students. Some members argued that it would be ideal to bring young and impressionable foreign students to the US, saying that "it would further the aim of greater understanding of the democratic system to choose students in their formative years during which time it would be easier to strengthen their interest in democratic principles which they would then reflect on their return to their native countries." Others, however, worried that that "when younger students were so chosen they often returned to their countries as misfits—unable to readjust to their native cultures." Rather than risk overdemocratizing young minds with the power of the American way of life, these members believed that it would be better to select "more mature students [who would] absorb an understanding of our institutions and . . . [would be] willing to go back and play a part in their own culture." These arguments carried the day, and Fulbrights were restricted to graduate students. But the notion that foreign grantees would themselves become agents of Americanization suggests just how transformative their experience in the United States was expected to be. It moved Fulbright, for instance, to flights of fancy.

"How often I have thought what a fine thing it would be if Mr. Stalin or Mr. Molotov could have gone to Robert College or Columbia in their youth," he wrote.[51]

Americans going abroad, on the other hand, would not be seduced by their exposure to foreign cultures. Instead, they would gain instrumental knowledge of the world and become a national asset for a country rising to world leadership. As William Benton put it, Fulbrighters would "become a reservoir of trained Americans, young men and women who know other nations and people." Importantly, that knowledge would not destabilize their underlying Americanism. In fact, as one member of the BFS asserted, Fulbrighters "will return to us with a more sympathetic understanding of other people and at the same time with a much deeper appreciation of our own institutions and our way of life."[52] Like Dorothy, American Fulbrighters would travel far, only to realize that there truly was no place like home.

No coherent model of cultural exchange could explain such a contradictory set of outcomes. Rather, the Fulbright Program's theory of cultural exchange rested on a deep faith that American culture itself was transformative; that its basic morality was universally recognizable and thus irresistible. Fulbright himself was remarkably explicit on this front. In 1944, he argued that giving foreigners the opportunity to study in the United States "does not mean that we seek to impose our own doctrines directly upon these peoples. It merely means that we have faith in the basic rightness of our Christian democratic civilization, and that if people are permitted to seek the truth through education and the free and unrestricted interchange of ideas, they naturally will develop a society compatible with our own." "My belief in the [Fulbright] program," he later explained, "is based on the assumption that when foreigners come to our shores what they see will be good. In spite of our occasional strange aberrations, I believe that America is a great country, that its virtues outweigh its faults. If the people of the world can understand us, they will throw in their lot with us."[53]

Such assumptions undermined the Fulbright Program's ostensible commitments to mutual understanding and bilateral cultural exchange. The implementation of the Fulbright Program tended to assume not a two-way transfer of culture, but an expanding sphere of American influence. Fulbright, for instance, took as his model of the ideal exchange student the example of a Turkish politician who had been educated at Columbia University, saying that "his mind is like a channel open and sympathetic, through which the thoughts and purposes of the West, especially America, can be presented to his people objectively and truthfully." In slipping from a metaphor of exchange to one of transmission, Fulbright revealed that his vision of cultural exchange assumed that free exchange would involve the export of American values.[54] At the end of the day, the Fulbright Program was understood to be a perfect mechanism for solidifying a liberal world order with the United States at its center.

Of course, that was just the theory. We don't know a great deal about the lived experiences of Fulbright scholars; historians are only beginning to uncover their stories. But as we might expect, the experiences of thousands of students and scholars studying abroad were incredibly varied, their trajectories far more discordant, dissonant, and diverse than the smoothly expanding appreciation of the United States that early administrators imagined. Some Americans fell in love while overseas, either with foreign cultures or particular foreigners. (Sylvia Plath, for instance, met Ted Hughes while at Cambridge on a Fulbright.) Some were plainly dissatisfied by their experiences, such as Dr. Walter Krause, an economist from Utah, who was so unhappy with the lack of heating in 1950s Australia that he lasted only two days at the University of Tasmania. And then there were those who were so alienated by their experiences in the United States that they became more opposed to the United States than ever before. As one administrator observed ruefully in 1951, "Some of our guests have left with a chip on the shoulder and a phobia against the U.S. and all it stands for."[55]

Even if the ultimate impact of the Fulbright Program was determined by the accretion of all these idiosyncratic, individual stories, and even if the real creators of the program's legacy were not Washington administrators in the 1940s, but, rather, the thousands of unsung scholars, students, and university officials who actually put exchange into practice, the origins of the program are nevertheless significant. They tell us a great deal about US attitudes toward the world order they thought they were creating. The geography and political economy of the program, as well as its contradictory theories of cultural exchange, meant that this program of "mutual understanding" was designed to constitute the United States as the center of an expanding liberal world order. And there was, at the end of the day, no negotiating with geography or with funding; some nations, organized as a new periphery circling the US educational metropole, had a Fulbright Program. Others did not. That such an unequal and hierarchical program was the main piece of international educational infrastructure created at the birth of the postwar order is deeply revealing. UNESCO lacked the funds to establish anything so grand; despite numerous proposals, nothing like a United Nations University was ever seriously debated, let alone created. Instead, the world paid for a nationalist exchange program centered on the United States.

Alongside the money for the Fulbright Program, surplus sales also set aside a tranche of foreign currency the United States could use to pay for real estate or building construction. The surplus disposal financed an explosion of US construction abroad, creating a vastly expanded network of US embassies and consulates that represented US power to the world in new ways. Built in prominent locations by flashy, modernist architects, the buildings themselves symbolized a rising American presence. And by providing accommodations to cultural centers and libraries, as well as a vastly expanding legion of foreign service employees, the buildings provided very useful locations for more substantial forms of US international power.

Historically, the United States had been reluctant to purchase international real estate. With democratic disdain for the aristocratic pomp of formal ambassadors and lavish embassies, it had expected ministers and consul generals to provide their own accommodations. (The ironic result was that only the wealthy could realistically afford one of these appointments.) And given the limited responsibilities of the consulates of the time, it was sufficient to lease premises for the limited staff they required. In 1910, the US owned diplomatic properties in only five locations—Bangkok, Beijing, Constantinople, Tokyo, and the International Zone of Tangier (the Sultan of Morocco had gifted this last building to the United States in 1821). In 1911, as the US began asserting itself in international affairs in new ways, Congress passed a bill to encourage the purchase of more properties. But the bill provided only a small pot of funds and failed to create an effective bureaucracy for foreign buildings, and by 1926, only six additional properties had been purchased (in Havana, Oslo, Paris, San José, San Salvador, and Santiago). The State Department had also been gifted properties in Panama City (by the War Department), Paris (by the former US ambassador), and London (by J. P. Morgan). Most overseas buildings continued to be leased; in the 1920s, the US consulate in Dublin was located over a saloon. Even though additional money began to flow in the late 1920s, the disruptions of the Great Depression, and then World War II, meant that the rate of expansion was slow. In 1932, the United States owned 40 buildings abroad; in 1946, it owned only 114.[56]

By 1952, however, the US owned 737 buildings overseas, with a further 128 under construction. It was an astonishing expansion, one that shaped the modern footprint of the US diplomatic apparatus. From 1900 until 1945, Congress had spent less than $20 million on embassy construction; from 1945 to 1960, it spent $215 million. And almost all of the new money came from foreign credits negotiated as part of the war surplus settlement; 97 percent of the 1946 appropriation, for instance, came from surplus sales. That meant that Congress was happy to let go of the purse strings because, as with the Fulbright Program, the money seemed free. Owning buildings overseas, asserted Senator Claude Pepper, would be a "very salutary use that we could make of our surplus property so that we will have something permanent to show for it." Unconcerned about costs, Congress delegated unprecedented authority to buy and build property abroad to Foreign Building Operations (FBO), a new bureaucracy within the State Department. As one of its key administrators later put it, the FBO had a "freedom to act, backed up by an organizational autonomy and independent appropriation, [that] was not enjoyed by many government agencies."[57]

And so in the years after World War II, when many nations were digging out from the rubble, the FBO went house-hunting. In Rome, it purchased the Villa Taverna and the Palazzo Margherita, which had previously been owned by the Fascist Party (the United States also unwittingly took possession of the building's rich art collections, which were in storage in the basement). In Egypt, where the US consulate was spread over three underwhelming buildings, the United States exchanged war surplus for two mansions in Cairo, as well as properties in Alexandria and Port Said. Among its many other purchases were a series of buildings on Grosvenor Square in London, a consulate in Nouméa (for $40,000 worth of surplus), and land in Algiers, Baghdad, Dakar, Hanoi, and Saigon.[58]

Money derived from surplus sales also created a giant fund to pay for the design, construction, and outfitting of new buildings. Foreign funds in six currencies paid for the construction of an embassy in Rio de Janeiro. Materials for the new embassy in Havana were sourced from around the world and paid for in each location by money derived from surplus sales—the steel came from Belgium, the cement from France, plastic partitions from England, travertine marble from Italy. Interior decorations, too, were sourced globally. Anita Moeller Laird, who was responsible for the interior design of US foreign buildings from 1949 to 1972, used foreign credits to decorate the embassies with china from Germany, crystal from Czechoslovakia, and silver from Peru.[59]

Perhaps most importantly, the FBO had the autonomy to hire private architects who revolutionized the design of US buildings abroad. Previously, when the United States had leased buildings, they had been indistinguishable in the visual landscape of foreign cities. On the relatively rare occasions that the US had constructed buildings, it had favored a colonial style, such the chancery in Canberra designed to look like a house in colonial Virginia, the American Legation in Monrovia based on the Baltimore home of a founding-era advocate of Black emigration, or the replica of the White House that housed the US consulate in Yokohama. (At one point, in fact, there had been plans to build "little White Houses all over the world," but apart from Yokohama, the only other one was in Baghdad, which had actually been designed by its owner, an Iraqi businessman who was leasing it to the State Department.)[60]

The FBO's postwar burst of construction after World War II, however, was overseen by men with a penchant for modernist architecture. Supervising FBO architect Leland King gave contracts to architects deploying the international style, which favored industrial materials such as glass and steel and which rejected ornamentation. It was a radical break with what had come before, and it associated US buildings with international trends in architecture. In Rio de Janeiro and Havana, for instance, new embassies were built by the prestigious Harrison and Abramovitz firm, which had previously designed the UN building; the new embassies were shining glass and marble office towers, with open interiors. In The Hague, Bauhaus architect Marcel Breuer, who had previously helped design the new UNESCO headquarters in Paris, designed an embassy that featured two blocks of offices, sheathed in imported limestone and raised over a recessed base, connected by a glass hall. The interior was sleek—with marble walls from the south of Switzerland, floors of Norwegian slate, rugs from India, curtains from Belgium, and Burmese Teak paneling in the library—all paid for by surplus funds, as was the land itself. The new embassy was constructed on a block of land that had been destroyed by accidental British air bombing in what was the second worst bombing in the Netherlands during the war; five hundred Dutch citizens died in the incident. That the US had calmly bought the location and thrown up a modernist sculpture to its own power struck some Dutch commentators as callous, and they were critical of the final building.[61]

There *were* deep problems with the designs, which were often inappropriate in their new settings. The uniquely trapezoidal windows in The Hague's embassy leaked air and water. The Rio de Janeiro building wasn't built to code, as was discovered when a fire broke out toward the end of construction. Air conditioning in the 1940s wasn't up to the task of cooling glass buildings in tropical climates—the embassy in Havana would get unbearably hot, for example—but when sunscreens were added to the outside of buildings, as was done in Quito, trespassers were provided with an easy way to climb into the building. Even without sunscreens, the new buildings weren't particularly protest-proof, as demonstrated when protesters lobbed rocks through the glass walls of a new building in Frankfurt.[62]

Nevertheless, the turn to modernist architecture made the United States look technologically sophisticated, experimental, wealthy, and, by virtue of a series of overdetermined metaphors between glass buildings and transparent governance, open to the world. As *Architectural Forum* put it in 1953, the new buildings provided "a colorful picture of a young, progressive and modern-minded America." The irony was that Congress, stacked with conservatives of various stripes, was in the same period deeply skeptical of modernist aesthetics. In 1946, when the State Department arranged an international tour of modernist art, Congress had attacked the paintings as un-American and forced the defunding of the art program and the premature cancelation of the tour. (The paintings themselves were sold off as surplus government property.) But the architectural program, sheltered from Congress because of its autonomous funding, proceeded unchecked into the early 1950s.[63]

Meanwhile, the buildings played an important role in facilitating the spread of US state power. Diplomatic relations were begun with new nations of the decolonizing world—the FBO built the embassies. A host of development officers, technical assistance consultants, and aid workers went out to modernize the world and help US allies in the Cold War—the FBO provided their office buildings and apartments. American tourists and businesspeople, traveling overseas in ever-greater numbers, needed help with passports, visas, and other consular services—they found them in buildings owned by the FBO.

The new buildings frequently housed libraries and information centers—in Rio de Janeiro, a one-floor, amoeba-shaped library jutted out from the front of the embassy; in Cairo, the library occupied a two-story mansion behind the embassy. In the 1940s, the United States built a wave of such libraries. During the war, propaganda agencies had built libraries in Latin America and the British Commonwealth, and the US Occupation authorities opened libraries in Germany and Japan, stocked at first with discards from the Army Service libraries. By 1953, the State Department was running 230 libraries, used by some twenty-seven million visitors every year, in seventy-five countries. They were significant cultural centers, hosting, for instance, music recitals, art exhibits, film screenings, discussion groups, and lectures. In Cairo, on Thursdays and Fridays, two junior librarians organized games and crafts for local children, during which time they also taught the children English.[64]

Above all, the libraries were a beachhead for American books and magazines. On average, they held ten thousand to fifteen thousand volumes, intended to give a "full and fair" view of American life through a carefully curated selection of magazines and reference works and literature, as well as a healthy smattering of anti-Communist texts like *1984* and *Darkness at Noon*. Before the war, the US had not been a major exporter of books; Britain, Germany, France, and Spain had dominated the international market. In 1941, Germany had exported books valued at $35 million, Britain $16 million, and the United States only $800,000, far less than Switzerland or Sweden. But now the US took the lead. Its book exports, helped on by three State Department programs, quadrupled between 1945 and 1960. One such program were the libraries, which were complemented by a Books in Translation program that subsidized and arranged for the translation of fifty million American titles and an Informational Media Guarantee program through which the US government repaid book exporters $83 million for sales in countries where their earnings were trapped in nonconvertible currency. (Tellingly, UNESCO tried to implement the same three programs to reconstruct the global distribution of books in these years, but strapped for cash, its programs were miniscule in comparison. Whereas the US built hundreds of libraries, UNESCO helped rebuild just one, a tiny library in Normandy. Its effort to build pathways through currency restrictions, a book coupon program, was worth $9 million, not $83 million, and its translation program, the Collection of Representative Works, focused mainly on translating non-Western classics into English and French and left funding and publication to foundations, learned societies, and book publishers.) State Department planners were happy to promote the export of US books because they saw them as a central mechanism to win over the same global elites who were the target of the Fulbright Program. "Relatively few persons in any foreign country read books at all, even when translated into the local language," conceded one administrator of the library program. "However, those who do read books tend to be influential out of proportion to their numbers . . . an opinion-molding minority, a clientele of leadership for our programs with wide influence upon the ideas and actions of their national groups. These are the people who condition the ideas of the broad masses of foreign populations."[65]

All these buildings would prove useful to more assertive forms of state power, too. The design of the Havana embassy featured a division between public-facing functions, like the library, which were placed in a one-story building on the street, and the offices for more sensitive operations, which were placed in a remote tower. That so many state employees worked and lived in these new buildings around the world—by 1957, there were ninety-nine thousand nonmilitary US government employees living abroad—meant that they provided useful cover for intelligence work. CIA agents, for instance, could work easily in the remote tower in Havana, as they did in many other embassies. (After designing the Havana embassy, Harrison and Abramovitz designed Langley, the agency's headquarters.) And as would become painfully clear during the Iranian revolution several decades later, the US embassy in Tehran had been a key staging ground for US interventions in Iran over the years. That embassy, paid for by surplus credits, had been built by the FBO between 1948 and 1951.[66]

The trading of war surplus also played a role in producing another important vector of US-dominated globalism in the 1940s: civil aviation. The war had been a boon to the US airline industry. Although it was the home of the Wright brothers, the United States had been a relative laggard in commercial aviation in its first decades, because it had been reluctant to support its air industry with the mail subsidies so essential to steady profit. Germany, France, the Netherlands, and the United Kingdom had taken the early lead—flight promised better connections to (and control over) distant colonies, as well as a way to bypass railroads that had been ravaged during World War I. But in the late 1920s, the United States began heavily subsidizing domestic and international air mail routes. Pan American Airways, in particular, emerged in the 1930s as the world's most powerful airline, with airports throughout the Western Hemisphere and across the United States' Pacific Empire. By the outbreak of the European war in 1939, the US had taken the lead in airplane production too.[67]

The war radically accelerated US dominance in the field. Factories mobilized for war churned out planes—three hundred thousand were produced in 1945, up from eight hundred in 1939. The British agreed to focus their relatively scarce productive capacities on combat aircraft and to rely on their American allies for transport planes—a division of labor that made sense during the war but that also set the United States up nicely for the postwar period. Meanwhile, the vast global supply networks of the war effort expanded the reach of US airlines. Before the United States entered the war, Pan Am had been secretly granted money from the President's

Emergency Fund to build almost sixty airports in the Western Hemisphere that could be quickly converted to military use. (The State Department simultaneously pressured Latin American governments to dislodge German airlines from their previous dominance of the region.) Pan Am flew supplies to British troops in North Africa from these bases; soon they would extend their routes into the Middle East via a string of newly constructed air bases. For the first time, a truly global air network had been built. And as US commercial airlines lent planes and pilots to the Army Air Transport Command, the United States was building the capacity for postwar dominance of civil aviation.[68]

What remained entirely unclear was what would be done with all this surplus air capacity—the bases, the planes, the navigational equipment—now that the war was over. The disposal would be intricately intertwined with important negotiations over the postwar regulation of the emerging civil aviation industry.

The airplane became a potent symbol for the possibilities of postwar internationalism. Flight seemed to promise new forms of communication, connection, and communion. Wendell Willkie had an early taste of the new domain of international air travel when he flew to Britain, the Middle East, the USSR, and China as Franklin Delano Roosevelt's personal representative in the winter of 1941–1942. And it consolidated his belief in the importance of global peace. "Continents and oceans are plainly only parts of a whole, seen, as I have seen them, from the air," Willkie reflected. "It is inescapable that there can be no peace for any part of the world unless the foundations for peace are made secure throughout all parts of the world." *One World*, Willkie's account of the trip, was also a manifesto for postwar internationalism that sparked the American imagination—its first printing sold out in forty-eight hours, and it became only the third work of American nonfiction to sell more than a million copies. Willkie worked with the Museum of Modern Art in New York City to provide the display text for its 1943 *Airways to Peace* exhibition, a show that was designed to prove that "in a world internationalized by the airplane, peace can only be built on dynamic idealism." Economist J. Parker Van Zandt, who claimed the airplane was a "magic wand," argued in 1944 that air travel "uproots the most ingrained habits and dissolves the stubbornest prejudice." "You're never the same again" he continued: "A new earth opens within the old: a new intimacy made possible between diverse peoples. And you share in the modern magic of aircraft that is fashioning a neighborhood of nations, transforming the whole world into an island community." As the *New York Times* put it, "Our whole conception of One World is bound up with the airplane."[69]

In reality, the relationship of air travel to international politics was much more complicated. It wasn't clear why or how flight led to global consciousness—after all, the period's most famous aviator, Charles Lindbergh, had turned out to be an anti-Semitic isolationist, not an idealistic One Worlder.

And more pragmatically, airplane technology only provided the capacity for new forms of global connection—the structure of the postwar aviation industry still had to be determined by politics and the interests of states. In the 1940s, there was little international collaboration in the governance of the air; states claimed unilateral sovereignty over their airspace. In the decades before World War I, the first international congresses to consider the laws of international flight had flirted with the idea of declaring the skies to be a free and open commons—freedom of the air, it seemed, could be like the freedom of the seas—but the British, drawing on common law property rights, had claimed sovereignty over its air space in statutes in 1911 and 1913. A 1919 Convention Relating to the Regulation of Air Navigation, negotiated as part of the Versailles settlement, likewise concluded that "every state has complete and exclusive sovereignty in the air space above its territory and territorial waters"—the military uses of planes had become all too apparent in the war for states to grant potential enemies free rein. The United States, which had signed the 1919 convention but failed to ratify it, claimed similar sovereign rights in its Air Commerce Act of 1926 and then signed the Havana Convention of 1928, which spread the same philosophy of air sovereignty throughout the Western Hemisphere.[70]

As a result, airlines could only fly over or land in the territory of a foreign state if they received permission. In the interwar years, a delicate game of give-and-take had carved out a few narrow pathways for international flight. Sometimes bilateral agreements could be reached—in 1936, Britain and the US had agreed that each could land two planes a week on the other's soil; a similar agreement allowed the United States to land four planes a week in France. Elsewhere, as in Latin America, diplomatic pressure could win unilateral concessions for foreign airlines. ("We have been moving heaven and earth to help Pan American airways," admitted one State Department employee in 1928.[71])

But access to the vast network of bases that the United States had constructed during World War II had been secured only for the duration of the war. "It will by no means be a simple matter for the US to secure from other countries rights of the . . . types that it needs or would like to have," concluded one US planning committee in the late stages of the war, adding,

> in many foreign nations there is great public sentiment against the granting of air base rights to the U.S. or any other country. The concession of rights that might be regarded as "sovereign" would in most countries become a political issue of major importance. The fact that we have built or improved new fields in those countries for war purposes by no means gives us the right, and in many cases does not even give us an equitable claim to the occupation and use of such fields for military or commercial purposes in peacetime.[72]

But without such landing rights, Assistant Secretary of State Adolf Berle informed the president, "our flying would be crippled, if not stopped, in the great areas of the world." Or as *Time* magazine put it, the US airlines risked ending the war like "a sprightly young man all dressed up in fine clothes but with few places to go outside of his own yard."[73]

The important question, then, was how to convert the new potential for international aviation into a functioning network. American attitudes to this question reflected broader attitudes to international order. Henry Luce's vision of an American Century implied a world open to American travel—he said that Americans needed the "right to go with our ships and our ocean-going airplanes where we wish, when we wish, and as we wish." Such unilateralist and expansionist attitudes were shared by Juan Trippe, the powerful head of Pan American Airways. Trippe wanted to use America's strong position to maximize its advantages, declaring: "We should keep ourselves free of any general commitments in favor of reciprocity, [and] we should seek landing rights without offering them. . . . We should successfully, and without jeopardizing our own position abroad, find plausible reasons to deny most requests and keep our concessions to a minimum." (The similarity in position was no coincidence. Trippe and Luce had been friends since their Yale days; by the 1940s, they regularly golfed together.)[74]

Vice President Henry Wallace, who championed an internationalist "Century of the Common Man" against Luce's American Century, also thought that "the solution of the air problem is absolutely indispensable to solution of the problem of world peace." But in an article in the *New York Times Sunday Magazine*, he dismissed calls for American predominance in aviation as the special pleading of "new American imperialists." Instead, he preferred the creation of a vast web of reciprocal air rights, overseen by a robust international regulatory organization; he also flirted with the idea of "internationalizing . . . the large airports." Clare Booth Luce used her maiden speech in Congress in 1943 to attack Wallace's plans for freedom of the air as "globaloney," a sign of the naïve internationalism of the "all-out postwar cooperationists" who wanted a "bigger and redder and more royal New Deal for the whole world." Like her husband, and like her friend Juan Trippe, Luce said that "we should maintain our position of international civil air supremacy." (Juan, in fact, had introduced Clare to Henry.) US air policy could be boiled down to a simple maxim, "We want to fly everywhere." Given such public clashes, civil aviation policy emerged as a central front in debates about the postwar order. A young William Fulbright, for instance, made his name as a liberal internationalist by devoting *his* maiden speech in Congress to an attack on Luce's cynical and self-interested vision of air policy.[75]

Planning within the Roosevelt administration fell between the extreme nationalism of Luce/Trippe and the robust internationalism of Wallace. Both the military and the New Dealers favored a strong American aviation industry, but they believed that a competitive, liberal international environment would best lock in American advantage. To the chagrin of Trippe, who hoped to maintain his prewar monopoly, a decision was made to open international routes to domestic American airlines, which had gained experience flying internationally as part of the war effort; Howard Hughes's TWA soon changed its name from Transcontinental and Western Air to Trans World Airlines. (In a last-ditch act of obstruction, Trippe had Senators Owen Brewster and Pat McCarran introduce legislation to create one "All American Flag Line" that would monopolize international flight and would be dominated by Pan Am. The bill went nowhere.) In 1943 and 1944, the Civil Aeronautics Board consulted with US air interests to draw up a map of desired postwar routes and identify the necessary landing rights.[76]

On the all-important question of how those landing rights were to be secured, there were two factions in the administration. Lloyd Welch Pogue, chairman of the Civil Aeronautics Board, favored negotiating for them bilaterally, which would allow the United States to use its economic and geopolitical weight to secure advantageous rights. But he was opposed by Adolf Berle, who was responsible for air policy within the State Department and who fancied himself something of a Grotius of the air age; Berle thought it would be better to create a multilateral institution that would universally guarantee landing rights for all nations. It was a real disagreement about tactics—and one with potentially large consequences for the structure of the international order—but it was only a tactical dispute, for both men sought American dominance. "American interests," said Berle, would be "short sighted as not to see that the doctrine of free air is their plainest road to superiority." Pogue disagreed. He concluded that the US "had immense advantages that we ought to be taking some credit for and some of these people [who sought a multilateral commercial agreement] were throwing it away."[77]

In November 1943, Roosevelt came down on Berle's side, and plans for a multilateral international agreement picked up steam. In late 1944, fifty-two nations came to Chicago for an International Conference on Civil Aviation that was intended to establish a permanent international body to manage the skies, as well as multilateral treaties to settle the issue of postwar landing rights. Held six months before the San Francisco conference and shortly after Bretton Woods and Dumbarton Oaks, this overlooked conference revealed early signs of the tensions that would plague postwar internationalism. The Soviet Union withdrew at the last minute, ostensibly to protest the presence of Portugal, Switzerland, and Spain at a conference that it believed should have been limited to anti-Fascist allies. The United States, meanwhile, proposed an international organization "giving a larger vote to the more important countries," in which the United States, the USSR, and Britain each had two seats on a permanent governing council; Brazil, China, and France were granted permanent seats; and the remaining six were allocated to Europe (three seats), the Americans (two seats), and Asia and Africa (sharing one seat between them). Latin American nations acted as a bloc to scuttle this proposal, insisting that the council be elected by all the member states. Based in Montreal—in the 1940s, Canada was a central hub in aviation politics because planes could fly the northern circle routes only if they could land in its territory—the International Civil Aviation Organization (ICAO) soon played an important, if low-key, role in monitoring technical standards and safety guidelines and collecting statistics. But it was a weak institution, with little coercive power over the commercial and geopolitical issues that were most important to international aviation.[78]

The central action at the conference concerned writing international laws to govern landing rights. In one sign of the close relationship of international flight to liberal internationalism, it became common in the period to refer to these various commercial concessions as the "Five Freedoms." The first two of these freedoms were straightforward: they were the right to fly over a country and the right to make an emergency landing in a country. These rights were basically required for international aviation, and by the end of the Chicago conference, all fifty-two nations had signed what they called a "Two Freedoms" agreement guaranteeing them.[79]

Things got much trickier when it came to the last three freedoms, for these concerned the economic lifeblood of the airlines: the rights to pick up and put down passengers. Here the conference fell apart because of a dispute between the United States and the British Empire, the two most powerful international aviators, each anxiously eyeing their postwar position. The US had the undeniable edge in postwar commercial capacity—in 1945, it had 72 percent of the world's air commerce; Britain had only 12 percent. But by virtue of its vast territory, the British Empire controlled vitally important landing rights around the world, which the United States needed to be able to fly globally. "Without British cooperation," observed one US planning document, "we could be denied access to many of the most important centers and would find it difficult to construct any around-the-world air service under the American flag." The British, meanwhile, had no intention of simply opening up their airspace to free-market competition with the American commercial juggernaut; if they were going to facilitate the expansion of American airlines, they wanted international regulation of air traffic to protect their own industry. As one of their planning documents put it, the "choice before the world lies between Americanisation and internationalisation. . . . It is difficult to doubt that it is under the latter system that British interests will best be served." And the question of aviation was close to an existential one for the empire. After the war, said Archibald Sinclair, British secretary of state for Air, "we shall be a small island of 45 million people in a world dominated by the great US of A . . . or we shall be the center of a great Empire which will be bound together by our air routes."[80]

The Americans had tried to square things away in bilateral talks before Chicago but had been unsuccessful. The Chicago conference soon devolved into an equally unproductive sidebar between the British and the United States. On Freedoms Three and Four, there was some wiggle room. The UK was willing to grant the US the right to deliver passengers from the US to the UK (Freedom Three) and to pick up passengers in the United Kingdom and deliver them to the US (Freedom Four) so long as there was some international quota set on these routes. The US was willing to agree to a quota, as long as it was fairly loose and would not overly interfere with their commercial success. But the intractable issue was the Fifth Freedom—the right of US airlines to pick up passengers in Britain and deliver them to a third country (say, France). The US airlines needed these rights to allow them access to the European mainland; the United Kingdom feared that US airlines would be able to outcompete them on these routes and thus undermine their industry. The US put considerable effort into demanding Fifth Freedom rights—at one point, Roosevelt wrote to Winston Churchill to suggest that a failure to come to terms might threaten future lend-lease deliveries. (Churchill protested, fairly, that this was "pure blackmail.") But no agreement could be reached. (Matters weren't helped by the fact that the heads of the two delegations took an intense personal dislike to each other, nor by a communication breakdown between the British delegation and its home office, which caused backsliding at a key moment.) In the end, only twenty nations at Chicago signed a "Five Freedoms Agreement," and only nine states ever ratified it.[81]

After Chicago, the United States was forced to shift strategy to gain its all-important Fifth Freedom rights. Berle's emphasis on multilateralism was out—as was Berle, who had fallen out of favor with the new secretary of state, Edward Stettinius, who just happened to be Juan Trippe's brother-in-law. Pogue and his preference for bilateral negotiations and US power politics were in the driver's seat. Pogue had long thought that the disposal of surplus wartime airfields could be "utilized as bargaining points in reaching agreements with other nations for postwar air commerce rights." Now it became policy to transfer airfields and air equipment to foreign governments as part of the broader settlement of war surplus and to extract in exchange "satisfactory bilateral air rights agreements," including fifth freedom rights. This was seen as one way "whereby the U.S. might receive some benefit, monetary or otherwise, from the nations that will be receiving a 'windfall' when these fields come into their possession."[82]

In 1944 and 1945, the United States successfully negotiated such bilateral agreements with eight smaller European nations, but the big challenge remained the British. In early 1946, the two met in Bermuda to hammer out a bilateral air agreement. The US was willing to use whatever leverage it had to gain Fifth Freedom rights. It suggested that "the allocation of surplus equipment to the British would . . . have to be contingent upon our working out a satisfactory air transport agreement." It threatened to bypass Britain entirely by relying on its recently signed air agreement with Ireland to create routes to Europe. (Churchill had been so outraged by this move that he wrote to Roosevelt to ask him to annul the agreement.) And then it threatened to hold up delivery of the recently negotiated $3.75 billion loan to the United Kingdom until an air agreement could be reached. The British buckled, signing an agreement that granted full Fifth Freedom rights to both nations without insisting on any quotas to regulate American transatlantic traffic. "We knew what we wanted when we came," concluded Colonel George Baker, head of the American delegation, "We have got it and more."[83]

Remarkably, some US senators were skeptical that the agreement best advanced US interests. Brewster, for instance, found the deal "incomprehensible to a Yankee"—he said that the United States should have claimed Fifth Freedom rights in the United Kingdom without offering reciprocity to the British by using the loan alone as leverage. McCarran agreed, "query[ing] where the fairness is and where the U.S. was protected in these deals"; he added, "We open up a territory furnishing 80 percent of the air traffic of the world, to unlimited flights, unlimited schedules, by a country that we know has furnished only about 20 percent of the air traffic of the world." The substance of those concerns reflected the long-standing interests of the two senators in protecting the prerogatives of Pan Am and domestic airlines, but it also revealed how nationalistic US aviation policy had become just fourteen months after the Chicago conference. While the agreement did allow the British some rights to compete with US airlines, these were dwarfed by the rights that the United States had won. The Bermuda agreement, like all aviation agreements, reserved the domestic market to domestic airlines; foreign airlines could pick up passengers in the United States, but only if they were flying them out of the country. This was a boon to the US. As Baker explained, an American airline could "pick up in the United Kingdom and set down on the continent anywhere; whereas, they [the British] can't pick up in New York or San Francisco and set down anywhere in our continent. So the over-all deal seemed very much in our favor." The balance sheet for international competition was similarly skewed to the United States. The British would be allowed to fly two routes from New Orleans (to Mexico City and to Cuba, and then down the West Coast of Latin America), which did allow them to compete on these routes with Pan Am. But in exchange, the US won the right not only to fly from London to Europe—considered a much more promising market—but also the right to fly from Calcutta and Bombay and Singapore and thus deep into Asia. "We believe we made a very good bargain," concluded Baker understandably, even if it fell short of the expectations of pugnacious nationalists like McCarran and Brewster. "Unfortunately," he explained to the senators, "in this world we seem to have to give at least something for everything we get."[84]

After Bermuda, the United States continued to successfully negotiate for bilateral agreements. It used the disposal of surplus wartime airfields as part of the leverage to construct a global network of routes. In Egypt, for instance, Pan Am and TWA required landing rights at Payne Field, which had been built by the US during the war. But the Egyptian government was reluctant to grant them Fifth Freedom rights, for it held out hopes of building up its own international airline, Misr Airways. Egypt also had some leverage, for with British funding, it had built its own Almaza airfield, which it hoped to designate as its international airport. Almaza was in a better location than the remote Payne Field (Almaza's proximity to Cairo meant, among other things, that employees could take a train to work), but its runways were not capable of handling the new, large planes that the US commercial airlines hoped to fly through the region. Meanwhile, the British, whose less advanced fleet *could* land at Almaza, proposed funding Misr Airways in exchange for exclusive air rights; by the time the British were ready to fly larger planes, they would have extended Almaza's runways. In short, the Americans risked being squeezed out—the Egyptians could deny American airlines Fifth Freedom rights and negotiate a protectionist air agreement with the British. But then the United States decided to transfer Payne Field, its equipment, and a number of surplus airplanes to the Egyptians as part of the overall surplus settlement. It was a good deal for the Egyptians, one that the British couldn't match. Payne Field was renamed for King Farouk and designated as an international airport, and the US was granted Fifth Freedom rights in Egypt; under a new name and new owners, Payne Field had been "maintain[ed] as a link in the chain of airfields built around the world during the war."[85]

In the rest of the world, too, the United States proved savvy in negotiating favorable aviation agreements. The Czechs were given a few thousand gallons of surplus aviation gasoline to sign over fifth freedom rights; Italy was granted ownership of wartime airfield installations in exchange for US rights; in exchange for ownership of US-built airfields on French soil, the French granted the US air rights to Paris, Marseille, Algiers, Tunis, Dakar, Pointe Noire, Brazzaville, Guadeloupe, Martinique, French Guiana, New Caledonia, Saigon, and Hanoi. Surplus disposal also helped accomplish the equally significant, if more mundane, task of technical standardization. Most of the world's navigational, air communications, and weather equipment had been built, and placed at key locations around the globe, by the US military—some 257 installations scattered across sixty-eight countries. A standard services agreement was drawn up in which this material was transferred to foreign governments (along with a pledge to train foreign personnel to run them and, if available, a year's supply of maintenance parts) if they agreed to maintain and operate it in keeping with US standards. Thus, the surplus disposal functionally fulfilled one of the central jobs for which the International Civil Aviation Organization had been created. "Today," observed the State Department in 1947, "a substantial part of the facilities being operated at international airports consists of US surplus military equipment. To this extent the work of the ICAO has been made easier."[86]

In all, the intertwined disposal of air surplus and negotiation of aviation agreements secured a world open to the expansion of US commercial airlines. By the middle of 1946, the United States was so pleased with the successes of its bilateral strategy that it announced that it was formally withdrawing from the multilateral five freedoms treaty it had proposed only two years earlier. At the end of the year, an aviation agreement with China removed the "last major obstacle to the operation of American around-the-world air services." It was the twenty-third bilateral agreement the US had signed since the Chicago conference had sputtered out.[87]

In theory, these agreements were almost all reciprocal—they allowed foreign airlines fifth freedom rights in the United States as well as providing for US expansion. But the reciprocity here was more theoretical than actual—and not only because of US geographical isolation. Even more importantly, most other nations lacked the commercial capacity to take advantage of their fifth freedom rights, at least in the immediate future. US airlines instantly gained three new routes through China, while the Chinese had no airline that could fly to the United States. And on the rare occasion when there was serious risk that the US would lose out in a free competition with a foreign airline, the US acted to protect its own interests, as negotiations with the Dutch revealed. The US had relatively little to gain from Fifth Freedom rights in the Netherlands—the market was small, and access to Europe was secured via other nations. But the Dutch airline KLM threatened to be a powerful competitor on transatlantic routes and on routes connecting the US East Coast to the Caribbean (via the Netherlands Antilles), particularly because it had built a business model bringing other central Europeans to the Netherlands before ferrying them overseas. So the US simply refused to grant KLM the four routes through the United States that it wanted—it limited them to two, which it made temporary and subject to revision. The Dutch had little leverage in response, apart from futile jeremiads against American hypocrisy. The issue remained a diplomatic sticking point into the 1970s.[88]

As a result of such hard-nosed bargaining, and the strategic use of the wartime surplus, the US aviation industry entered the postwar period with the landing rights and air routes to take advantage of its massive commercial capacity. Its airlines would dominate international aviation for decades.

In all, the surplus disposal had turned into an unexpected windfall for the United States. "The return which has been obtained for overseas surplus," boasted Secretary of State James F. Byrnes in 1946, "has already far exceeded the realization hoped for . . . [and] it has been possible to effect this realization on terms which will result in a substantially greater direct and immediate benefit to the American taxpayer than we had believed possible."[89] Material that had been considered almost worthless a little more than a year before had been almost miraculously converted into new networks for American cultural expansion: an educational exchange program centered on the United States, a string of gleaming new buildings, and a global civil aviation network welcoming to US airlines. Each of these networks, in its own way, was structured by unilateral US power and nationalist self-interest. Each was designed to promote the expansion of US power rather than any truly international exchange of information. And though their creation had cost the United States very little—in fact, these networks cost only a small percentage of the moneys the US received from its surplus—they were nevertheless sufficient to displace and marginalize more genuinely internationalist endeavors aimed at the same ends. The Fulbright Program and US embassy buildings would do more to remake flows of global information than UNESCO; bilateral US air negotiations were more important to postwar aviation than the international treaty proposed at Chicago. At the dawn of the postwar order, international cultural networks were thus shaped more by unilateral US power than by multilateral institutions. The material excess of US war production, it turned out, was simply too powerful a mechanism of cultural globalization.

CHAPTER THREE

PASSPORTS, VISAS, AND THE POLITICS OF INTERNATIONAL TRAVEL

In September 1945, the magazine *Free World* announced in a special issue devoted to the end of the war the creation of a column devoted to travel. The magazine, a bastion of left-liberal internationalism, predicted a new "round-the-world flow of tourists," and so promised to bring to readers "every bit of information available about the opening up of travel facilities, transportation, hotel and other arrangements." Such prosaic information was presumed to contribute directly to the stability of the new international order. "It is our faith," declared the editors, "that travel on a vast scale will give more guarantees of lasting peace than armies, or navies, or bombs. By understanding, the peace of the world will be made to endure."[1]

Similar sentiments were widespread among the liberal elites responsible for constructing the postwar order. Frederick Ogilvie, economist and director-general of the British Broadcasting Corporation, asserted in 1946 that travel "can do more than any other single agency to promote international understanding and goodwill, breaking down prejudices and hatreds and laying foundations for an enduring peace." Chinese diplomat Wu Nan-Ju agreed, arguing in 1947 that "the free intercourse and personal contact between peoples were the only grounds on which international peace could be based." Freedom of movement was also a central plank of the postwar US vision of a liberal international order, for it, too, saw the movement of people as fundamentally intertwined with the free flow of ideas. "International travel," declared one group of postwar planners in the US government, "is of the greatest importance in promoting friendship and improving cultural relations among nations."[2]

Yet at the same time, the United States tightly regulated the movement of people across its own borders. In the 1940s, the obscure Passport

Division within the State Department denied passports to hundreds of Americans, preventing international travel that security-minded officials determined was "not in the best interests of the United States." And a similarly obscure Visa Division carefully screened foreigners seeking to travel to the United States, denying visas to all whom it considered security risks. There was a clear contradiction between this expansive regime of border protection and the promotion of international travel as a key to world peace. When he was denied a passport to travel to Palestine in 1948, Irving De Witt Talmadge understandably complained that such practices were "an infringement of the free flow of information principle of the United Nations which this country has pledged itself to uphold."[3]

These competing policy imperatives would come to a head in a forgotten series of international conferences and congresses in the late 1940s that sought to liberalize international visa and passport requirements. These conferences were a central arena in which international liberals tried to construct a world order based on understanding and free flows of information. Serious effort was made to draft binding multilateral treaties that would allow individuals to travel without documents, and plans were laid for the creation of a UN organization devoted to the principles of free travel. At first, US delegates to these conferences were enthusiastic about this program of travel liberalization—they tended to come from sections of the state interested in promoting international commerce, and they saw free travel as a way to promote the tourism industry and thus globalize the international economy. But then conservative, security-conscious officials within the Visa and Passport branches of the State Department opposed any efforts to reduce their regulation of the border. What emerged from this philosophical and bureaucratic clash was a hypocritical policy. The United States asked other nations to reduce their border controls to allow the free international movement of US citizens, but it would make no reductions of its own national security regulations at the border.

Because of postwar America's economic and geopolitical might, this policy was successful, with significant repercussions for the development of postwar travel rights. The United States could use its economic leverage to force other nations to accept more US tourists without liberalizing its own border regime. Other nations, hungry for US tourist dollars, obliged. As a result, the proposed UN Travel Organization was delayed for decades, the United States maintained severe ideological barriers at its border, and what had been imagined as a global order of border liberalization emerged in a piecemeal fashion, most notably in Europe. As a new era of international travel dawned, the mobility rights of individuals remained deeply structured by geopolitical power.[4]

Those seeking to travel internationally in the 1940s faced considerable bureaucratic obstacles. Traveling across national borders required documents—a lot of documents, as Harvard law professor Sidney Post Simpson discovered in 1946 when he surveyed entry requirements in thirty-four Western Hemisphere nations: 22 required health certificates; 20 required a smallpox vaccination certificate; 18 needed varying degrees of proof of financial solvency; 23 needed photos; 19 required a police certificate of good conduct (an oddly useless document, because one could go to any police department to issue a certificate that you had no criminal record in their particular jurisdiction). The specific requirements varied from nation to nation: some wanted photos from the front, some from the side; Surinam required one photo, Venezuela, fourteen. And those were the *entry* requirements. Many states also required documentation for exit. Travel to multiple nations thus required a panoply of documents. In 1946, one air pilot reported that he had carried 155 different papers on one flight.[5]

Such travel requirements were a relatively new phenomenon. "Before 1914," observed the United Nations Economic and Social Council, "the international traveler could, except in certain countries, move about freely without passport or visa." The middle decades of the nineteenth century had seen the birth of what is often called an era of free migration, as nations of Western Europe rolled back border restrictions and allowed free international movement. In truth, this was a brief and partial period of liberalization. The late nineteenth century also saw the rise of new forms of border control aimed at restricting the movement of large categories of people: Asians in the Pacific, Eastern Europeans seeking to move to the West, immigrants who were seen as carriers of dangerous diseases and ideologies. But for travelers of the right background, it was an era of relatively free movement, and borders could be crossed without documentation.[6]

The outbreak of World War I saw the rapid imposition of a host of passport and visa requirements that affected all travelers. States around the world paid new attention to the movement of individuals. They sought to exclude spies and saboteurs and to prevent potential draftees from fleeing abroad; if neutral, they sought to prevent traveling citizens from coming to harm in war zones and potentially embroiling them in the conflict. Such regulations were not relaxed after the armistice. In interwar decades of rising geopolitical conflict, economic protectionism, and dictatorial government, security concerns remained high. And as exemplified by the implementation of strict quotas on immigration to the United States in the 1920s, states seeking to restrict migration on racist grounds became ever more concerned with documenting the movement of individuals across their borders—it was only once the borders were closed to permanent immigrants that a new system of travel documentation became required to distinguish visitors from potentially "illegal" immigrants. In a more material sense, too, the interwar rise of tourism was a consequence of the closing of the borders: international steamship companies turned to tourists to fill the third-class steerage compartments that had once housed migrants. And then, with the outbreak of World War II, new emergency wartime restrictions on entry and exit were instituted.[7] By 1945, therefore, travelers faced the accumulation of decades worth of restrictions and regulations.

Meeting these various documentary requirements took considerable time and effort. In post–World War II Colombia, approval of visa requests sometimes involved sending a wire to the foreign office in Bogota, which could take up to twenty days to respond. In El Salvador, travelers needed to pay $1 for a visa, deposit three photographs, and report to local police within forty-eight hours of arrival; individuals staying longer than seven days needed to be fingerprinted for an identification card for emigration, which needed to be countersigned by the Office of Foreign Relations. The process could take three to four days "sitting around in offices and wasting time," according to one frustrated traveler. (Moreover, he reported to the State Department, "the treatment one receives from the petty officials is very unpleasant.")[8]

For travelers on business, for whom time was money, such delays were particularly frustrating. With the rise of air travel, it was now possible to imagine ever more ambitious itineraries, hopping quickly from one country to the next. Bureaucratic delays that had only been annoying while waiting for one's ship to leave port became intolerable when they interfered with more finely calibrated schedules. In 1947, the American Legation in Addis Ababa wrote to the secretary of state to complain that the export manager for Reynolds Metal Company had lost half of his only day in town to the finicky task of getting exit permits from Ethiopia and a visa for Eritrea—time that could have been spent making business connections. In 1946, the Air Transport Association (ATA) likewise produced a long document outlining the "maze of regulations" faced by travelers. Tellingly, the imagined protagonist in the ATA's document was a man making his first international flights who had been told to travel to three countries "to make a preliminary study in some field of business."[9]

During World War II, as such travel documents became a symbol of all that was wrong with the old regime, many began to imagine that the postwar order would do away with them. For instance, when US bomber pilot Gary Davis renounced national citizenship and declared himself to be the "first world citizen," he symbolically marked the occasion by printing himself a self-designed "World Passport." Davis may have seen himself striding boldly into a postnationalist future, but most hoped for a return to a passportless past. This is what Ernest Bevin had in mind when he famously announced that his foreign policy could be reduced to the desire to "go down to Victoria Station, get a railway ticket and go where the hell I like without a passport or anything else."[10]

It was that attitude that led to the formation of a number of new organizations lobbying for the global liberalization of travel regulations. The International Chamber of Commerce formed a Committee of Experts on Consular and Customs Formalities in Transportation in 1946 that sought a radical simplification and reduction in travel regulations to secure "with the least possible delay . . . the return to the pre-1914 regime. e.g. the abolition of the compulsory passport" and "the elimination of all visa requirements." The International Touring Association likewise hoped for a "return to the system used before the First World War." In 1946, leading American manufacturers, airlines, railroads, shipping companies, and travel agencies formed a Committee for World Travel that had a single, specific objective echoing Bevin's vision of passport-free travel: "any American desiring to take a trip abroad for business or pleasure should normally be able to obtain all necessary documents on the same day he decides to make the trip."[11]

The most important of these postwar initiatives was an International Conference of International Tourist Organisations, which met in London in September 1946. With delegates and observers from forty-one countries, it was the largest-ever conference of travel organizations—a decade earlier, only fourteen nations had attended a precursor meeting—and the gathered delegates were in the mood to take bold steps to liberalize international travel. Ahmed Seddik Pasha, representing the Egyptian State Tourist Administration, called for the world to abolish visas and "return to the status quo before 1914 when we were all happy and when everything went very well." ("Hear, hear!" responded the delegates.) When another delegate suggested that that was not practical, Australian journalist Thomas Dunbabin objected. "I do not see why we cannot," asserted Dunbabin, because "all these wretched restrictions do not prevent anything harmful happening."[12]

Given such sentiments, the delegates passed a host of resolutions calling for the easing of customs and tariff barriers, the gathering of standardized tourist statistics, and the promotion of international travel. Tellingly, they also called for the creation of an international organization to work to reduce tourist barriers and created a committee charged with bringing it into being. (As T. C. Choi from China explained, "Everybody will agree that mere discussion at this conference will not produce any concrete results unless we call upon some international organization to give effect to the resolutions.") All these measures were passed unanimously. Objections to the proposed organization sought only to make it more robust: Scotland wanted it to have a larger budget so that it would not feel like "playing with a Meccano set"; Egypt and Lebanon wanted assurances that European states would not dominate.[13]

Nevertheless, beneath the surface of such liberal consensus lurked deeper tensions. The only resolution that did not win unanimous approval was perhaps the most important: "at the earliest possible moment steps should be taken for the immediate simplification of visas and passports and for the ultimate abolition of visas." Even the inclusion of a distinction between simplification and abolition struck some delegates as a sellout. "We are either convinced or we are not that visas are necessary," fumed Seddik from Egypt. "Why the talk about simplification? . . . If we are convinced that visas are useless we should ask our governments to act and to abolish them." But the hedging remained in the resolution, and even then, it failed to win support from New Zealand, Romania, and, most importantly, the United States. ("Efforts were made by the delegation," reported the Americans afterward, "to eliminate the words 'ultimate abolition of visas' from the resolution. . . . These efforts were unavailing.") The position of the United States would come to be very important.[14]

Still, given all the other activity in 1946, this momentary lack of unanimity seemed little more than a blip in the move to liberalize travel. All these groups saw themselves as heirs to interwar efforts to roll back passport and visa requirements. In 1920 and 1926, League of Nations conferences on passports and customs formalities had advocated a return to the pre-1914 regime, and league surveys suggested that there had been tentative movement in this direction before the international crises of the 1930s. Similarly, Inter-American Travel Congresses, held in 1939 and 1941, had sought to reduce passport and visa requirements and "make the Western Hemisphere a single great tourist area where travelers may move about freely and easily."[15]

It was not long before the United Nations took up the issue of travel. In May 1946, the Temporary Transport and Communications Commission of the Economic and Social Council recommended that an international conference be held to work toward liberalizing world travel. To prepare the way, it called for a Meeting of Experts to be held in early 1947 to develop specific policy proposals and then charged its secretariat to prepare an agenda for these meetings. The agenda, drawing from the London conference, proposed a variety of measures to reduce and simplify passport requirements, visa requirements, and frontier formalities (such as customs and baggage inspections). Expert delegates from thirty-two nations, plus a number of observers, would gather in Geneva in April 1947 to debate these agenda items and set the stage for a future conference that would commit the United Nations to freedom of movement.[16]

At first, officials within the US government supported this drive toward the multilateral reduction of travel restrictions. Averell Harriman's Department of Commerce, in particular, was "vitally interested in the encouragement of international travel as one of the most important elements in our foreign trade." Harriman was so enthusiastic for two reasons. "First," he explained in December 1946, "we want to make it as easy as possible for businessmen to travel." This was hardly a surprising position for Harriman. He was, after all, a child of corporate privilege, a highly successful international banker and venture capitalist, and one of the first Americans to own a private plane. Commerce, moreover, had long been a promoter of international business. Harriman's second interest in travel appeared to be more populist. "We want to encourage tourist as well as commercial travel," he said. But on closer examination, this was also a matter of simple economics. Travel, Harriman explained, "has been our greatest 'commodity' import in peacetime and has furnished far more U.S. exchange to customer countries than any other commodity item."[17]

This was an important, if initially counterintuitive, piece of accounting. When Americans spent money abroad as travelers, this spending was logged as an *import* in the national balance of payments. Americans were sending money overseas; in exchange, they were, in essence, importing the experience of being overseas. As an official within the Department of Transportation and Economic Development in the Office of Inter-American Affairs explained, "expenditures made by US tourists in a foreign country are an import on our part, because we are importing goods and services, and an export on the part of the country in which the dollars are spent." And lest the implications of that bookkeeping were misunderstood, he pointed out that, at least in the case of Latin America, "it is pretty safe to say that every tourist dollar we spend there soon returns to us for the purchase of products of our own industries." Or, as Harriman put it, tourist travel was a "means of placing dollar exchanges abroad to help pay for exports from the US."[18]

Encouraging Americans to travel abroad thus appeared to be a crucial mechanism for overcoming the dollar gap. It was an important way to recirculate dollars, providing foreign nations with the capital to invest, to develop, and, ultimately, to support America's export economy. In fact, studies within the US government soon suggested that foreign travel had a peculiarly important role in the foreign account balance. In 1937, which was considered "neither a heavy nor a light travel year," gross foreign travel expenditures amounted to $472 million, circulating more dollars to the world than any other imported commodity. (The three closest contenders were paper base stock, at $254 million; rubber, at $252 million; and textiles, at $250 million.) Between 1920 and 1940, US travelers abroad had deposited more than $8 billion overseas.[19]

Now, with the postwar economy booming and the dollar gap looming, foreign travel seemed to promise unprecedented rewards. If foreign travel grew at the same rate as the national economy, something like $1.25 billion might be spent overseas in 1946. And more optimistic planners spied a "historic pattern" in which travel expenditures grew faster than the national economy as travel costs dropped with the rise of new forms of transportation and as ever-larger numbers of American workers received ever-longer paid vacations.[20]

Travel also promised more specific economic rewards to those in the travel industry. US travel agencies and commercial airlines met privately with the Commerce Department, encouraging it to relax travel regulations. Owen Brewster, widely derided as the "Senator from Pan-Am" for his close ties to the airline, introduced legislation to Congress to reduce travel restrictions. Juan Trippe, keen to reap the benefits of Pan Am's new global network, publicly called for "World Prosperity through International Travel"—he was adept at translating his own economic interests into the more palatable language of liberal internationalism. "For we Americans," he added, "foreign travel is a cultural, political and economic necessity if our country is to fulfill its responsibility of world leadership."[21]

More broadly, US administrators thought that international tourism promised a painless mode of economic development for countries receiving American tourists. "In many respects," opined one State Department memo, tourism "is an economic resource which involves no real depletion of natural resources. It is an especially important factor in under-developed countries since its development requires relatively little investment in imports." In January 1946, a US Department of Commerce publication extolled the developmental benefits of international tourism in more quotidian terms. If five hundred tourists to Brazil spent $10 a day for ten days, it would be worth as much to its national economy as exporting a $50,000 cargo of rubber—"as almost everyone will agree," it added, "selling food, souvenirs and entertainment to the tourists would be a more agreeable occupation for the Brazilians than trying to extract $50,000 worth of rubber from the Amazonian jungles." And whereas making $5 from banana exports cost Guatemalans a great deal of risk and labor, the country could "enrich itself by that same $5 with almost no effort at all—merely by encouraging Mr. Smith to tour around the country with a camera for one day photographing donkeys, Indians, and volcanoes." If Guatemala "enriched itself," it also meant that it didn't need any resources redistributed from wealthy nations like the United States. Even better, relying on tourism to develop foreign economies seemed not to interfere with American economic interests. "Unlike commodity imports," observed one journalist, "tourist spending abroad may be expanded indefinitely without raising any question of serious injury to domestic industry." International tourism, in short, promised a frictionless world of capital accumulation—a liberal economist's dream of rising tides and free exchanges, of value without labor, of growth without exploitation.[22]

American enthusiasm for smoothing away obstacles to travel after World War II was thus heightened; and despite superficial similarities with earlier, interwar efforts, the existence of the dollar gap meant that the United States had new and distinctive interests in the issue. In the late 1930s, when the US first began sending delegates to Inter-American Travel Congresses, it had wanted only to "overcome the unfavorable trade balance in the travel account." To balance the amount of money US tourists were spending overseas, it sought to lure Latin Americans—and their money. In other words, before the war, economic conditions had incentivized the US to lure in foreign travelers. Now, economic conditions meant that the United States was interested only in promoting the foreign travel of its citizens. This would shape American policies in important ways.[23]

In sum, for American advocates in the immediate wake of World War II, promoting the free movement of travelers and tourists promised to harmonize the world economy. In a radio broadcast in October 1946, William Clayton, then undersecretary of state for Economic Affairs, said that the booming US expenditure on foreign travel would "by itself" amortize American international loans over the next twenty-five years. The month before, the executive secretary of the Executive Committee on Economic Foreign Policy had gone as far as to suggest that "American foreign travel . . . may be no less important than the [International Monetary] Fund, the [World] Bank, or the exchange control provisions of the draft charter in freeing world trade."[24]

To pursue these important goals, an interdepartmental Committee on Foreign Travel (CFT) was created in the executive branch. Charged with "promot[ing] . . . travel that will bring about better international relations," the committee was placed under the directorship of Herbert Wilkinson of the Commerce Department.[25] Wilkinson, a US delegate to the London Conference of Tourist Organisations, was a champion of the department's liberal vision for free international movement. A native of South Dakota, Wilkinson appeared to be a recent convert to the cause, his enthusiasm itself a sign of the recent US discovery of the importance of free travel to international liberalism. After studying law and economics at Cornell, Johns Hopkins, and Georgetown, Wilkinson had joined the Agricultural Adjustment Administration as an economist during the New Deal and then worked as chief of export control for the Board of Economic Warfare before joining the navy in 1943. As was typical of so many minor government officials, war service marked a transition from domestic interwar work to international postwar work. In 1945, Wilkinson had joined the Office of International Trade.[26]

Under Wilkinson's chairmanship, the CFT began to outline a program for the reduction of visa and passport restrictions. It wanted to put the United States on record as "favor[ing] a universal return to the pre-1914 practice of permitting travel without passports." And as long as passports continued to exist, the CFT opined that state control over their issuance should be relaxed—they should be valid for at least five years and renewable upon application. The CFT also favored a worldwide reduction in visa requirements. At the 1946 London conference, Wilkinson had followed policy instructions that the United States wanted other nations to waive visa requirements for US citizens, but that it would not waive its own. ("We would like to receive for American travelers all possible concessions," explained one internal policy memo, but "we are unable under existing legislation to offer reciprocity on some points.") Now, the CFT argued that it would not be enough for the "US to sit back and watch other nations eliminate restrictions unilaterally"—the United States would also need to reduce its restrictive practices to produce a more liberal world. To pursue these goals, and to help create a liberal postwar order, the CFT even imagined the creation of a World Travel Charter and a UN World Travel Organization. "A peace which should enable all men to traverse the high seas, the air and all lands without hindrance as envisioned by the Atlantic Charter," it said, "requires collective action by the nations to remove barriers to international travel."[27]

These deliberations of the CFT in the winter of 1946–1947 were the high point of US interest in liberalizing travel. This small group of policy makers saw the upcoming Geneva meetings as an opportunity for the United States to participate in a worldwide effort to return to the era of free movement and to create a multilateral UN institution devoted to promoting that cause. Wilkinson's CFT did not pursue these goals simply out of altruism or self-sacrifice. Rather, its agenda was the culmination of the Commerce Department's economic goals, which were seen to be completely compatible with these abstract liberal principles. As Herbert Wilkinson put it, "There does not appear to be any conflict between the objectives of promoting trade and scientific and cultural understanding."[28]

But travel policy was more complicated than that. Behind the scenes, sections of the State Department were beginning to question the CFT's liberal policy agenda. Through the end of 1946, it had primarily been the economic offices of the State Department that had been interested in the question of international travel, and they had tended to see things in much the same light as the Commerce Department. But as the rest of the State Department discussed travel policy in the run-up to the Geneva meeting, a greater diversity of opinions emerged. In January 1947, a decision was made to establish an intradepartmental committee that would meet fortnightly to articulate a more coherent set of State Department policies on travel and then present them to the CFT. In February, at the first meeting of this new Travel Policy Committee (TPC), chairman Paul Nitze made clear just what had been missed by the liberal internationalists on the CFT, noting that "it must also be borne in mind that the complete elimination of travel barriers in order to facilitate trade cannot be undertaken without sufficient consideration being given to the security aspects of such programs."[29]

Quickly, Nitze's committee moved to remedy the oversight. At its next meeting, representatives from the Visa Division and the Passport Division joined the TPC.[30] Both divisions were central components of the national security state. To understand how they changed US travel policy in the late 1940s, it is necessary to understand how these organizations had developed and how they were accustomed to regulating the border.

Both the Passport and Visa Divisions had been born in the flurry of security activity around World War I that began creating the infrastructure to protect the nation from subversives. In 1917, amid dark warnings from intelligence officials that German agents were passing into and out of the nation, a travel control act was passed "to control the transmission of information in and out of the country." Congress simply authorized the president to issue proclamations regulating the entry and exit of all persons in the interests of public safety. (According to the bill's sponsor, Representative Henry D. Flood, it was "essential that the executive have wide discretion and wide authority" because "no one can foresee the different means which may be adopted by hostile nations to secure military information or spread propaganda and discontent.") On August 8, President Woodrow Wilson proclaimed that no citizens or aliens would receive the necessary documents to cross the border "unless it shall affirmatively appear that there are adequate reasons for such departure or entry and that such departure or entry is not prejudicial to the interests of the United States." Violating the order was punishable by fines of up to $10,000 or twenty years in prison.[31]

These regulations lingered after the armistice, even though everyone had understood them to be temporary. ("This is strictly a wartime proposition," A. W. Parker of the Bureau of Immigration had testified to Congress at the time.) In 1921, after Congress had rejected multiple appeals from the administration to make the visa regulations permanent, an obscure rider to the Diplomatic and Consular Appropriations bill accomplished this sea change in US border policy—all foreigners now needed a visa to enter the country. And although the end of the war meant that US citizens no longer needed a passport to leave the nation, it was nevertheless increasingly important to hold a passport because many other nations had, like the United States, maintained their own entry controls.[32]

The Visa and Passport Divisions therefore blossomed in the interwar period. With the introduction of racial quotas to limit immigration in 1924 came the creation of new categories of nonimmigrant visas so that merchants, students, and tourists would not count toward their country's respective quotas. This produced a new task of bureaucratic policing, handled by consular officers advised by the Visa Division. (In a sign of the period's extreme caution about border control, being issued a visa just meant that you had the right to apply for entry at the border. Border officials would double-check the work of consular officials and could still bar entry.) Meanwhile, a series of executive orders, as well as the Passport Act of 1926, gave the secretary of state broad and undefined authority to decide who could and could not be issued a passport as well as the process for making those determinations.[33]

One of the primary ways both the Visa and Passport Divisions exercised their new powers was by regulating the movement of suspected radicals. Antianarchist laws that barred entry to those who advocated the overthrow of the government by force, or were members of organizations that did, applied to both immigrant and nonimmigrant visas alike. And although those laws didn't specifically bar members of the Communist Party, it was assumed by all, including the attorney general, that they were intended to do precisely that. (This is why the repeated efforts of conservative

Congressmen Hamilton Fish and Martin Dies to pass anti-Communist immigration laws repeatedly died in Congress in the early 1930s.) And so a wide variety of radicals were denied entry to the United States. To take one particularly evocative example, in 1925, S. J. Saklatvala, an Indian-born member of the British Parliament, was denied a visa to attend a meeting of the Interparliamentary Union in Washington, DC. Saklatvala was a member of the Communist Party, an advocate for the global working class, and a noted critic of the British Empire; upon learning that he could not travel to the United States, he asked, pugnaciously, "Is America afraid of the truth?" The American Civil Liberties Union and the Communist Party protested the exclusion, and Senator William Borah attempted to remove authority over visas from the State Department. But the incident blew over—the British were happy to deny the anticolonial Saklatvala a platform, and Secretary of State Frank Kellogg remained unrepentant, explaining that there was "no reason" that Saklatvala "should be considered exempt from the immigration law any more than the humblest immigrant." (Coincidentally, William Fulbright was studying at Oxford on his Rhodes Scholarship during the incident and heard Saklatvala give a talk to the American Club that descended into an anti-American protest. The young Arkansan was struck less by the visa issue than he was by the behavior of the "ruffians and asses" in the protest. "Never fear me becoming anglicized," he wrote his mother, "[the British] really aren't so 'hot' after all."[34])

The Passport Division was similarly keen to deny passports to suspected radicals, but it had been issued no standards to do so and was simply making up policy as it went along. "Our decisions where radicals are concerned," complained an internal memo in 1920, "are impressionistic and contradictory." To standardize things, the division simply borrowed a definition of radicalism from the 1918 immigration act, replacing the word "alien" in the act with "citizen." As simple as that, it had just developed a broad policy to limit the movement of American citizens. That policy stood until 1931, when Secretary of State Cordell Hull spontaneously and unexpectedly reversed it—he was worried that denying passports to Communists would give radical critics of the United States "evidence that our Government is a class government in the hands of the capitalist classes." The reversal was accomplished simply, swiftly, and unilaterally. "As I understand that I have complete discretion in the matter," Hull declared, "I think it is wiser not to refuse the passport."[35]

In the rising geopolitical tensions of the late 1930s, both divisions gained expanded powers over travel. The Passport Division sought to limit the rights of Americans to travel to particular regions of the world.

As war broke out in Ethiopia, Spain, and China, the State Department stamped passports invalid for travel to these regions—ostensibly a move designed to preserve neutrality, but one which also reflected a new interest in policing citizens' international political engagement, allowing travel only for internationalist agendas compatible with those of the executive branch. And while the Passport Division's reach turned out to be larger than its grasp (foreign governments did not enforce the stamps), and while some two hundred volunteers for the Spanish Civil War were denied their passports (roughly four thousand Americans did fight for the republic), an executive order in 1938 gave legal imprimatur to the new practice.[36]

At the same time, amid fears of German spies and saboteurs, increased control was exercised over foreigners traveling to the United States. An Alien Registration Act provided new powers to deport radicals and required all aliens applying for visas or currently within the United States to register with and be fingerprinted by the state. In June 1940, control over immigration was transferred from the Department of Labor to the Department of Justice to allow, as attorney general Robert Jackson explained, "a more strict control of the privilege of entering this country." No one would be issued a visa unless it "affirmatively appears to be for the American interest."[37]

Then, in June 1941, the Visa and Passport Divisions successfully lobbied for yet further powers. The Visa Division was worried that when foreigners visited the United States, they "might have carried back some valuable information to Germany," such as a German technician who had been working on a defense project in Buffalo and then returned to repair a German phenol plant that had been bombed by the British. The head of the Passport Division, Ruth Shipley, also wanted tighter controls. "When a person has to have a passport to get to certain places," she told Congress, "then you have the opportunity to find out why he is going and where he is going and what he is going to do will be inimical to the best interests of the US or against the public safety." On June 20, Congress passed a law requiring consular officials to deny visas to aliens whom they believed would "endanger the public safety of the U.S." The next day Congress quietly amended the 1918 Travel Control Act so that the president would have the authority to issue a proclamation requiring a passport not only during a state of war, but also during the "unlimited national emergency" that Franklin Delano Roosevelt had declared on May 27, 1941. On November 14, the president issued just such a travel proclamation. No citizens would be allowed to leave the nation without a passport, and foreigners would not be allowed to leave without an exit permit.[38]

The Passport and Visa Divisions exercised their new authorities by issuing a host of restrictive regulations. Passports were denied to ever-larger categories of travelers. In April 1941, the *New York Times* reported that the issuance of passports had "dwindled to a trickle" because of "the restrictions and microscopic scrutiny to which each application is subjected." Later that year, the Passport Division required the revalidation of all passports in an attempt to minimize fraud and to remove passports "from the hands of persons engaged in activities not in the best interests of the United States." (There was particular concern about a bogus passport ring in Athens.) The new passports, which had to be revalidated every six months, featured a new security measure, the fingerprints of the issuing officer. In all, the war introduced what the State Department called a "radical change in the Division's functions." Whereas the interwar Passport Division had, according to the State Department, been ostensibly committed to protecting the individual citizen while traveling abroad, its "principal purpose" was now "to safeguard and maintain the security of the state."[39]

The Visa Division, too, was transformed by the war. In the first twenty years of its existence, it had grown slowly—the 17 individuals who staffed the organization in 1918 had expanded to only 27 by 1938. By October 1940, it had 47 employees. But then, in the rush of new regulations, the staff mushroomed. By the middle of 1942, the Visa Division was employing 278 people who were so overworked by the heightened scrutiny that they were giving all visa applications that they logged 27,400 hours of overtime. Working in conjunction with the FBI and counterintelligence officials, they were zealous in denying visas to individuals they considered to be security risks. In September 1942, for instance, they rejected 800 of the 1,100 applications they reviewed.[40]

By the end of the war, these obscure offices in the State Department had accumulated tremendous powers over the ability of individuals to travel. Swollen beyond recognition by repeated delegations of authority, they entered the postwar period with incredible discretion to regulate international travel. Communist artists, intellectuals, and political figures were routinely denied visas in the late 1940s: Brazilian architect Oscar Niemeyer, Mexican painter David Alfaro Siqueiros, and the "Red Dean" of Canterbury, Dr. Hewlett Johnson, to name just a handful. In 1948, Ukrainian and Belarussian delegates to the UN Human Rights Commission were denied visas to attend meetings responsible for drafting the Universal Declaration of Human Rights. The Passport Division, meanwhile, issued passports only to those whose travel it believed to be in the best interests of the United States. In 1948, even Congressman Leo Isacson was denied a passport to go to Paris on a fact-finding mission about US policy in Greece. Isacson had criticized early Cold War foreign policy, and the Passport Division believed that issuing a passport to the government representative was "not in the interests of the government."[41]

Because the Passport and Visa Divisions were understood to be protecting national security and engaging in foreign affairs, they were not subject to the various procedural protections that were becoming the norm of the growing regulatory state. Decades of jurisprudence had established that foreigners could not claim constitutional rights to enter the nation. In 1938, when a Canadian anarchist appealed his exclusion on the grounds that it interfered with First Amendment rights, the appeals court ruled simply that "we have the right to exclude whomever we wish and for any reason whatsoever." In short, as one member of the Visa Division had explained to a congressional committee in 1926, the only meaningful way to appeal a visa denial was to go to your foreign office and begin "raising a howl."[42]

Although the Passport Division's work more directly implicated the rights of US citizens, it, too, acted without procedural restraint. Americans denied a passport were provided no explanation for the decision—they were only informed that their "travel abroad at this time would be contrary to the best interests of the United States." They could not appeal the denial, nor could they assess or contest the evidence the State Department used. To make its decision, the Passport Division simply turned to its own vast files. By 1946, when it made plans to convert its records to IBM punch cards, it had some two thousand four-drawer filing cabinets stuffed with papers dating to 1925. (According to the *New York Times*, the files were storied in a "dank dungeon . . . rat and termite infested.") The division also consulted with the FBI and developed its own staff of investigators to look into suspicious applications. It then made its decision according to its own logic. In 1940, the *Saturday Evening Post* concluded that these were "practically star-chamber proceedings."[43]

One individual had ultimate authority over those proceedings. Ruth Shipley headed the Passport Division for an astonishing twenty-eight years, from 1927 until 1955. By the 1940s, this Maryland-born daughter of a Methodist minister had established a stunning amount of authority in the masculine world of the State Department. She was, in the words of one journalist, "one of the most influential figures in the federal government" and an "indestructible landmark on the Washington scene." The *New York Times* referred to her "complete discretion" over the issuance and denial of passports. She was "completely unmovable" once she had reached a decision on a passport case, and she could decide "as automatically as you step on the gas or apply the brakes." Magazine headlines captured the highly personalized authority Shipley had accrued: *Reader's Digest* dubbed her the "State Department's Watchdog"; according to *Colliers*, "You Don't Go If She Says No." Shortly after World War II, Eleanor Dulles had applied for passports to allow her children to accompany her as she worked with the US mission to reconstruct the Austrian economy. But Shipley, who had decided that postwar Europe was no place for children, rejected the applications, and her decision could not be challenged. Dulles, no shrinking violet, found her dealings with the Passport Division a "harrowing experience." She said that Shipley "was a tartar and a despot."[44]

Whereas Shipley's constant presence symbolized the stability of the Passport Division, the Visa Division seemed defined by flux. Between 1918 and 1934, ten people cycled through the role atop the organization; three more took a stab at the job between 1934 and 1946. Meanwhile, as it moved offices ten times in its first thirty years, it became known as a "peripatetic" bureaucracy, a "division on wheels." But beneath the turmoil were a cohort of midlevel bureaucrats who had similar tenures to Shipley and who exercised considerable control over the day-to-day operations. Perhaps the most important of them was Robert C. Alexander, who had joined the visa division in 1928. By World War II, he had risen to become an assistant chief. He oversaw the Anti-American Activities section of the Visa Division, which was responsible for security policies, and also the issuance of exit permits. And with his legal background, he served as the division's main legal and technical advisor, with responsibility for drafting regulations and codifying precedent in internal procedures.[45]

Shipley and Alexander entered the postwar period with astonishing powers over the rights of individuals to travel, and they exercised their discretion in keeping with their avowedly conservative political leanings. Shipley, for instance, should be seen as a central figure in the history of the countersubversive state, bound to the national security branches both by ideology ("One of the things I believe in," she boasted in 1953, "is refusing passports to communists") and by blood: one brother, Alexander Bielaski, was the director of a precursor to the FBI; the other, Frank, directed investigations for the Office of Strategic Service; and a sister, Alice, had a thirty-year career with the Army's G-2 division and the CIA.[46]

Alexander, meanwhile, played a central role in aligning the Visa Division with the countersubversive priorities of the rising national security apparatus. In the late 1930s, he had been outraged that liberal pressure groups had criticized the division's draconian refugee policies. Those policies had stranded many to the cruelties of Fascism and war, but Alexander attributed the criticism to certain individuals who were "either swayed by abnormal humanitarian impulses or inspired by the propaganda from Berlin." He oversaw a secret wartime treaty with Panama that allowed the US to make the decisions about who could enter Panama so that alleged Axis agents could be away from this key strategic location. In the early postwar period, he represented the State Department in the running of Operation Bloodstone and was responsible for securing visas for the former Nazi assets being brought into the United States.[47]

In the 1940s, Alexander was also playing a significant role in the emerging politics of the second Red Scare. In July 1948, he went before a congressional committee to allege that hundreds of undesirable Communists were infiltrating the United States with visas to work at the United Nations. His claims that individuals "trained in terrorist activities in Moscow" were "roaming" in New York were picked up in the conservative media, which then were busy attacking the UN. (The *Chicago Tribune* editorialized that "few tears would be shed if the whole UN spy base and arena for acrimony were got off American soil.") To quiet the matter, Secretary of State George Marshall established a three-person committee that spent a month investigating Alexander's claims. It concluded that Alexander's testimony had been "irresponsible in its lack of factual support" and formally reprimanded him. But the assistant chief of the Visa Division was unrepentant. "In light of all the facts in the cases I have recently examined," he was forced to concede, "I am prepared to testify that the danger to our national security up to this time appears to be more potential than actual or immediate." He nevertheless remained concerned that if tolerance of "subversive classes coming into the country with permission to travel all over the country . . . is allowed to go on, the security of the Nation might be jeopardized."[48]

In short, Alexander and Shipley were committed to managing the border in alignment with a deeply politicized vision of America's national security and geopolitical interests. So when representatives from the Visa and Passport Divisions took their seats at the second meeting of the State Department's TPC on February 25, 1947, a significant shift occurred. Alexander himself represented the Visa Division at all future travel policy meetings; Shipley sent her number two, John Scanlan. With their arrival, the prerogatives of the national security state were being belatedly incorporated into the American agenda on international travel. But they were being incorporated through what one internal document called a "somewhat anomalous organizational structure" that reflected and reinforced the philosophical divisions within the US bureaucracy—the Commerce Department's CFT "emphasiz[ing] economic aspects of travel" in its liberal policy prescriptions and the State Department's TPC focusing on "security considerations." The stage was set for a confrontation.[49]

When the economic liberalism of the CFT and security considerations of the TPC clashed in planning meetings in February and March 1947, it turned out to be anticlimactic. The national security interests won out—representatives from the security organizations had well-established reputations as experts in travel policy, and the zero-risk logic of national security arguments stacked the deck against experimentation in the threatening geopolitical climate. So as the State Department rewrote US policy for the upcoming Meeting of Experts, it rolled back the more liberal tendencies of the CFT proposals. For instance, whereas the CFT had said that the United States should go on record as favoring, in principle at least, the abolition of passports, the State Department demurred, stating that the "universal abolition of the passport . . . is not desirable at present." And whereas the CFT had argued that bilateral passport reductions should be "encouraged," the State Department believed that to be too bold and out of step with US interests. Instead, the US went to Geneva arguing that bilateral agreements should only be "explored."[50]

At Geneva, the United States found other nations, such as France and the United Kingdom, equally unwilling to abandon passports altogether. Greece, Poland, and Turkey, in particular, were very concerned about regulating the movement of peoples for reasons of political security. Even so, the final resolution of the conference was more liberal than the US policy. Although the gathered experts said that a return to pre-1914 conditions "might well be kept in view as an ultimate objective," it was not "feasible" at present—a noticeable difference from the US position that it was not "desirable." And whereas the US had said only that the bilateral or multilateral agreements to waive passport requirements should be "explored," the gathered international experts thought that they should be "encouraged."[51]

This was all fairly symbolic stuff—the dispute was over words and sentiments, not policy—but the subtle maneuvering captured a significant process. CFT's more liberal policy had been more in line with international attitudes to travel regulation. Official US policy, as developed by the State Department, was far more protective of state prerogatives and made the United States something of an outlier.

At the conference, this pattern repeated itself. The UK and Canada wanted passports to be issued for five years and renewable for a further five; the CFT had also wanted passports of a five-year duration. The

United States, on the basis of State Department briefings, explained that it would not issue passports valid for more than two years because the Nationality Act of 1940 allowed the state to withdraw citizenship, which meant that the United States needed the right to review passports more frequently. With the support of France and Denmark, the United States ensured the committee settled on recommending a two-year minimum duration, with a recommendation that passports be valid for five years if possible. Similarly, whereas other nations wanted to reduce passport fees, the United States, following State Department instructions, argued that its relatively high $10 fee could not be changed without congressional legislation, which was unlikely given the large national debt. (By way of contrast, Great Britain charged $2.52 for a passport, Portugal charged $3.67, and Switzerland issued them for free.) Rather than advocate a specific reduction in passport fees, the committee recommended only that passport fees should not raise revenues, but only cover administrative costs. (In the aftermath of the meeting, the US did report to the United Nations that its passport fee only covered costs. In reality, the Passport Division was a revenue generator. In 1927, it brought in $1.5 million, even though it only cost $124,000 to run. By the early 1950s, Shipley could boast to Congress that that "we take care of a lot of other departments" because "we have a tremendous surplus over our costs.") Similarly, although the delegates had agreed that passports were supposed to be valid to travel for all foreign countries "except in special or exceptional circumstances," the US reported that its policy of restricting travel whenever the Passport Office said that there were "good reasons" to do so lived up to the spirit of the agreement.[52]

The nationalist position of the US delegation was made most clear in discussions about the radical reduction of visa requirements. This was the most significant issue on the table at Geneva; although everyone thought that completely eliminating passports was, at best, a long-term goal, reducing visa requirements seemed more practical in the short term. In fact, Belgium was already holding negotiations with Scandinavian nations, the United Kingdom, and Denmark to abolish the need for visas for travel between them. And nations in the Caribbean had stopped requiring visas for passengers arriving on a tourist vessel. At the London conference, there had been favorable discussion of a proposal to replace visas with a nonimmigrant identity card, issued by a citizen's home country, that would allow free movement of cardholders throughout all nations participating in the practice. Those nations would lose the ability to screen foreign visitors and make unilateral decisions about which individuals would receive an entry visa and which would not.[53]

But the United States was "unequivocally opposed to the abolition of the pre-entrance examination requirement for the acquisition of a US visa." The ostensible reason, as Dean Acheson briefed the delegation to Geneva, was that any form of automatic transit visa would "frustrate the present Quota act." Given the hard quotas established by the 1924 immigration act, the US needed to prescreen all visitors. Otherwise, there was a risk that individuals might "resort to various non-immigrant disguises in an attempt to evade the quota restrictions." Prescreening prior to departure not only secured the regime of immigration restriction, the Americans argued, it was also humane and efficient. It prevented the need for deporting inadmissible visitors once they had arrived in the United States, sparing them "inconvenience, expense, and . . . stigma." And it saved the transportation companies the expense of returning the illegitimate traveler to their home, as US law required.[54]

Given these concerns, the favored US position at Geneva was that the experts should recognize "that a distinction exists in visa requirements between countries which have and those which do not have quantitative immigration restrictions." Entrance visas should be abolished in "countries having no quantitative immigration restrictions"; they should be maintained in those, like the US, that did. This was an effort to preserve American autonomy from international liberalization by allying with the other white, settler colonial nations that had constructed racist regimes of immigration restriction in the late nineteenth century. But it was a surprisingly unproductive strategy. Like the United States, South Africa and Canada favored entrance visas because they helped regulate immigration, but South Africa conceded that "if the general feeling of the meeting was that the visas as such should be abolished, South Africa would not stand out." And although Australia supported the need for visas to restrict immigration, it did not want to protect only the prerogatives of nations with quantitative limits because its restrictionist regime did not rest on quotas. The United States failed to build a coalition in favor of its distinction.[55]

The United States thus failed to carve out an exemption for itself from the conference's general recommendation that visa requirements be liberalized via bilateral negotiation "with the general abolition of visas as its ultimate objective." This was, as the delegation reported to the State Department, an "important non-acceptance of U.S. policy," and it meant that the US now had to oppose efforts to multilaterally reduce travel restrictions. In an international meeting on travel policy in October 1947, when Belgium filed a motion to implement the resolutions of the Geneva meeting, the United States had to file a reservation about the section "calling for a gradual suppression of entry visas."[56]

In the Western Hemisphere, too, the US was finding itself increasingly isolated in its nationalist desire to control the entry of travelers. The replacement of entry visas with an internationally recognized tourist card was regularly debated at Inter-American Conferences on travel in the 1940s. (As one State Department document pointed out, the card "appeared on various occasions under different names," but always sought the same outcome: "to do away with passports and visas for nonimmigrant travel and have in lieu thereof one travel card.") The Inter-American Tourist Card had first been proposed by Argentina in 1939 at the San Francisco conference, when the United States had been able to ward it off by citing the risk of Nazi infiltration. But the idea of the card had the support of a number of states in the Americas, as well as US airlines, and the United States struggled to kill it. At the Panama Congress in 1947, George Shaw, chief of the US delegation, opposed proposals for the card with such repeated recalcitrance that he earned the nickname "Mr. Molotov." By the time of the 1949 meeting in Argentina, twenty-two nations supported an Inter-American Travel Card. No longer able to simply stonewall, the US now accepted a resolution in favor of the card, but only after it inserted language that the card would be subject to existing legislative requirements. Given the stringency of US visa laws, this gutted the resolution and allowed the United States to nominally vote in favor of it. As the *New York Times* reported, the proposed Inter-American Tourist Card "came into being with the virtually fatal handicap of a US 'joker' [clause] which just about destroyed its meaning."[57]

The increasingly lonely and increasingly virulent US opposition to the Inter-American Tourist Card was instructive for two reasons. First, it laid bare the real reasons that the United States was so keen to maintain visa requirements. In the UN context, as the State Department's Solomon Silver explained in an internal 1947 debate about tourist cards, the US had defended the need for visas "by stating that they are necessary for the US to enforce its quantitative immigration restrictions." But given that the Western Hemisphere was exempted from the quota system, "the argument set forth in the UN paper . . . would not apply" in the Inter-American context. As Silver delicately put it, this placed the United States in a "vulnerable position" in Inter-American debates, because the "underlying reason, which is one of security, as to why such a card cannot be adopted has been avoided in the past." It was the unilateralist interests of the national security state, at the end of the day, that dictated US opposition to eliminating visas; the effort to protect the racist prerogatives of the immigration system were, in this case, considered the more palatable cover story.[58]

National security opposition to freedom of travel ran deep. Because of the need to protect the atomic secret from foreign agents, argued the chief of the Visa Division in 1946, relaxation of visa restrictions would be "premature." The problem with free entry, another State Department official argued, was that "aliens are generally lost to sight after being admitted," and "since our chief concern is security," it was therefore imperative that US consular officials continued to review all foreign visitors. A 1948 overview of State Department travel policy concluded that "given the present state of the world," US interests in reducing travel restrictions should pursue a "cautious course until freedom from fear in a political and military sense is more nearly achieved."[59]

The anxiety of the mid-tier security bureaucrat—the fear cloaked as hard-nosed realism—was best captured by Robert Alexander:

> If there were no Communists in the world, no smugglers of narcotic drugs, no white slave traffic, no international gangsters or lesser crooks, no subversive agents of any power with designs upon another, in short, if we had arrived at the millennium, we could safely go a long way in abolishing all sorts of restriction upon international travel . . . but in the light of actual conditions throughout the world today it is indeed remarkable that international travel is as free as it is from extremely nationalistic controls.[60]

In the lead-up to a conference in Bogota in 1947, at which the abolition of visas was once again on the agenda, Alexander complained that there was "too much loose talk in recent years about abolishing restrictions on international travel," talk that he attributed to "three principal sources": "airlines being interested in monetary gains exclusively," Communists seeking "leeway to carry on their subversive activities," and "inexperienced governmental authorities . . . imbued with an idealistic imagination that we are living in One World."[61]

As Alexander's sneering dismissal of one-worldist liberals underlined, US opposition to the Inter-American Tourist Card was also significant for a second reason: it revealed the hypocrisy that structured US policy on international travel. *New York Times* correspondent Milton Bracker correctly identified the "paradoxical position" of the US at the 1949 Inter-American Travel Congress: while the United States complained about red tape in Colombia and Honduras, it also refused to countenance any international efforts to liberalize its own borders. (As Harvard law professor Sidney Simpson observed, there was an added irony in that the US "system of burdensome requirements" had provided the "basic pattern" for visa restrictions throughout the hemisphere.) An internal State Department discussion captured the basic problem in 1947 when it said that there was a need to explain "why the U.S. cannot adopt a continental tourist card and, at the same time, why it is to the benefit of other countries to adopt such a card. . . . Our prime objective is the waiver or simplification of a visa requirement for US citizens traveling abroad."[62]

In short, the United States wanted other nations to reduce their border restrictions, but it did not intend to reduce its own. Foreign need for US dollars would provide incentive enough for foreign nations to open their borders to American tourists. Behind closed doors, policy makers were remarkably candid and remarkably consistent in repudiating any need for reciprocity. Said Averell Harriman in 1946, "We feel that an international conference will produce some desired changes on the part of other countries, even though the US may not be ready to reciprocate fully for reasons of immigration policy, simply because other countries are so anxious to get dollar exchanges." Said Will Clayton that same year, "Although this country is not in a position to make substantial concessions in its requirements for the entrance of foreign visitors, the representatives should support the lowering of such requirements by other countries with regard to American visitors in order to encourage increased dollar expenditures by American travelers abroad." And Ruth Shipley added in 1947, "It should be borne in mind that many countries are willing to make especially favorable agreements with us, needing as they do the American dollar, without reciprocity on our part."[63]

Given such attitudes, it was not surprising that soon after the Geneva meeting, the United States began to lose interest in international efforts to relax travel restrictions. A sequel to the 1946 London conference of tourist organizations had been scheduled for Paris in October 1947. On its agenda was the creation of an "International Union of Official Travel Organizations" (IUOTO)—a permanent body devoted to travel, as had been mooted at London and Geneva. But in the run-up to the Paris meeting, American officials disagreed over whether to even send delegates. Members of the CFT remained committed to the idea: Wilkinson believed that a failure to send delegates would signal a retreat from previous commitments and undermine American efforts to liberalize travel; representatives of the Civil Aeronautics Board hoped for not only official US representation, but also representation for commercial interests such as American Express.[64]

But the State Department was skeptical and wanted to send only observers—not representatives—to the Paris conference. Its rationale for this position is not entirely clear. As one representative on the Travel Policy

Committee put it just weeks before the meeting, the State Department had approached its policy on an international travel organization "to date, with considerable vagueness." Now, it began to argue that the proposed IUOTO occupied an unsatisfying gray zone. The State Department had adopted a policy that intergovernmental organizations should be established only through the United Nations. If the IUOTO was to be an intergovernmental organization, it would contradict that policy and should be opposed. On the other hand, if the IUOTO was not to be an intergovernmental organization but rather an organization of private or quasi-governmental agencies devoted to travel, the United States had no one organization to represent it and thus could not participate. This was a curiously formalistic policy position, and it was not entirely convincing to members of the CFT. If the policy was to associate all international organizations with the United Nations, Wilkinson argued, why not join the IUOTO and work to bring it into the UN orbit? (For this reason, the CFT had intended to argue at Paris that the body should be renamed the World Travel Organization, which it said was "more dignified, more descriptive of purpose, and more in line with the nomenclature of organizations cooperating with the UN.") And if the US lacked one organization that could represent travel interests in international settings, that could be solved by simply creating one. In late 1947, in fact, Wilkinson and the CFT would propose that the Commerce Department create a Federal Travel Council, composed of government and industry representatives. Opposed by the State Department, the proposal went nowhere. "Such an organization," argued Alexander of the Visa Division, "is unnecessary and would constitute an unwarranted interference with the function of industry. It would in effect be a socialization of the travel industry."[65]

The impasse between the CFT and the State Department came to a head in an impromptu meeting just before the Paris conference; the date and participants went unrecorded, and although minutes for the meeting were kept, they were unusually condensed, written in a truncated and informal summation. Rehashing the dispute and confused by the State Department's new obstructionism, members of the CFT suspected that there must be some ulterior motive. Pushed to explain the department's position, George Canty cited (in the clipped and confusing grammar of the minutes): "Budgetary reason. We don't want to encourage selling of United Nations. We don't want to meet situation of intergovernmental travel organization until such time as need for it. Political situation I heard of none. I know of no political reason." As vague as that is—what does "selling" mean, was that a typo for "swelling"?—it is the closest documentary evidence we have. And perhaps concerns over cost were all there were to it. But budgetary concerns were also, in their own way, political—they just meant that the costs of the organization outweighed the potential benefit. Given the recent experiences in Geneva and at Inter-American organizations, the benefits of international organization to the United States had to appear marginal, for the State Department had realized that it could not control the outcomes of international meetings and that the rest of the world was not in complete alignment with its policy agenda.[66]

Whatever the precise rationale, when the CFT and the State Department compromised on a policy for Paris, State won. Wilkinson was dispatched to Paris as a representative, but with instructions that he could not vote on the creation of an international organization and that he should explain the State Department's objections to the form of the new international body. In the four-day conference at the Sorbonne, discussion of the IUOTO turned out to be controversial on multiple fronts, particularly the membership of the organization and whether colonies would represent themselves (the British position) or be represented by the colonial power (the French position). A number of nations wanted changes to the membership of the IUOTO before they would join it; a Belgian effort to commit the new organization to a return to the pre-1914 tourism regime was debated but proved too controversial to adopt. Making matters even murkier, the minutes of the conference were kept so poorly that the US filed an objection to their accuracy. Nonetheless, out of the mess, the IUOTO came into being late in 1947. True to policy, the United States abstained from either voting for or joining the new organization.[67]

Thereafter, US attitudes to international organization in the travel field were deeply ambivalent. When it seemed that the United Nations might develop a more serious regulatory stance, as had been promised at Geneva, US officials expressed considerable hostility. For this reason, when a sequel to the Geneva meeting was being proposed in late 1947, officials within the State Department asserted that "U.S. policy is to kill such a conference" and ensure no further discussion of the issue. Similarly, in 1950, when the UN secretary-general requested information on how nations were implementing the recommendations of the Geneva meeting, Robert Alexander stressed "the provisions of the charter which leave domestic immigration laws by member states outside the scope of the authority of the UN."[68]

Meanwhile, much international activity began to focus on the more agreeable issue of tourist promotion. The United States was happy to let interested officials participate in these endeavors. In 1950, even as the United States was dismissing UN calls for information on travel restrictions, it participated in the fourth session of the UN Transport and Communications Commission, which sought to standardize road signs and signals.[69]

And despite initial objections, the United States had joined the IUOTO in 1949, largely because the organization had revealed that its primary interests were in collecting and standardizing statistical information about tourism. In 1950, Wilkinson was elected head of the IUOTO, with the creation of an institution for research his signature policy. Soon the IUOTO, which operated on a tiny budget of $37,000, was devoting most of its energy to publishing a bimonthly *World Travel Review* and a regular volume of *World Travel Statistics*. Earlier dreams that such an organization would multilaterally reduce travel restrictions did linger in the perfunctory passage of resolutions urging the liberalization of visa, passport, and customs rules. Covering the 1952 IUOTO conference, the *New York Times* observed with appropriate cynicism that the passage of such resolutions was "usual on such occasions." But having ticked this box, the 126 delegates at the conference focused more of their attention on creating an International Institute of Scientific Travel Research, debating the establishment of a uniform classification system for hotels (based on the French system of assigning one to four stars), and anticipating the impact of tourist-class transatlantic flights. A pale imitation of the powerful UN travel organization that had been imagined in 1945 and 1946, the IUOTO trundled along in such a fashion until 1970, when it was reorganized as a World Travel Organization in anticipation of closer collaboration with the United Nations. And although it did begin working with UN development programs in the mid-1970s, it did not become formally affiliated with the United Nations until 2003.[70]

In the absence of a robust international institution, postwar engagement with the problem of travel restrictions took place on a bilateral or regional basis. As a result, liberalization was highly uneven. The most significant developments came in Western Europe, where sixteen Marshall Plan nations took advantage of the 1948 IUOTO meeting to create the European Travel Commission (ETC). Headed by the Belgian writer Arthur Haulot, who had played a central role in the 1946 London conference on tourist liberalization, the ETC was designed to establish freedom of movement among Marshall Plan nations. Encouraged by US Marshall Plan officials, recovering Western European states allocated to the ETC $140,000 of scarce dollar resources, which funded an advertising campaign to encourage Americans to think of taking a multinational trip to the continent rather than visiting just France or Italy. It used Marshall Plan funds to modernize aged and war-damaged hotel stock so that lodging would be more appealing to American tourists. And it worked with its member states to reduce customs duties and visa requirements to make it easier for tourists, especially Americans, to travel around Europe. By 1949, Americans in Western Europe did not need visas unless they were going to Iceland, Greece, Portugal, or Turkey. By 1950, Haulot boasted that visa restrictions had been reduced by 90 percent in Western Europe since the war and that customs regulations had been standardized and been brought into close alignment with US norms. As visa restrictions were rolled back, postwar dreams of unrestricted travel lingered, albeit on a regional rather than a global scale. In 1957, the Tourism Committee of the Organization for European Economic Cooperation declared the "the final goal, the pure and simple abolition of passports, is not merely a utopian aim." Eventually, these efforts would lead to the creation of the Schengen Zone.[71]

All this had been accomplished without any need for the United States to reduce its own border requirements. As Colonel Theo Pozzy, head of Marshall Plan travel policy—appointed to the position by virtue of his ties to Senator Owen Brewster—explained in 1949, the European desire for tourist dollars meant that "many countries are willing to make concessions to US tourists without requiring reciprocal treatment of European travelers in the U.S." That year, for instance, France eliminated its visa requirements for Americans without insisting on US reciprocity. But if one thought only of the bottom line, it was a deal that worked. By the end of the year, American tourist spending accounted for 25 percent of Western European dollar earnings.[72]

Travel industry advocates, witnessing what was happening in Europe, hoped that it might provide a model for the Western Hemisphere. When the Air Transport Association suggested to the Commerce Department in 1949 that the American Republics should unilaterally abolish visas to increase the flow of American dollars, however, it was advised that "though this had been done successfully with several European countries, it would be inadvisable to approach the Latin Americans in this way." Efforts to this effect *were* made: a Committee on the Facilitation of Inter-American Transportation asked Latin American nations at the Buenos Aires Inter-American Travel Congress to follow the lead of Belgium and Italy and reduce visa requirements for Americans; in 1950, representatives of the Commerce Department and the Pan American Union made a joint tour of South America to encourage governments to unilaterally reduce travel barriers. But even when these entreaties were somewhat successful, they could not be disentangled from the ongoing US reluctance to reduce its own border restrictions. Latin American nations would lower their regulations only if the United States reciprocated. In 1950, for instance, Ecuador replaced a complicated entry regime with a simple tourist card that would cost US citizens only $1. But it introduced this measure only in anticipation of reproposing the controversial inter-American tourist card at the next Pan-American conference.[73]

The question of travel liberalization in the Western Hemisphere, in short, could not be separated from more divisive political questions. At the fifth Inter-American Travel Congress in 1954, debates about reducing travel restrictions and promoting tourism were sidelined when representatives of the Arbenz government in Guatemala accused the United States of waging a "campaign of pirates"—it was scaring off tourists by stoking fears that Guatemala was Communist. The normal business of the conference resumed only when the Guatemalan delegates were forced to return home on short notice: their government had been overthrown in a CIA-backed coup. Some of that business, such as ongoing tinkering with plans for the Pan-American Highway, was uncontroversial. But when the tourist card came up again, the result was predictable. "The United States is willing that other nations have this facilitated entry," declared the US delegate, "but will not permit it herself for security reasons."[74]

As European travel became easier for Americans, therefore, travel in the Western Hemisphere remained tied up with travel restrictions. In 1952, the president of the American Society of Travel Agents estimated that travel to South America amounted to only about 1 percent of European traffic, a problem he attributed to "complex documentary requirements which have no parallel today anywhere else in the world." Efforts to reduce requirements, he regretted, had accomplished little, although perhaps this was unsurprising; as he said, "One cannot in good conscience point the finger at South America without mentioning some of the regulations that reverse the procedure when visitors from South America try to come to the US."[75]

In fact, while the United States was encouraging other nations to eliminate border restrictions, it was actually tightening its regulations. The United States allowed entry without travel documents in only a handful of cases, which were established on an emergency arrangement. Because it lacked the capacity to issue visas for the seventy million annual border crossings from Mexico or Canada, it allowed citizens of those nations to enter without visas. (It could also exclude suspect aliens at the land border without needing documentation to determine where to deport the individual.) Immediately after World War II, the US had extended this practice to Cuba, allowing visa-free entry for Cubans traveling to the United States for twenty-nine days or less. (The US lacked sufficient consular personnel to screen the fifteen thousand Cubans visiting the United States each month.) But in 1950, in response to Senate pressure, the State Department and the Immigration and Naturalization Service decided to reinstitute visa requirements "as a security measure": they again wanted to bar the entry of Communists. Wilkinson and the Commerce Department complained that it was a "step backward" in the effort to liberalize travel; the Department of the Treasury wondered, "Could the U.S. ask other countries to be less burdensome with respect to their visa requirements if the U.S. reinstated visa procedures?" But the State Department was nonplussed by these considerations of principle, thinking about the issue only in terms of power politics and American economic might. "The value of U.S. tourism to Cuba," declared the State Department's H. H. Kelly, "would be a strong force in preventing Cuba's imposing any barriers to tourists." He was right. Cuba initially threatened to respond in kind, but three months later, on the eve of enacting new restrictions, Cuba quietly decided to continue to waive visa requirements for US citizens.[76]

The outcome of the Cuba affair encapsulated the uneven politics of travel liberalization after World War II. In the absence of a global, multilateral commitment to easing international travel, the structure of postwar travel restrictions was shaped by geopolitical and economic power. As the world experienced a postwar boom in travel—435,000 Americans had gone overseas in 1947; more than a million did so in 1955, and more than two million in 1964—pathways into and out of nations were shaped by the prerogatives of powerful states. In some regions, such as the emerging European Community, travel restrictions were eased; in others, they were tightened. This was a decisive divergence, one that has shaped travel policy into the present—the two regions with the lowest barriers to entry today are the Caribbean and Western Europe, both areas that liberalized border controls in the 1940s in an attempt to lure US tourist dollars. The net result of this uneven process of travel liberalization was a "global mobility divide" above and beyond the economic inequalities that shape the opportunity to travel. Holders of European and North American passports have more rights to enter other states without a visa than holders of passports from other nations. (For instance, by the 2000s, Finns, Danes, and Americans had the passports with the most "power"—they could enter 130 countries without visas. Iranians, by contrast, could enter only 14 countries without visas, and Vietnamese travelers only 18.) Had the politics of the 1940s gone differently, had a serious multilateral institution developed with the authority to reduce travel regulations across the globe, such inequalities would have been mitigated.[77]

The Cuba affair also revealed the highly self-interested fashion in which the United States had engaged with the international politics of free travel in the 1940s. It had been primarily interested in ensuring the rights of its citizens to travel freely so as to help create a more balanced global economy. In this regard, it had been successful. After World War II, sixty-nine countries waived visa requirements for visiting Americans.[78] But the United States was simultaneously committed to maintaining unilateral control over its own borders. So while most US citizens experienced increasing international mobility after World War II, the United States itself was a far more closed space to international travelers. For liberal advocates of travel, like Wilkinson, the United States had adopted a frustratingly hypocritical policy, one that seemed to undermine the cultural exchange and international harmony that mobility was supposed to produce. But in economic and geopolitical calculation, US policy was perfectly rational: it maximized the circulation of US tourist dollars without impinging on the rights of the US state. Meanwhile, for the cautious, conservative guardians of national security, the primary concern was protecting US interests from what it imagined as a wide variety of anti-American travelers who could take advantage of the new era of mobility to harm American interests. In the 1940s, such concerns were already powerful enough to distinguish the United States as a state that had successfully exempted itself from postwar liberalization.

CHAPTER FOUR

PRESS FREEDOM, PROPAGANDA, AND THE GLOBAL FLOW OF INFORMATION

In 1943, Arthur Sulzberger embarked on an "aerial odyssey halfway around the globe" on a mission for the Red Cross. In only seven weeks, the publisher of the *New York Times* covered 29,000 miles, stopping in Cairo, Tehran, London, and Moscow. The experience led Sulzberger to conclude that the "world is trembling from what might be called the Revolution of the Age of Communication." "You can't do what I did and see what I did and come home an isolationist," he asserted; and he believed that newspapermen, in particular, had a renewed responsibility to "travel and see the world and see its problems." (Raymond Clapper, the famed journalist, put the point more romantically. He predicted that after the war "a kind of constant worldwide cruising will be a necessary activity for the American press. . . . Flying reporters, flying editorial writers, flying columnists, the eyes and ears of the American people, have a job ahead of them which can be one of the great adventures of American journalism.") Such flying US journalists, Sulzberger declared, also promised a broader transformation of world communications. Asked if he thought the American concept of press freedom would spread in the postwar world, he replied, "If I didn't believe that, I would lie down now and die."[1]

Many US politicians and news executives shared Sulzberger's hopes that the postwar order would see a reorganization of the international flow of news, as well as the globalization of American press freedom. Kent Cooper, head of the Associated Press (AP), thought that "the whole structure of human rights in a world of free men, with governments of their own choosing, rests upon one basic right: the right to know. . . . World understanding can be achieved only if news flows freely to all countries and may be freely published in them." In 1944, Congress passed a resolution calling for "the worldwide right of interchange of news." (It had been cosponsored by William Fulbright, who argued that the "unhampered flow of truthful news throughout the world" would help produce the "better understanding of one another [that] must be brought about among the nations of the world if peace is to endure.") The American Society for Newspaper Editors (ASNE) similarly sent a Committee on Freedom of Information on a four-month, eleven-country tour with the "the idea of spreading the gospel of the First Amendment among the people of foreign lands."[2]

War with Axis dictatorships had heightened belief in the moral necessity of global press freedom. Many Americans thought that the free flow of information was essential to preventing the rise of future dictatorships. "It seems probable," opined one commentator, "that such cancers as fascism and Nazism could not have prospered in a world where news was not poisoned by nationalistic propaganda." And many other nations, emerging from decades of depression, colonial occupation, and dictatorship, welcomed the opportunity to reimagine the global flow of news. "We all keep dreaming of a New World," Turkish officials told ASNE's Committee on Freedom of Information, "but you certainly have started the best sort of pioneer work to make the dream come true." Given such enthusiasm, the United Nations soon resolved to hold a conference to improve the global flow of news. Philippine representative Carlos Romulo, who had proposed the conference, declared that freedom of information was the "touchstone of all the freedoms to which the UN is consecrated."[3]

The United Nations Conference on Freedom of Information was held in Geneva in the spring of 1948. Largely forgotten today, it was at the time a unique centerpiece of the emerging international order. A rare early UN conference devoted to a specific issue, it was charged with drafting the press freedom clauses of the Universal Declaration of Human Rights and the Covenant on Human Rights (the only clause singled out for such unique attention), as well as writing a multilateral Convention on Freedom of Information that would legally bind all nations to specific measures to improve the flow of news. Over three weeks, six hundred delegates from fifty-seven nations discussed measures ranging from the professional standards of foreign correspondents to the global distribution of newsprint, from censorship laws to the visa regulations governing journalists.

But the delegates discovered that they deeply disagreed about how information should flow through the postwar order and even about the meaning of the concept "freedom of information" itself. American proponents of global press freedom had assumed that their crusade centered on the expansion of a set of interconnected rights. The term they hit upon to capture this cluster of rights—*freedom of information*—was something of a neologism, but they assumed it mainly involved the extension of American-style press freedoms. They wanted to ensure not only that journalists were free from government censorship, but also that journalists had both freedom of access to sources and freedom to send their news from one country to another. Other nations, it turned out, were less enamored of that vision. Many wanted some way to ensure that neither propaganda nor false news would be circulated. And nations from the decolonizing world worried that they were about to be swamped by US news; for them, global press freedom required not the spread of the US media, but the building up of their own news infrastructures. They argued that globalizing "freedom of information," that freeing the world from nationalist propaganda, might also require placing certain limits on the expansion of the United States.[4]

In the end, there was no way to transcend these differences, and the effort to write international press laws collapsed—little of the international infrastructure that had been discussed so passionately ever came into existence. But the trajectory of these forgotten debates nevertheless provides a great deal of insight into US attitudes to world order in the late 1940s. It reveals that US dreams of free flows of information were concerned primarily with the export of US news to the world, not the import of information into the United States—an interest shaped directly by the economic incentives of the US news agencies. It shows how limited the US vision of global press freedom really was, and how brittle the US commitment to multilateral institutions turned out to be when it lost control of the terms of the debate. And it shows how a campaign to free the world from state propaganda ended up, when filtered through the geopolitical lens of the Cold War, justifying an expansive new US propaganda program.

Efforts to improve global press freedom were hardly new. The AP's Cooper, perhaps the most important American advocate of the issue, had in fact urged the Woodrow Wilson administration to write global press freedom into the World War I peace settlement. But nothing came of his efforts, which just about summed up the trajectory of the many early attempts to create an international infrastructure to regulate the world's news. A World Press Conference, for instance, had been established at the 1893 World's Columbia Exhibition held in Chicago and met roughly annually until World War I, but it went no further than debating such matters as international telegraphic charges, freedom of the press, and the establishment of a world bureau of correspondents. Then a Press Congress of the World was created as an offshoot of the 1915 Panama-Pacific International Exposition in San Francisco. It, too, sought to globalize press freedom, but only passed a number of motions that were never implemented. Between 1927 and 1933, under the aegis of the League of Nations, a series of meetings had been held between press experts to create rapid and cheap news transmission to deal with the problem of global public opinion. In 1932, for instance, the secretariat of the league had written to 130 press organizations in sixty-four countries to collect suggestions to prevent the "spread of false information which may threaten to disturb the peace"—but nothing practical had emerged. In 1947, casting a jaundiced eye over this history, one journalist concluded that "a universal pattern of high-mindedness and futility has favored these conversations. They have always begun on a note of idealism, always proceeded toward pious resolutions and have, with one or two exceptions, always resulted in inaction."[5]

Still, despite the long history of idealist efforts to rid the world of propaganda, Cooper's activities in the 1940s are better understood as a new act in the political economy of international newsgathering. Cooper had actually attended the 1927 League Conference on Press Experts, but he thought it was insignificant. The real action—and the reason that Cooper happened to be in Europe at the time of the conference—took place behind the scenes, in contractual negotiations among the four largest international news agencies. The global flow of news was, in fact, subject to international control in the first half of the twentieth century. But control didn't lie in the idealist minds of international organs. It was tightly grasped in the calculating hands of the private news agencies: the AP, France's Havas, Britain's Reuters, Germany's Wolff.

These news agencies had emerged in the mid-nineteenth century. They acted as wholesale providers of news, providing a regular service of information to individual newspapers that subscribed to them—such a subscription gave an individual paper much wider coverage than it could itself manage, at a much lower cost. Newspapers depended on agencies for international news, in particular, because it relied on both a far-flung and expensive network of correspondents and, even more importantly for the timely circulation of information, access to the new technology of the telegraph. The considerable cost sunk into establishing these networks, and the economies of scale that accrued to the most dominant news agencies, meant that the international circulation of news had to pass through a very narrow bottleneck, dominated by a handful of news agencies that were keen to maintain their near monopolistic control. In 1870, the three major European agencies—Havas, Wolff, and Reuters—signed a formal cartel agreement whereby the world supply of news was divided into territories, each assigned to one of the agencies, which would have sole responsibility for supplying news from there to both of its international partners; it would also be the sole recipient of news from them, with a monopoly to sell international news within its territory. The flow of news had been carved into imperial segments—Reuters supplied the news to and from the vast British Empire, as well as East Asia; Havas covered the French Empire, Spain, and Latin America; Wolff had the smaller German and Austro-Hungarian empires, as well as Scandinavia and Russia. The cartel, said Cooper, was the "first, the greatest, and the most powerful international monopoly of the nineteenth century." It lasted until the 1930s.[6]

The United States was noticeably absent from the cartel at first; it was a minor player in international news. Havas, Wolff, and Reuters benefited from close collaboration with their governments, which wanted to encourage the export of news and so provided the agencies with important subsidies, as well as cheap rates, on government-owned cables. The AP, which emerged as the dominant domestic news agency in the United States, enjoyed neither of these privileges in the nineteenth century, in part because the US was a laggard in constructing cable—a fact that could cause considerable geopolitical embarrassment; as the United States expanded into Cuba and the Philippines in 1898, it had to rely on French and British cables to communicate with its troops.[7]

The AP nevertheless had a large enough domestic market that it was brought into the cartel as a junior partner in 1887, responsible for the United States. But the United States lacked the right to directly export its news to nations with which it wanted diplomatic and commercial ties. As Frank Noyes, the president of the AP, complained to Congress in 1913, nations in Central and South America "secure their news of the U.S. by way of Europe, and it consists mainly of murders, lynchings and embezzlements. The antipathy to the U.S. by these countries is undoubtedly largely due to the false perspective given by their newspapers." Similar complaints were made about the flow of news into East Asia, where it was alleged that Reuters blocked, filtered, and slanted US news so that it was prejudicial to US interests. Proponents of American expansion thus became invested in the export of US news.[8]

They were provided an opportunity when war broke out in Europe. Havas refused to supply Wolff news to Latin American newspapers, because it didn't want to spread German propaganda. The Latin American newspapers, still interested in German news, then turned to the United

States to fill the gap. The AP, bound to respect Havas's monopoly rights in Latin America, demurred, but a rival US agency, the United Press (UP), was happy to oblige because it was not a part of the cartel (it was also seeking to challenge the AP's domestic supremacy and wanted new international markets). The US government provided the UP with diplomatic support as it sought clients south of the border and also helped negotiate the all-important cheap telegraph rates on newly built American cables. (By the 1920s, after a surge of construction, the United States owned about a quarter of the world's cable network. Britain, which had owned 70 percent of the world's cable in 1887, still owned 50 percent.)[9]

The turmoil of World War I thus forced a renegotiation of the cartel agreement. Following Germany's defeat, Wolff had its international empire divided between the victors, and the AP, to head off the threat of the UP, was granted rights to compete with Havas in South America. Still, the cartel agreement held strong—the AP's territory had expanded, but not by much, especially when compared with Reuters and Havas. When Cooper became head of the organization in 1925, he was champing at the bit to expand further. The cartel agreement was renegotiated in 1927 to recognize the AP as an equal party for the first time. In the early 1930s, Cooper made a bilateral deal to exchange news with a Japanese news agency, which had recently modeled itself on the AP, thus dislodging Reuters from its monopoly there. Shortly thereafter, the AP and the UP jointly pledged that they would no longer abide by any exclusive exchange agreements and would sell to all who wanted to purchase their services.[10]

The US agencies had announced the end of the cartel. The challenge they now faced was finding a way to compete with European news agencies that were deeply entrenched in their vast holdings across Africa, Asia, Europe, and the Middle East.

The disruption and devastation of World War II did much to level the playing field. During the conflict, the international flow of news was structured more by wars of propaganda than by commercial competition. The Office of War Information, responsible for the vast US propaganda effort, collaborated with the news agencies to distribute their news into new markets. It coordinated and paid for the export of a daily news service and even went as far as to subsidize foreign news agencies that wanted to subscribe to US news agencies. The United States had also finally found a way to bypass British dominance of the communications infrastructure, having built a globe-straddling wireless network that allowed it to spread information without cable.[11]

Meanwhile, the news supply in much of the world was devastated. German and French news agencies, having been discredited by association with the Nazi and Vichy regimes, had disappeared when those governments collapsed; much of their infrastructure had been destroyed during the war. More broadly, journalists had been killed at high rates over the previous decade. Many had died as war correspondents or in the violence and starvation that war had brought. And many had suffered political execution—either at the hands of occupying governments, or, following liberation, at the hands of their own countrymen for collaboration. As a result, as the UN Educational, Scientific, and Cultural Organization (UNESCO) put it in 1947, "there [wa]s a recognized need for qualified journalists" throughout the world.[12]

Spared the destruction, the US news agencies licked their chops. In 1945, both the AP and the UP organized new divisions "for more effective sales to the world market." The directors of the AP gave Cooper a $1 million annual budget to turn the agency into a global institution.[13]

For all the idealist talk of mutual understanding, American interest in global freedom of information therefore rested on a base of material self-interest. "Like most big business executives," the *Economist* observed tartly, Cooper "experiences a peculiar moral glow in finding that his idea of freedom coincides with his commercial advantage."[14]

The crusade for global freedom of information quickly made its mark on the agenda of the young United Nations. To the disappointment of American advocates, the San Francisco conference did not write an explicit freedom of information provision into the UN Charter. But freedom of information was soon debated in the General Assembly, in the Economic and Social Council, and within the Commission on Human Rights.[15]

That Cooper and his colleagues thought that they needed the support of the United Nations to ensure the expansion of American news was significant. The news agencies were not the only US media companies looking to expand into the world in the wake of World War II. The American film industry, too, was seeking unfettered access to foreign markets—among other things, it wanted to export a backlog of movies that had built up during the Depression and the war. And just like the news industry, the film industry turned to the State Department to help in that endeavor. In particular, it wanted help tearing down quota walls that foreign nations had constructed to protect their film industries from US dominance.

But whereas the news industry saw itself as an insurgent, trying to wrest control of the world market away from the European powers, the film industry saw itself as a natural global heavyweight, which simply needed help recapturing the global predominance that had been earned decades earlier. The United States had actually been an importer of films in the first years of the medium in the 1900s—France had been the global power—but the disruptions of World War I soon gave the US an insurmountable advantage. Just prior to the war, the US had exported 32 million feet of film and imported 16 million feet; by the 1920s, it was exporting 235 million feet and importing only 7 million feet. By that point, 95 percent of the films shown in the United Kingdom were American, as were 80 percent of the films shown in South America and two-thirds of the films shown in Italy and the Dutch East Indies. The once mighty France was in the same boat—77 percent of the films shown in the mainland were from the US, as were more than half of the films shown in France's Southeast Asian colonies. But then, in the 1930s and 1940s, foreign nations had built quota walls to roll back US hegemony and develop their own film industries. The challenge now was to remove these barriers and to allow the natural economics of the business to return the United States to global dominance.[16]

As a newly created Motion Picture Export Association worked with the State Department to accomplish this goal, its various strategies reflected such confident assumptions. Although it made some efforts to establish export markets through multilateral agreements—it put out feelers to the State Department to see if film might be included in freedom of information agreements; it tried to use the nascent international free trade infrastructure to bar quotas and tariffs on film—it quickly moved on when these turned out to be dead ends. Instead, it worked closely with the State Department to negotiate favorable bilateral trade agreements with foreign governments, ensuring that the US film companies were able to effectively bypass quota laws and foreign currency restrictions. In 1948, Congress added a helping hand when it enacted the Informational Media Guarantee Program, in which the US government promised to repay Hollywood in US dollars any earnings trapped overseas in nonconvertible currency. The strategy was successful. By 1949, the United States had captured 56 percent of the European film market, 62 percent of the African market, 64 percent of the South American market, 47 percent of the Asian market, and three-quarters of the film markets in Central America and the Pacific. By the 1950s, with 40 percent of Hollywood's revenues coming from overseas, the United States was itself importing very few foreign films.[17]

By contrast, the interest of the US news agencies in international agreements was more sustained and more intense. The news industry seemed uncertain of its ability to dominate the field without the establishment of a favorable regulatory environment, in which foreign markets would be opened to them by mutual consent and binding international law. Whereas the film industry's foreign policy was expressed primarily in the language of free trade, the news industry's foreign policy was expressed primarily in the language of mutual understanding and international liberalism. Whereas the film industry largely pursued its goals through economic institutions, the newspaper industry went to the highest political branches of the new international government.

That the campaign for Freedom of Information turned so decisively to the United Nations was one more legacy of the relatively belated rise of the United States as a global power in the news industry. In 1941, when Henry Luce had proclaimed an American Century, he had justified US world leadership by noting that American mass culture had already created "an immense American internationalism. American jazz, Hollywood movies, American slang, American machines and patented products, are in fact the only things that every community in the world, from Zanzibar to Hamburg, recognizes in common." What Luce referred to as "American jazz" and "Hollywood movies" were complex cultural hybrids, of course, produced by artists from all over the world and incorporating an equally diverse range of aesthetic and social influences—describing the *content* of these cultural forms as simply or straightforwardly "American" is inadequate. But even if Luce was being crudely nationalistic in his assessment, it was telling that he could not include the news media in his list of these "very human ways" in which the United States already was a world power.[18]

In 1941, it simply wasn't possible for even a brashly boosterish news media executive like Luce to imagine that US news had already created an American Century—that remained an aspiration. Thus the turn to the United Nations to globalize an industry that remained, by its own lights, troublingly parochial. The US press services "represent the one great oasis of objectivity in an international desert of propaganda and government influence," observed Oregon newspaper publisher Palmer Hoyt in 1946. "There is only one thing that can save civilization and that is the unhampered release of objective news—American style—between the nations." Never mind that we "will hear charges of American imperialism," he continued. "Our obligation is to extend freedom of the press to the entire world. If we fail, then all fail."[19]

The messianic quality of the news industry's international vision reflected its insurgent character and also added a sheen of moral righteousness to its quest for international agreements. Globalizing American news seemed a more serious affair than globalizing other forms of commercial media. (For this reason, the State Department rebuffed efforts from the film industry and comic book publishers to latch onto the freedom of information campaign to help them with their export problems.)[20] And so it was conducted as a political matter of the utmost importance.

This had important consequences for the institutional development of the United Nations. "Freedom of information" was a broad enough concept that international oversight could have included debate about a host of issues and the whole range of media. By rights, it should have been taken up by UNESCO, whose constitution had charged it with developing "such international agreements as may be necessary to promote the free flow of word and image." But the US news agencies, which understood themselves to have different needs and a greater significance than the other media industries, had gone directly to the United Nations itself.[21]

This made plain just how marginalized UNESCO had become. In December 1945, Archibald MacLeish learned that freedom of information was being discussed at ECOSOC rather than at UNESCO. In a series of irate letters, he complained to Dean Acheson and William Benton that this would leave UNESCO a "pretty dead duck," just weeks after it had been created. MacLeish had hoped that UNESCO could play a role in reforming or regulating the global flow of information and had rested that hope on the organization's ability to win the respect and cooperation of the media industries; he knew that the only "wampum" it could offer them in exchange was "its active assistance in the removal of the bars and blocks of freedom of communication." But the United States had divided the jurisdiction. Important questions about telecommunications, central to the political economy of the media, were split off into a series of "technical" organizations.[22] And the "principle of freedom of communication" had been turned over to the Commission on Human Rights, which, lacking an administrative organ of enforcement, "can do nothing but declare and exhort." UNESCO, MacLeish concluded glumly, "is crippled if not actually destroyed as the great new agency of international understanding which was planned in London." He was right. UNESCO's only contribution to reforming the postwar media landscape was a minor convention that exempted a limited class of "Visual and Auditory Materials of an Educational, Scientific or Cultural Character" from taxes and customs duties. Signed by only sixteen nations, it quietly went into force in 1954.[23]

Meanwhile, as the United Nations took up the subset of issues about press freedom that had come to dominate the "freedom of information" debate, it became clear just how contentious the US vision really was. In the middle of 1946, the United Nations created a Sub-Commission on Freedom of Information, staffed by fifteen experts. It was soon roiled by acrimonious exchanges between US and Soviet delegates. Ironically, this clash was itself a product of the decision to pursue freedom of information through the UN rather than UNESCO; the Soviets did not join UNESCO until 1954. At the United Nations, though, debates about the globalization of news media became fatefully intertwined with the burgeoning Cold War.[24]

For a brief moment after World War II, it had actually seemed that the campaign for a free flow of information might provide a bridge to reduce tensions between the United States and the USSR. In November 1945, at a diplomatic banquet, Soviet Foreign Minister Vyacheslav Molotov had toasted the AP's Moscow correspondent with a wish "for better understanding of one another" and then announced the abolition of Soviet censorship on foreign correspondents. But as Cold War tensions ratcheted up, international journalism became a central site of ideological conflict. Only one month later, incensed by what he said were inaccurate stories in the *New York Times* and the *Daily Herald*, Joseph Stalin overturned Molotov's policy and reimposed a censorship regime. It soon tightened drastically. As some Western journalists were charged with espionage and subversion and expelled from the emerging Soviet Bloc in 1946 and 1947, they became symbols of increasing distrust between the two powers. For Americans, the expulsions proved the tyrannical illiberalism of the Soviets and their efforts to mold public opinion. For the Soviets, by contrast, the need for the expulsions suggested the perfidy and warmongering of the capitalist American press. Criticism of the "bourgeois press" of the United States became a stock feature in Soviet political commentary, satire, and even drama. Konstantin Simonov's 1947 stage play *The Russian Question* narrated the story of an American journalist who was fired by his corrupt capitalist bosses when he tried to tell the truth about how wonderful the USSR actually was. The play was personally endorsed and promoted by Stalin and won the Stalin Prize in Literature and the Arts. Such disputes over the press had serious diplomatic repercussions. When an AP reporter in Warsaw complained that his dispatches were being censored, Dean Acheson retaliated by suspending a $90 million loan to Poland.[25]

These US-Soviet clashes over press freedom soon disrupted UN discussions about global freedom of information. In 1947, as both the Sub-Commission on Freedom of Information and the UN General Assembly worked to lay the groundwork for the forthcoming conference on the matter, Soviet delegates argued that any international laws guaranteeing press freedom also had to allow for states to censor so-called warmongering. Soviet Deputy Foreign Minister Andrey Vishinsky, who repeatedly accused conservative American publishers like Gannett and Hearst of falsely stirring up international tensions, argued that such a measure was both essential to world peace and hardly offensive to even American traditions of press freedom, which after all banned obscenity, dishonest advertising, and libel. "Which is the greater evil," he demanded, "advertising colored water as medicine or a campaign of man-hating and enmity toward peace-loving nations?"[26]

Because the Soviets wanted to pass the measure with an explicit condemnation of American warmongering, they could not get it approved. But they did not give up, deploying every parliamentary trick they could think of. The warmongering resolution has "haunted us in various guises and disguises in a dozen committee rooms," complained Philippine representative Carlos Romulo, it was a "cat with nine lives." The whole incident was, as one journalist pointed out, "a flagrant example of bare-knuckle diplomacy" that was transforming the United Nations from a site of universalist idealism to one of international power politics.[27]

For American observers, it raised worries about the upcoming Geneva conference. For State Department policy maker Lloyd Free, debates at the United Nations revealed that "most of the countries of the world do not see eye-to-eye with America on freedom of information." Because of that fact, *Editor and Publisher*, the newspaper industry journal, now suspected that the Geneva conference might threaten global press freedom rather than advance it. "Russia would like to eliminate all the free press," it editorialized. "Russia's big opportunity to make some progress in this direction comes next March in Geneva." Only a year earlier, American journalists had seen the United Nations as a site through which they could project their vision of global freedom of information. Now they worried that Geneva could result in having "a completely foreign concept of press freedom imposed on the rest of the world" and that the new machinery of international law that was supposed to liberalize news exchanges could turn into a "dangerous weapon for suppression and censorship." Then they had an even more troubling thought: if things went poorly at Geneva, *Editor and Publisher* noted anxiously, "American journalists stand to lose more freedoms than the rest of the world will gain in any final international press agreement."[28]

As optimism faded, the status of the Geneva conference declined. Eleanor Roosevelt rejected an invitation to head the delegation; early plans to send James Byrnes, Dean Acheson, and Adlai Stevenson came to naught. When William Benton, recently retired from his role as head of propaganda operations in the State Department, was offered the position, he was also tempted to demur. "I am not hopeful of any international agreements on key issues at this conference," he wrote to Hugh Baillie of the UP, "Is there anything that gives you hope?" But in the end, Benton accepted because the matter was "so crucial to international understanding *for the long run.*" In any case, he had "hammered at this theme" for too long to quit now.[29]

As Benton's delegation was briefed during their voyage to Geneva, they learned that the State Department was also concerned that the rest of the world would be hostile to the US agenda for the conference. That agenda was based on what the State Department dubbed the "classical concept of freedom of information" and focused on breaking up "existing monopolies of misinformation—particularly those of a governmental nature—so as to permit the flow of true information." But "the adoption of US views will be impeded," the State Department worried, "by the growing fear of American 'cultural imperialism' which has swept the world in recent months." In that context, "reiteration of the classical theory of freedom of information—no matter how fervently—will not seem a convincing answer to current problems." There was a real risk that the "U.S. will find itself in a state of lonely grandeur, while the great majority of delegations adopt compromises which, in fact, compromise freedom of information itself."[30]

There was a great deal of truth in this assessment. The US vision of global press freedom *was* out of kilter with the attitudes of most of the other nations. But while the United States dismissed these alternative visions as nothing more than departure from high principle, they actually reflected serious consideration of two of the knotty problems that bedevil liberal conceptions of press freedom to this day. The first concerned the best ways to prevent the spread of misleading propaganda. The Americans, following the philosophy of the modern First Amendment, presumed that if unregulated information flows were increased, truth would emerge out of the marketplace of ideas. In the 1940s, many other nations, like many pundits concerned about "fake news" today, thought such attitudes naïve. If states deliberately sought to spread propaganda, if journalists recklessly reported falsehoods, how would truth emerge? To increase the spread of truth, they believed that there needed to be some mechanism to guarantee that the flow of news was not only free, but also responsible to the common good.[31]

The second problem was posed by global inequality. Classical visions of press freedom, built around negative liberties, provide a poor way to protect the rights of the less powerful from the more powerful—it is the rich who find it easiest to win a competition in the free market. It was therefore easy for the United States to insist that breaking down barriers to the flow of news was the only prerequisite for freedom of information—given their economic clout, they would likely dominate the deregulated international news flow thus created. The rest of the world, however, would struggle to compete—or to build up alternative sources of information. The result, as one French delegate put it, would be a "monopoly of information in favor of those who are best supplied. It could result in a sort of mass media imperialism." In all, as Julian Huxley, director-general of UNESCO, put it, the US vision of classical liberalism seemed a lot like the advocacy of a "laissez-faire anarchy" that was "incompatible with the true nature of liberty and could only derive from a blindness to the real needs of the world."[32]

The United States failed to adequately engage with these concerns. Although the problems of irresponsibility and inequality are politically and intellectually discrete, the United States treated them as intertwined facets of an illiberal "trend toward 'cultural isolationism' [that] must be combatted." And it dismissed that trend as a by-product of "Communist propaganda based on anti-U.S. nationalism." Therefore, the US delegation concluded that it needed to take a pugnacious attitude into the conference—it had to avoid being "maneuvered" into a defensive position by the Soviets, and it had to "head off compromises with middle of the road nations." The result was that the United States came to Geneva—a conference about the *exchange* of information—with a deep unwillingness to negotiate or to hear alternative viewpoints. "This is no conference about money or wheat or radio frequencies where divergent viewpoints must and should be compromised," Benton announced to the conference's opening session. "This is a conference about principles essential to free men."[33] The United States assumed that it represented the worldly manifestations of those principles and its task was to extend them, undiluted, to the rest of the world. Such an attitude, particularly when undermined by the various ways that US practice itself fell short of liberal principles, would ultimately doom this effort to globalize press freedom.

Take, for instance, the discussion about the best way to purge propaganda from the international flow of information. A number of states believed that the United Nations needed to do something to proactively improve the quality of information circulated by the press. The French proposed the creation of an international information council at the UN, composed of professional journalists, which would issue an international press card to foreign correspondents to allow them reportorial access. The card could be withdrawn in the case of professional misconduct. The French also proposed that nations should sign a treaty that would provide an international "right of reply," a legal right for an aggrieved party to place a correction in a newspaper if it felt that it had been inaccurately represented. The right of reply had a long history in France and Latin America as a way to encourage responsible journalism; a similar law lay forgotten on the books in Florida and would be dusted off by media reformers in the early 1970s as a way to democratize the US press. (In 1974, the US Supreme Court ruled it an unconstitutional interference with the First Amendment.) In the French proposal, foreign governments would have the right of reply to misrepresentations in foreign newspapers and the right to petition the United Nations to enforce that right. It was popular among Latin American delegates, who said it would provide a way for relatively powerless countries to defend their "honor" and "prestige" when they were treated contemptuously in the newspapers of more affluent nations.[34]

Nations also hoped to preserve the right of their domestic governments to regulate toxic news circulating within their polities. This issue came up during discussions about the freedom of information clause in the proposed Covenant on Human Rights. The covenant was intended to be the binding, legal partner to the Universal Declaration of Human Rights; whereas the declaration was simply a nonbinding statement of ideals, the covenant was supposed to outline what, precisely, states could and could not do with regard to the exchange of information. This distinction made the covenant much more important than the declaration, but it also meant that the drafting of the covenant bogged down for decades, leaving the declaration alone as the unenforceable centerpiece of the international human rights regime. In 1948, however, no one knew that the covenant would become so delayed, and the debate at Geneva was contentious. The text of the clause had to guarantee freedom of expression, yet it also had to work out what forms of regulation were acceptable. Observing that the "right of freedom of expression carries with it duties and responsibilities," the Second Article of the covenant allowed the imposition of "penalties, liabilities or restrictions limiting this right." It then listed the seven grounds on which such restrictions were acceptable: defamation, obscenity, copyright infringement, inciting a crime, interfering with a trial, "expressions which incite persons to alter by violence the system of government," and circulating "matters which must remain secret in the vital interests of the State." The Indian delegation then inserted an additional, eighth form of legitimate restriction: it allowed states to punish "systematic diffusion of deliberately false or distorted reports which undermine friendly relations between peoples and states."[35]

All these proposed legal regulations stemmed from the belief that the simple exchange of news would be insufficient to eradicate propaganda and that governing organizations had some role to play in policing the limits of expression. Their proponents at the United Nations were motivated by recent political experiences within their nations. India, for instance, was concerned about the turmoil of the 1947 Partition, in which irresponsible journalism had fanned the flames of ethnic violence. France, struggling to purge Vichy collaborators from its press and reflecting ruefully on its tolerance of antidemocratic speech in the interwar period, was likewise comfortable insisting that the right to free speech was not absolute.[36]

The United States, however, opposed all these measures. It feared that an international press council would "develop into an instrumentality of censorship and control." It worried the Indian clause on censoring false reports would open the door to regulation of its news agencies by foreign governments. (It would, complained *Editor and Publisher*, "condone all the journalistic malpractices behind the Iron Curtain.") And it was concerned that the right of reply treaty would have allowed foreign governments a way to "force their viewpoints into the vast American press." As the US delegate Erwin Canham explained, "A compulsory right of correction would have been a one-way street, running against the U.S." Rather than legal regulation, the United States argued that it would be better to increase the flow of information and let competition in the marketplace drive the bad information out. It was willing, therefore, to entertain a noncompulsory right of reply, which would simply add more news to global exchanges. And its preferred legal remedy to improve the press was an International Convention for the Gathering and Transmission of News, which would guarantee the rights of foreign correspondents to travel across borders and to report freely and without censorship in foreign nations.[37]

The problem for the United States was that while it presented itself as a champion of classical press freedom at Geneva, it was also deeply committed to preserving its many regulations against foreign propaganda. This hypocrisy was plainest in its proposed treaty on the free movement of journalists. The draft treaty was intended to "encourage the freest possible movement of foreign correspondents" and so declared that "contracting states shall impose no special or unusual restrictions on the entry into, residence in, exit from and transit through the territories of each other of certified correspondents," which seemed a straightforward piece of liberal globalism. But it also clarified that states retained the authority to administer "their respective laws and procedures" relating to the entry of journalists.[38]

In the case of the US, as we have seen, visas were routinely denied to a variety of individuals whose entry was believed to endanger the public safety of the United States—restrictions that also applied to journalists. As the State Department briefed the delegation to Geneva, under antiradical immigration laws "visas are normally denied to any alien, including a correspondent, who is a member of the Communist Party." The attorney general did have discretion to allow the conditional entry of individuals who were otherwise ineligible for visas, and some correspondents were allowed in on this basis. But this normally involved the imposition of specific regulations on these individuals. All Soviet correspondents to the United States, for instance, were restricted in their movements in precisely the sorts of ways that the United States claimed it wanted to eradicate. For example, Soviet correspondents in Washington, DC, were required to reside within a forty-mile radius of the White House, and they all had to register their itineraries with the Justice Department. When French Communist Pierre Courtade, who worked for the popular Communist daily *L'Humanite*, was provided entry to cover the United Nations in October 1947, he was prohibited from leaving the area of the United Nations, which made it hard to report on diplomatic happenings in Washington. He was also required to pledge that he would not write anything "anti-American." Courtade confessed, "My problem is to cover the UN without offending the U.S."—failure to do so would result not in censorship, but in deportation.[39]

The willingness of the United States to regulate the activities of even UN correspondents revealed the limits of its ostensible commitment to the free movement of journalists. In theory, the UN Headquarters Agreement, negotiated between the United States and the United Nations in 1947, guaranteed that the United States would allow journalists accredited by the UN to enter the country if the UN consulted with the US about its accreditation process. The agreement was part of the quid pro quo that turned the UN headquarters into international space even though it happened to be firmly on New York soil. When implemented, however, the agreement revealed that the United States was unwilling to concede control over its borders to the international organization. In the few months between the time that agreement went into effect at the end of 1947 and the start of the Geneva conference the following March, the United States had already arrested two UN correspondents, interned them on Ellis Island, and begun deportation proceedings. The affair created a minor international incident. The UN charged that the US had violated the Headquarters Agreement by acting unilaterally. The US argued that the UN had not properly vetted or accredited the two correspondents and that it would not have accredited them if it had properly consulted with the United States—neither correspondent, the US believed, was legitimate.

One of them, Syed Hasan, had entered the country on a student visa to pursue a master's degree in international affairs at Columbia University, but then took up a position as a correspondent for the Communist Indian newspaper *People's Age*, technically violating his student visa. The other, Nicolas Kyriazidis, had been accredited as a UN correspondent for two Communist papers in Athens, but after both had been shut by the Greek government, he had switched his employment to work part time for *Demokratis*, a small Communist paper in Cyprus, for which he was not accredited. Despite the Headquarters Agreement, the United States insisted that it had in "no way yielded up its sovereign rights to investigate, to hold hearings, and to deport alien journalists or persons holding themselves as such if the circumstances warrant." After a hurried one-day conference, all seven hundred preexisting UN credentials were voided, and the UN and US came to new terms to formalize the process of consultation. Moving forward, the UN would prove to be deferential to US advice as to which journalists to accredit, and under what terms.[40]

In short, what the United States really cared about was the free movement of its journalists in *other* countries. The State Department knew that this was a "possible source of embarrassment" at Geneva. "The US," it predicted, "will have to safeguard its position in limiting the rights of outright Communists to enter this country and at the same time endeavor to broaden news coverage throughout the world." This hypocrisy was not lost on the delegates. As long as the proposed laws on freedom of movement allowed for the unilateral application of immigration laws, pointed out the Soviet Bloc, then they weren't worth much—they contained, as one Polish delegate put it, "no concrete provisions."[41]

American opposition to legal restrictions on foreign propaganda, such as the Indian ban on false reporting or the French proposal for an international press council, faced similar problems. While the US delegation argued that any attempt to draw distinctions between true news and fake propaganda was a form of statist interference with classical press freedom, the United States itself was more than comfortable in drawing such distinctions and engaging in expansive press censorship. The military governments occupying the former Axis nations provided the most extreme examples. In the US zone of Germany, where the press operated under license from 1945 to 1949, the US government banned nationalist, pan-German, and Fascist views; in Japan, a legion of six thousand US censors scoured the press for signs of militarism. These were exactly the kinds of anti-Fascist content restrictions that the United States claimed to oppose because of their tendency to turn into tools of repression for undemocratic governments. Perhaps the United States had a point—in both Germany and Japan, criticism of the US occupation was banned.[42]

More significantly, the United States also had in place a number of laws that sought to protect its domestic public from foreign propaganda. Licenses to operate US broadcasting stations were limited to American citizens—Congress feared that aliens could use them to spread subversive propaganda. Section 305 of the 1930 Tariff Act prohibited the importation of seditious materials. The Foreign Agents Registration Act of 1938 mandated that all persons acting as agents of a foreign government had to register with the government and provide the Justice Department with copies of any materials they circulated to the public, as well as a list of the recipients. In 1940, the attorney general ruled that sections of that act, in combination with obscure provisions in the Espionage Act, also allowed the US Post Office to seize and destroy propaganda that had been mailed to US citizens from abroad unless the foreigner was registered under the Foreign Agents Registration Act, a most unlikely situation given the law was designed for foreign agents within the United States. The 1940 Alien Registration Act, known as the Smith Act, made it illegal to "advocate, abet, advise, or teach the duty, necessity, desirability or propriety of overthrowing or destroying any government in the United States by force or violence," or to "print, publish, edit, issue, circulate, sell, distribute, or publicly display any written or printed matter" that did so. As the Geneva conference met, the Justice Department was preparing its successful prosecution of the leadership of the US Communist Party under the statute. Eleven people were indicted in July 1948, and their convictions upheld by the Supreme Court in the famous *Dennis* case of 1951. By 1956, a further ninety-eight people would be convicted under the law.[43]

For all that the United States proclaimed itself opposed to statist interference in the global flow of information, it had no intention of making international commitments that would interfere with these laws. In fact, behind closed doors, the State Department was primarily concerned not that the language of the proposed Covenant on Human Rights would allow too many restrictions on press freedom, but "whether or not we could continue to enforce quite a number of laws which we now feel are both legitimate and highly desirable." The US delegation was particularly concerned about whether the draft covenant would allow the censorship of information relating to atomic energy. So rather than trying to specify in the covenant all the reasons that it might want to censor information, the US instead believed that it would be better to rewrite the clause with a general provision that would allow states to limit the press in any case that was "clearly defined by law" and that was also "based on the rights of others or on the protection by law of the freedom, general welfare and security of all." For a delegation simultaneously claiming that the Indian "false reporting" statute was too broad, this sweeping proposal was an odd move. As one British delegate pointed out, this general clause "would justify any existing practice, or any which a state might find it convenient to introduce, in order to render freedom of expression illusory."[44] It wasn't a winning proposition, and it did much to undermine US opposition to India's proposal. At the end of the day, US efforts to prevent other nations from censoring their news couldn't be squared with its own desires. It failed to prevent other nations from insisting that improving the free flow of information around the world required some measures to regulate illiberal propaganda.

The United States had similar problems defeating proposals at Geneva that sought to redress the inequalities of the global flow of news. Delegates from nations like India and China were understandably concerned that simply promoting the flow of information would leave them disadvantaged, and powerless to prevent the influx of news written by the West. The head of the Chinese delegation, P. C. Chang, who had played a central role in drafting the Universal Declaration of Human Rights, explained the basic problem to the US delegation in a private meeting. "Underdeveloped countries," Chang pointed out, "were of the opinion that if the conference did not go beyond resolutions assuring the freedom of movement and transmission of news, [they] would have no chance in a highly competitive field. He was glad to realize that the US was in a position to send almost any number of correspondents abroad, but he felt that such a proposition would not meet with the undivided enthusiasm of underdeveloped countries which did not have means of sending many correspondents abroad." Simply removing barriers to the flow of information would mainly mean "that economically powerful counties might penetrate less well-developed states by the extension of their own system." Hansa Mehta, the Indian activist who had helped write women's rights into the Universal Declaration of Human Rights, explained the inadequacies of the Western news agencies when viewed from the decolonizing world:

> Both in the matter of carrying news from India to other countries and bringing in news from other countries our experience has been that this service has been rendered not with the primary object of informing the people of India of activities abroad which would contribute

> materially to her own development, nor with the object of promoting better understanding between the people of the world . . . but with other motives I need not elaborate here. Of America we know a great deal of gangsters in Chicago and film stars in Hollywood. In the other direction, India was known as a land of mystery, fabulous splendor, elephants and snakes. It needed a world conflict of the magnitude of the last war to break down these barriers. We are willing and anxious to throw open all sources of information and all facilities to competing agencies providing we are assured that those who will survive in the field will serve the object which we are gathered round this table to secure.[45]

To create a more balanced, accurate flow of news, delegates from these nations asked for assistance in building up their own news capacity. S. A. Brelvi, of India, suggested that there was a need for wealthier nations to equitably distribute the "supplies of physical facilities and technical equipment for the dissemination of information between all countries." A Pakistani delegate agreed, saying that without such material resources, "it would be impossible for the population of industrially undeveloped countries to reap the full benefits of the wide distribution of information."[46]

The most important of these resources was newsprint, which was in short supply. The war had disrupted the production and transport of this most elementary material. Without paper, one could not start a newspaper; without cheap paper, journalism couldn't flourish. But the global newsprint supply, shaped by market forces, was deeply uneven. The United States, with 6 percent of the world's population, consumed 63 percent of the world's newsprint supply—and used more than half of it to print advertisements. (Even so, the booming US press had an insatiable demand for newsprint. Between 1943 and 1958, Congress held twelve investigations into newsprint shortages in the US.) The advertising inserts in US newspapers in the late 1940s were larger than entire editions elsewhere; according to one study, the United States used as much newsprint every day as India consumed in a year.[47] Newsprint shortages did not just shape the political economy of journalism; they also opened the door to political interference in the press. From Soviet-dominated Poland to Juan Perón's Argentina, states were adept at using scarcity as a tool to discipline the press. The US also knew how to play this game—in Italy, the CIA funneled newsprint to anti-Communist papers in the run-up to the important 1948 election; the next year, Communist newspapers in Occupied Japan saw their monthly newsprint allocation cut from 86,000 pounds to 20,000. As Dutch diplomat (and former editor and future high commissioner for refugees) Gerrit Jan van Heuven Goedhart put it in 1947, "The situation with regard to the available amount of newsprint is so desperate, that it, in fact, completely frustrates freedom of information, however beautifully phrased it may be."[48]

A number of nations argued that an international organization should redistribute these resources. But the United States was deeply opposed to the idea, which it considered another form of interference with its laissez-faire philosophy. When Carlos Romulo of the Philippines and Devdas Gandhi of India both proposed the creation of a global pool of newsprint which could be allocated by an international board, one American commentator acknowledged: "that idea will appeal to the 'have not' nations, but to the 'have' nations, of which we are one, it is not too welcome." The United States instead preferred to solve the problem by "developing further sources of newsprint in other areas [of the world] rather than lopping off part of the existing supply." At Geneva, the United States relied on parliamentary foot-dragging to stymie any effort to include discussions of resource inequality in the Covenant on Human Rights (it said that the subject was a "detail" best left out of a "document intended for posterity"), but it failed in its effort to block a motion that the United Nations should explore the explore the possibility of newsprint redistribution in the future. The US was the only nation to speak out against it.[49]

The exchanges revealed the United States to be both inflexible and isolated on the issue of global inequality. "The poor countries are being asked to give in these conventions," complained Chang, "and the rich countries are not proposing to give us anything." Privately, the US delegation knew that they were driving an unfair bargain. In his confidential report after the conference, William Benton confessed with considerable relief that Chang had not pushed on this "potentially important issue . . . very hard—perhaps not as hard as he should have."[50]

The clash between all these different visions of press freedom produced a stalemate at Geneva. The US was unwilling to compromise on its laissez-faire vision. Other nations remained adamant that improving the international flow of news required addressing inequality and propaganda. Discussion became interminable, predictable, formulaic. Afterward, US delegate Zechariah Chafee quipped that the United Nations could save a great deal of time if it adopted an "algebraic theory" of debate. Delegates could simply state a letter rather than give speeches: Americans could say "A" to argue for classical liberalism, "B" could stand for the French and middle-of-the-road position on press responsibility, the Soviet Bloc could say "C" when it wanted to outline the evils of monopoly capitalism and the perfections of communism, and so on.[51]

Amid the grandstanding at Geneva, the only meaningful victory for the United States came in the committee charged with writing Article 19 of the UN Declaration of Human Rights. The Soviets had proposed that freedom should come with responsibilities to the public, suggesting that "freedom of speech and freedom of the press shall not be used to advocate fascism or aggression; to sow racial, national or religious hatred, to disseminate false information or to incite the nations to mutual enmity." In the face of US opposition, it was voted down, 18–5. A milder French proposal, which held that anyone who used their right to free expression "shall be answerable in cases defined by the law for abuses of that freedom," was also defeated, albeit by a closer margin: ten delegates voted against, three for, and ten abstained. Instead, the US version was adopted by seventeen votes to none (with the six nations of the Soviet Bloc abstaining). It emphasized a laissez-faire vision of press freedom and made no mention of limitations, specifying that "everyone shall have the right to freedom of thought and expression; this right shall include freedom to hold opinions without interference and to seek, receive and impart information and ideas by any means and regardless of frontiers."[52]

In one sense, Article 19 did mark a noteworthy departure from the First Amendment of the US Constitution, which provides no guarantees of the right to "receive ideas" and focuses exclusively on the rights of the speaker. Throughout the twentieth century, progressive reformers struggled, with little success, to expand the First Amendment to protect the rights of the audience.[53] It is likely that the existence of such language in the Universal Declaration of Human Rights reflects in part a spike of attention such receiver rights attracted at the midcentury—Chafee, for instance, served on the Hutchins Commission on Press Freedom, which was exploring the meaning of press freedom for media consumers, at the same time that he was engaged in debates at the United Nations. It also seems likely that the language on receiving ideas was a form of subtle deference to more collective notions of press freedom that the United States defeated at Geneva. But perhaps most significantly, it reflected the ambitions of US proponents of global press freedom, who primarily imagined that it would be foreigners who wanted the "right to receive" information coming across their borders from the United States. It was a vision of rights that dovetailed perfectly with the geoeconomic ambitions of the US news agencies.

In any case, Article 19 was just a statement of ideals. Where the rubber hit the road, in the concrete provisions of international law, the United

States could not prevail. When the Geneva conference drew to a close, the delegates had not been able to reconcile or consolidate the competing visions of press freedom, so they simply approved a multitude of conflicting proposals: three different versions of an international convention on press freedom, more than forty separate resolutions, and a still-contentious version of the Covenant on Human Rights, which lacked US approval because it allowed the censorship of false propaganda.

The US delegation was surprisingly happy with its work, largely because it had been focused on making sure that the Soviets had not been able to dominate proceedings and had accomplished that goal—the delegation boasted afterward that it had been "surprisingly easy to outmaneuver the Soviets." The "atmosphere [at Geneva] was far more favorable to us than at any other UN meeting since 1945," concluded Canham. "We are winning the cold war."[54]

In focusing on the Soviets, however, the United States failed to notice the more meaningful divisions in the international order that had opened up at Geneva. The real obstacle to the US vision for global press freedom came not from the Soviet Bloc, but from the decolonizing world. As the various motions from Geneva wormed their way through the UN bureaucracy—they had to be debated and approved at the Human Rights Commission, then at the Economic and Social Council, then at the General Assembly's Third Commission, and then at the General Assembly as a whole—nations from the Global South became increasingly militant in calling for measures to ensure that global press freedom would amount to more than what Raul Noriega of Mexico called a "one-way affair, designed almost exclusively to assist U.S. information agencies." Merging concerns about inequality and irresponsibility, they sought to insert into the draft press freedom laws protections for their nascent news agencies, the right to reply to false reports in Western papers, and the right to ban false propaganda. At first, the Americans were incredulous, and dismissive, of this emerging bloc—Canham waved off the "have-not nations" because they "have not large powerful press associations or the concept of the free press." But the have-not nations turned out to have a majority in the United Nations, and they won vote after vote on the issues. The dynamics were revealed in a 1949 vote, in which Mexico successfully inserted a mandatory right of reply into the proposed US treaty on newsgathering. The United States opposed the move, as did twelve of its allies, almost all of them European. But even though the Soviet Bloc abstained, the motion passed when it received twenty votes from such nations as Afghanistan,

Brazil, China, Egypt, Haiti, India, Lebanon, Nicaragua, Panama, Peru, Thailand, and Venezuela. To the surprise of the Americans, a North-South axis had displaced the East-West clashes of the Cold War. "We soon found we could vote down the Russian bloc," reflected the UP's Hugh Baillie, "but we could not handle opposition from nations we had thought were on our side."[55]

In response, the United States decided to oppose any effort to extend press freedom through the United Nations. Former champions of global press freedom had become disillusioned. Baillie said that the proposed US convention had "been captured by the enemies of freedom of the press and distorted into a monstrosity for control and regulation of the press." Chafee said that it had been so transformed by "crippling amendments" that "it would be better not to have any convention at all." Conservative critics went further, worrying about protecting the United States from the United Nations. "The American people are today confronted with the question," suggested Elisha Hanson, attorney for American Newspaper Publishers Association, "as to whether, in an attempt to give greater liberty to other peoples in the world, they will destroy their own." By 1952, the State Department had decided that the proposed laws coming out of Geneva had "grown into such a monster that there is just nothing that we can do but to oppose it with everything we have."[56]

The open opposition of the United States more or less closed the window on any meaningful chance to write global press freedom laws. The US worked quickly to close down the Sub-Commission on Freedom of Information in 1952 and to shuffle debate about the issue offstage. Instead of writing international law, the United Nations was now to focus on fact-finding, tasks that were delegated to UNESCO as well as a UN rapporteur. After thirty-three sessions of discussion, which had taken place in nine different organs of the UN, the crusade for freedom of information sputtered to a halt. Apart from Article 19 of the Universal Declaration of Human Rights, it had produced only a minor treaty in 1952 providing nations the right to send a reply to foreign governments in the case of inaccurate reports—when it went into force in 1962, it had been ratified by only Cuba, El Salvador, France, Guatemala, Sierra Leone, the United Arab Republic, and Yugoslavia; only seven more nations ever joined it.[57] The Freedom of Information Crusade had produced only a smattering of the legal infrastructure it had once promised.

The failure of the US news agencies to inscribe their global aims into international law didn't prevent them from expanding. Their sheer economic capacity ensured that they quickly became global institutions. In 1944, the AP had sold news to thirty-eight countries; by 1952, it was selling to seventy. In accordance with their free-market philosophy, the US news agencies now often sold directly to foreign papers rather than coming to agreements with foreign news agencies—as had been the case in the old cartel agreements and was still the practice of Reuters, as well as the newly formed Agence France-Presse (AFP). By 1952, the UP had 1,183 clients in seventy-six countries; the AP had more than 3,500. The UP and the AP didn't, it turned out, need a global press treaty to move into new markets. They just needed a world without a cartel agreement.[58]

The US news agencies were expanding, but they could not expand everywhere, for the global news market remained geopolitically segmented. "Although agreements between the world agencies no longer exist," observed UNESCO in 1953, "in fact their freedom of action remains largely theoretical; new distribution zones have appeared, corresponding to political and ideological spheres of influence." Central America, Kuwait, and Saudi Arabia were dominated by the US agencies; Eastern Europe and Communist China—with a combined 30 percent of the world's population—relied on the Soviet Union's TASS bureau for their news. Meanwhile, the European news agencies clung to old centers of strength: Reuters and the AFP remained dominant in their colonial spheres in Africa, and the US agencies lacked an Arabic language service and couldn't compete with its European rivals in the Middle East. What was different about the post–World War II order was that much of the world lay outside of one of these exclusive spheres of influence. By the early 1950s, 40 percent of the world's population lived in regions that received news from the American, French, *and* British news agencies: Canada, Egypt, India, Pakistan, Turkey, Vietnam, much of South America, and most of Western Europe. A further 8 percent of the world's population received all the Euro-American news plus news from TASS. The 203 million citizens of such nations as Afghanistan, Indonesia, Iran, and Japan could thus be said to be the main beneficiaries of the newly globalized and newly competitive international news market.[59]

American citizens, on the other hand, remained unusually dependent on US news agencies for news of the outside world. The cartel was long buried, and there was no law barring US newspapers from subscribing to foreign news agencies, but few newspapers saw any need to take on the cost. And so very few did—just a small number of prestigious papers that took out a Reuters subscription and a tiny handful of French-language papers in New England that subscribed to the AFP. Meanwhile, very few newspapers could themselves afford a stable of foreign correspondents; in the early 1950s, only six newspapers, in three cities, did so. Other papers could purchase their coverage—the *New York Times* foreign coverage was syndicated to thirty-one papers—or hire correspondents on special assignment. The flow of news into the United States thus remained dominated by the AP and the UP and shaped by their geographic footprint. The AP, for instance, maintained seventy-two foreign bureaus: twenty-nine in Europe, eighteen in Latin America, thirteen in Asia, twelve in Canada, and none in Africa.[60]

In all, as the news market globalized, it did so in highly uneven ways. The US news agencies expanded into newly competitive markets, although they could not fully displace their old European rivals. Still, the Americans had firmly established themselves as global powers. Into the 1960s, Reuters, the AFP, the AP, and the renamed UPI (United Press International) provided something like 90 percent of news that was printed or broadcast in the world. Nations from the Global South remained, just as they had predicted at Geneva, unable to control their depiction in the news flow. A 1952 study, for instance, found that the US press gave very little coverage to India, much of which focused on the "bizarre or outlandish," such as "eccentric maharajas, mystics, sacred cows, tigers, cobras [and] child brides." In such ways did news flow out of the United States much more easily than it flowed in. That was in perfect keeping with the economic ambitions that had underscored the quest for global press freedom from the beginning.[61]

Ironically, the more important legacy of the failure of the Geneva conference was that it helped legitimize a rapidly expanding US propaganda program. In the early part of the 1940s, the United States had an ambivalent relationship with propaganda—although it found propaganda distasteful in principle, it quickly rolled out large-scale propaganda programs when it thought that they would be geopolitically useful. In 1938, the State Department had created a Division of Cultural Relations to expand influence in Latin America; in 1940, it was joined in this effort by a new Office of the Coordinator of Inter-American Affairs. After the United States joined the war, the Office of War Information pumped books, pamphlets, movies, and radio programs through a vast global network. In 1945, Harry Truman had made the decision to continue some form of postwar propaganda, albeit on a smaller scale—an Office of International Information and Cultural Affairs was created, with a much-reduced budget.[62]

Still, the idea of a permanent peacetime propaganda program remained controversial. In January 1946, a State Department Memorandum on the

Postwar International Information Program called for ongoing government participation in spreading US information abroad—one of its central proposals was the creation of a seven-thousand-word daily news bulletin to be sent to parts of the world not currently purchasing US news. It was based on a similar practice adopted during the war, when the AP and the UP had provided news to the Office of War Information free of charge to be sent overseas (in fact, the practice was still in operation at the time the new plan was proposed, because the news agencies had agreed to a State Department request to continue it for six months after the end of the war). But within days of the proposal, both the AP and the UP announced that they would no longer supply news to the state, for they said it smacked of propaganda and would discredit their campaign at the UN for a global flow of free information. "Of course we desire to be completely disassociated from the State Department's propaganda program," huffed the UP's Baillie. "We have campaigned all over the world for freer flow of news among nations."[63]

The issue roiled the newspaper industry, which argued angrily about whether the state could play a role in spreading their news to the world. Did it help global press freedom by increasing the proportion of the world receiving "objective" US news? Or did it hurt global press freedom by discrediting US news as just another form of propaganda? Symbolically, the three members of ASNE's globe-trotting Freedom of Information Committee split three ways on the issue. One supported the program as of a piece with their campaign at the United Nations, while another opposed it as an undemocratic propaganda program. The third, seeking a compromise, wanted reforms to ensure that the State Department would not tamper with the news. A special commission appointed by ASNE revealed just how tentative the press was about embracing propaganda. Edwin James, managing editor of the *New York Times*, believed that this issue "comes nearer a 51–49 proposition than anything I have been up against." Oveta Culp Hobby, the executive director of the *Houston Post*, who would soon serve as a delegate to the Geneva conference, agreed, saying, "I cannot recall a problem about which I have had as many conflicting responses."[64]

The fate of the press freedom campaign at the United Nations helped resolve such doubts. As hopes for a multilateral press treaty faded and as foreign nations called for regulations on the US press, unilateral US propaganda began to seem a justifiable, and possibly necessary, technique to ensure that the rest of the world would benefit from access to the uniquely free press in the United States. Erwin Canham, for instance, had supported the AP boycott of the State Department's informational campaign in 1946—he was opposed to propaganda. But when he returned from Geneva in 1948 to accept the presidency of ASNE, he had become a more militant Cold Warrior and begun to embrace the State Department ("which showed [at Geneva]," he said, "a complete, aggressive, vigilant awareness of the meaning of press freedom in American terms"). ASNE members greeted his election by pledging support for State Department propaganda programs "for the purpose of disseminating truth through the world."[65]

The reaction to the Geneva campaign was not the main cause of the rise of propaganda in the late 1940s. The Cold War was always going to result in a clash of ideas, and Congress had already begun expanding propaganda activities prior to the Geneva conference (most notably when it passed the Smith-Mundt Act in January 1948). But the campaign at the United Nations was nevertheless significant to the history of Cold War propaganda. A number of important individuals moved back and forth between the two campaigns, such as William Benton, who had earlier overseen the State Department's nascent postwar propaganda programs and had returned from Geneva to take up a Senate seat where he continued to advocate for what he called a "Marshall Plan in the field of ideas." Similarly, the American Newspaper Guild president Harry Martin so impressed the State Department with his performance as a delegate at Geneva that he was soon appointed as director of labor information for the Marshall Plan. (As Acheson put it, "Martin had made a name for himself in the Government by going into an international propaganda encounter and pitching a no-hitter.") In his new role as government propagandist, Martin oversaw the production of news features and radio programs designed to win the hearts and minds of Europe's working class, a task he saw as perfectly in keeping with his earlier efforts to free the world's flow of news from propaganda. And Canham was soon serving on the Advisory Commission on Information, which was responsible for overseeing Cold War propaganda policy.[66]

The title of that body—the Advisory Commission on *Information*—was also significant, for it revealed the intellectual contortions that had come to define US attitudes to propaganda and free information. When the United States spread media content to the world, that content was understood to be a contribution to global freedom of information because the US spread the truth, not propaganda. This self-serving distinction predated Geneva—World War II, after all, had given birth to the Office of War *Information*. But it would course through Cold War propaganda programs, from the "Campaign of Truth," announced by Truman in a speech to ASNE in 1950, to the United States Information Agency (USIA) created by President Dwight D. Eisenhower to centralize propaganda efforts in

1953, to the much-studied Congress for Cultural Freedom, in which the CIA secretly funded cultural organizations ostensibly dedicated to combating statist domination of the culture. And Geneva played a crucial role in legitimizing this equation of American propaganda with truth, because it was where the relationship between American press practice and global freedom of information had been most seriously debated. US commentators had left Geneva convinced that the rest of the world simply didn't appreciate the liberal virtues of the US press and that the United States alone understood the concept of "freedom of information." Rather than pursue dialogue about the quality of information it was spreading around the world, the United States had emerged with a hardened commitment to global soliloquy.

And so a statist propaganda program was embraced as continuation of efforts to create world understanding through the spread of free information. Letters to Truman revealed how commonsensical this had become by 1950. The self-described "Librarian and American Citizen" Elizabeth Hodges wrote to her president to "applaud your great campaign of truth speech" and to "thank you for stressing the importance of increasing world understanding in the interests of peace." J. Scott Pike wrote that both he and his wife "were favorably impressed" with the campaign because "we feel that getting the truth across to the common people of the entire world is by far the best means of winning the Cold War." J. H. Bowers of Memphis, Tennessee, suggested that the "Campaign of Truth" could be easily augmented. For "those countries having a coastline and unfavorable to us," he suggested, "why not stuff through a hole in a plastic tube or bottle truthful information and drop them into the incoming tide outside the three mile limit. News spreads rapidly." It is tempting to dismiss such sentiments as naïve or simplistic, but they had surprising purchase even among ostensibly hard-nosed Cold Warriors. A preferred activity of CIA-funded émigré groups in the 1950s was to attach propaganda leaflets and fake newspapers to balloons, travel to the borders of the Soviet Bloc, and let them float over the Iron Curtain. Some agents were so enamored with the idea that they drove their superiors mad. "If you send me one more project with goddamned balloons," growled CIA chief Walter Bedell Smith to one of his underlings in the early 1950s, "I'll throw you out of here." By the time the practice stopped in the wake of the Hungarian uprising in 1956, some three hundred million pieces of propaganda had been floated into Eastern Europe.[67]

American propaganda agencies were soon pumping all sorts of information into the world. By 1950, for instance, the US was spending $80 million a year to send information to ninety-three countries. It mobilized all the powerful media industries—it showed films to an audience of four hundred million, distributed sixty million pamphlets, and broadcast radio programs in forty-five languages. The USIA consumed the majority of the ink and paper that were being imported into South East Asia in the 1950s to print millions of copies of periodicals and hundreds of translations of American books. USIA officers also proved adept at planting news stories in foreign newspapers; in Paris, for instance, they had contractual arrangements with five news agencies; and from Cairo, they were sending 3,500 column inches each month to 110 newspapers and 40 magazines and were publishing a twelve-page weekly paper in Arabic. They also took advantage of their global networks to launder their stories—when they wanted to convince Iceland about the importance of the North Atlantic Treaty Organization, for instance, the USIA planted stories in Scandinavian and British newspapers and waited for Icelandic news to pick them up, unaware of their origins. Meanwhile, propaganda and public relations agencies were attached to all sorts of aid and technical assistance programs, and covert psychological warfare proceeded apace. It all acted as a force multiplier for the already dominant position of the US media in the global flow of information. And, focused on exporting information, it did nothing to improve the flow of foreign news into the United States. In fact, although Congress had explicitly insisted that propaganda produced under the Smith-Mundt Act could not be disseminated to the American public, there was inevitable cross-contamination, as domestic newspapers picked up stories that had originated as propaganda plants overseas or paid attention to media events planned to capture international attention.[68]

In short, the propaganda wars of the 1950s further polluted the international flow of information—all the information spread this way was politically motivated, some of it was outright fraudulent, and its sheer mass distorted the political economy of information in myriad ways. Although US practitioners saw propaganda as a way to spread objective information throughout the world, it in fact did nothing to address the underlying problems and inequalities of global information that had been aired at Geneva; if anything, by soaking up resources and using US dollars to subsidize media production, it exacerbated the dependence of the Global South on US media forms. And as all this propaganda sloshed around the world, it distracted from the many ways that information remained tightly regulated by nation-states engaged in geopolitical struggle.

In a 1953 speech to the United Nations, for instance, Eisenhower announced a new plan to transfer atomic material to an international agency which would be devoted to agricultural, medical, and energy uses of nuclear power—it was called “Atoms for Peace.” Little came of the plan, which was soon replaced by thirty-eight bilateral agreements to export nuclear reactors from the United States. But implementation had never been the main point of the speech. It had been conceived of as a way to maintain support for the US nuclear program in the face of rising concerns about fallout from weapons tests; publicizing peaceful uses of atomic energy was seen as a way of directing attention away from such anxieties. And so the propaganda machinery pumped the plan throughout the world—the Voice of America broadcast Eisenhower’s speech in thirty languages; films of the speech went to thirty-five countries; it was printed in newspapers around the world; and television programs (like *The Magic of the Atom*) and mobile exhibits about the program were created and distributed widely. Although the public information campaign was known as “Operation Candor” inside the administration, the government was using publicity to distract the public from the massive, and highly classified, buildup of the US nuclear arsenal. In fact, Eisenhower remained opposed to a “policy of candor toward the American people” on atomic matters and instructed Lewis Strauss of the Atomic Energy Commission to keep the public “confused as to fission or fusion.”[69] Only five years after the Geneva conference, that was what remained of the US quest for “global freedom of information.”

CHAPTER FIVE

THE FEAR OF FOREIGN CULTURE IN COLD WAR AMERICA

In 1957, to celebrate the seventy-fifth birthdays of two famous artists, two retrospective exhibitions were arranged. The Museum of Modern Art in New York City prepared a retrospective on the career of Pablo Picasso; at the same time, a retrospective on the career of Rockwell Kent toured the Soviet Union. Kent is today almost entirely forgotten, but the American author, painter, illustrator, and adventurer was famous in the mid-twentieth century. His paintings hung in the Metropolitan Museum of Art, the Whitney, the Corcoran, and the Frick; he had illustrated thirty-seven books, including popular editions of *Moby-Dick*, the *Bridge of San Luis Rey*, and *Leaves of Grass*; his memoirs of travel and exploration sold well. He was also a controversial political figure—an outspoken critic of American capitalism, an international pacifist, and a lifelong socialist with an Emersonian streak. Like Picasso, Kent combined the figure of the artist and the man of politics. Kent had publicly supported the Spanish Republic, participated in Henry Wallace's 1948 presidential campaign, pleaded the Fifth before Joe McCarthy, and been issued, in 1943, one of two lifelong memberships in the International Longshoreman Worker's Union—the other went to the renowned actor and singer Paul Robeson. The work of both artists therefore helped to symbolize a leftist, pacifist variant of post–World War II internationalism. Exhibitions of Kent and Picasso paintings were central events in the Khrushchev-era thaw in Soviet culture, where they represented a new openness to Western culture. A large Picasso mural decorated the UNESCO conference room in Paris, and a tapestry of *Guernica* would later decorate the UN General Assembly. A Rockwell Kent mural, depicting a thriving, peaceful world stitched together by air travel, decorated the House of Representatives Commerce Committee's hearing room—painted in 1944, it was called *On Earth Peace.*[1]

But in 1957, neither Picasso nor Kent was able to attend their respective exhibitions because the US government wouldn't allow either of them to travel. Kent could not leave the United States—he had been denied a passport because he was suspected of Communist sympathies. Picasso could not enter the United States—he had been denied a visa in 1950, when he had tried to head a "Partisans of Peace" delegation to the United States, which the State Department said consisted of "communists and fellow travelers." As the *New York Times* concluded, "Art appeared yesterday to do better in crossing international borders than the artists who create it."[2]

That 1950s America was hostile to foreign culture is not exactly a secret. The second Red Scare was defined by its attempts to cast domestic dissent as illegitimate foreign influence—there was a reason, after all, that it was called the House *Un-American* Activities Committee. And the hunt for subversives and spies was justified as an effort to protect American culture from international interference. But this fear of the foreign, this anxiety about internationalist networks, has been hiding in plain sight, and we have missed its significance to the history of cultural globalization. At a moment when the United States was acting as a truly global superpower, it had, in important ways, isolated itself from foreign ideas, culture, and information. Even as American culture and dollars and military force penetrated nations around the world, the US itself was surprisingly parochial, insulated from international currents. In fact, the conservative guardians of national security expended considerable effort to police the flow of ideas and people across the US border and to maintain the purity and autonomy of American culture—visa and passport restrictions ratcheted up in the 1950s, as did efforts to exclude un-American ideas from the public sphere and hostility to international organizations. These practices had particular efficacy because the influence of foreign culture on the US had already withered as a result of economic and demographic developments: the booming US media industries had little need to import material; and two generations after the closing of the border, remarkably few US residents had been born overseas, which had ruptured familial and experiential connections with international cultures. By the end of the 1950s, an effort to reconnect with international culture thus became a front for civil libertarian activism, as journalists, intellectuals, artists, and citizens sought the right to travel without government restriction and to import ideas. Although they had some success, it was a slow and difficult process. And the fact that US citizens needed to go to court to win such rights reminds us just how truncated connections to the world had become, even in a decade in which the United States had declared itself leader of the "free world."

The Cold War saw an efflorescence of mechanisms to control the movement of culture across US borders. During the Korean War, President Harry Truman invoked the Trading with the Enemy Act to enforce sanctions against China and North Korea, making it difficult to purchase cultural goods—magazines, paintings, books, even stamps—from these nations without special approval. The sanctions lasted for decades, during which time they were also extended to Cambodia, Cuba, and Vietnam.[3]

Similarly, in 1951, officials in the US Post Office and the Department of Justice decided that it was essential to intercept and destroy mail of the "propaganda type" from behind the Iron Curtain. Taking authority from an obscure 1940 attorney general's ruling, which itself relied on a combined, and clever, reading of obscure sections of the Espionage Act alongside the Foreign Agent Registration Act, customs officials began destroying thousands of items without informing intended recipients. The presumption was that any material from behind the Iron Curtain was illegal propaganda, a clunky system that produced absurdities. In St. Paul, a customs official who did not speak Russian was looking for Communist propaganda with only the aid of a Russian dictionary. One graduate student never received a German edition of Karl Marx's correspondence—the books had been destroyed at the border. Research libraries began noticing that they were no longer receiving issues of items they subscribed to; in 1955, their issues of *The Economist* were delayed by an overzealous official. In the same year, the American Friends Service Committee realized that it never received five hundred copies of a pamphlet about the 1954 coup in Guatemala that it had ordered from the United Kingdom. The pamphlet, which argued that there had been no Communist threat in Guatemala and that the United States had intervened to help big business, had been written by a British member of Parliament and published by the "Movement for Colonial Freedom," which had roughly sixty members of Parliament in its ranks. But the Post Office had seized the material as propaganda nonetheless. When the Friends threatened to sue, the Post Office released the material and announced a change in policy: recipients would now be notified when material was impounded, and a list of individuals entitled to receive such material was developed. It was an improvement, but it involved the Post Office in complex decisions about which Americans had rights to receive foreign information. University presidents were asked to vouch for the legitimacy of those asking for research materials from the Soviet Bloc—seventy-five copies of Lenin's *State and Revolution*, required reading for a history course at Brown, were released only when the university assured the Post Office of the bona fides of the course and the professor. Individuals who were politically suspect—a wide category amid the paranoia of the second Red Scare—were out of luck. So were the less well connected. Those the Post Office perceived to be too poorly educated to be using the foreign material for research purposes did not receive it. One retired Coast Guard officer in New England, whose hobby was studying navigational problems affecting the Russian navy, was denied magazines from Russia—his postmaster told him he was "unqualified."[4]

Meanwhile, travel regulations blossomed. The Visa and Passport Divisions were central agencies of the countersubversive state, having accrued considerable authority during the interwar period. In 1952, they were moved into the Bureau of Security and Consular Affairs, where they were overseen by the anti-Communist Scott McLeod.[5] They had been sharing information with the FBI for decades and would continue to do so well into the 1960s—they asked the FBI to investigate suspicious applicants, and the FBI in turn relied on the Passport Division to keep an eye on travelers it was monitoring. The travel bureaucracy was thus a crucial cog in the mutually reinforcing machinery of suspicion that continually ratcheted up pressure on suspected radicals. In 1953, for instance, CBS correspondent Winston Burdett was denied a passport on the basis of an earlier, inconclusive FBI investigation into his political sympathies (which had involved reviewing his previous passport applications). The denial produced a new round of investigation by the Senate Internal Security Subcommittee, before which Burdett named names, triggering yet another round of investigations.[6]

The Visa and Passport Divisions also used their reputations for hawkish monitoring of the border to expand their powers. In part, they did so by lobbying for new legislative authority. The 1950 Internal Security Act—which required members of organizations deemed to be Communist fronts to register with a new Subversive Activities Control Board and allowed for detaining Communists in camps in times of emergency—also sought to prevent suspected Communists from either entering or leaving the country. On the visa front, the Internal Security Act barred the entry of aliens who were members of or affiliated with the Communist Party or any other totalitarian party or any organization ordered to register as subversive, as well as all who advocated world communism and those deemed likely to break the espionage, sabotage, or public disorder laws, to join a group designated as subversive, or to otherwise criminally threaten national security. Meanwhile, once an organization had been ordered to register with the Subversive Activities Control Board, it would become illegal for any member of that organization to use, or even apply for, a passport. (The punishment was a fine up to $10,000 or five years in jail.) These passport and visa rules were transferred into the Immigration and Nationality Act of 1952, along with the 1918 Travel Control Act, which was quietly expanded to give the president the right to issue proclamations limiting travel in "any national emergency" (it had previously been limited to either wartime or the specific emergency that President Franklin D. Roosevelt had declared in 1941). In 1953, relying on the State of Emergency that he had declared during the Korean War, Truman issued a proclamation calling for "utmost diligence" in regulating the entry of foreigners and requiring that Americans needed a valid passport to depart from or enter the United States.[7]

Both the 1950 Internal Security Act and the 1952 Immigration Act had been sponsored by Patrick McCarran, the virulently conservative senator from Nevada, who was closely allied with the equally conservative bureaucrats in charge of travel. Ruth Shipley said that "McCarran and the un-American committees have done a grand job." McCarran in turn said that many of the "protective measures against subversives" that were featured in his bill "came from the mind of Shipley."[8]

But it turned out that these laws didn't do a great deal to meaningfully expand the authority of the Visa and Passport Divisions; rather, they simply gave legislative imprimatur to practices that the travel bureaucracy had already adopted. The 1950 Internal Security Act, for instance, explicitly barred Communists for the first time; but since the 1920s, the Visa Division had been assuming that Communists were barred by the antianarchist laws. Meanwhile, as Truman explained in his failed veto of the act, while advocates "claimed that this bill would deny passports to communists, the fact is that the Government can and does deny passports to Communists under existing law." The only clear new power was barring registered Communists from applying for passports—but this section never really went into effect. Efforts to order the Communist Party to register were caught up in legal challenges until 1961. Then, when the passports of Herbert Aptheker and Elizabeth Gurley Flynn were revoked in early 1962, the pair successfully appealed to the Supreme Court, which ruled Section 6 of the Internal Security Act unconstitutional.[9]

Still, if the new laws did not do a great deal to create new powers for the travel bureaucracy, they indicated approval for its already sweeping powers and were a clear encouragement to enforce them enthusiastically. The Visa Division immediately picked up its workload—by 1951, it was reviewing 3,623 cases per month, a 659 percent increase from the previous year. The State Department began restricting all travel to sections of the Communist world. The use of such "area restrictions" dated to the interwar period, when the State Department had tried to restrict travel to Spain, Ethiopia, and China, but they blossomed in the Cold War. Passports were stamped invalid for travel to Yugoslavia in 1947; to Hungary in 1949; to Bulgaria in 1950; and to Czechoslovakia in 1951. In 1952, the State Department declared that passports were not valid for travel to Albania, Bulgaria, China, Czechoslovakia, Hungary, Poland, Romania, or the USSR unless specifically endorsed. The order was loosened in 1955, although travel was still banned to Albania, Bulgaria, and what the State Department artfully dubbed "those portions of China, Korea and Vietnam under Communist control." For six months after the Suez Crisis, the State Department stopped issuing passports for travel to Egypt, Israel, Jordan, and Syria. And in January 1961, after the US broke diplomatic relations with Cuba, it banned all travel to Cuba apart from that considered "in the best interests of the United States, such as [by] newsmen or businessmen with previously established business interests."[10]

Even while the passport provisions of the Internal Security Act were tangled up in legal challenges, the Passport Division plowed ahead in deciding who could and could not receive passports. In early 1951, the Passport Division asked the State Department's legal advisor to clarify the meaning of the Internal Security Act. "For some time," the resulting legal opinion observed, "it has been the general policy of the Department to refuse passports to Communists generally as persons whose presence abroad would be inimical to the best interests of the U.S." The new act "merely makes what was before a discretionary right of refusal mandatorily exercisable in certain specified contingencies." And, in the opinion of the legal advisor, "it would be appropriate and consistent with the spirit of the Internal Security Act to deny a passport, whether or not an organization has in fact registered" under the act. Shipley took this message to heart. When Congress asked Shipley if her division was enforcing the ban on passports for those listed by the Subversive Activities Control Board, her answer was instructive: "There is no such list, yet, but the spirit of the McCarran Act is quite strong in the interests of security." She added, "We were given a legal opinion, which we asked for, that it was our duty to carry out the spirit of the act . . . we have done quite a good job on it. We have stopped a good deal of travel." In December 1951, Shipley again boasted that the department "is endeavoring to carry out the spirit of the McCarran Act [and] has refused or withdrawn passport facilities in hundreds of cases." As attorney Leonard Boudin observed archly, "This is the first time to the writer's knowledge that a precise statute is to be enforced not by its letter but by its spirit."[11]

As a result, visas were routinely denied to suspected Communists—in 1951, a Dutch historian, coming to work on a Rockefeller Grant, was denied a visa because he had been a member of the Communist Party in the 1920s; the next year, Graham Greene suffered a long delay in the issuance of his visa because he had been a member of the Communist Party for four weeks in 1923. Meanwhile, passport denial also ratcheted up. We don't know exactly how many passports were denied in the 1950s—the Passport Division was notoriously secretive and didn't even order tabulating equipment until 1955—but even if a full census of passport denials existed, it would understate the impact of the practice. We will never know how many Americans, afraid to have their passports denied, decided never to apply for one. (In 1958, Robert Murphy, deputy undersecretary of state, testified to Congress that the "greatest value of having authority to deny is not in the number of actual applications that are actually denied; the value of having such authority is that the Communist Party and its various apparatus, knowing that authority exists, do not apply for passports.") But we know that passports were denied to the same sorts of individuals who were otherwise pilloried and persecuted in the second Red Scare. After their run-ins with the Hollywood blacklist, Ring Lardner Jr., Donald Ogden Stewart, Edward G. Robinson, and Carl Foreman were all denied passports in the 1950s. Minor New Deal officials, such as Walter Packer and Charlotte Towles, had their passports denied after being criticized by McCarthyite politicians. And many left-leaning private citizens found themselves denied passports for political activity. Walter G. Bergman, for instance, had his passport revoked while lecturing in Denmark in 1953; Bergman, director of instruction research at the Detroit Public School System, had earlier been attacked by Martin Dies's House Committee on Un-American Activities for attending a Moscow summer school in 1934. Similarly, a graduate student in anthropology was denied a passport needed for a 1955 research trip to Africa because of his involvement in a Communist-dominated union ten years before.[12]

Passport and visa control thus followed the broader contours of antiradical policing in these years—the same assumptions of guilt by association, the same suspicion of dissent, and the same reliance on anonymous informants and confidential testimony. When Shipley finally explained to Linus Pauling why she had repeatedly denied the famous chemist a passport, for instance, she stated that her office had knowledge of allegations that Pauling was a "concealed member of the Communist Party"—unspecified allegations that it valued above Pauling's signed affidavits to the contrary. Shipley also listed twenty-three other allegations that Pauling had followed the Communist Party line: he had spoken at a rally against the H-bomb, given a speech opposing the "witch-hunt and communist scare" of the Hollywood Ten, called for the end of anti-Russian and anti-Communistic propaganda, claimed that there was no reason for dismissing a Communist as a professor, written to the president asking for the commutation of the Rosenbergs' death sentences, and so forth. As Pauling pointed out in an appeal, these activities all fell well within the exercise of his First Amendment rights. But they were sufficient, in Shipley's eyes, to prove that his travel abroad "would not be in the best interests of the United States."[13]

Travel control was thus an important, underappreciated front in the political persecution of dissidents in the second Red Scare. But it was even more significant for what it revealed about the desires of the US state to regulate the flow of information across its borders during the Cold War. Travel control articulated most powerfully around forms of internationalism that sought to animate alternative visions of global political community, targeting networks that sought to connect to foreign cultures without relying on the US state. In particular, travel control played a central role in disrupting and delimiting the movement of Black internationalists, who had struggled over previous decades to create a transnational political movement organized around racial justice and anticolonialism, as well as the international scientific community, committed to the global circulation of knowledge.[14]

In the wake of World War II, efforts to reestablish international scientific communications were flourishing. American security officials closely regulated the movement of scientists across their border, however; many people were asked questions about their political beliefs, and all were required to list, under oath, every organization with which they had been associated in the previous fifteen years. As a result, apparently half of all foreign scientists who wanted to enter the United States experienced some visa difficulties; hundreds of scientists were simply denied visas because officials were suspicious of their affiliations. For instance, the Hungarian biochemist Albert Szent-Györgi, winner of the Nobel Prize in Physiology or Medicine, was denied a visa in 1947 because he had headed the Hungarian-Soviet Cultural Society. E. B. Chain, codiscoverer of penicillin, was denied a visa because of a trip he had made to Eastern Europe as part of a UN group promoting the production of penicillin. The French Association des Travailleurs Scientifiques had made its way onto official blacklists because of suspicions about its president, and scientists who had been members were routinely denied visas; unfortunately, about 70 percent of French scientists had been members at some point. As the Federation of American Scientists pointed out, such visa policies "are contrary to the fundamental principles of our political philosophy which is based upon openness and freedom of information and movement." The damage they must have done to international scientific exchange, and to American science in particular, is difficult to quantify. They certainly made it very difficult to organize international scientific conferences in the United States. Twelve officials were prevented from attending an International Congress of Pure and Applied Chemistry in New York in 1951. Of twenty-four scientists invited to a University of Chicago Congress on Nuclear Physics, ten had visa delays and two were barred completely. By 1955, four international science unions that had been planning conferences in the United States had decided to relocate them.[15]

Shipley's Passport Division similarly interfered with the international travel of American scientists. In 1951, the Federation of American Scientists was sufficiently concerned about the "considerable interference with scientific travel by the State Department" that it formed a seven-member Passport Committee. Edward Condon, an advocate for placing atomic energy under civilian and international control, was denied a passport to travel to the 220th anniversary of the Russian Academy of Sciences. Martin Kamen was three times denied a passport to lecture at the Weizmann Institute of Science in Israel because he had chatted with a Russian scientist about leukemia while he was doing radioisotopic research for the Manhattan Project. While some of these passport denials, as in the case of Linus Pauling, are best understood as forms of political censorship, all scientists came in for additional scrutiny—the Passport Division made "additional checks" on chemists and physicists, and in 1950, the Atomic Energy Commission began building a list of all persons with access to classified information to "be used for control of their future foreign travel." Discussing the Geneva conference to liberalize travel policy, Paul Nitze had made clear the important role of passport restrictions in protecting national security interests in atomic energy. "One of the primary channels through which such information is released," he observed, "is by the movement of persons."[16]

Meanwhile, the two most famous cases of passport denial targeted perhaps the two most famous Black internationalists of the period: W. E. B. Du Bois and Paul Robeson. In July 1950, the State Department issued a "stop notice" at all ports to prevent Robeson from departing the country, and J. Edgar Hoover instructed the FBI to seize Robeson's passport. Relying on the broad powers of the Travel Control Act, the State Department even prevented him from traveling to Canada, normally possible without a passport. Unable to perform as planned at a convention of the United Mine, Mill, and Smelter Workers, Robeson was forced to sing and speak to the conference by telephone from Seattle. A few months later, a concert was arranged at Peace Arch Park on the Canadian border, and from the back of a truck parked on US soil, Robeson performed to some twenty-five thousand Canadians. Similarly, in 1951, after Du Bois was indicted for failing to register under the Internal Security Act for his activities in anti-imperialist and antinuclear organizations, the State Department withdrew his passport. Although Du Bois was soon acquitted, he was denied a passport until 1958; his wife, Shirley Graham Du Bois, likewise found herself denied a passport for her activism. Among other events, the ban forced Du Bois to miss the Bandung conference. Other Black activists, such as Ira De Reid and Harold Cruse, were similarly denied passports. Meanwhile, scholars, activists, and journalists from the Caribbean and Africa could enter the United States only if their visa applications were approved. In the mid-1950s, Trinidadian radicals C. L. R. James and Claudia Jones both ran afoul of the visa authorities and found themselves interned on Ellis Island before being deported.[17]

As the regulation of scientists and Black internationalists revealed, the US government was carefully policing the globalization of culture. Only certain ideas and people were allowed to flow freely across the US border; some international networks were to be disrupted, blocked, and marginalized. The highly visible policing of Black internationalists, for instance, destabilized what had been a vibrant circulation of ideas across the Black Atlantic. In the expatriate Black community in Paris, rumors swirled that the US consul was employing fifty plainclothes informers to monitor the cafés and find grounds to deny passports. In 1952, Richard Wright refused to return to the United States for a book tour until there were signs that "a man can get his passport without being too scared."[18]

By contrast, international travel that accorded more closely with the foreign policy prerogatives of the US was carefully shepherded around potential legal obstacles. In 1949, the CIA was granted authority to provide permanent residency to up to one hundred foreigners a year, even if they were otherwise ineligible for entry (as was the case, for instance, with former Nazi collaborators). One of the reasons Truman had opposed the visa regulations in the 1950 Internal Security Act was that its definition of totalitarianism was so broad that it would have prevented "Spanish businessmen [and] students" from entering the country. To maintain close relations with its allies in Spain, Italy, and Germany, the law was subsequently revised to ensure that it did not apply to Falangists or to those who had been rank-and-file members of the Nazi or Fascist parties. More broadly, the attorney general retained considerable authority to waive visa regulations on a selective basis. And the passport office's notoriously opaque practices gave individuals like Shipley wide discretion in adjudicating what sorts of travel were and were not in the "best interests" of the United States. "We have no standard practice where things can go through a machine," Shipley explained of her decisions to issue student exchange passports in 1952. "You have to look at the students to see whether any of them are going to one of these communist countries."[19]

Such monitoring and filtering of international connections served multiple functions. It allowed the US government to monopolize the domain of foreign affairs to ensure that citizens could not develop alternative networks that would interfere with Cold War calculations or geopolitical grand strategy. Shipley made this goal perfectly explicit when she told Robeson that in speaking out about colonialism, he was "meddling in matters within the exclusive jurisdiction of the Secretary of State." Robeson had "been for years extremely active politically on behalf of independence of the colonial peoples of Africa," explained the State Department in 1952, which interfered with the president's role as the "sole organ" in the "field of international relations." Although decolonization "may be a highly laudable aim," the State Department concluded, "the diplomatic embarrassment that could arise from the presence abroad of such a political meddler, traveling under the protection of an American passport, is easily imaginable."[20]

Control over the flow of information and people also allowed the US state to carefully manage its image abroad. An opening-night performance of *The Crucible* in Brussels symbolized the general trend. The playwright, Arthur Miller, had been, ironically, denied a passport to travel to the debut, so when the crowd cried out to applaud him, his place was taken by the US ambassador—officially sanctioned representatives, not private citizens, were to represent the US overseas. As Du Bois put it in a letter to the first Congress of Black Artists and Writers in Paris in 1956, "Any Negro-American who travels abroad, must either not discuss race conditions in the U.S. or say the sort of thing which our State Department wishes the world to believe." Less controversial Black Americans thus represented the United States: at Bandung, Adam Clayton Powell Jr., not Du Bois; Louis Armstrong and Dizzy Gillespie, not Paul Robeson, touring abroad—often as part of State Department cultural outreach programs.[21]

Meanwhile, the propaganda agencies of the US state were favored targets of red-baiting congressional conservatives, eager to find evidence that New Dealers were using taxpayer money to smuggle subversive material abroad. McCarthy launched congressional investigations into the Voice of America; he claimed that there were thirty thousand books by subversives on the shelves of US libraries overseas and dispatched Roy Cohn and David Schine on a highly publicized tour to ferret them out. Under pressure, the State Department ordered the libraries to purge books by "any controversial persons, communists, fellow travelers, etc."—books by Thomas Paine, Howard Fast, Lillian Hellman, W. E. B. Du Bois, Paul Robeson, Dashiell Hammett, Theodore Dreiser, and Rockwell Kent were hastily taken out of circulation. Of course, such efforts to clean up the international image of the United States did much more to sully it; in the chaotic library investigations, eleven books were literally burned. US Fulbrighters visiting Australia in 1953 found themselves forced to explain the Red Scare to their hosts, who had the impression that "McCarthy is the most important person in the U.S." One grantee reported that Australians asked the most questions about "household appliances, clothes, and book-burnings or witch-hunts."[22]

Finally, all these restrictions on travel, particularly when combined with the prohibitions on importing "propaganda" from abroad, had the consequence of delimiting the flow of information to the American public. In the early 1950s, for instance, one left-wing journalist was denied a passport to travel to Italy to report on land reform—he was told that nothing "constructive" would come of it. When individuals were prevented from traveling abroad to research, report, observe, or simply talk to foreigners and when foreigners were prevented from coming to the United States or sending their books and articles to American readers, the range of ideas accessible to the US public was narrowed. As journalist William Worthy put it, "Travel control is thought control and intellectual control."[23]

It is difficult to measure the effect of such border controls on American political culture—trying to quantify the movement of ideas through the vast and complex public sphere in the United States of the 1950s is impossible. But such conscious policing of the border was layered on top of a culture that had been rendered surprisingly parochial and insulated from global influence by broader trends of demography and political economy. Although we associate immigration restriction with the nativist 1920s, the closing of the border had its largest impact on the nation's demographics in the 1950s and 1960s—by 1960, only 5.4 percent of the population had been born overseas, down from 14.7 percent in 1910. And because of the racist quotas of the immigration regime, only 5 percent of those foreign-born residents came from Asia and only 0.4 percent from Africa—84 percent of US residents who had been born abroad in 1960 came from either Europe or Canada. With the partial and ironic exception of US personnel at foreign military bases, there were remarkably few US residents with ongoing ties to many regions of the world, let alone experiences of living in them—and the racism of the period marginalized many of those that did. Tourism, focused on short vacations, was a poor substitute and was concentrated, in any case, in Western Europe.[24]

As a result, public attitudes to foreign cultures were relative blank slates and highly dependent on depictions in the media. Yet the US media industries in the 1950s were importing very little content; reaping the benefits of a booming consumer economy, as well as a vibrant export market, they were saturated with American-made content. (Their executives also assumed that there would be little American demand for foreign content.) The result was a media system that was surprisingly closed, creating an Americanist echo chamber. More than half of the world's records, for instance, were made and sold in the United States at the time; pop music was a distinctly American phenomenon. The movie industry, too, was dominated by Hollywood—the United States was spending only between $4 and $15 million a year to import movies in the 1950s, while it was exporting between $120 and $215 million a year. Most of the movies it imported came from Western Europe and Japan, and with a few notable exceptions—such as the Brigitte Bardot vehicle, *And God Created Woman*—they were shown in only a small network of art house cinemas because they were often denied the seal of approval by the Motion Picture Production Code necessary to play in the major movie houses. Code authorities, with a prurient fear of European sexual mores, as well as close ties to the domestic studios, thus acted as nationalist protectionists. Only a tiny number of foreign films were distributed widely, and a number of them, such as *The Bridge on the River Kwai*, had been jointly produced with Hollywood and hardly constituted either a meaningful break with standard Hollywood fare or an exposure to foreign cultures.[25]

Meanwhile, the new medium of television was perhaps the most effectively nationalized culture industry in US history. In 1954, 82 percent of the television sets in the world were in the United States; the rest of the world combined did not match the number of American television sets until 1963. The sheer size of the domestic market, as well as its head start on rivals, skewed the emerging international market for television shows—sales were "one-way traffic," as the *Baltimore Sun* reported in 1963. *I Love Lucy* was being shown around the world; *Dragnet* and *Kit Carson* had large audiences in Japan. But the United States was not importing television content—into the early 1970s, only 1 percent of American programming was imported, a uniquely low figure. In the United Kingdom, 12 percent of content was foreign, as was 23 percent of Dutch television and 39 percent of Mexican television. Australia was importing more than half of its television content, as were Iraq, Israel, Malaysia, and Nigeria. Guatemala imported an astonishing 84 percent of its television content.[26]

The dynamics in the all-important newspaper industry were less extreme but reflected similar trends. Between 12 and 15 percent of the news that the AP supplied to daily newspapers concerned international developments. In 1952, an international study calculated that US newspapers devoted ten inches of white space to foreign news, less than the space devoted to sports news (thirteen inches) and only about a quarter of the space devoted to local news (thirty-eight inches). A 1961 study of six Ohio newspapers found that they devoted only 6.7 percent of their coverage to international news, 28 percent of which focused on Western Europe. Readership surveys suggested that "the average American reads very little of the foreign news published in his favorite newspaper"—of the 18.5 minutes per day the average reader spent with a paper, they spent fewer than 2.5 minutes on the foreign news. At the height of the Korean War, 56 percent of respondents in one survey could not correctly identify Syngman Rhee, and 79 percent did not know what "NATO" stood for.[27]

Unlike the television or movie industries, the US news industry was not unusually parochial; all nations, understandably, favor the coverage of domestic politics in their daily press. A comparative study in 1964 found that high-end newspapers in the United States devoted between 9 and 17 percent of their white space to foreign news, only marginally less than British papers, in which foreign news took up between 13.8 percent and 20.8 percent—and the US newspapers were 55 percent larger than their British counterparts, more than making up for the difference. The problem was that the flow of news into the United States was, whatever its size, inadequate to the global scale of US foreign policy. The most perceptive students of the US press had understood this problem at the dawn of the postwar order. During its 1945 deliberations, the Hutchins Commission on Press Freedom had realized that the United States would be a postwar superpower. ("We will be ruling the world," observed Reinhold Niebuhr bluntly.) That just raised the stakes for guaranteeing that the democratic subjects at the heart of the new world order would be fully informed about global affairs, lest the entire edifice lose legitimacy. It was an overwhelming, intimidating problem, as one of the early drafts of the commission's report put it,

> to ask the American people in their exercise of power through opinion to make up their minds concerning the border conflicts and nationalistic and imperial demands in Transylvania, Singapore, Iran, Ecuador and Iceland can be done with confidence only if we have unusual and wholly responsible means of popular adult information and enlightenment on these matters.[28]

As the range of US interests and interventions proliferated in the 1950s, it would prove impossible for the US press to stay abreast of them all. There were only so many US foreign correspondents in the world—a little under three hundred in 1950, and four hundred to five hundred in the mid-1960s—and they were clustered in the obvious locations: London, Rome, Paris, and Tokyo. There were no US correspondents in Prague, Bucharest, Riyadh, Khartoum, or Beijing; in 1963, CBS's Africa bureau chief lived in London. Explained one journalist, "He can get to any spot in Africa quicker than anyone sitting down on the continent itself (barring the latter's immediate area). And his family can enjoy a fairly normal life with good schools for the children." In 1963, something like 50 percent of US correspondents were in Europe, 20 percent in Latin America, 20 percent in Asia and Australia, and a combined 10 percent in the Middle East and Africa.[29] Preparation for many locations was hard to come by: more than half of the correspondents received their first foreign assignment before they could speak a foreign language, and two-thirds of US correspondents in Central and East Asia confessed that they had "no understanding [of the language] to speak of." And so reportage could be stretched to cover only a small fraction of the places in which the US state was geopolitically and economically involved. In 1952, between two-thirds and three-quarters of the eighty-thousand words being sent into the US via the wire services each day centered on a handful of issues and locations: the Korean War, the United Kingdom, France, Japan, West Germany, Italy, and international organizations. The rest of the world competed for the remaining real estate on the wire, much of which would not be picked up by the daily paper. Even less of it would be read by citizens skimming the headlines over morning coffee.[30]

The consequence was that the American public's knowledge of vast parts of the globe, including some of the most consequential fronts of the Cold War, was shallow, fleeting, and partial. With little concrete knowledge of places like Korea or Indonesia or decolonizing Africa, it became easy to see them as little more than empty stages for sentimental, self-regarding acts of colonial uplift.[31] And it was easier to translate the specificities of their histories and politics into broader, more abstract narratives such as the global clash between the forces of capitalist freedom and communist tyranny. It all made public debate about many parts of the world vulnerable to manipulation by small numbers of partisan advocates, particularly if they were well connected to key cultural and political institutions. The names by which such networks were known—the China Lobby, the Georgetown Set—revealed both their prominence and their modus operandi.

Public attitudes to Vietnam in the 1950s and early 1960s, for instance, were deeply shaped by tiny networks of advocates, such as the American Friends of Vietnam, who believed that the United States needed to prop up the Ngo Dinh Diem government as a bulwark against Communist aggression or the small group of Saigon correspondents who favored, like their sources in the US military, a more aggressive US policy in rolling back Communist insurgents. So emaciated was the flow of information about Vietnam to the United States that one man could play a profound role in shaping middlebrow attitudes to the country: Tom Dooley, a Catholic doctor famed for his humanitarian work in the country. With help from William Lederer, who had met the doctor while serving as a Navy public information officer in Haiphong—and who had ties to the CIA and *Reader's Digest*—Dooley wrote an exaggerated, stylized, and sentimental account of Vietnamese politics, full of atrocities committed by the North Vietnamese government against Catholics and praise for the benevolence of US involvement. Published in 1956, *Deliver Us from Evil* was a critical and commercial success. It went through twenty prints, and its anti-Communist message reached millions more when it was excerpted in *Reader's Digest*. The United States Information Agency (USIA) arranged for its worldwide distribution. Dooley became a regular on television, radio, and the speakers' circuit and was soon appearing in US magazine polls as one of the ten "most esteemed" men in the world. There were few alternative voices, which meant that Dooley "contributed to the malformation of our knowledge and moral judgments about Southeast Asia," as one journalist put it later, and played a crucial role in creating a "climate of public misunderstanding that made the war in Vietnam possible." Those paying attention, in other words, were likely to be misinformed about conditions in Vietnam. The broader public, feeling little reason to pay attention, was likely to be uninformed. By 1964, when there were only 603 Vietnamese residents in the United States, two-thirds of the public confessed to having given little or no thought to Vietnam. The year before, *New York Times* correspondent Scotty Reston had told Congress that "we are engaged in quite a war in Vietnam and this country hasn't the vaguest idea that it is in a war."[32]

There were some individuals whose lived experience brought them into contact with foreign nations, peoples, and ideas. Bob Browne, for instance, spent six years in the late 1950s working as a foreign aid officer in Cambodia and Vietnam. When he returned to the United States in 1961, his knowledge of Southeast Asia provided a platform for important antiwar and civil rights activism. He also returned with a Vietnamese-Chinese wife, Huoi; they were one of thousands of interracial married couples created by the movement of American civilian and military personnel throughout the world and which did slow, subterranean work in the reconstruction of American ideas about race. Still, appreciating the significance of Browne's struggles to inform the US public about the realities of US policy in Southeast Asia requires understanding the considerable obstacles he came up against. Knowledge of the region was minimal. When Browne was first sent to Cambodia in 1955, his briefers in the State Department could not locate a single other person who had lived there to meet with him. When he returned to the United States, Americans asked him if Vietnam was in East or West Africa; they often assumed that Huoi was Japanese. So although we should not overstate the enclosure of American culture in the postwar period—such projects of containment are never stable or absolute; individual artists, activists, and intellectuals always probe for cracks and connections; lived experience is messy and sprawling—neither should we underestimate its surprising efficacy, at least in the short term.[33]

In fact, with US connections to the world so withered, when so little information about key sites of Cold War conflict was placed before the public, and when most of that emerged from small networks of partisan "experts," efforts to police travel and the circulation of news took on outsized significance. They worked as one more barrier to public understanding of US foreign entanglements, and they prevented individuals from building their own expertise. This in turn limited the range of people who might speak to broader publics.

The policing of the flow of information fell most heavily on certain dissident groups, acting as yet another mechanism of intimidation and marginalization. Reinserting the partisan dynamics of security regulation into our histories of the US public sphere of the 1950s and 1960s thus helps clarify an important moment in the development of US political culture. There is a residual tendency to narrate the middle decades of the twentieth century as a rise of internationalism or as a transition from parochial detachment in the interwar years to engagement with international affairs in the postwar years. But for radical Black internationalists, for leftists, and for a number of scientists, the experience was almost the complete opposite: a period of free international travel, of engagement with a host of internationalist movements and causes, was replaced in the 1940s by a period of enforced parochialism. Those denied a passport, like Robeson, experienced this in its most extreme form, which they conceptualized as form of incarceration. Losing the ability to travel, Robeson said, made him a "a prisoner in his native land."[34]

The US fixation on controlling the flow of ideas and people also helps us rethink the history of US foreign relations in the 1950s. Even as the United States proclaimed itself leader of the free world, it remained deeply suspicious of international entanglement and worked to insulate American culture from foreign contamination. By the early 1950s, a broad network of conservatives had moved into open hostility to the UN system, which they said was seeking to undermine US cultural autonomy. More precisely, they charged that the UN was seeking to promote communism and that it threatened to promote racial equality in the United States. Frank Holman, president of the American Bar Association, claimed that the Universal Declaration of Human Rights was written on "pink paper" and would "promote state socialism, if not communism, throughout the world." He was also upset that the Human Rights Commission included only three representatives of "English-speaking countries" and said that the UN genocide conviction could be used to trump up charges against a white motorist who accidentally hit a Black pedestrian. In 1953, Secretary of State John Foster Dulles announced that the US would no longer participate in efforts to write an international human rights covenant—he praised the American Bar Association for raising concerns that the United Nations was trying to impose "socialistic conceptions" on the United States.[35]

UNESCO inspired similar contempt. In 1950, UNESCO issued a "Statement on Race," which declared that race was a "social myth" rather than a "biological fact." Under pressure from Dutch, British, and US biologists, UNESCO retreated quickly, issuing a revised statement the next year that conceded that racial differences did have a scientific basis. But within the United States, the damage had been done. The Daughters of the American Revolution (DAR) denounced the United Nations as socialist for preaching equality. In 1951, two-thirds of its activity in Texas focused on the UN; in Illinois, the DAR sponsored an essay contest on why the US should not belong to a world government. In Los Angeles, a UNESCO educational exhibit was displayed only after portions challenging racial difference were removed as "propaganda," and the use of UNESCO materials in schools became the object of grassroots protest. In 1952, the Women's Breakfast Club of Los Angeles complained that UNESCO materials being taught in public schools were "subversive and un-American" and "designed to destroy the love for America as a sovereign nation," and the Veterans of Foreign Wars charged that studying UNESCO in schools was a communist plot to undermine patriotism in favor of "one world citizenship." Under such pressure, Los Angeles banned the teaching of UNESCO materials in its schools. A racist textbook later used in Louisiana cited the UNESCO statement as evidence of the "equalitarian dogma" being pushed by dishonest scientists onto a vulnerable public.[36]

This hostility to international organizations led the United States to try to police the loyalty of US employees of the United Nations. Senator James Eastland said that the UN was a "nesting place for American subversives"; Pat McCarran said that it was a "haven for spies and communists." This was a forgotten front of the second Red Scare and another example of how the United States was willing to engage with international organizations only if it could bend them to its will. In 1952, McCarran's Internal Security Subcommittee was busy investigating the loyalties of Americans working at the United Nations, and a special grand jury orchestrated by Roy Cohn was looking for evidence of subversion. The pressure of defending UN employees during the angry hearings drove Abraham H. Feller, the UN general counsel, to suicide. Truman then created an International Organizations Employee Loyalty Board, which investigated almost four thousand Americans, and created new loyalty procedures. When employees pled the Fifth, the United Nations fired them or put them on compulsory leave. In 1954, when the board began investigations of Americans stationed at international offices, it created a minor diplomatic incident: French and Swiss politicians objected to the practice taking place on their soil, and seven UNESCO employees refused to appear before the loyalty board and were fired by Luther Evans, director-general of UNESCO, who happened to be American. The UNESCO Staff Association opposed the US loyalty investigations, seeing them as an effort to "castrate the UN and make it the kept eunuch of Republican foreign policy." After much back-and-forth, the UN Administrative Tribunal ruled that the seven employees had to be reinstated, which led to a new round of conservative complaints that the United Nations had established a "sort of super sovereignty" that elevated UNESCO above the United States. American relations with international organizations had devolved into a wrestling match over power and control.[37]

Conservative nationalists similarly feared that cultural exchange programs would open the door to foreign ideas that would undermine American culture. When Congress debated the educational exchange provisions of the Smith-Mundt Act in 1947, Clare Hoffman did not want to "authorize the expenditure of . . . millions to bring teachers of communism here." John Rankin agreed, believing it to be "not only ridiculous but dangerous to bring into this country either students or instructors from behind that iron curtain." Another congressman was concerned that "student and communist agents, slick tongued, and smooth commentators, may come to this land for no other purpose than to propagandize and attempt to change the minds of American youth." Liberal Californian Democrat Chet Holifield saw things differently, wondering if conservative critics had

> any faith in the principles of democracy, in the fundamental tenets of our country . . . have we anything to be afraid of in allowing these people to come over here? Are you actually in your hearts afraid that they are going to convert American democracy into communism or to fascism . . . I wager, if anything, the conversion will be on the other side of the fence. . . . I say we will bring the light that will work miracles in their lives, I have no fear of these interchanges. I say to those that do have fear: 'O ye of little faith.'[38]

The dispute revealed a fundamental division that helps us rethink the partisan politics of globalization in the early Cold War. What appeared superficially to be a clash between conservative nationalists and liberal internationalists was in reality a clash between two different assumptions about the power of American culture. The conservatives thought that American culture was vulnerable to international influence and needed protecting; the liberals thought that American culture was so powerful as to need no protection. Seen in this light, it was liberals who were the ebullient nationalists, assuming that American culture was destined to spread throughout the world; the anti-Communist conservatives were, ironically, more willing to countenance that exchange might involve a two-way flow of ideas—an idea that terrified them. Similar clashes echoed across the Cold War. In 1953, Fulbright publicly defended his program when McCarthy tried to red-bait it. Beyond his general distaste for the senator from Wisconsin, Fulbright shared Holifield's faith in the power of American culture. Fulbright said that "the highly emotional attacks upon communism and Russia by some of our public orators is an indication of the weakness of their faith in our system."[39]

Superficially, it seemed that Fulbright's more optimistic nationalism dominated US policy in the 1950s and 1960s. Exchange programs proliferated in the Cold War: 3,500 students participated in a farm youth exchange program; the Ford Foundation funded business, media, and labor exchanges to "strengthen the free world and promote international understanding"; Henry Kissinger organized a summer school at Harvard, where he hosted foreign intellectuals; airlines funded student exchange scholarships, for which students had to submit essays on "how jet-age transportation and communication can speed world peace." In 1956, Eisenhower launched the People-to-People Campaign to encourage all Americans to help promote "world understanding" by creating grassroots connections to the world, such as sending books overseas or collaborating with sister cities and foreign hobbyist associations (the New Jersey Garden Club sent fifty dogwood trees to Niigata and fifty rose bushes to Seoul). From July 1957, a pamphlet signed by Eisenhower was included in all passports, encouraging Americans to think of themselves as representatives of their country and to engage in meaningful cultural exchanges when abroad. In 1961, in an effort to build more exchange programs in the Global South, the Kennedy administration established the Peace Corps and also reorganized the Fulbright Program, which now needed to expand beyond the geographic confines of the surplus disposal. In the late 1950s, the sale of agricultural surplus had allowed the Fulbright to expand into fifteen nations, mostly in Latin America. Now the Fulbright-Hays Act created a more permanent funding base for the program. (The United States nevertheless continued to look for ways to offload the costs, asking its partners to pick up part of the tab. In 1962, Germany agreed to fund 80 percent of US-German exchanges over the next five years; by the end of that decade, the fourteen European nations involved were collectively paying more for the program than the United States.) The logic of all these programs rested on the optimistic belief that exchange would spread American culture throughout the world. "Mutual understanding and freedom are contagious," testified Assistant Secretary of State Philip H. Coombs in Senate hearings on the Fulbright Program in 1961.[40]

But behind the scenes, the protective, paranoid security branches did a great deal of work to ensure that these programs were not turned to "un-American" purposes. Students and scholars selected for a Fulbright were screened by the Passport Division or the FBI before they could travel; they were also asked to swear loyalty oaths. In 1957, the director of the State Department's International Educational Exchange Service boasted that screening was so thorough that there had never been a security incident caused by an exchange visitor in the United States. Tentative efforts to establish exchange programs with the Soviet Union in the 1950s saw similar scrutiny, on both sides of the Iron Curtain. American visitors to the Soviet Union were barred from entering 30 percent of the landmass of the USSR; 27 percent of the United States was closed to Soviet visitors. Those visitors required special visa clearances, which were issued only warily—in 1955, the National Security Council concluded that the USSR was more liberal in its visa policy to Americans than the United States was to Soviet applicants. Given US dominance of international air networks, Soviets often had to pass through US airports even when traveling to third destinations, such as conferences in Latin America or the 1956 Olympics in Melbourne, and—because they were deemed to pose "a severe risk to the security of the U.S."—they had to remain in the custody of US officials at any time they were not on the plane, a practice known as "bonded transit." In 1955, John Foster Dulles understandably said he "had the feeling that everyone wants to penetrate the Soviet Union, but no one wants the Soviet Union to penetrate us."[41]

Fears of subversive, un-American globalization were thus inextricably intertwined with hopes that exchange would lead to the expansion of American culture. Even as some sections of the State Department proclaimed the importance of free movement to liberal internationalism, other sections of the state and other sections of the State Department policed the movement of ideas and people across borders. At the very least, this was hypocritical. Perhaps it also provided the precondition for the liberal triumphalism of the State Department's public posture—it was much easier to promote "liberal internationalism" when one could be sure that only acceptable networks were being internationalized, when one could rest easy that subversives were being filtered out.

Critics were quick to point out the contradictions of US policy. Senator Hubert Humphrey worried that passport denials might "irreparably damage our international standing by giving the impression that we do not practice at home what we preach abroad." Carl Ackerman of the Columbia School of Journalism complained to the attorney general that visa restrictions "will make needless enemies in Latin America and elsewhere, . . . may invite retaliation . . . and will isolate American universities from all world trends and opinions not approved by you." Even Whittaker Chambers was struck by the problem, writing to William Buckley that "the spectacle of an artist like Paul Robeson, denied a passport by his own government, makes us traduced of other nations."[42]

Many worried that the United States was coming to resemble its Cold War nemesis. Protesting new visa regulations in 1948, Representative Arthur G. Klein worried that these "totalitarian rules" were a "step toward the Russian viewpoint." In 1952, the *Washington Post* editorialized that "the harsh fact of the matter is that the U.S. is getting to be, like Russia, a place where international meetings can no longer be held." Comparisons with the Iron Curtain soon proliferated. In the *Virginia Law Review*, Reginald Parker argued that excluding citizens from "going abroad and getting acquainted with the outer world is indeed the central meaning of the phrase 'iron curtain.'" Truman declared that the McCarran Act was establishing an American "iron curtain." The *Bulletin of the Atomic Scientists* said the United States had built a "paper curtain." Victor Weisskopf, who had worked on the Manhattan Project, complained that the McCarran Act was constructing a "Uranium Belt" and that American travel policy was "strengthening a growing attitude which considers America and Russia both equally evil powers."[43]

But although critics could point to the gap between the United States' practices and the rhetorical commitments to a liberal-internationalist order of free movement, they could not appeal to international organizations to liberalize American policy. UNESCO had been marginalized, no international infrastructure had emerged from the Freedom of Information campaign, and international travel organizations had been diverted to less controversial matters. A three-week UN conference on tourism in 1954, for instance, settled for producing two conventions designed to make it easier for tourists to travel with cars and a variety of specified personal possessions (one portable gramophone with ten records, one nonpowered bicycle, two tennis racquets) without paying import duties. Haitian delegate Ernest George Chauvet did propose a clause banning racial discrimination against tourists in hotels and restaurants. As the *New York Times* noted, this could have "easily prove[d] embarrassing to many countries where segregation is practiced," and it was quickly watered down to a technical point that discrimination would be barred specifically in the assessment of customs duties. (Even so, the resolution was passed with "many abstaining votes.") To preserve its border controls, the United States had defanged international arenas in the late 1940s; thereafter, those institutions provided no avenue to meaningfully challenge visa and passport practices.[44]

Pressure to reform Cold War policy flowed instead through domestic channels. Efforts to reconnect with the world were a central front of civil libertarian political struggle in the late 1950s and early 1960s. A small cluster of students, journalists, activists, and intellectuals made travel, and the importation of knowledge about the world, deeply political acts. Perhaps the most prominent among them was William Worthy, a Black American journalist who had been educated at Bates College and the University of Oslo, worked as A. Philip Randolph's public relations assistant, and become deeply involved in pacifist and civil rights activism. In the 1950s, while working for the *Baltimore Afro-American*, he reported on the Korean War, the Montgomery bus boycott, and the decolonization of Asia, including the Bandung Conference. These experiences, understood through his broadly anti-imperial and antiracist politics, led him to conclude that the United States was the "most hated nation in the world today"—although, he added, the "newspaper fooled folks" in the United States would never know it. (They were "being taken for one gigantic counter-revolutionary ride by the righteous smokescreens emanating from Washington's propaganda mills," he noted.) Worthy thus became increasingly critical of the inadequate flow of information about the world. "Our daily papers, giant weekly news magazines, radio and television networks will not, and psychologically cannot, report the hard facts and bitter truth from Africa, Asia and Latin America," he said. To provide a better supply of information to the public, Worthy felt it was necessary to report firsthand from places like Communist China, North Korea, and North Vietnam, which brought him into direct conflict with State Department's travel regulations. "For the courts and the press to permit any Secretary of State to function as assignment editor," he argued, "is to scrap the First Amendment, and to lower an ostrich-type curtain over throbbing areas on the map." By 1960, Worthy was involved with the Fair Play for Cuba Committee—a central organ of the emerging New Left—which sought to tell the American people "what really is happening in Cuba" by taking journalists and writers to witness the revolution themselves, thereby countering the misinformation circulating within the United States.[45]

Alongside their efforts to bring new information to the public, activists like Worthy sought to reduce US travel restrictions and bring US policy into alignment with its ostensible commitments to liberal internationalism. The most prominent conflict concerned the travel of US journalists to Communist China—between 1949 and 1956, none had traveled there. Following the revolution, Mao's China had expelled all journalists from countries that had not established diplomatic relations with the new regime, but in 1954, it began sending out feelers to individual US newspapers to see if they would send correspondents. These invitations were rebuffed, however, because in 1952, the United States had barred all travel by American citizens to China. A second round of Chinese invitations was more successful—in 1956, William Worthy and two correspondents from *Look* magazine traveled to China without passports. The State Department, knowing that it was a "test case" for its travel ban and worrying that "if no punitive action is taken, the ban on travel to the China mainland will collapse rapidly," therefore revoked the passports of all three journalists upon their return. Because the travelers were journalists, the action raised questions about press freedom. Newspaper industry trade journal *Editor and Publisher* held that "the U.S. government, once dedicated to penetrating or tearing down

Iron Curtains wherever they exist around the world has now resorted to erecting its own brand of curtain around the American people." Mainstream media organizations called for a statute protecting the free movement of journalists, and Humphrey introduced such a bill to Congress.[46]

It was a striking inversion of arguments for the free movement of journalists that the United States had championed at the Geneva conference on press freedom nine years earlier. And although Humphrey's proposed statute went nowhere, the strategy seemed to bear fruit. In August 1957, citing public pressure, the State Department announced that it would allow a select group of twenty-four journalists to travel to China, although only for a seven-month trial period, so that they could see if the Chinese were manipulating the journalists or allowing free reporting. The State Department never explained how it planned to make this judgment, but this effort to expand the travel rights of US journalists was soon undermined by US insistence on carefully managing its own borders. The Chinese would grant entry visas to US correspondents selected by the State Department only if Chinese correspondents of its own choice were granted reciprocal rights to enter the United States.[47] But the US wanted to maintain its right to deny entrance visas to individual Chinese journalists under the anti-Communist provisions of the McCarran-Walter Act, and so matters deadlocked. They then became disastrously intertwined with broader diplomatic posturing—in March 1961, China insisted it would grant American journalists visas only if the United States withdrew armed forces from Taiwan. As a result, no US journalists would enter China until the normalization of relations in 1971, when three were granted visas to cover the visit of the US table tennis team. Even then, it would take until 1979 for the first US news bureaus to open in China. Domestic political pressure, in short, was no match for the tectonic forces of geopolitics.[48]

Increasingly, those Americans interested in freedom of movement and freedom of information therefore turned to the courts in the 1950s, developing constitutional arguments that border controls interfered with their rights as American citizens. It was a far different strategy from the multilateralist, institutionalist politics of liberalization that had been envisioned in the late 1940s. And although this legal strategy did produce some successes, its shortcomings remind us of the limits of national constitutionalist claims in a globalizing world.

The denial of passports to American citizens produced the first and most successful wave of legal challenges. Because it directly affected the liberties of US citizens, and because it bore a family resemblance to other civil liberties violations in the second Red Scare, it was an easy step to claim that being denied a passport was unconstitutional and an interference with what was increasingly dubbed a "right to travel." The Federation of American Scientists, for instance, claimed that the "passport should be recognized as a right of the U.S. citizen, not merely a privilege." Law journals ran articles exploring "the constitutional right to travel" and the "right to go abroad."[49]

While that made perfect rhetorical and political sense, it was entirely unclear which constitutional right, in particular, was being violated. Drawing on the nascent idea of a "right to know," some argued that the right to travel derived from the First Amendment because the ability to travel to gather information and speak to foreigners was essential to freedoms of expression and association. Other advocates of the right to travel drew on domestic "right of locomotion" cases, in which the Supreme Court had recognized the right of citizens to move between the states. Yet others sought to base it on classical texts, making reference to the right to go abroad found in the Magna Carta (clauses 41 and 42 recognized rights "to any person . . . to go out of our kingdom, and to return") or Blackstone's legal commentary ("Everybody has, or at least assumes, the liberty of going abroad when he pleases").[50]

The first legal challenge to the passport regime simply combined all these potential arguments. In 1950, Paul Robeson argued that when the secretary of state had relied on discretionary authority to deny him a passport, it had violated the First, Fifth, Ninth, and Tenth Amendments, as well as Article I, Section 9, and Article III of the Constitution. In the face of State Department assertions of its unreviewable discretion over foreign affairs, the court dismissed, claiming a lack of jurisdiction.[51]

Beginning the next year, however, a more targeted claim was more successful. In 1951, Anne Bauer, a naturalized American citizen who had previously worked for the Office of War Information and the US Military Government in Occupied Germany and who now worked as a freelance journalist in Paris, had her passport revoked. The State Department provided no reasons for the decision beyond the standard assertion that her activities were "contrary to the best interests of the U.S." Without a passport, Bauer was required to return to the United States, so she argued that being denied a passport without a hearing violated her right to due process. (The State Department continued to argue that issuance and revocation of passports fell solely within the domain of foreign affairs, which meant that the executive branch had "absolute discretion" in the matter.) In a 2–1 decision in July, the US District Court for the District of Columbia sided with Bauer, drawing on the right to travel domestically to recognize a constitutional right to travel internationally. (The court held, "It is difficult to see where, in principle, freedom to travel outside the U.S. is any less an attribute of personal liberty. Especially is this true today, when modern transportation has made all the world easily accessible.") It was an admittedly narrow decision. Bauer had claimed only the right to a hearing, not a passport, and the ruling granted "wide discretion" to the State Department on passport matters. Still, it was significant that, for the first time, a court had ruled that State did not have "absolute discretion." A passport could not be denied without due process.[52]

The decision kicked off six years of legal tussling about what, exactly, due process should look like in a passport case. Shortly after the *Bauer* decision, and in light of public criticism of some of its more famous denials, the Passport Division announced new regulations, which included a Board of Passport Appeals. But they were largely superficial changes—the Passport Division still gave itself broad powers to deny passports, required appellants to sign an affidavit that they were not a Communist, provided appellants no access to confidential information used to make passport decisions, and reserved to the secretary of state final, nonreviewable decision-making authority. That such a process looked like reform testified primarily to how arbitrary passport policy had been. It was no wonder that little use was made of the new procedures. Ten months after the ostensible creation of the Board of Appeals, Shipley explained that it hadn't even established its operating procedures—no appeals had yet made it that far.[53]

Still, the *Bauer* decision was an important chink in the armor of the Passport Division's authority. A series of cautious lower-court decisions in subsequent years began to define appropriate procedures in passport cases—what a "hearing" had to entail, what information should be provided to citizens. When its prerogatives were challenged by the courts, the State Department responded by issuing the passport in question rather than subjecting itself to court-ordered procedure—it could thus claim only to have exercised its own judgment in the cases. The State Department still asserted that its authority was complete, and it was still adamant that it was acting properly in the national interest. In 1956, in fact, the chief of the Passport Legal Division argued that the "present attack on the passport policy is a part of a general Communist offensive against the security policies of the U.S. Government." As late as 1957, the US Court of Appeals for the DC Circuit upheld the denial of passports to suspected radicals on security grounds. The secretary of state, concluded the court, "may preclude potential matches from the international tinderbox."[54]

One of the two "matches" in question in that case was artist Rockwell Kent. (The other was Walter Briehl, a psychiatrist who had sought to travel to mental health conferences in Geneva and Istanbul and who had refused to sign a noncommunist affidavit.) The always pugnacious Kent was happy to serve as a test case for Leonard Boudin, who had built a reputation on passport denial cases (including his own) and emerged as one of the most important civil libertarian attorneys of the period—he would later represent Daniel Ellsberg in the Pentagon Papers case. Boudin and Kent appealed the denial to the Supreme Court, where, in 1958, the legality of the entire passport apparatus was considered for the first time. Previous court challenges had focused only on claiming certain procedural rights. Now the court was asked to consider whether the State Department's authority over travel was itself legitimate.[55]

In a 5–4 decision, the Supreme Court ruled that passport denial was an illegitimate interference with a Fifth Amendment right to travel. The majority decision, written by civil libertarian William Douglas, stopped short of ruling on the extent to which that right could, in constitutional terms, be curtailed. Instead, apparently to hold together a slim majority, Douglas focused on the "extent, if any, to which Congress has authorized its curtailment." Based on a selective reading of the historical vagaries of passport law, he concluded that the Passport Division had not been delegated as much authority over passports as it had claimed.[56]

The ruling rendered the Passport Division's regulations invalid, making it possible for even alleged radicals to receive passports. In the next month, passports were issued to roughly sixty applicants who had previously been denied them. On July 5, Kent received his passport and promptly visited the Soviet Union to see an exhibit of his art. He subsequently published *Of Men and Mountains: Being an Account of the European Travels of the Author and His Wife, Sally, Following Their Release from Continental Imprisonment.* Passports were also issued to the Du Boises, who promptly departed on a one-year international tour. "I felt," W. E. B. Du Bois wrote, "like a released prisoner."[57]

The narrow proceduralism of the *Kent* decision meant that it stopped well short of establishing a constitutional right to travel, however, as Justice Douglas soon found out. In June 1959, the State Department denied Douglas a passport to travel to China not because it thought that the liberal justice was ideologically suspect, but because it was banning all travel to China. *Kent* ruled that the State Department did not have the right to deny passports to individuals on the basis of ideology; the question now was whether the State Department had the right to bar travel to entire regions.

It soon became clear that the courts thought that area restrictions were a legitimate form of travel regulation, as the legal struggles of William Worthy demonstrated. In early 1957, Worthy reapplied for the passport that the State Department had confiscated after his unsanctioned 1956 trip to China. It denied the application because Worthy had refused to pledge that he would abide by area restrictions. (The two *Look* journalists did make that pledge and were reissued their passports.) Backed by the American Civil Liberties Union, Worthy took the matter to court, arguing that area restrictions interfered with his constitutional rights to travel and report, which made them no different than the ideological restrictions that had been ruled unlawful in *Kent*. But the DC Circuit Court of Appeals argued that the "point here presented in no wise resembles the matter decided by the Supreme Court in *Kent v. Dulles*" because "no beliefs, associations, or personal characteristics are involved." And it ruled that "the right here involved is not a right to think or speak; it is a right to be physically present in a certain place." Thus area restrictions did not impinge on the rights of US citizens; they were a valid form of foreign policy, and their efficacy was best judged by the executive branch, not the judiciary. "Unless almost the whole of our foreign policy and the titanic domestic burdens being presently borne by our people are devoid of factual foundation, there is presently in the world a deadlock of antagonistic forces, susceptible of erupting into a fatal cataclysm," the court warned in a classic piece of Cold War jurisprudence. "In foreign affairs, especially in the intimate posture of today's world of jets, radio and atomic power, an individual's uninhibited yen to go and to inquire may be circumscribed. A blustering inquisitor avowing his own freedom to go and do as he pleases can throw the whole international neighborhood into turmoil."[58]

In late 1959, the Supreme Court declined to hear Worthy's appeal. It simultaneously dismissed similar complaints from Congressman Charles Porter, who had wanted to travel to China to explore US policy, and from Waldo Frank, who had been invited to lecture in Beijing on Walt Whitman. And in 1965, in a five-to-four ruling, the Supreme Court upheld the constitutionality of area restrictions when it approved the denial of a passport to Louis Zemel, a leftist ski operator who wanted to travel to Cuba to "acquaint [himself] at first hand with the effects abroad of our Government's policies, foreign and domestic, and with conditions abroad which might affect such policies." Hoping to "satisfy [his] curiosity" and become a "better informed citizen," and represented by Leonard Boudin, Zemel argued that the travel ban was an unconstitutional interference with both his First Amendment rights and his Fifth Amendment right to travel. The majority decision, written by Chief Justice Earl Warren, dismissed these arguments. Unlike the ideological denials at stake in *Kent*, Warren thought that the restriction on travel to Cuba was a reasonable policy "supported by the weightiest considerations of national security." And although Warren conceded that preventing travel to Cuba "renders less than wholly free the flow of information concerning that country," he nevertheless argued that this did not interfere with the First Amendment because it was a regulation of action, not speech. "There are few restrictions on action," Warren asserted, "which could not be clothed by ingenious argument in the garb of decreased data flow. . . . The right to speak and publish does not carry with it the unrestrained right to gather information."[59]

Activists committed to internationalism nevertheless continued to travel to restricted areas and continued turning to the courts to uphold their rights to do so. Between 1957 and 1961, Worthy made four trips to Cuba without a passport—after the last one he was jailed for violating the Immigration and Nationality Act of 1952, which made it illegal to enter the United States without a valid passport. The jailing created a controversy. A Committee for the Freedom of William Worthy picketed outside the UN building, whose Sub-Commission on the Prevention of Discrimination and Protection of Minorities debated the matter; and in Cuba, Ghana, and Uganda, it was seen as evidence of US racism. In 1964, a unanimous US Court of Appeals for the Fifth Circuit overruled Worthy's conviction on the grounds that citizens had a Fifth Amendment right to return home that could not be subject to criminal penalty. Three years later, in *United States v. Laub*, a case concerning the travel of students to Cuba, the Supreme Court ruled that there were no criminal penalties for traveling *to* a restricted area, either—Congress had never passed a law creating such penalties, and the State Department could not create them simply by administrative fiat.[60]

Still, the Passport Division would not go quietly. On the same day the *Laub* decision was handed down, it announced that it would rely on administrative rather than criminal penalties to enforce its restrictions. If passport holders traveled to restricted areas, the State Department would confiscate their passport upon their return, and it would reissue the passport only if they pledged that they would abide by the area restrictions in the future. This would have the effect of grounding those travelers within the United States. Once again, activists challenged these policies by going overseas and then to court. In January 1966, pacifist scholar Staughton Lynd, radical historian Herbert Aptheker, and Students for a Democratic Society leader Tom Hayden went to North Vietnam on a "fact-finding and investigating mission"; on their return, their passports (and some of their papers) were seized. Lynd, represented by Boudin, challenged the action. Almost two years later, in December 1967, the US Court of Appeals for the DC Circuit ruled that the State Department's policy was invalid because it interfered with Lynd's right to travel, as established in the *Kent* decision. To do so, it cleverly narrowed the substance of *Zemel*'s ruling that the State Department had the right to institute area restrictions. *Zemel*, the court explained, meant only that the State Department could attach conditions to the use of the passport document itself, not to the travel of the citizen. If Lynd promised that he would not use his passport in restricted areas, he could *himself* travel to restricted areas without threat of sanction. The highly legalistic decision undermined the State Department's capacity to enforce its travel bans.[61]

Yet while it considered an appeal of *Lynd*, the State Department continued to seize the passports of those who traveled to restricted areas for another three months; it also lobbied Congress for legislation authorizing it to criminally punish unauthorized travel. It continued to stamp all passports with misleading instructions that suggested that travel bans continued—only citizens familiar with the law would understand the intricacies of the post-*Lynd* landscape. It remained the case, moreover, that traveling without a passport was still a risky maneuver, unlikely to appeal to any but the most politically committed citizens. That meant that many citizens in the late 1960s abided by bans on travel to such places as Cuba, North Korea, North Vietnam, China (until 1971), or the nations of the Middle East (for a nine-month period following the 1967 Six-Day War).[62]

Despite the legal successes of civil libertarians, in other words, the Passport Division clung tight to whatever power it could. Since 1955, the office had been under the control of Frances G. Knight, a protégé of McCarthyite political networks and Shipley's hand-picked successor. Like her mentor, Knight was a formidable bureaucratic infighter—"a woman so powerful, cagey, and persistent," Sanford Ungar observed, "that she has often been compared with J. Edgar Hoover." When the liberal and well-connected Assistant Secretary of State Abba Schwartz sought to end travel restrictions and remove Knight in 1966, he was hauled before Knight's conservative allies on the Senate Internal Security Subcommittee to answer questions about his apparent disinterest in policing travel and soon found himself stripped of authority over passports and forced out of the administration. In 1971, Knight's office maintained a "lookout list" of 250,000 suspected subversives whose travel it reported to law enforcement, and Knight continued to argue that the issuance of passports was a matter of political judgment best left in her skilled hands. "Let's face it," she explained, "all of those hippies look alike, and there is also the problem of ethnic sameness." Knight's tenure lasted twenty-two years, until 1977.[63]

Civil libertarians had much less success challenging the visa regime. Had challenges to the passport regime been built on the basis of protecting the right of the US citizen to know about foreign affairs, they would have provided a platform to liberalize visa policy. But because they had focused on protecting the rights of Americans to travel, these victories could not be translated to visa cases, for those concerned the travel of foreigners, who could not make constitutional claims. In 1903, when Clarence Darrow had represented the first anarchist deported for ideological reasons, he had tried to argue that antisubversive immigration laws interfered with First Amendment rights. But foreigners could not claim a First Amendment right to enter the country. To challenge the constitutionality of visa denial, one therefore had to find a way to argue that it interfered with the rights of Americans.[64]

The most important effort to do so was made in 1970, when Communist intellectual Ernest Mandel was denied a visa to lecture at US universities. (On his agenda were lectures at Princeton, Amherst, the New School, MIT, Columbia, and Vassar; a talk in New York on "Revolutionary Strategy in Imperialist Countries"; and a Stanford conference on Technology and the Third World, where he was to debate John Kenneth Galbraith.) The Belgian Mandel freely, and proudly, admitted that he advocated world communism, which rendered him technically inadmissible under the antisubversive provisions of the Immigration and Nationality Act. In 1960 and 1968, though, he had been admitted under the waiver program, and in 1970, the State Department had again recommended to the attorney general that Mandel's ineligibility be waived "in the interest of free expression of opinion and exchange of ideas." But the Immigration and Naturalization Service (INS) rejected the recommendation, claiming that during Mandel's 1968 visit, he had "abused the opportunities afforded him to express his views in this country." This sounded ominous, but what the INS called "flagrant abuses" were exceedingly minor. For example, Mandel had spoken at more universities than his visa application indicated. And although one of the conditions of his 1968 waiver had been a prohibition against speaking at venues where contributions were solicited for political causes, Mandel had spoken about French student demonstrations at a cocktail party at the Gotham Art Theatre, at which French student posters were later auctioned to raise funds for the legal defense of the protesters. Even if those were technically violations of his visa, Mandel was not aware that his visa had been issued under the waiver program and was unaware that these conditions had been attached to his entrance.[65]

A number of American university professors who had invited Mandel to speak—including Noam Chomsky, Richard A. Falk, and Norman Birnbaum—thus went to court to force the attorney general to admit Mandel. They argued that being deprived the opportunity to "hear his views and engage him in a free and open academic exchange" interfered with their First Amendment rights. In 1971, in a New York District Court, they won a 2–1 decision—as Judge John F. Dooling put it, "the admission of Mandel is but a lever by which the constitutional rights of his prospective citizen audience are to be given effect." The decision was one of a number of cases from the late 1960s and early 1970s that sought to reorient the First Amendment from a focus on the rights of the speaker to the rights of the audience. In 1965, for instance, a unanimous Supreme Court had ruled that postal regulations that restricted the delivery of Communist propaganda to American citizens were unconstitutional. At the time, the Post Office was requiring individuals who wanted to receive what it deemed to be foreign propaganda to request that it be delivered. But the majority opinion, written by Justice Douglas, concluded that such a requirement was an abridgement of the right to receive information through the mail, one that was likely to deter some Americans from requesting certain material, and hence an abridgement of the recipient's First Amendment rights. With the District Court's decision in *Mandel*, it seemed that the rising tide of respect for the First Amendment in the post–World War II United States was about to provide a constitutional mechanism to end ideological exclusion at the border.[66]

But the government appealed, and in 1972, in a 6–3 decision, the Supreme Court reversed, ruling that one could not claim a right to hear a foreign speaker. The executive had clear authority to exclude aliens, the majority concluded, and if it exercised that authority on "the basis of a facially legitimate and bona fide reason, the courts will neither look behind the exercise of that discretion, nor test it by balancing its justification against the First Amendment interests of those who seek personal communication with the [foreigner]." The decision reflected the ongoing deference of the courts on matters of foreign policy and national security. In dissent, in fact, Justice Thurgood Marshall argued he knew of no precedent for this "unusual standard" of deference. "Nor," he added, "can I imagine (nor am I told) the slightest justification for such a rule." Marshall believed that the "briefest peek behind the Attorney-General's reason for refusing a waiver . . . would reveal that it is a sham" and was certainly insufficient to justify interfering with First Amendment rights. "If Americans want to hear about Marxist Doctrine, even from advocates," Marshall concluded, "government cannot intervene simply because it does not approve of the ideas." Excluding Mandel "directly prevented the free interchange of ideas guaranteed by the First Amendment."[67]

The US state continued to deny visas on a wide range of ideological grounds. Gabriel García Márquez was denied a visa between 1963 and 1971; Pablo Neruda couldn't get one between 1966 and 1972. In the 1970s, approximately seven hundred to eight hundred individuals were denied visas each year. Many thousands more were let in only after receiving waivers from the attorney general—a process that continued to allow the imposition of a variety of specific restrictions. The process was time-consuming, alienating, and shot through with the arbitrary and occasionally capricious decisions of a large bureaucratic mechanism. Historian Eric Hobsbawm, for instance, was granted a waiver to teach at MIT in the late 1960s, despite FBI concerns about his Communist Party membership, but only after a lot of back-and-forth. In addition, the terms of his waiver required prior approval for travel outside the Boston region. (To Hobsbawm's relief, a nonplussed university administrator turned a blind eye to the requirement.) Unsurprisingly, some foreigners took umbrage and simply turned down invitations to speak to American audiences. The impact of these visa policies on the flow of information to the United States, while impossible to quantify, was thus considerable.[68]

It all underscored the ways that US visa policy continued to diverge from the ostensible US commitment to a world structured by freely moving ideas and people, as was made clear by the dissenting opinions in the *Mandel* case. In a direct echo of the liberal-internationalist philosophy that had been in vogue in the 1940s, Marshall asserted that "the progress of knowledge is an international venture." The simple fact that Mandel had been invited to the US confirmed for Marshall the truth of that philosophy because it "revealed that individuals of differing world views have learned the ways of cooperation where governments have thus far failed." Yet, as Justice Douglas put it in his dissent to the decision, "the Attorney General stands astride our international terminals that bring people here to bar those whose ideas are not acceptable to him." Mandel himself concluded that it all betrayed the American government's "lack of confidence . . . in the capacity of its supporters to combat Marxism on the battleground of ideas." The more confident ruling class of nineteenth-century Britain, he observed sharply, had let Marx himself live among them for forty years.[69]

In such ways did a fear of foreign culture course through the United States at the height of the nation's global power. While the US proclaimed to the world its belief in the free flow of information, global connections were carefully monitored, filtered, and policed. "Somehow it is strange to hear the State Department say," sang Phil Ochs his 1964 "Ballad of William Worthy," "You are living in the free world, in the free world you must stay." As national security policing layered on top of an American culture that was exporting a great deal and importing very little, cultural globalization took on a curiously lopsided quality in the 1950s and 1960s—the world became much more familiar with the US than the US was with the world. Even as the nation's economic and military footprint was expanding, American culture became oddly solipsistic, regarding itself as the center of a global liberal order. (As Ochs put it sarcastically, "Try not to worry if someday you should hear, the whole world is off limits, visit Disneyland this year.")[70] In many ways, the isolation of American culture from international influence was only a fleeting moment, a product of the bright glare of US commercial affluence in the immediate aftermath of World War II. But even if it couldn't last, these were formative years for the mass culture industries and for contemporary political culture—many Americans continue to view them nostalgically as both a "golden age" and the norm from which subsequent history is but a departure. To "make America great again" is to return it to this image of the 1950s.

Patterns of culture and habits of mind with lasting consequences were set in place in these years. In 1966, in a moment that symbolized the globality and simultaneity of modern communications technologies, 400 million people around the world watched the World Cup final played between England and West Germany. In the United States, however, it was available only on tape delay, and only 2.4 million viewers tuned in—an audience so disappointing that the US networks declined to buy the rights to the 1970 World Cup. Six months later, the first Super Bowl was played in Los Angeles before a television audience of 65 million Americans. When Green Bay beat Kansas City, the Packers were proclaimed "world champions" of a sport that was played nowhere else in the world.[71]

CONCLUSION

THE UNFULFILLED PROMISE OF CULTURAL GLOBALIZATION

In the last third of the twentieth century, American culture was once again becoming integrated into global flows; it ceased to be as insulated, and as exceptional, as it had been in the decades after World War II. As with the nation's earlier isolation, basic trends in demography and political economy did much of the heavy lifting. Reform of the immigration system in 1965 transformed the demographics of the country—a shift with profound consequences still playing out today. By 2013, 13 percent of the nation's population was foreign born, up from 4.7 percent in 1970. Of this foreign-born population, 26 percent emigrated from Asia; 24 percent from Mexico; and 24 percent from Latin America. Immigrants from Europe and Canada, who had made up 85 percent of the foreign-born population in 1960, constituted only 14 percent half a century later. A more multicultural United States, with many more first-generation immigrants, meant many more connections to cultures around the world for both immigrants and nonimmigrants alike. This change was rendered most visible in the proliferating mosaic of restaurants and ethnic groceries in the United States, but it also created new demand for foreign-language films and newspapers, as well as much else in the media and cultural ecosystem.[1]

Meanwhile, as the culture industries developed in much of the rest of the world, a reservoir of new content was built up, a great deal of which eventually found its way into the US media. It is remarkable how much of the cultural history of the late twentieth century involved foreign regeneration of the American culture industries—from the British Invasion's breathing new life into the extinguished fires of rock 'n' roll, to the influence of Akira Kurosawa and the French New Wave on the New Hollywood directors of American film's 1970s golden age, to the rise of anime from Japan and martial arts films from Hong Kong. Individual fans and artists—the Beatles and Bruce Lee, 1960s film school buffs and late-1970s anime clubs—did much in the face of resistance from the commanding heights of the US culture industries. (US record labels even declined to exercise their early options to the Beatles because they could not imagine anyone topping US pop music or buying a foreign derivative. Early reviews dismissed the mop-tops as a "musical anachronism" that was "achingly familiar"; the *New York Times* confidently predicted that Beatlemania would not cross the Atlantic because "it is dated stuff. Hysterical squeals emanating from developing femininity really went out coincidental with the payola scandal and Presley's military service.") But once a market had been established, US culture industries were quick to capitalize. "World music" and "world literature" soon emerged as genres—the very abstraction of these labels testifying to the global quest for content, as well as ongoing US indifference to serious engagement with the specificities of foreign cultures.[2]

Still, even though the social and cultural life of the United States were becoming re-entwined with global cultural currents, there remained a deep skepticism toward efforts to reform or reorganize the dynamics of cultural globalization. Despite the economic and demographic trends, the effort to reconnect the United States with global currents remained political. Radical activists in the United States continued to try to forge connections with their global comrades, struggling to overcome the obstacles placed in their way by the security branches of the US state. A newly militant Global South took advantage of its majority at UNESCO to call for a New World Information and Communication Order, which sought to displace Western domination of international media in favor of a more universal, egalitarian flow of culture. And as détente came to define European relations, efforts were made at Helsinki to revitalize the flow of information across the Iron Curtain. The US state remained skeptical of these efforts: it continued to insist on policing radical forms of travel; it was hostile to the Helsinki agreements until it realized it could deploy them as a lever to open the Soviet Bloc to American culture: and it was so enraged by developments at UNESCO that it quit the organization in 1984. Well into the 1980s, the US state continued to pursue the same uneven approach to cultural globalization that had defined its policy in the 1940s: it simply wanted to export certain forms of American culture, a policy it called "liberal internationalism."

An effort to connect to the world was a central preoccupation of the radical social movements of the late 1960s. From Malcolm X's pilgrimage to Mecca to the embrace of Mao Zedong and Che Guevara by the New Left, radical Americans sought to reimagine themselves as part of a global majority rising to power—one that was about to dislodge the racist, patriarchal, and/or capitalist hegemony of the United States in favor of a more globalist, inclusive world order. In the context of an American political culture that was remarkably isolated from the Second World and the Global South, this was a project that required establishing new cultural networks. Travel became political precisely because it ran on unsanctioned tracks and because it created opportunities to provide new flows of information to the American public. It was no accident that the Fair Play for Cuba Committee, with its efforts to bring the "truth" of Cuba to the American public, served as a crossroads for so much nascent countercultural intellectual activity in the early 1960s—its members included James Baldwin, Allen Ginsberg, Lawrence Ferlinghetti, Norman Mailer, and William Appleman Williams. Robert F. Williams's first trip to Cuba was organized by the Fair Play for Cuba Committee (his fellow travelers were LeRoi Jones and Harold Cruse). When Robert and Mabel Williams later went into exile in Cuba, and then China, they devoted their time to the publication of the *Crusader* newsletter and Radio Free Dixie; playing jazz and blues music alongside its news coverage, the radio program promoted Black nationalism across national borders. The two-hundred-odd Americans who traveled to North Vietnam on solidarity tours as part of such organizations as Women Strike for Peace or the Du Bois Clubs had similar goals of forging international connections. One of the most significant was the eleven-person US People's Anti-Imperialist Delegation to China, North Korea, and North Vietnam in 1970. Headed by the Black Panther Party's minister for information, Eldridge Cleaver, who was in exile in Algeria after a brief stint in Cuba, the delegation's politics were deeply concerned with the flow of information. Cleaver had first been invited to North Korea, for instance, to participate in an International Conference of Journalists of the Whole World in the Fight against US Imperialist Aggression. The delegation symbolically accepted prisoner-of-war mail from the North Vietnamese government to return to the United States. And when Alex Hing sought to explain the mission in the Asian American journal *Gidra*, he emphasized the novel flows of information, the global connections, which would be produced, stating that "the information we will gather and our experiences with the Korean people and Korean culture should be extremely exciting."[3]

It is striking how many of these activists saw themselves as developing alternatives to existing, US-dominated networks of communication and propaganda. The Williamses, for instance, were familiar with the politics of international communication in the 1950s. They were, for example, critical listeners to Voice of America and Radio Free Europe, and Robert had sought work as an information officer within the Marines, only to be denied by racist hiring practices. In 1969, when the Venceremos Brigade was organized to take volunteers to Cuba to labor in solidarity with the revolution, it was also intended to provide new modes of education for young Americans who could communicate the truth about Cuba to the American public—advocates of the program dubbed it an "illegal Peace Corps." In the same years, leftists in the United States were trying to develop forms of cultural infrastructure, such as the Underground Press Syndicate, the North American Congress on Latin America (which aimed to provide the New Left with more accurate information about political relations in the Western Hemisphere), or Third World Newsreel (which aimed to be a "revolutionary communications network of, by and for Black and Third World people of America"). Informational politics, in short, were central concerns of the globalist left. It was no accident that when Cleaver's faction of the Black Panther Party split off in Algeria in 1971, it renamed itself the Revolutionary Peoples Communications Network, with the goal of exchanging information among leftist groups around the world.[4]

Although the efforts of these radical activists suggested a new interest in globalizing the United States, their impact should not be overstated. They were experiments on the margins; they never remade the mainstream media. And although the existence of new forms of political travel reflects the relative decline of travel policing since the mid-1950s, these trips were still being conducted in the shadow of the security state, which still sought to blame domestic dissent on foreign interference. Senator John McClellan, for instance, blamed racial uprisings in the late 1960s on Moscow, which he said had created an "espionage or sabotage school in Ghana, Africa, for colored people"; Lyndon Baines Johnson, as president, wanted the security branches to "carefully look at who leaves this country, where they go, why they are going." The FBI continued to monitor and harass radical activists, as when it forged letters between Cleaver and Huey Newton to hasten the growing divide between the international and domestic wings of the Black Panther Party. When the Castro regime began to sour on the Williamses in the mid-1960s, they were denied travel documents to return to the United States and instead continued their exile in China. They would not return to the US until 1969, at which time Robert was questioned about his political activities before a Senate subcommittee.[5]

The State Department's area restrictions had been stripped of their legal power by the late 1960s; but choosing to travel without a passport nevertheless remained a risky and provocative act that only the most committed were willing to undertake—it was, in large part, what made these trips so political. It was also why such travelers were subject to harassment and persecution upon their return. Staughton Lynd, for instance, may have won his legal battle with the State Department about his right to travel to North Vietnam, but the incident cost him his academic career. After Yale President Kingman Brewster suggested that Lynd had provided "aid and comfort" to the enemy, Lynd was denied tenure. In coming years, he was offered employment at five other schools, only to have each offer vetoed by university administration, and he left academia for a long career as an activist and public intellectual. Similarly, Jane Fonda was met with accusations of treason when she returned from a controversial tour of North Vietnam in 1972. Congress even flirted with legislation that would punish such trips with up to five years in jail.[6]

In short, although the bridges that were built between the United States left and the decolonizing and socialist world in the late 1960s were important, they primarily remind us just how isolated and policed these forms of cultural globalization remained. We should not, therefore, be surprised that there was a tendency among the left in these years to romanticize or exoticize foreign nations that they knew very little about—they were struggling to overcome an international communication system geared primarily to exporting American culture.

The overall flow of information in the world remained deeply lopsided in the 1970s. American television companies sold twice as many programs overseas as all other countries combined; US commercial channels still imported only 1 percent of their programming. The Associated Press (AP) sent ninety thousand words a day from New York to Asia; nineteen thousand words a day went the other way. For every one hundred wire items Venezuela received from the United States, it sent back only seven, and those seven went back via the US-owned AP and UP. Beneath these uneven flows lay an equally uneven distribution of communications capacity. By 1977, 48 percent of all radio receivers were in North America; 3 percent were in Africa; and 12 percent were in Asia. In the same year, Africa consumed some 900 kilograms of printed paper per one thousand inhabitants per year, whereas North America consumed some 67,000 kilograms per one thousand inhabitants. In the 1970s, as critics were observing, it still made some sense to claim that "the media are American."[7]

In the 1970s, UNESCO made a controversial effort to redress these inequalities and decenter the United States in a series of calls for what became known as a "New World Information and Communication Order

(NWICO)." In a decade-long process, in roughly one hundred meetings held in forty-two countries, governments and media groups sought to diagnose the inadequacies of the global communication order and to imagine pathways and policies for reform. This preoccupation with addressing material inequalities in educational and cultural flows was best understood as a return of the redistributionist vision of cultural globalization that had been repressed at UNESCO's founding in the 1940s and that had derailed the freedom of information campaign at the United Nations.[8]

UNESCO had not exactly ignored the problem of cultural inequality in the 1950s and 1960s. At the urging of the United Nations, it had undertaken a series of studies and fact-finding conferences that helped clarify the stunning shortages of communications capacity in much of the decolonizing world. In the early 1960s, it found that some 60 percent of the world's population lacked access to what it determined to be the minimum media needs of a modern nation. Observing that this created a "mass thirst for knowledge" and an "information famine," UNESCO estimated that some $3.4 billion would need to be spent to provide just ten newspaper copies, five radio receivers, two television sets, and two cinema seats per one thousand inhabitants. Although UNESCO did begin a program of technical aid to help remedy these problems, its tiny budget meant that its efforts were dwarfed by vast flows of development aid coming from private foundations, nation-states, and other agencies of the UN. Moreover, all these communication development programs were dominated by modernization theorists, such as Wilbur Schramm and Daniel Lerner, who believed the main goal was providing technical assistance to foreign governments to help them "catch up" to the model of the US—the problem could be solved by simply extending American-style media systems into new terrain, a neat piece of generosity that seemed to promise only benefits to the US, and its allies, in the geopolitical and ideological clash with Communism. (It was telling that Schramm and Lerner's ideas, as well as their status, were shaped directly by their role in early Cold War propaganda efforts. Lerner, for instance, drew on his work assessing the effectiveness of Voice of America broadcasts in the Middle East to generate his theories about the role of mass communications in his landmark book *The Passing of Traditional Society*.) More radical solutions thus remained effectively sidelined throughout the period. "The high degree of participation by such American advisers as William Schramm [sic]," observed the State Department in 1970, "has helped mold the [communications development] program in accordance with our recommendations."[9]

By the beginning of the 1970s, however, a newly militant Global South transformed the tenor of UNESCO debate by calling for a more foundational rethinking of the structure of international communications. Decolonizing nations had long sought to both build up their own educational and cultural capacities and to establish cultural exchanges between themselves that were not mediated via old colonial centers. The Final Communiqué of the Bandung Conference, for instance, called for the promotion of "cultural cooperation among countries of Asia and Africa" to aid in the "acquisition of knowledge of each other's country, mutual cultural exchange and exchange of information." In 1953, the Egyptian government began broadcasting a "Voice of the Arabs" program; in an effort to reach Egypt's African neighbors, Radio Cairo was soon broadcasting in Swahili. Similarly, Fidel Castro launched the Prensa Latina news service shortly after the Cuban revolution and Radio Havana a year later, and they were soon exchanging news with Egypt's Middle East News Agency and Yugoslavia's Tanjug.[10]

Amid the broader geopolitical and cultural transformations of the 1970s, this interest in cultural decolonization blossomed into a critique of the broader structure of international communications. As new nations emerged from colonialism, they formed a powerful voting bloc in international organizations, including UNESCO—between 1960 and 1965, thirty-seven new countries joined UNESCO, where they made up one-third of the membership. Just as the Third World bloc at the United Nations called for a New International Economic Order (NIEO), so did their colleagues in UNESCO call for a New International Information Order. (Mahmood Masmoudi, Tunisia's delegate to UNESCO and one of the key advocates of a NWICO, said that it was the "natural corollary" to the NIEO.) And just as the emergence of dependency theory asserted that technical assistance programs led not to economic development but to ongoing domination by the West, so, too, did a new critique of "cultural imperialism," articulated by journalists and scholars such as Armand Mattelart, Ariel Dorfman, D. R. Mankekar, Eleazar Diaz Rangel, and Herbert Schiller, assert that the spread of Western culture was producing new forms of cultural exploitation and subordination.[11]

A crescendo of international conferences and meetings called for a new approach to cultural globalization. In 1973, the Fourth Summit of the Non-Aligned Movement in Algiers called for the "reorganization of existing communication channels which are the legacy of the colonial past." The delegates asserted, "It is an established fact that the activities of imperialism are not confined solely to the political and economic fields but also cover the cultural and social fields, thus imposing an alien ideological domination over the peoples of the developing world." In 1976, a meeting of journalists in Mexico decried the "systematic deformation of the reality of third world countries" in global news media, and a Non-Aligned Symposium on Information in Tunis argued that the only way to remedy the "disequilibrium" in global informational exchanges was to "obtain the decolonization of information and initiate a new international order in information." UNESCO's General Conference, meeting in Nairobi at the end of the year, drafted a "Declaration of Fundamental Principles Governing the Use of the Mass Media in Strengthening Peace and International Understanding and in Combating War Propaganda, Racism, and Apartheid." The declaration, which turned out to be the high-water mark of the NWICO movement, called for the cultivation of a "two-way flow of news."[12]

The US was deeply critical of these proposals, arguing that they were Soviet-backed attempts to dominate the organs of international communication. "The evidence is conclusive," asserted Roscoe Drummond in the *Christian Science Monitor*, that "UNESCO . . . is in the destructive grip of an alliance of 'third world' and communist countries" who sought to "use UNESCO as a tool to restrict the flow of news and information in every way it can." The United States was particularly upset by article 11 of the proposed UNESCO declaration, which was based on a Soviet draft and which made states responsible for the media within their jurisdiction; to US commentators, the clause would allow foreign states, many of them undemocratic, to control the information coming into and out of their countries. As it had at Geneva in 1948, the United States opposed redistributionist policies by presenting itself as a global champion of civil liberties. The State Department helped establish a World Press Freedom Committee that staged a counterconference to UNESCO's San José meeting and asserted that the proposals for a NWICO posed "potential danger to the press of the entire world."[13]

NWICO was a complex formation, and there is no doubt that some of its ostensible advocates were dictatorships cynically seeking cover for repressive domestic policies. (There were also dictatorships, such as those of Brazil and Uruguay, that joined the United States in attacking NWICO as a Marxist threat to freedom of expression.) But to focus purely on the rhetorical grandstanding would be to ignore NWICO's most significant efforts to re-network the world's communications infrastructure. Working journalists and state officials met in workshops and conferences across the Global South to discuss such pragmatic issues as access to news reports and subscription services, cable and satellite transmission rates, training programs for journalists and camera crews, and the creation of shared libraries of news film. In January 1975, a Non-Aligned News Agencies Pool was established that collected news from members and redistributed them via the facilities of Tanjug, the Yugoslavian news agency. By 1981, it had eighty-three members and was adding something like forty thousand words a day to news exchanges in the Global South. The year 1975 also saw the establishment of a Caribbean News Agency, and a Pan African News Agency was established, with UNESCO support, a few years later. As historians excavate these efforts, we will get a clearer sense of both the political stakes of the moment and the role of NWICO in resculpting global flows of information.[14]

In the 1970s, however, the United States treated these proposals to expand communication as no different than statist proposals for propaganda and censorship. At UNESCO's Nairobi conference in 1976, for instance, Venezuela agreed with the US that Soviet-inspired calls for state sovereignty over the international flow of news were anathema—Venezuela also preferred freedom from state censorship. But it simultaneously insisted that there was a need to correct North American bias in the news, and so it favored the creation of a Third World News Pool. ("Why," asked Luis Penalver, Venezuela's minister of education, "should we rely exclusively on foreign news sources, which represent powerful economic interests, to hear about our own neighbors?") But to US critics of NWICO, this was all just hair-splitting. "The Third World News Pool," argued George Beebe, chair of the World Press Freedom Committee, "will be a worthless government propaganda machine."[15]

The hostility of the US to any attempt to reimagine the institutions and networks of global culture doomed the NWICO debate. At Nairobi in 1976, conflict over NWICO became so intense that it looked as though UNESCO would fracture. To defuse the matter, Amadou Mahtar M'Bow, UNESCO's new director-general and the first African to head a UN organization, worked to defer it by creating new committees to study the issues. In 1978, a revised Declaration of Mass Media, which had dropped the controversial article 11, was passed by acclamation. (M'Bow declared this "one of the most moving moments of my life," although many nations grumbled that the statement had become so anodyne as to be meaningless.) And in 1980, after years of meetings, a blue-ribbon commission on global communications issued its optimistically titled report *Many Voices, One World*. The report provided a detailed survey of the inequalities that marred global communication flows and that had spurred demands for a NWICO. But even though it concluded with eighty-two recommendations to improve the situation, these strove so hard to avoid controversy that they largely sidestepped the difficult, substantive policy questions and ended up satisfying no one. In any case, the recommendations didn't even make it onto the agenda of the 1980 UNESCO General Conference and were never implemented in a sustained program.[16]

Four years after Nairobi, the only concrete step that UNESCO had taken to actually implement a NWICO was the creation of an International Program for the Development of Communications, a program of technical assistance that had been proposed by the United States as yet another "Marshall Plan" for information and that raised understandable concerns that it represented nothing more than the same old developmental policy that NWICO had been intended to overcome. Remarkably, the incoming administration of Ronald Reagan was skeptical of even this US-originated development program. Rather than paying its contributions directly to the program, as did all other nations, it insisted on holding them in trust in the United States Information Agency (USIA)—it wanted to maintain the ability to release funds only to projects of which it approved.[17]

Although proposals for NWICO had thus been defanged, by this point a coalition of US journalists, politicians, and conservative think tanks was actively calling for the United States to withdraw from UNESCO. They made a number of interrelated charges. The Reagan administration, which was conducting a broad review of US involvement in multilateral organizations so as to both reassert US leadership and limit US expenditures, argued that UNESCO was a bloated, inefficient, and corrupt bureaucracy that was squandering US contributions. (In fact, UNESCO's budget remained tiny; it was about two-fifths of Stanford's budget. In 1984, the entire US contribution was just 0.05 percent of the $92 billion that Reagan had added to the defense budget in his first term.) There were also accusations that UNESCO had become inappropriately "political" and that its criticisms of Israeli archaeological practices in Jerusalem were a sign of anti-Semitism. (Between 1974 and 1976, when UNESCO had excluded Israel from membership in its European regional group, the US had refused payment to the organization.) And there were repeated complaints that NWICO threatened to interfere with the free flow of information and encourage censorship of the US press. When a UNESCO working group, discussing protections for journalists in war zones, proposed issuing ID cards to journalists, for instance, this move was seen as an attempt to license the press, even though the working group had abandoned the proposal. In response, the heads of news media organizations held a conference at the French resort town of Talloirs at which they issued a declaration criticizing UNESCO and underscoring their commitment to the "free flow of information." In 1982, when authorizing the State Department's budget, Congress added an amendment, sponsored by

Tennessee Republican Robin Beard, that would block funding to UNESCO if it threatened press freedom. The Senate had already voted 99–0 to disapprove of NWICO.[18]

At the end of 1984, after years of threats, complaints, and accusations, the US left the organization. Gregory Newell, assistant secretary of state for international organizations, claimed that UNESCO had displayed an "endemic hostility toward the institutions of a free press, free markets and, above all, individual human rights." Whatever the specifics of those charges—and contemporary State Department reports made clear that no UNESCO policies "pose[d] any active, direct threat to a free press"—the real issue was one of power, not principle. As UNESCO membership expanded and then become more militant, the United States lost control of the organization. Tellingly, alongside its denunciations of NWICO, the United States had been simultaneously seeking ways to reestablish control. In July 1984, Newell had written to M'Bow to outline the kind of reforms that might have allowed the United States to maintain its membership. They included a criticism of the one-nation, one-vote structure, which was seen to "not sufficiently reflect minority interests"—by which he meant the minority of wealthy states. The US wanted to add procedural checks on UNESCO's democratic process that would give great powers like itself a weighted vote. It proposed a veto power over contentious issues, to be allocated on a geographic basis; a requirement that an 85 percent vote would be required by the board to approve UNESCO's program; and a requirement that the budget needed approval from major donors (nothing would be passed without a vote from nations representing 51 percent of the contributions to UNESCO). UNESCO, which had the broadest representation of any UN organization, was unsurprisingly unwilling to entertain these revanchist proposals. But even that could serve a purpose, for the US was hoping that its departure would have a "ripple effect" throughout the UN. "If we drop out of UNESCO," said one State Department official, "you will see a lot of other organizations straighten out their act."[19]

When the United States left UNESCO, it joined a small and unflattering club of ex-members—Poland, Hungary, and Czechoslovakia had quit the organization during the Cold War tensions of the early 1950s; South Africa had left the organization in 1956 in protest of UNESCO's antiracism initiatives. Observing the US departure from what it had once trumpeted as a core organ of liberal internationalism, journalist James Traub said that "there was something painfully instructive in our isolation." "The days when the US ran UNESCO, and everything else, are over," he concluded: "The radical conservatives in ascendancy in Washington do not seem to accept this."[20]

At the same time that UNESCO was trying to reorganize international flows of information between the Global North and South, a new effort was being made to reorganize flows of information and people between the capitalist West and the Communist East: the Conference on Security and Cooperation in Europe, which ultimately led to the 1975 Helsinki Final Act. Hammered out in grueling discussions between thirty-three European nations from both East and West, as well as Canada and the United States, the Final Act was the highpoint of détente. To stabilize relations across the Iron Curtain, the act contained a sequence of agreements, organized into three baskets. Basket 1 provided, at long last, diplomatic recognition of the post–World War II Eastern European borders—the desire to achieve such recognition was what led the USSR to suggest the conference in the first place, and the Soviets were pleased with the result. But in exchange, the Soviets had allowed the west to introduce guarantees of human rights, and Basket 3 called for "increased cultural and educational exchanges, broader dissemination of information [and] contacts between peoples" in order to "contribute to the strengthening of peace and understanding among peoples."[21]

Such international recognition of the rights of individual citizens to travel and to receive information from abroad created an opportunity for dissident groups within the Soviet Union to mobilize, and they were soon deploying the Helsinki agreements to protest against their repressive regimes. The first of them, the Moscow Helsinki Group, was founded in 1976; the next year, Charter 77 emerged in Czechoslovakia; and in 1980, Solidarity demanded that the Polish government abide by the Helsinki agreements. All of these organizations, increasingly bound together in a transnational network, played central roles in the collapse of Communism in the late 1980s. In the long run, the Helsinki Final Act therefore played an important part in legitimizing and fostering efforts to liberalize the political culture of the Soviet Bloc. We can see now that the Helsinki Act was perhaps the most meaningful moment in the long history of efforts to undermine communism through the spread of ideas, information, and the free movement of people. It was the rightful heir to the 1940s crusade for global freedom of information.[22]

The irony was that the United States was largely uninterested in the provisions of Helsinki that guaranteed the free flow of information and played little role in writing them. Western European nations such as France and West Germany had insisted on the Basket 3 provisions, and as they did so, they sounded a lot like US liberal internationalists of an earlier period. George Pompidou, for instance, said that "the more contacts we have with the East, the more liberty will become contagious." Some members of the

State Department agreed with their European colleagues, but they were stymied by Secretary of State Henry Kissinger, who dismissed the importance of cultural exchange and the free flow of information. "Being able to buy the *New York Times* in Moscow," he scoffed, "won't change the Soviet system." He thought that the Basket 3 agreements were a "meaningless psychological exercise," that they were "frivolous," and that they would "lead to nothing." Kissinger's vision of foreign policy was built upon "realist" respect for the sovereignty of great powers, and he was inclined to dismiss the entire spectacle of negotiations at Helsinki. "I don't care what they do," he said. "They could write in Swahili for all I care. . . . I don't believe that a bunch of revolutionaries who have managed to cling to power for 50 years are going to be euchred out of it . . . by the kind of people negotiating in Helsinki." When Leonid Brezhnev became frustrated with Western European insistence on guaranteeing the free flow of information, he complained to Kissinger, and between them, the two sought to add language insisting on respect for domestic sovereignty. (They had Finland introduce the compromise language to hide its origins.)[23]

Even after the final negotiations, US domestic commentary remained critical, thinking that the agreement did nothing but recognize the borders of Eastern Europe and thus legitimized Soviet domination. Newspapers urged President Gerald Ford not to sign the final agreement because it won nothing for the United States; George Kennan called it "a lot of nonsense" and an "exercise in semantics." When Ford did sign the agreement, he received flak from both of his political rivals in 1976. "I think we lost in Helsinki," declared Jimmy Carter. "We ratified the takeover of Eastern Europe. We got practically nothing in return." Ronald Reagan, challenging Ford on behalf of a resurgent Republican right, agreed, saying, "I am against it and I think all Americans should be against it." It was no accident that the gaffe that grievously harmed Ford in the 1976 presidential debate concerned Soviet domination in Eastern Europe—Helsinki was considered to be an un-American agreement.[24]

It didn't take long for Americans to realize that the Basket 3 agreements actually provided them with a useful tool to attack the Soviet Union. After a delegation of congressional members met with dissidents on a post-Helsinki tour of the USSR, they passed legislation to establish a committee to monitor Soviet compliance with its new obligations to respect human rights. Once in office, President Carter embraced these parts of the Helsinki agreement as a sign of American strength over the Soviets, not a sign of capitulation to them—one of his National Security Council staffers recalled that Carter's human rights policy was a "very pragmatic tactic, to really beat up morally on the Soviets." Beginning with the Belgrade follow-up meeting in 1977, US delegations to subsequent meetings of the Helsinki process began reading into the conference record evidence of the Soviet Union's poor record of compliance.[25] This offensive deployment of the Basket 3 agreements continued under Reagan.

For a brief moment, it seemed that the effective weaponization of the Basket 3 agreements would require reform to US policy as well, so as to avoid charges of hypocrisy. In March 1977, noting that the United States was "culpable in some ways" for violating Helsinki's guarantee of free movement, Carter removed restrictions on travel to Cuba, North Vietnam, North Korea, and Cambodia. The next year, the Passport Act was reformed to limit the imposition of area restrictions to times of war or to protect the public health or physical safety of US citizens.[26]

But these reforms turned out to be partial and fleeting. Travel control soon reemerged. In 1980, during the Iranian hostage crisis, Carter barred travel to Iran. Tellingly, he did so not by relying on the now-revised and delimited Passport Act, but by invoking the International Emergency Economic Powers Act—control over financial transactions with Iran provided a way to effectively delimit travel. (The order exempted journalists, although William Worthy was one of the few who took advantage of it.) The Reagan administration relied on the same economic powers when it reinstituted a travel ban to Cuba in 1982, and in 1984, the Supreme Court upheld the legality of this new form of travel ban; drawing on the *Zemel* precedent, it argued that travel control was "justified by weighty concerns of foreign policy." The same powers were subsequently used to bar travel to Libya. The ban on travel to Cuba, which was both expanded and placed on a statutory basis in the 1990s, would not be loosened until the Obama administration. The Reagan administration even reanimated political control over passports when it revoked, with Supreme Court approval, the passport of Philip Agee, the dissident former CIA agent.[27]

Reforms to US visa policy in the Carter years were even more ineffectual. In 1977, Carter did announce that he was conducting a "broad-scale review" intended to liberalize travel to the United States—the Helsinki Agreements made it particularly important that the immigration laws barring members of proscribed organizations like the Communist Party were not used to interfere with the admissions of Soviet Bloc visitors. The only result of this process, however, was the tepid 1977 McGovern Amendment to the immigration laws—it didn't remove the bar but encouraged the attorney general to make increased use of a right to "waive" this prohibition. And in 1979, the law was amended once again to reapply a bar on members of "purported labor organizations in countries where such organizations are in fact instruments of a totalitarian state." In any case, by focusing only on the bar on membership of proscribed organizations, the McGovern Amendment left in place a still capacious range of prohibitions on the entry of those who were adjudged to be prejudicial to the public interest or the safety or the security of the United States. Hundreds of individuals were thus prevented from entering the United States in the 1980s: Hortensia Allende, Salvador's widow; Tomas Borge, Nicaragua's interior minister; General Nino Pasti, a former NATO representative who was prevented from giving speeches critical of the deployment of US cruise missiles; environmentalist Farley Mowat, who had belonged to a pro-Cuba committee a quarter-century before; Olga Finlay and Leonor Rodriguez Lescano, who were barred from presenting information on Cuban family policy to a New York City Commission on the Status of Women; 350 Japanese delegates, including Hiroshima survivors, who were prevented from attending a UN-affiliated conference on nuclear disarmament. In 1980, asked to explain the denial of a visa to leftist playwright Dario Fo, the State Department revealed the ongoing sensitivity of the United States to criticism from overseas: "Fo's record of performance with reference to the United States is not good. He has never had a good word to say about us."[28]

During the 1990s, amid the heady triumphalism after the fall of the Soviet Bloc, it became all too easy to once again equate American cultural expansion with cultural globalization. "Soft power" was in vogue, and the United States was an "information superpower." David Rothkopf, recently departed from the Department of Commerce, called for the United States to become the "dominant power of the Information Age . . . by breaking down the barriers that divide nations." Similarly, the German editor Josef Joffe told readers of the *New York Times Sunday Magazine* in 1997, "America has the world's most open culture, and therefore the world is most open to it." And as he championed free trade with China in March 2000, President Clinton announced, "In the new century, liberty will spread by cell phone and cable modem."[29] In truth, things were much more complicated than this revived American exceptionalism suggested. The multimedia firms spreading "American culture" to the world were themselves strange global hybrids, tied into international corporations with allegiances to no nation-state, such as Sony or Rupert Murdoch's News Corporation.

As the war on terror emerged, it became all too apparent that alternative, dissonant globalizations were at work. (The surprised refrain "Why do they hate us?" captured the shock of this realization.) In fact, the rise of Islamic fundamentalism suggests the vulnerabilities of the sorts of cultural networks the US had created in the wake of World War II: Sayyid Qutb, the intellectual godfather of the Muslim Brotherhood, had been radicalized by his alienating experiences as a foreign exchange student in Denver in the late 1940s; Iranian revolutionaries in 1979 took hostages in the American Embassy that had been built in the postwar burst of surplus-funded construction; from the 1960s to 9/11, the air networks central to global travel also became sites of terrorism. But these unanticipated forms of blowback were easily contained, culturally at least, by ramping up the surveillance and security state—no-fly lists updated travel controls for a new era.[30] Insulating the homeland seemed to allow the United States to maintain its outsized cultural, military, and economic footprint in the world's affairs without importing unwanted ideas or actors. This familiar trade-off meant that it was still possible to call this uneven form of exchange "cultural globalization" and to think that America's role in the world was guided by something called "liberal internationalism."

The surprise presidency of Donald Trump seemed a sharp break from this. Nationalism replaced internationalism: America came first; walls replaced flows; international institutions that gave the US a "raw deal" were to be defunded. The world, in short, was a hostile place, inimical to the values of the heartland. But apart from the rhetorical denunciation of "liberal internationalism," there was much that was familiar in the Trump administration's policies. Trump's travel ban, for instance, was a new form of visa control, which suspended the issuance of visas to applicants from Iran, Libya, North Korea, Somalia, Syria, Yemen, and Venezuela—some 135 million people. After two failed efforts to ban the entry of Muslims, the administration ultimately claimed that the order was a national security measure, and the Supreme Court upheld its constitutionality, citing the *Mandel* decision as justification for its deference to executive branch decisions about who could enter the country, as well as the historical precedent of Carter- and Reagan-era visa bans.[31] As the ban disrupted the movement of families and migrants and tourists, it severed cultural connections. It also, as had visa policy in the past, interfered with student exchanges, international conferences, and the travel of academics, which were all subject as well to the administration's capricious desires. For example, a decision was made not to renew work visas for journalists employed by Voice of America; similarly, a hastily announced policy that would have required international students to take classes in-person in the fall of 2020 if they wanted to remain in the US sent students and administrators scrambling—before it was retracted in the face of legal challenge. On top of the general antipathy to immigration, rising tensions between China and the US began to restrict the flow of people between the two nations. New restrictions were placed on the sorts of Chinese students and researchers who could study in the United States, and a cascading series of tit-for-tat restrictions on journalists led to new limits on the number of Chinese journalists who could work in the US, as well as on the length of their visas.[32]

Meanwhile, reflecting its general antipathy to international organizations, the Trump administration once again withdrew the United States from UNESCO—citing, once again, the "anti-Israel bias" of the organization. After leaving UNESCO in 1984, the US had rejoined it in 2002, as part of the George W. Bush administration's charm offensive at the United Nations in the lead-up to the war on Iraq. But in 2011, when UNESCO accepted Palestine as a member, the United States had cut off funding, as required by legislation from the early 1990s that barred American financing to any UN agency that accepted Palestine as a full member. This created a major financial crisis at UNESCO and cost the US its voting privileges in 2013. (By 2017, the US owed UNESCO $550 million.)[33] And as the coronavirus pandemic swept the world in 2019, the US announced its intention to withdraw from the World Health Organization, one more sign of its retreat from multilateral institutions and a familiar reprise of long-running conservative skepticism to the UN. But in a striking departure from the past, the US is also finding itself involuntarily isolated from international networks. As foreign nations began to cautiously reopen their borders after the lockdowns that greeted the first wave of the pandemic, they refused to admit Americans, on the understandable grounds that the disease remained out of control in the United States.[34] It is, perhaps, a taste of things to come, a glimpse of a globalizing world in which the US is a peripheral, pariah state—not the center of the system and no longer free to dictate terms to the less powerful.

Whatever may come next, a clearer history of the politics of cultural globalization reminds us of the exclusionary, nationalistic, and self-interested currents that structured America's engagement with the world even at its moment of "liberal" ascendancy. Taking seriously the shortcomings of the US commitment to the international exchange of ideas also reminds us of the deep unevenness and inequality that has marked cultural exchange across the second half of the twentieth century. Cultural globalization remains an incomplete project, one barely begun in the twentieth century, and reflecting on the role of the United States in that unfinished history raises important questions. At the end of the day, what was "liberal" about "liberal internationalism"? And what would it take to create a truly free flow of information around the world?

ACKNOWLEDGMENTS

I finished writing this book in the long months spent at home during the COVID-19 pandemic. The enforced isolation was probably good for getting me through the final stretch, but it cast into relief all the people and institutions whose help over the years got me close enough to see the finish line. It's a pleasure to thank them here.

I've been thinking about international cultural flows for as long as I've been a historian—my first stab at examining the origins of the Fulbright Program came in my first seminar as a PhD student at the University of Chicago in 2004, where Mae Ngai and Jim Sparrow offered much advice and encouragement. Since then, I've discussed the ideas that made their way into this book with more colleagues, friends, workshop groups, and conference panels than I can count, let alone mention here—my thanks go to you all.

The impact of some conversations on the manuscript, though, has been so profound that they are easy to remember. An early version of the Fulbright material in chapter 2 was published in *Diplomatic History*, where it was much sharpened by two anonymous reviewers; my thinking about the Fulbright was reinvigorated by a stimulating conference (and subsequent volume) on Fulbright's legacy organized at the University of Arkansas by Alessandro Brogi, Giles Scott-Smith, and David Snyder. The *Journal of American History* sent an early version of chapter 1 out for review—the anonymous reviewers didn't care much for it, but although I didn't end up resubmitting the article, their comments spurred a number of new lines of thought and research that very much improved my analysis. Dina Fainberg and Diana Lemberg answered some questions I had based on their excellent work, which helped clarify some important points. Laura Weinrib generously gave chapter 5 a careful read and helped sharpen it in a number of places. Paul Kramer's support for my work has meant a great deal for many years—among many other acts of generosity, he invited me to present a version of chapter 1 at Vanderbilt and arranged for me to meet with Sarah Nelson, which led to many inspiring and illuminating conversations with Sarah about international communications politics. Conversations with Paul, as well as with Emily Marker, Lincoln Mullen, and Matt Karush, also helped convince me that my various projects on cultural globalization made sense as a book.

Above all, my work as a historian has been shaped by my good fortune to have the Department of History and Art History at George Mason University as my home. The department is a remarkably collegial and supportive environment in which to write history. I have benefited from conversations with many colleagues about various aspects of this book and received very helpful feedback on chapter 4 from participants in the Modern History Workshop. Brian Platt has been a selfless chair, and Emily Gibson, Carrie Grabo, Susie LeBlanc, and Sue Woods handle the business of the department with remarkable skill and cheer—their tireless work created the space I needed to write. I've also been fortunate to teach a wide range of graduate reading seminars and undergraduate courses over the past seven years, which provided a wonderful opportunity to think through the history covered in this book. Conversations with Justin Broubalow about his own excellent work on American immigration politics helped clarify my thinking for chapters 3 and 5. And to all my students—especially the graduate students, whose energy and enthusiasm in discussing works of history in our evening classes constantly amazes me—I give many thanks for helping me work so much of this history out in the classroom.

Financial support, much of it from George Mason, was also essential in conducting the research for the book. A Mathy Junior Faculty Fellowship gave me a semester off to devote to research in 2016, and a Nancy Weiss Malkiel Fellowship from the Institute for Citizens and Scholars allowed me to spend a pleasant part of that fateful fall in Paris. A departmental travel grant allowed me to tack a whirlwind trip to the Kew Archives on top of a conference trip to London in 2017, and expert help from the archivists there helped me make the most of my time. The work of George Oberle and all the librarians at George Mason has always been crucial to my research; it wouldn't have been possible to finish this book without the extraordinary efforts of libraries and presses across the country to make material available online during the pandemic.

I couldn't have asked for a better experience with a press than I've had with Tim Mennel and Susannah Engstrom at the University of Chicago Press. Tim has been an enthusiastic, perceptive reader of my work, and his brilliant line edit tightened everything up tremendously; the entire process has run much more smoothly than I could have hoped. Two anonymous reviewers provided helpful notes on places where my first draft needed sharpening—thank you.

Closer to home, the pandemic has shrunk our world, revealing just how important some relationships are. Justin Evans, Judy Choi, Persy, and Claudia have become family—sharing food, wine, and conversation with them provided essential escape from the worst moments of writing and 2020. In our regular Zoom calls, my parents in Sydney never fail to ask how the book is going; while I'm glad to tell them it is done, I'll be even happier when I can tell them in person.

Emily Jane Weaver's influence is on every page of this book. In part, that's because she let me read the manuscript to her during an improbably enjoyable series of pandemic happy hours—her impeccable taste and astute comments improved it in more ways than I can count. It's also because Em has been supporting this project for years. When I spent long days writing and researching, she was always understanding; when I prattled about war junk, or passports, or newsprint, she always asked thought-provoking questions; and when I needed to travel overseas for research, Em adjusted her work—and sleep—schedule to travel with me. So although this book has been a big part of my life for years, Em's enthusiasm for the world has kept it from taking over—I remember our time in Paris more for our ongoing quest for pastry than for my hours in the archives. Em, I love our life together—thank you. This one's for you.

ABBREVIATIONS

AM Archibald MacLeish Papers, Library of Congress, Washington, DC

APP Gerhard Peters and John T. Woolley, American Presidency Project, online at http://www.presidency.ucsb.edu/

BSC Entry A1 1507: Bureau of Security and Consular Affairs Records Relating to Visas, 1946–1953, Record Group 59: Records of the State Department, National Archives and Record Administration II, College Park, MD

CFT Entry 211: Committee on Foreign Travel Documents, 1945–1952, Record Group 353: Records of Interdepartmental and Intradepartmental Committees, National Archives and Record Administration II, College Park, MD

CFTWP Entry 214: Committee on Foreign Travel Working Papers 1946–1952, Record Group 353: Records of Interdepartmental and Intradepartmental Committees, National Archives and Record Administration II, College Park, MD

CIES Council for International Exchange of Scholars Records, Special Collections of University of Arkansas Libraries, Fayetteville, AR

CR Conference of Allied Ministers of Education Records, UNESCO Archives, Paris, France

CT *Chicago Tribune*

CR corr. Conference of Allied Ministers of Education Correspondence Files, UNESCO Archives, Paris, France

ECEFP Entry 212: ECEFP Foreign Travel Subcommittee: Minutes, 1946–1952, Record Group 353: Records of Interdepartmental and Intradepartmental Committees, National Archives and Record Administration II, College Park, MD

ECEFP corr. Entry 208: ECEFP Foreign Travel Subcommittee: General Correspondence, 1945–1949, Record Group 353: Records of Interdepartmental and Intradepartmental Committees, National Archives and Record Administration II, College Park, MD

EP *Editor and Publisher*

FRUS *Foreign Relations of the United States*

HC Commission on Freedom of the Press Records, Special Collections Research Center, University of Chicago Library, Chicago, IL

HFSD US Department of State, Office of Foreign Liquidation Commissioner, *The History of Foreign Surplus Property Disposal, 1945–1949*. This multi-volume internal history of the OFLC was never published, but it is available in the Library of Congress: https://lccn.loc.gov/50060163.

HN Entry 496: Records of Harley A. Notter, Record Group 59: Records of the State Department, National Archives and Record Administration II, College Park, MD

IND *Investigation of the National Defense Program, Hearings before a Special Committee Investigating the National Defense Program, Part 36: Surplus Property Abroad*, December 1945 and January 1946

JWF J. William Fulbright Papers, Special Collections of University of Arkansas Libraries, Fayetteville, AR

KEW The National Archives, United Kingdom

LP Leo Pasvolsky Papers, Library of Congress, Washington, DC

NYT *New York Times*

OIC Entry 5536: Office of International Conferences, Administrative Files 1928–1967, Record Group 43: Records of International Conferences, Commissions, and Expositions, National Archives and Record Administration II, College Park, MD

P47 Entry P47: Records Relating to the Air Coordinating Committee, 1945–1952, Record Group 59: Records of the State Department, National Archives and Record Administration II, College Park, MD

RCEPFF Entry P34: Records of Conference of Experts on Passport and Frontier Formalities, Record Group 43: Records of International Conferences, Commissions, and Expositions, National Archives and Record Administration II, College Park, MD

RG 59 Record Group 59: Records of the State Department, National Archives and Record Administration II, College Park, MD

RG 197 Entry A1 21: Office of the Chairman, General Records, National Archives and Record Administration II, Record Group 197: Records of the Civil Aeronautics Board, College Park, MD

TPC Entry 483: Travel Policy Committee Documents, Record Group 353: Records of Interdepartmental and Intradepartmental Committees, National Archives and Record Administration II, College Park, MD

UNESCO CR UNESCO Central Registry Collection, AG8—Secretariat Records, UNESCO Archives, Paris, France

UNESCO PC Preparatory Commission of UNESCO Records, 1945–1947, AG 3, UNESCO Archives, Paris, France

UNFOI Entries A1 720–24: Records Relating to UN Conference on Freedom of Information, Record Group 43: Records of International Conferences, Commissions, and expositions, National Archives and Record Administration II, College Park, MD

WP *Washington Post*

NOTES

INTRODUCTION

1. "People Must Speak to People," *NYT*, February 18, 1945, SM5; Scott Donaldson, *Archibald MacLeish: An American Life* (Boston: Houghton Mifflin, 1992), 371–94.

2. See, for instance, Robert Jervis et al., *Chaos in the Liberal Order: The Trump Presidency and International Politics in the 21st Century* (New York: Columbia University Press, 2018).

3. Amid a vast literature, influential accounts include E. F. Penrose, *Economic Planning for the Peace* (Princeton, NJ: Princeton University Press, 1953); Robert A. Divine, *Second Chance: The Triumph of Internationalism in America during World War II* (New York: Atheneum, 1967); Elizabeth Borgwardt, *A New Deal for the World: America's Vision for Human Rights* (Cambridge, MA: Belknap Press of Harvard University Press, 2005); Melvyn Leffler, *A Preponderance of Power: National Security, the Truman Administration and the Cold War* (Stanford, CA: Stanford University Press, 1992); Benn Steil, *The Battle of Bretton Woods: John Maynard Keynes, Harry Dexter White, and the Making of a New World Order* (Princeton, NJ: Princeton University Press, 2013); Robert Latham, *The Liberal Moment: Modernity, Security and the Making of the Postwar Order* (New York: Columbia University Press, 1997); Patrick J. Hearden, *Architects of Globalism: Building a New World Order during World War II* (Fayetteville: University of Arkansas Press, 2002); G. John Ikenberry, *Liberal Leviathan: The Origins, Crisis and Transformation of the American World Order* (Princeton, NJ: Princeton University Press, 2011); Mark Mazower, *Governing the World: The History of an Idea, 1815 to the Present* (New York: Penguin, 2012), esp. 191–213; and Stephen Wertheim, *Tomorrow, the World: The Birth of U.S. Global Supremacy* (Cambridge, MA: Harvard University Press, 2020).

4. "Congress Adopts World Free News Resolution," *EP*, September 23, 1944, 12; "Freedom of Information," *EP*, October 26, 1946, 84; 79th Cong., A2353 (April 26, 1946).

5. In a helpful formulation, John Fousek has dubbed this ideology "nationalist globalism." John Fousek, *To Lead the Free World American Nationalism and the Cultural Roots of the Cold War* (Chapel Hill: University of North Carolina Press, 2000).

6. For similar arguments that globalization and internationalism were radical projects not of the Euro-American core but of the decolonizing and socialist worlds, see Johanna Bockman, "Socialist Globalization against Capitalist Neocolonialism: The Economic Ideas behind the New International Economic Order," *Humanity* 6, no. 1

(2015): 109–28; Adom Getachew, *Worldmaking after Empire: The Rise and Fall of Self-Determination* (Princeton, NJ: Princeton University Press, 2019); Susan Pedersen, *The Guardians: The League of Nations and the Crisis of Empire* (Oxford: Oxford University Press, 2015).

7. Robeson Taj Frazier, *The East Is Black: Cold War China in the Black Radical Imagination* (Durham, NC: Duke University Press, 2015), 81.

8. Classic statements seeing globalization as domination are Herbert Schiller, *Mass Communications and American Empire* (Boulder, CO: Westview, 1992); and Ariel Dorfman and Armand Mattelart, *How to Read Donald Duck: Imperialist Ideology in the Disney Comic* (New York: International General, 1975). The inadequate attention they pay to the processes of cultural reception, and more multidirectional flows of culture, has been effectively critiqued; see Fred Fejes, "Media Imperialism: An Assessment," *Media, Culture and Society* 3 (1981): 281–89; Tamar Liebes and Elihu Katz, *The Export of Meaning: Cross-Cultural Readings of Dallas* (New York: Oxford University Press, 1990); Ulf Hannerz, "The World in Creolisation," *Africa* 57 (1987): 546–59; Arjun Appadurai, "Disjuncture and Difference in the Global Cultural Economy," in *Modernity at Large: Cultural Dimensions of Globalization*, ed. Arjun Appadurai (Minneapolis: University of Minneapolis Press, 1996), chap. 2. But simply emphasizing reception, hybridity, and multiplicity ignores important power dynamics—see Jan Nederveen Pieterse, "Globalization as Hybridization," in *Global Modernities*, ed. Mike Featherstone et al. (London: SAGE, 1995), 45–68; John Tomlinson, *Cultural Imperialism: A Critical Introduction* (London: Pinter, 1991); Colin Sparks, "Resurrecting the Imperial Dimension in International Communication," in *Internationalizing "International Communication,"* ed. Chin-Chuan Lee (Ann Arbor: University of Michigan Press, 2015), 157–77.

9. Influential historical accounts of particular moments and places in which culture has crossed borders include Andrew F. Jones, *Yellow Music: Media Culture and Colonial Modernity in the Chinese Jazz Age* (Durham, NC: Duke University Press, 2001); Uta G. Poiger, *Jazz, Rock, and Rebels: Cold War Politics and American Culture in a Divided Germany* (Berkeley: University of California Press, 2000); Brian Larkin, *Signal and Noise: Media, Infrastructure, and Urban Culture in Nigeria* (Durham, NC: Duke University Press, 2008); The Modern Girl around the World Research Group, *The Modern Girl around the World: Consumption, Modernity, and Globalization* (Durham, NC: Duke University Press, 2009); Victoria de Grazia, *Irresistible Empire: America's Advance through 20th-Century Europe* (Cambridge, MA: Belknap Press of Harvard University Press, 2006); Christina Klein, *Cold War Orientalism Asia in the Middlebrow Imagination, 1945–1961* (Berkeley: University of California Press, 2003); Melani McAlister, *Epic Encounters: Culture, Media, and U.S. Interests in the Middle East since 1945* (Berkeley: University of California Press, 2001).

10. For arguments about the need to replace a naturalized language of flow, circulation, and connection in favor of a history of uneven structures and unequal actors, see Frederick Cooper, "What Is the Concept of Globalization Good For? An African Historian's Perspective," *African Affairs* 100 (2001): 189–213; Augustine Sedgewick, "Against Flows," *History of the Present* 4 (2014): 143–70; Stefanie Gänger,

"Circulation: Reflections on Circularity, Entity, and Liquidity in the Language of Global History," *Journal of Global History* 12 (2017): 303–18.

11. My approach is indebted to work on the political development of communication in the domestic United States, such as Paul Starr, *The Creation of the Media: Political Origins of Modern Communications* (New York: Basic Books, 2004); Richard R. John, *Spreading the News: The American Postal System from Franklin to Morse* (Cambridge, MA: Harvard University Press, 1995).

In the field of US foreign relations, the study of "public" or "cultural" diplomacy has flourished and takes into account the political construction of institutions of cultural exchange. But the significance of public diplomacy programs in these years is better understood when embedded in a broader history of cultural globalization. For influential accounts of US cultural diplomacy, see Reinhold Wagnleitner, *Coca-Colonization and the Cold War: The Cultural Mission of the United States in Austria after the Second World War* (Chapel Hill: University of North Carolina Press, 1994); Jessica C. E. Gienow-Hecht, *Transmission Impossible: American Journalism as Cultural Diplomacy in Postwar Germany, 1945–1955* (Baton Rouge: Louisiana State University Press, 1999); Penny M. Von Eschen, *Satchmo Blows Up the World: Jazz Ambassadors Play the Cold War* (Cambridge, MA: Harvard University Press, 2004); Laura Belmonte, *Selling the American Way: U.S. Propaganda and the Cold War* (Philadelphia: University of Pennsylvania Press, 2008); Nicholas Cull, *The Cold War and the United States Information Agency: American Propaganda and Public Diplomacy, 1945–1989* (Cambridge: Cambridge University Press, 2008), 22–62; Walter L. Hixson, *Parting the Curtain: Propaganda, Culture, and the Cold War, 1945–1961* (New York: St. Martin's Press, 1997), 1–14; Frank A. Ninkovich, *The Diplomacy of Ideas: U.S. Foreign Policy and Cultural Relations, 1938–1950* (Cambridge: Cambridge University Press, 1981); Justin Hart, *Empire of Ideas: The Origins of Public Diplomacy and the Transformation of U.S. Foreign Policy* (New York: Oxford University Press, 2013); Kenneth Osgood, *Total Cold War: Eisenhower's Secret Propaganda Battle at Home and Abroad* (Lawrence: University of Kansas Press, 2006).

CHAPTER ONE

1. "Report on Needs of European Countries for Scientific Instruments and Laboratory Equipment," July 1946, CR, Vol. 6(2), 26–34.

2. UNESCO, *The Book of Needs of Fifteen War-Devastated Countries in Education, Science and Culture*, Vol. 1 (Paris: UNESCO, 1947), 21–28, 30, 49, 74, 93; *Book of Needs*, Vol. 2 (Paris: UNESCO, 1949), 13, 119, 76, 30; Professor Chen Yuan, "Memorandum on Losses in China," November 27, 1945, UNESCO PC, Vol. 6.

3. Commission of Enquiry on Special Educational Problems in the Liberated Countries, "Report from the Director," n.d., CAME/A/145, CAME records, Vol. 2(2). Historians have recently begun reexamining reconstruction on its own terms, rather than treating the period through the lens of the Cold War; see Ian Buruma, *Year Zero: A History of 1945* (New York: Penguin, 2013); Ben Shephard, *The Long Road Home: The Aftermath of the Second World War* (New York: Anchor Books, 2010); and

Mark Mazower, Jessica Reinisch, and David Feldman, eds., *Postwar Reconstruction in Europe: International Perspectives 1945–1949* (*Past and Present* Supplement 6, 2011). Educational reconstruction has not figured in these histories, with the exception of Charles Dorn, "The World's Schoolmaster: Educational Reconstruction, Grayson Kefauver, and the Founding of UNESCO, 1942–1946," *History of Education* 35 (May 2006): 297–320.

4. "UNESCO Constitution [November 16, 1945]," http://portal.unesco.org/en/ev.php-URL_ID=15244&URL_DO=DO_TOPIC&URL_SECTION=201.html.

5. The paradigmatic statement is in Akira Iriye, *Cultural Internationalism and World Order* (Baltimore: Johns Hopkins University Press, 1997). See also F. R. Cowell, "Planning the Organization of UNESCO 1942–1946, A Personal Record," *Journal of World History* 10 (1966): 210–56; H. H. Krill de Capello, "The Creation of the United Nations Educational, Scientific and Cultural Organization," *International Organization* 24 (Winter 1970): 1–30; and Walter H. C. Laves and Charles A. Thomson, *UNESCO: Purpose, Progress, Prospects* (Bloomington: Indiana University Press, 1957). More critical histories of UNESCO emerge in James P. Sewell, *UNESCO and World Politics: Engaging in International Relations* (Princeton, NJ: Princeton University Press, 1975); Philip W. Jones, *International Policies for Third World Education* (London: Routledge, 1988).

6. De Capello, "Creation," 2–7; Malcolm Robertson to Ministers or Acting Ministers of Education, October 28, 1942, Draft Report of Second Meeting of CAME, January 19, 1943, Draft Report of Fifth Meeting of CAME, July 27, 1943, all in CR, Vol. 1.

7. Draft Report of Conference, November 16, 1942, CR, Vol. 1; "Standard List, First Part," June 13, 1944, "Standard List, Second and Final Part," June 23, 1944, "Standard List of Material for 25 Pupils," July 7, 1944, all in CR, Vol. 8; "First Re-equipment Needs for One Medical School in Czechoslovakia," n.d., CR, Vol. 6(1); Walter Kotschnig to Charles Thomson, December 15, 1945, box 17, untitled folder, HN.

8. UNESCO, *Book of Needs*, Vol. 1, 17; "Assistance for the Teachers in Schools in Liberated Areas by Next September," n.d., CAME/A/120, Minutes of First Meeting of Emergency Aids to Teachers Committee, July 7, 1945, CAME/A/132, both in CR, Vol. 2(2); "Notes Compiled by the Ministry of Education on Improvisation by Teachers," September 1945, CAME/EAT/2, UNESCO PC, Vol. 6; Draft Report of 8th Meeting of CAME, February 4, 1944, CR, Vol. 1; Audio-Visual Aids Commission, "Report of Work," n.d., CAME/A/144, CR, Vol. 2(2); Draft Report of 14th Meeting of CAME, October 18, 1944, Draft Report of 20th Meeting of CAME, October 3, 1945, both in CR, Vol. 1; "Inter-allied Book Center," *Times*, September 29, 1944, State Department Decimal File 800.42/10–244, box 3253, RG 59.

9. Draft Minutes of First Meeting Commission on Scientific and Laboratory Equipment, October 19, 1943, CAME/D/1, Draft Minutes of 12th Meeting Commission on Scientific and Laboratory Equipment, July 11, 1944, Draft Minutes of First Meeting of the Technical Subcommittee, April 5, 1944, CAME/D/47, all in CR, Vol. 5.

10. Draft Report of Conference, November 16, 1942, CR, Vol. 1; "Paper C," n.d., CAME/A/12, CR, Vol. 2(1); Malcolm Robertson to Ministers or Acting Ministers of

Education, October 28, 1942, CR, Vol. 1; Draft Minutes of 15th Meeting of Commission on Scientific and Laboratory Equipment, September 26, 1944, CR, Vol. 5; Sewell, *UNESCO and World Politics*, 43–45; "Report on Needs of European Countries for Scientific Instruments and Laboratory Equipment," July 1946, "Science Commission, Matters of Broad Principle Arising Out of Its Work," February 26, 1945, both in CR, Vol. 6(2); Draft Minutes of 7th Meeting of Commission on Scientific and Laboratory Equipment, March 21, 1944, CAME/D/43 CR, Vol. 5.

11. Draft Minutes of Fourth Meeting of Commission on Scientific and Laboratory Equipment, February 1, 1944, CAME/D/29, Draft Minutes of 2nd Meeting of the Technical Subcommittee, May 16, 1944, CAME/D/73, both in CR, Vol. 5; CG Beasley to Judd, October 22, 1943, Dyer to Grimmett, n.d., Grimmett to Dyer, April 15, 1946, all in box 9, folder: British Empire, CR corr.; Quayle to Beasley, February 15, 1944, CR, Vol. 6(1); Draft Minutes of 26th Meeting of Books and Periodicals Commission, February 10, 1944, CR, Vol. 2(1); UNESCO, *Book of Needs*, Vol. 2, 14; FWH Smith, Under Secretary of State Burma Office to Huxley, August 5, 1944, Huxley to Smith, September 6, 1944, Minutes of "Burma Office Representative on the CAME," August 9, 1944, all in LC 440/440/453, FO 924/26, Kew.

12. No author to Drzewieski, "Various Questions Concerning Reconstruction," September 12, 1947, "Work Programme During the General Conference," October 23, 1947, both in box 40, folder: X07.55 REC, UNESCO CR; UNESCO, *Book of Needs*.

13. "Proposal to Establish an International Centre for the Preservation and Consultation of Dissertations," n.d., CAME/A/98, CR, Vol. 2(2); Draft Report of 16th Meeting of CAME, March 7, 1945, CR, Vol. 1; F. R. Cowell to Richardson, February 27, 1945, box 1, File: Commission of Enquiry on Special Education Treatment, CR corr.; United Nations Information Organisation, *Allied Plan for Education: The Story of CAME* (London: UN Information Organisation, 1945), 16–33.

14. De Capello, "Creation," 18; Cowell, "Planning the Organisation," 220; M. Butts, "International Bureau of Education, Geneva," December 20, 1944, CAME/A/84, CR, Vol. 2(2); Jan Opocensky, "The Beginnings of UNESCO, 1942–1948," (unpublished manuscript, UNESCO Archives), Vol. 1, 8–14; "Plans for the Creation of an Inter-Allied Bureau for Education," n.d., CAME/A/48, CR, Vol. 2(1).

15. E. George Payne to Cordell Hull, May 11, 1943; "Statements and Resolutions of Institute on Educational Reconstruction in Central and Eastern Europe," April 8, 1943, Decimal File 800.42/220, Grayson Kefauver to Sumner Welles, April 5, 1943, Decimal File 800.42/208, all in box 3247, RG 59; Draft Minutes of 2nd Meeting of the Technical Subcommittee, May 16, 1944, CAME/D/73, CR, Vol. 5.

16. "US Group in London for Education Talks," *NYT*, April 4, 1944, 17; Winant Telegram, September 4, 1943, doc. 970, *FRUS* 1943, General Vol. 1.

17. Box 17, untitled folder, HN; Sarah Ellen Graham, *Culture and Propaganda: The Progressive Origins of American Public Diplomacy, 1936–1953* (Burlington, VT: Ashgate, 2015), 115; Mr. Gore-Booth, minutes of a talk with M. Achilles of European Division of State Dept, December 18, 1943, L 55/23/410, FO 370/885, Kew; S. M. Bruce to Secretary of State Rt. Hon. Viscount Cranborne, March 29, 1944, ED 42/17, Kew; Initialed, illegible memo, April 5, 1944, ED 42/22, Kew; Harold Butler, British

embassy to RA Butler, January 31, 1944, ED 42/22, Kew; "Tentative Proposals to Be Made to the British, Chinese and Russian Governments and the Other Governments Represented in the Conference," January 10, 1944, Gideonse to Benjamin Gerig, October 29, 1943, "The Transformation of the Present Conference of Ministers of Education into an Educational and Cultural Commission of the UN," January 11, 1944, all in box 17, untitled folder, HN.

18. Charles Thomson to Shaw, "Proposals to Be Made to the British Govt Regarding CAME," January 7, 1944, box 17, untitled folder, HN.

19. Eugene Brown, *J. William Fulbright: Advice and Dissent* (Iowa City: University of Iowa Press, 1985), 16–18; Randall Bennett Woods, *Fulbright: A Biography* (New York: Cambridge University Press, 1995), 80–82; "Participation of the United States in Emergency Educational and Cultural Rebuilding of the War-Torn United Nations," *Department of State Bulletin* 10, no. 249 (April 10, 1944): 299.

20. "Conference of Allied Ministers of Education in London," *Department of State Bulletin* 10, no. 254 (May 6, 1944): 413.

21. Winant to Secretary of State, April 17, 1944, doc. 537, *FRUS*, Vol. 1; Draft Report of Open Meeting, April 12, 1944, Draft Report of Second Open Meeting, April 14, 1944, both in CR, Vol. 1.; "Suggestions for a United Nations Organization for Educational and Cultural Reconstruction," n.d., CR, Vol. 7; Kefauver to Thomson, April 26, 1944, Decimal File 800.42/576, box 3251, RG 59.

22. Hull to Winant, April 17, 1944, Document 538, "Recommendations of the American Education Delegation on Educational Rehabilitation," April 29, 1944, Document 540, both in *FRUS*, Vol. 1.

23. Wright to Huxley, September 25, 1944; Huxley to Wright, December 29, 1944, LC 1419/269/454, FO 924/24, Kew; Frank Ninkovich, *Diplomacy of Ideas: U.S. Foreign Policy and Cultural Relations, 1938–1950* (New York: Cambridge University Press, 1981), 78–82; Stephen Wertheim, "Instrumental Internationalism: The American Origins of the United Nations, 1940–3," *Journal of Contemporary History* 54 (April 2019): 279; Robert A. Divine, *Second Chance: The Triumph of Internationalism in American during World War I* (New York: Atheneum, 1967), 185, 216; Stettinius to Eleanor Roosevelt, November 23, 1944, doc. 545, *FRUS* 1944, General, Vol. 1; Joseph Grew, "Proposed Setting Up of International Education Office," February 6, 1945, box 4, folder: Memoranda of conversations 1945, LP.

24. Shephard, *The Long Road Home*, 54–57, 154–55, 228; Ninkovich, *Diplomacy of Ideas*, 82.

25. "Proposals for Dept of State Policy on Participation by the US Government in a UN Educational and Cultural Organization and in a Program of Educational and Cultural Reconstruction," n.d., box 17, folder: Education Drafts (1 of 2), HN; WRR to Miss Goodfellow, October 16, 1944, ED 121/270; John G. Winant to Anthony Eden, August 18, 1944, ED 121/270; Wright to Huxley, September 9, 1944, LC 827/269/453, FO 924/24; Sir A. Cardogan to John Winant, November 25, 1944, ED 121/270; Wright to Huxley, September 25 1944, Huxley to Wright, December 29, 1944, both in LC 1419/269/454, FO 924/24; Michael Huxley to Michael Wright, December 7, 1944, LC 827/269/453, FO 924/24, G. H. Hall to R. A. Butler, October 11,

1944, ED 121/270, T. Gurney to Lord Halifax, Washington, December 22, 1944, LC 1346/269/453, FO 924/24, all in Kew.

26. Tentative Chinese Proposals for a General International Organization, August 23, 1944, doc. 422, Informal minutes of meeting no. 3 of the joint steering committee held at 11:15 a.m., October 4, 1944, doc. 495, Memorandum by undersecretary of state to secretary of state, October 3 1944, doc. 493, all in *FRUS*, Vol. 1. James Reston, "China Plan Given at Dumbarton Oaks," *NYT*, October 3, 1944, 1; Paul Gorden Lauren, *The Evolution of Human Rights: Visions Seen* (Philadelphia: University of Pennsylvania Press, 1998), 160–63; Marilyn Lake and Henry Reynolds, *Drawing the Global Colour Line: White Men's Countries and the International Challenge of Racial Equality* (New York: Cambridge University Press, 2008), 341; Robert Hilderbrand, *Dumbarton Oaks: The Origins of the United Nations and the Search for Postwar Security* (Chapel Hill: University of North Carolina Press, 1990), 240; Stephen C. Schlesinger, *Act of Creation: The Founding of the United Nations, A Story of Superpowers, Secret Agents, Wartime Allies and Enemies, and Their Quest for a Peaceful World* (Boulder, CO: Westview, 2003), 47.

27. Glenda Sluga, *Internationalism in the Age of Nationalism* (Philadelphia: University of Pennsylvania Press, 2013), 101; Mary Ann Glendon, *A World Made New: Eleanor Roosevelt and the Universal Declaration of Rights* (New York: Random House, 2001), 13–14; Lauren, *Evolution of Human Rights*, 178–85.

28. Marika Sherwood, " 'There Is No New Deal for the Blackman in San Francisco': African Attempts to Influence the Founding Conference of the United Nations, April–July, 1945," *International Journal of African Historical Studies* 29 (1996): 81; Marika Sherwood, "The United Nations: Caribbean and African-American Attempts to Influence the Founding Conference in San Francisco in 1945," *Journal of Caribbean History* 29, no. 1 (1995): 41, 43; Marika Sherwood, "India at the Founding of the UN," *International Studies* 33 (1996): 417–18; Adom Getachew, *Worldmaking after Empire: The Rise and Fall of Self-Determination* (Princeton, NJ: Princeton University Press, 2019), 87.

29. Carol Anderson, *Eyes off the Prize: The United Nations and the African American Struggle for Human Rights, 1944–1955* (New York: Cambridge University Press, 2003), 49–50, 86–87.

30. "Principal Proposals by Other Governments and Arguments against Them," n.d., box 5, folder: International Organizations - UN Proposals for, LP; Schlesinger, *Act of Creation*, 123; Ninkovich, *Diplomacy of Ideas*, 84; "Anti-Lynch Bill Rocks Senate," *New York Amsterdam News*, November 20, 1937, 1; "Tom Connally of Texas Is Dead," *NYT*, October 29, 1963, 1; "Tom Connally on Democracy," *Chicago Defender*, January 18, 1947, 14; Anderson, *Eyes off the Prize*, 3–4, 45; Ruth B. Russell, *A History of the United Nations Charter: The Role of the United States 1940–1945* (Washington, DC: Brookings Institute, 1958), 784–85.

31. "Proposals for Dept of State Policy on Participation by the US Government in a UN Educational and Cultural Organization and in a Program of Educational and Cultural Reconstruction," n.d., box 17, folder: Education Drafts (1 of 2), HN. Kefauver to Johnson, January 9, 1945, Decimal File 800.42/1–245, box 4128 RG

59; Cable from Washington to Foreign Office, January 21, 1945, ED 121/270, Earl of Halifax to Foreign Office, March 3, 1945, FO 924/132, both in Kew. "Tentative Draft Constitution for a United Nations Organization for Educational and Cultural Reconstruction," n.d., CAME/A-53; "US Proposals as Amended at the 7th Meeting of the Drafting Committee, March 8, 1945," both in CR, Vol. 7. The March date on this final document appears to be incorrect; based on other documents, it is from mid-April.

32. "Draft Report on the ILO Comments upon the Tentative Draft Constitution," n.d., CAME/A/101, "Revised Draft Statement to Accompany the Draft Constitution," n.d., CAME/A/111b, both in CR, Vol. 2(2). Minutes of 1st Meeting of Drafting Committee, January 29, 1945, CR, Vol. 7; WRR to Goodfellow, February 7, 1945, ED 121/270, Kew.

33. Hovde to Kefauver, April 10, 1945 500.CC/4–445, filed with 800.43/2–145, Anderson to Kefauver, April 17, 1945, Decimal File 800.42/4-/1245, both in box 4128, RG 59; Luther H. Evans, *The United States and UNESCO* (Dobbs Ferry, NY: Oceana Publications, 1971), 33; Bryan J. Hovde, "Proposed Position of the U.S. Delegation: The Problem of Aid to Reconstruction of Educational and Cultural Facilities," October 20, 1945, box 17, folder: Education Drafts (1 of 2), HN; *International Office of Education, Hearings before Committee on Foreign Affairs on H. Res. 215*, 79th Cong. 47–49 (May 10, 15, 17, 1945); *Membership and Participation by the United States in the UNESCO: Hearings before the Committee on Foreign Affairs on H. J. Res 305*, 79th Cong. 5 (April 3–5, 1946); 91 Cong. Rec. 11,000 (November 26, 1945) (statement of Rep. Merrow).

34. WRR to Goodfellow, February 7, 1945, ED 121/270, Proposed United Nations Organisation for Educational Reconstruction, March 3, 1945, FO 924/32, both in Kew; Grew to Johnson, March 6, 1945, Decimal File 800.42/3–245 box 4128, RG 59.

35. Sewell, *UNESCO and World Politics*, 71–78, Alfred Zimmern to Miss N. Parkinson, British Council, September 13, 1945, ED 121/269, Kew.

36. Archibald MacLeish, "Report to the Secretary of State from the Chairman of the US Delegation," in *"The Defenses of Peace": Documents Relating to UNESCO*, Part 1, US State Department Publication 2457 (Washington, DC: Government Printing Office, 1946), 7–8; Kefauver to Hovde, September 27, 1945, Decimal File 501.PA/9–2745 45, box 2232, RG 59.

37. Bryan J. Hovde, "Proposed Position of the US Delegation: The Problem of Aid to Reconstruction of Educational and Cultural Facilities," October 20, 1945, "Suggested Position to Be Taken by the US Delegation on the Problem of Reconstruction and Rehabilitation," November 4, 1945, both in box 17, folder: Education Drafts (1 of 2), HN.

38. *Conference for the Establishment of UNESCO*, November 1–16, 1945, UNESCO doc. ECO/CONF./29, 141, 147–48. Luther H. Evans, member of the US delegation and later UNESCO director-general, kept notes on the delegation meetings that were often more detailed than the official minutes. His notes were later published in Evans, *The United States and UNESCO*, 101–6.

39. Charles Dorn and Kristen Ghodsee, "The Cold War Politicization of Literacy: Communism, UNESCO, and the World Bank," *Diplomatic History* 36 (February 2012): 373–98; Luther Gulick to Dean Acheson, April 24, 1944, Decimal File 800.42/525, box 3250, RG 59; "UNRRA: Note by Foreign Office," attached to Draft Report of 7th Meeting of CAME, December 7, 1943, Draft Report of 20th Meeting of CAME, October 3, 1945, both in CR, Vol. 1. "Suggested Position to Be Taken by the US Delegation on the Problem of Reconstruction and Rehabilitation," November 4, 1945, box 17, folder: Education Drafts (1 of 2), HN; *Conference for the Establishment of UNESCO*, 148–49.

40. "UNRRA School Aid Projected by US," *NYT*, November 10, 1945, 6; *Conference for the Establishment of UNESCO*, 149–50; Summary of Minutes of Delegation Meeting, November 9, 1945, 9 a.m., Decimal File 501.PA, box 2233, RG 59; Evans, *The United States and UNESCO*, 107–12.

41. *Conference for the Establishment of UNESCO*, 151; MacLeish to Acheson, November 10, 1945, Decimal File 501.PA/11–1045, box 2233, RG 59; Evans, *The United States and UNESCO*, 79–80, 101–6.

42. MacLeish to Acheson, November 10, 1945, Decimal File 501.PA/11–1045, box 2233, RG 59; Evans, *The United States and UNESCO*, 1–2, 101–6, 112–17; US Department of State, *"The Defenses of Peace,"* Part 2, 15.

43. MacLeish to Acheson, November 10, 1945, Decimal File 501.PA/11–1045, box 2233, RG 59; Evans, *The United States and UNESCO*, 125–27.

44. MacLeish to Benton, November 12, 1945, Decimal File 501.PA/11–1245, box 2233, RG 59; Verbatim Record of the Fourth Meeting of the Technical Subcommittee on the Needs of War-Devastated Areas, February 8, 1946, UNESC/Prep.Com/Tech .Sub.Com./.P.V.4, UNESCO PC, Vol. 6.

45. For this reason, the Polish delegates tried on the last day of the Fifth Commission to revert to the name Interim Commission, but the amendment was voted down, 19–5. *Conference for the Establishment of UNESCO*, 151.

46. "Instrument Establishing a Preparatory Educational, Scientific and Cultural Commission," and "Summary and Analysis of UNESCO," in US Department of State, *"The Defenses of Peace,"* Part 1, 7–8; Part 2, 37.

47. MacLeish to Benton, November 16, 1945, Decimal File 501.PA/11–1545, box 2233, RG 59; Cowell, "Planning the Organisation," 226; "Summary Report on UNESCO Conference," December 3, 1945, included in Benton to Secretary of State, December 5, 1945, doc. 374, *FRUS* 1945, General: The United Nations, Vol. 1.

48. Record of the 12th Meeting of the 5th Session of the Preparatory Commission, July 12, 1946, UNESCO/Prep.Com/5th Session, P.V.12(1), UNESCO PC, Vol. 2.

49. Joseph Needham, "Memorandum on an International Science Cooperation Service," July 1944, Joseph Needham, "Place of Science and International Scientific Cooperation in Postwar World Organization," March 15, 1945, both in CR, Vol. 6(2); Sewell, *UNESCO and World Politics*, 77–79; Simon Winchester, *The Man Who Loved China: The Fantastic Story of the Eccentric Scientist Who Unlocked the Mysteries of the Middle Kingdom* (New York: HarperCollins, 2008).

50. Joseph Needham, "Place of Science and International Scientific Cooperation in Postwar World Organization," March 15, 1945, CR, Vol. 6(2); "First Statement of the Conception of an International Science Cooperation Service, in a Letter from Dr Needham," December 29, 1943, box 3, folder: CAME, UNECO and the Origins of UNESCO, CR corr.; Sewell, *UNESCO and World Politics*, 48–51.

51. Record of the 12th meeting of the 5th session of the Preparatory Commission, July 12, 1946, UNESCO/Prep.Com/5th Session, P.V.12(1), UNESCO PC, Vol. 2; "Revised Progress Report on the Programme of UNESCO," August 16, 1946, UNESCO/Prep.Com/51 (rev 1), UNESCO PC, Vol. 1; Verbatim Report of the Fourth Meeting (resumed) of the Technical Subcommittee of the Preparatory Commission, February 13 1946, UNESC/Prep.Com/Tech.Sub.Com./.P.V.4 (1) UNESCO PC, Vol. 6.

52. "Summary of Proposals Received by the Secretariat Concerning the Future Work of UNESCO," February 6, 1946, UNESCO/Prep.Com/22, "Organization of an International Campaign against Illiteracy," April 12, 1946, UNESCO/Prep.Com/24, "Proposal for a Textbook on World History Submitted by the Mexican Delegation," April 12, 1946, UNESCO/Prep.Com/25, "Recommendations for the Program of *UNESCO* in the Educational Field: Proposals Submitted by the United States Government," May 21, 1946, UNESCO/Prep.Com/46 all in UNESCO PC, Vol. 1.

53. UNESCO, "Freedom of Information and Illiteracy," March 9, 1948, UN Doc e/conf.6/26, box 3, folder: Econf6, UNFOI; Sewell, *UNESCO and World Politics*, 117; Record of the First Meeting of the 5th session of the Preparatory Commission, July 5, 1946, UNESCO/Prep.Com/5th Session, P.V.1.(1), UNESCO PC, Vol. 2.

54. Fourth Meeting of the Technical Subcommittee on the Needs of War-Devastated Areas, February 8, 1946, UNESC/Prep.Com/Tech.Sub.Com./.P.V.4, UNESCO PC, Vol. 6; A. F. Myers, "Whither UNESCO?," *Journal of Educational Sociology* 20 (1946): 22–23.

55. Graham, *Culture and Propaganda*, 144; Sewell, *UNESCO and World Politics*, 127; 92 Cong. Rec. 5,384 (May 21, 1946); *Minutes of General Conference First Session*, 1946, UNESCO/C/30, 90–106; Sewell, *UNESCO and World Politics*, 118; Opocensky, "The Beginnings of UNESCO," 138–52; Laves and Thomson, *UNESCO*, 46–47.

56. "Educational, Scientific and Cultural Rehabilitation and Reconstruction," November 4, 1946, UNESCO/Prep.Com/Tech.Sub.Com./52 (Rev.1) UNESCO PC, Vol. 6; Position paper on UNESCO's program in Educational, Scientific and Cultural Relief and Rehabilitation, November 19, 1946, Decimal File 501.PA/11-1346, box 2238, RG 59; *Minutes of General Conference First Session*, 90–106, 260–63; UNESCO, *Report on the Effectiveness of the Reconstruction Programme: 1947–1948–1949*, UNESCO Publication 732 (Paris, 1950), 45; Laves and Thomson, *UNESCO*, 71–76; "Report of the Director-General," September 20, 1947, UNESDOC 2 C/4; Bernard Drzewieski to Huxley et al., "Transfer of Funds in the 1947 Budget," October 20, 1947, Bernard Drzewieski to Acting Director General UNESCO, "Reconstruction Program for 1949," June 10, 1948, both in box 40, folder: X07.55 REC, UNESCO CR.

57. Laves and Thomson, *UNESCO*, 77–78; "Preliminary Work Plan for *UNESCO* International Volunteer Work Camps Project," n.d., Summary record of the 8th meeting of the Official and External Relations Commission of UNESCO, July 1950, Jaime Torres Bodet, Untitled Memorandum, January 22, 1951, all in box 213, folder:

361.9 A 01: 369.4 A 075/02; First Meeting of TICER, September 23–24, 1947, box 214, folder: 361.9 A 01 TICER 06 "47" Part 2; "Summary Records of TICER General Conference," January 11–12, 1950, TICER/Conf.5/SR 1.2.3.4, box 215, folder: 361.9 A 01 TICER 06 "50" all in UNESCO CR; "Report of Fact-Finding Committee on TICER," December 15, 1949, TICER/Conf.5/2, UNESDOC.

58. Iriye, *Cultural Internationalism and World Order*, 147–48; Laves and Thomson, *UNESCO*, 7–8; Sewell, *UNESCO and World Politics*, 81, 99, 121, 227; Marian Neal, "United Nations Technical Assistance Programs in Haiti," *International Conciliation* 81 (1951): 81–122; Joseph Watras, "UNESCO's Programme of Fundamental Education, 1946–1959," *History of Education* 39 (2010): 219–37; Chantalle F. Verna, "Haiti, the Rockefeller Foundation, and UNESCO's Pilot Project in Fundamental Education, 1948–1953" *Diplomatic History* 40 (2016): 269–95; Jan Opocensky, "The Beginnings of UNESCO" 135–36; Dorn and Ghodsee, "The Cold War Politicization of Literacy," 373–98.

Fundamental Education had a complex genealogy and could also be traced to colonial education schemes that sought to provide vocational training for colonial laborers rather than formal education for national citizens. Phillip W. Jones and David Coleman, *The United Nations and Education: Multilateralism, Development, and Globalisation* (London: Routledge, 2005), 30.

59. Watras, "UNESCO's Programme"; Sewell, *UNESCO and World Politics*, 227.

60. "CIER," January 17, 1950; "The Work of the Commission for International Educational Reconstruction," September 1947; Snyder to Drzewieski, September 4, 1947; George N. Shuster and Ethel B. Gilbert, "USA Voluntary Giving," March 15, 1950, all in box 212, folder: 369. A 01 (73), UNESCO CR; Laves and Thomson, *UNESCO*, 71–76; "Commission for International Educational Reconstruction," July 8, 1946, UNESC/Prep.Com/Tech.Sub.Com./41, UNESCO PC Vol. 6; *Report on the Effectiveness of the Reconstruction Programme*, 17; "Report of the New York Unit of the Reconstruction Service for the Year 1950," April 17, 1951, box 40, folder: X07.55 REC, UNESCO CR.

61. China, apparently, was not surveyed. "The Work of the Commission for International Educational Reconstruction," September 1947, "Important Note on Expenditures by Organizations in the United States for Educational Reconstruction in Particular Countries," n.d., Shuster and Gilbert, "USA Voluntary Giving," all in box 212, folder: 369. A 01 (73) UNESCO CR.

62. Of the $22 million in aid that CIER could track in 1949, 25 percent was spent on vocational instruction, 15 percent on educational fellowships, and 15 percent on medical instruction and international work camps. Only $31,000 was spent on audiovisual aids and $179,000 on laboratory equipment—combined, less than 1 percent of the total; CIER didn't know what a further $7 million was spent on. *Report of the Director General on the Activities of the Organization from October 1949 to March 1950*, UNESDOC 5/C3 (Paris, 1950), 70–77. Shuster and Gilbert, "USA Voluntary Giving"; "Report of the New York Unit of the Reconstruction Service for the Year 1950," April 17, 1951, box 40, folder: X07.55 REC, UNESCO CR; Minutes of the Third Meeting of CIER, January 23, 1947, box 212, folder: 369. A 01 (73), UNESCO CR.

63. "Report on Aid to Devastated Countries by Various Agencies in the US," December 5, 1945, UNESC/Prep.Com/Tech.Sub.Com./8, UNESCO PC, Vol. 6; Huxley

to Luce, April 22, 1947, Emeline B. Nollen to Huxley, May 27, 1947, Minutes of the Third Meeting of CIER, January 23, 1947, all in box 212, folder: 369. A 01 (73), UNESCO CR; "Outline for the Reconstruction Programme for the Years 1951 to 1955," n.d., box 40, folder: X07.55 REC, UNESCO CR.

64. Richard H. Pells, *Not Like Us: How Europeans Have Loved, Hated, and Transformed American Culture Since World War II* (New York: Basic Books, 1997), 49; Julian Bach, *America's Germany: An Account of the Occupation* (New York: Random House, 1946), 150–68; Harold Zink, *The United States in Germany, 1944–1955* (Princeton, NJ: D. Van Nostrand, 1957), 193–214; Alonzo G. Grace, *Basic Elements of Educational Reconstruction in Germany* (Washington, DC: Commission on the Occupied Areas, American Council on Education, 1949); Buruma, *Year Zero*, 279, 301; Preston, "The History of U.S.-UNESCO Relations," 82; "Summary of the Report of the US Education Mission to Japan" and "Summary of the Report of the US Education Mission to Germany," both in *International Conciliation* 25 (January 1947): 20–33; Edward R. Beauchamp, "The Development of Japanese Educational Policy, 1945–85," *History of Education Quarterly* 27, no. 3 (Autumn 1987): 302–5; Okazaki Masafumi, "Chrysanthemum and Christianity: Education and Religion in Occupied Japan, 1945–1952," *Pacific Historical Review* 79, no. 3 (August 2010): 393–417.

65. Jessica Wang, *American Science in an Age of Anxiety: Scientists, Anticommunism, and the Cold War* (Chapel Hill: University of North Carolina Press, 1999), 15–16; James Chace, "Sharing the Atom Bomb," *Foreign Affairs* 75, no. 1 (1996): 129–44; Martin J. Sherwin, *A World Destroyed: The Atomic Bomb and the Grand Alliance* (New York: Vintage, 1977), chap. 4; Barton J Bernstein, "The Quest for Security: American Foreign Policy and International Control of Atomic Energy, 1942–1946," *Journal of American History* 60 (1974): 43; Joseph Manzione, "'Amusing and Amazing and Practical and Military': The Legacy of Scientific Internationalism in American Foreign Policy, 1945–1963," *Diplomatic History* 24 (January 2000): 34, 40; Victor Sebestyen, *1946: The Making of the Modern World* (New York: Vintage, 2016), 309–10; Jeffrey A. Engel, *Cold War at 30,000 Feet: The Anglo-American Fight for Aviation Supremacy* (Cambridge, MA: Harvard University Press, 2007), 46.

66. Chace, "Sharing the Atom Bomb," 134, 138; Bernstein, "The Quest for Security," 1028; Michael J. Hogan, *A Cross of Iron: Harry S. Truman and the Origins of the National Security State, 1945–1954* (New York: Cambridge University Press, 1998), chap. 6, 238; Ira Katznelson, *Fear Itself: The New Deal and the Origins of Our Time* (New York: Liveright, 2013), 429–36; MacLeish to Acheson, December 17, 1945, box 1, folder: Dean Acheson, AM; *Membership and Participation by the United States in the UNESCO: Hearings before the Committee on Foreign Affairs on H. J. Res 305*, 79th Cong. 29 (April 3–5, 1946); 92 Cong. Rec. 5,385 (May 21, 1946); Frank E. Samuel Jr., "Technical Data Export Regulations," *Harvard International Law Club Journal* 6 (Spring 1965): 125–65.

67. John Gimbel, "Project Paperclip: German Scientists, American Policy, and the Cold War," *Diplomatic History* 14 (July 1990): 343–66; John Gimbel, "The American Exploitation of German Technical Know-How after World War II," *Political Science Quarterly* 105 (1990): 295; Christopher Simpson, *Blowback: The First Full Account of*

America's Recruitment of Nazis, and Its Disastrous Effect on Our Domestic and Foreign Policy (New York: Weidenfeld & Nicolson, 1988), chap. 2; Sebestyen, *1946,* 244; Rachel Pawlowicz and Walter E. Grunden, "Teaching Atrocities: The Holocaust and Unit 731 in the Secondary School Curriculum," *History Teacher* 48 (2015): 271–94; Nicholas D. Kristof, "Unmasking Horror—A Special Report: Japan Confronting Gruesome War Atrocity," *NYT*, March 17, 1995, 1; Laves and Thomson, *UNESCO*, 95–96.

68. *"The Defenses of Peace,"* Part 2, 30.

CHAPTER TWO

1. J. W. Fulbright, "Isolation and Foreign Policy: Commencement Address at Gettysburg College," April 26, 1943, 5, box 2, file 1; Fulbright, Address at American Design Awards Luncheon, May 1, 1946, Fulbright Papers, box 4, folder 11; J. W. Fulbright, "Peace through Education," November 1944, box 3, folder 27, all in JWF. Randall Bennett Woods, *Fulbright: A Biography* (Cambridge: Cambridge University Press, 1995), 107–9, 121; "End All Wars by Education: Fulbright's Back to School Plan," *Daily Express*, April 13, 1944, Decimal File 800.42/8–844, box 3251, RG 59.

2. Harry P. Jeffrey, "Legislative Origins of the Fulbright Program," *Annals of the American Academy of Political and Social Science*, Vol. 491, May 1987, 37; Lonnie Johnson, "The Making of the Fulbright Program, 1946–1961," in *The Legacy of J. William Fulbright: Policy, Power, and Ideology*, ed. Alessandro Brogi, Giles Scott-Smith, and David J. Snyder (Lexington: University of Kentucky Press, 2019), 152; National Humanities Center Steering Committee on the Future of the Fulbright Educational Exchange Program, *Fulbright at Fifty; Meeting the Challenge of the Next 50 Years* (National Humanities Center, Research Triangle Park, July 1997), iv.

3. Johnson, "The Making of the Fulbright Program," 153.

4. *HFSD,* Vol. 1, viii; *HFSD*, Vol. 2, Part 1, Unit 2: Europe, 27, 222–24; Peter Edson, "Surplus Education," *News*, July 30, 1946, box 58, file 13, JWF.

5. Haynes Johnson and Bernard M. Gwertzman, *Fulbright: The Dissenter* (Garden City, NY: Doubleday, 1968), 108. This is the origin of this account, and the reference, entirely unhelpful, is to a "private letter from Fulbright to a scholar, Fulbright files." Woods also emphasizes the garden party, drawing on Johnson and Gwertzman as well as an interview with Fulbright. See Woods, *Fulbright*, 130. That Fulbright introduced legislation to Congress the very next day also makes this story implausible.

6. Benjamin Fine, "Education in Review," *NYT*, September 23, 1945, 77.

7. *To Amend the Surplus Property Act: Hearings before the Committee on Expenditures in the Executive Departments*, 79th Cong. 97 (1946); *IND*, 19775; "Statement of John W. Snyder, Director of War Mobilization and Reconversion on Foreign Disposal," September 24, 1945, box 8, file 6, JWF.

8. *HFSD*, Vol. 1, iii; *HFSD*, Vol. 2, Part 4, 1, 19; *IND*, 19703, 19790; *HFSD*, Vol. 2 Part 2, 144–46; *HFSD*, Vol. 2, Part 5, 2.

9. *HFSD*, Vol. 2, Part 3, 3, 11; *HFSD*, Vol. 2, Part 7, 33–37; *HFSD* Vol. 2, Part 2, 198–99; *HFSD*, Vol. 2, Part 4, 19; "Exhibit 46, Chemical Warfare Technical Service Report of Surplus Declarations" in *IND*, 20425.

10. *IND*, 19533, 19535, 19549–50, 19556–57, 19574; 19626, 19790, 20179–81; *Special Committee Investigating National Defense: Executive Session with War and Navy Departments on Overseas Surplus Property*, May 9, 1945, 48, 51; "Statement of John W. Snyder"; "Final Report of Special Representative for Southeast Asia and Review of Activities between 30 August 1946 and 14 August 1947," August 30, 1947, box 1, file: Final Report, Special Representative Southeast Asia, Entry A1 401, RG 59; *HFSD*, Vol. 1, 124, 238; H. Wendell Endicott, "Call and Conference with R. W. Hadley Far Eastern Division Goodyear Tire and Rubber Export Company," October 31, 1945, box 9, file: Pacific Area Conference Reports, Entry 401, RG 59; Gerald F Barry, "General Reports on Malaya (including Singapore)," October 14, 1946, box 1, file: 1 November–1 December, Entry 401, RG 59.

11. *IND*, 19929–31, 19900–19904, 20022, 20032; *HFSD*, Vol. 2, Part 1, 10; Office of Field Commissioner, Shanghai, "Historical Report: 1 September to 1 October," xii, box 77, folder: China History September 1946, Entry 401, RG 59.

12. *IND*, 19623–25, 19655, 20002; *HFSD*, Vol. 2, Part 6, 23–24.

13. H. Wendell Endicott, "Memorandum," October 1945, box 8, file 6, JWF.

14. Thomas B. McCabe to Senator Fulbright, December 17, 1945, box 8, file 6, JWF.

15. *HFSD*, Vol. 1, iii, 7–8, 140–44; *Special Committee Investigating National Defense: Executive Session Overseas Subcommittee with State Department*, January 31, 1945, 70.

16. *HFSD*, Vol. 1, iii–iv, 13–14, 20–22; *Investigation of the National Defense Program, Subcommittee Session on Overseas Surplus Property*, May 29, 1945, 5–14; Harry S. Truman, Exec. Order No. 9630: Redistribution of Foreign Economic Functions and Functions with Respect to Surplus Property in Foreign Areas, September 27, 1945, APP; *To Amend the Surplus Property Act*, 79th Cong. 288–89.

17. "Statement by J. William Fulbright of Arkansas," September 1945, box 8, file 6, JWF Fulbright to John W. Swarthmore, February 11, 1946, box 11, file 1, JWF; *Foreign Educational Benefits and Surplus Property, Hearing before a Subcommittee of the Committee on Military Affairs*, 79th Cong. 2 (1946); *To Amend the Surplus Property Act*, 79th Cong. 292; *HFSD*, Vol. 1, 115–16.

18. 91 Cong. Rec. 12,123 (December 15, 1945); *Foreign Educational Benefits and Surplus Property, Hearing before a Subcommittee of the Committee on Military Affairs*, 79th Cong. 14 (1946); Jeffrey, "Legislative Origins of the Fulbright Program," 45–46; Woods, *Fulbright*, 128–34; Johnson, "The Making of the Fulbright Program," 157; 92 Cong. Rec. 10,214–15 (July 26, 1946).

19. *HFSD*, Vol. 1, 140–49; *Report to Congress on Foreign Surplus Disposal*, January 1949, US State Department Publication 3400 (Washington, DC: Government Printing Office, 1949), 7.

20. *HFSD*, Vol. 1, 53–55; "Notes from Staff Meeting," May 7, 1946, box 10, file: Pacific Area Reports of Conference, Leo R. Priwatley to Office of Inspector General, Exec HQ, US Army, Peiping, n.d., and Frank H. Hurst, "Certificate," April 2, 1947, both in box 11, file: Shanghai Reports, Historical, Kilburn R. Brown to Commissioner Endicott, "History 26 October 1945, 0930," October 26, 1945, box 9, file: Pacific Area Conference Reports, all in Entry 401, RG 59, *HFSD*, Vol. 2, Part 4, 34.

21. *HFSD*, Vol. 2, Part 4, 62–64; *Report to Congress on Foreign Surplus Disposal*, July 1949, US State Department Publication 3559 (Washington, DC: Government Printing Office, 1949), 8.

22. *HFSD*, Vol. 1, 166–76; *HFSD*, Vol. 2, Part 1, 60–62, 113–31; *HFSD*, Vol. 2, Part 4, 43–46, 68–71, 73–78, 82.

23. Office of Field Commissioner, Shanghai, "Historical Report: 1 September to 1 October," Exhibit 26, folder: China History September 1946, box 77, Entry 401, RG 59.

24. A further $30 million in debts was returned to the United States, to be used to pay US flag vessels to transfer goods to China. *Report to Congress on Foreign Surplus Disposal*, October 1946, US State Department Publication 2655 (Washington, DC: Government Printing Office, 1946), 21.

25. Jeffrey, "Legislative Origins of the Fulbright Program," 43; *Report to Congress on Foreign Surplus Disposal*, January 1947, US State Department Publication 2722 (Washington, DC: Government Printing Office, 1947), 9.

26. "Property Abroad," *WP*, April 24, 1946, 6; "A Good Swap," *NYT*, September 14, 1946, 4; "Student Exchange," *Toledo Blade*, August 10, 1946, box 58, file 13, JWF.

27. Institute of International Education, *Building Roads to Peace: Exchange of People between the United States and Other Countries* (New York: Institute of International Education, 1948); "A Weapon for Peace," *NYT*, December 25, 1946, 28.

28. William I. Nichols, "America's Next Move," *This Week*, July 15, 1945, 8, box 58, file 13; "U.S. Representative Fulbright Says Education Is Vital to Permanent Peace," box 58, file 25, "Address by Sen. J. W. Fulbright on Drew Pearson Program," July 31, 1949, box 7, file 28, all in JWF.

29. Tamson Pietsch and Meng-Hsuan Chou, "The Politics of Scholarly Exchange: Taking the Long View on the Rhodes Scholarship," in *Global Exchanges: Scholarships and Transnational Circulations in the Modern World*, ed. Ludovic Tournes and Giles Scott-Smith (New York: Berghahn, 2017), 38; Eckhardt Fuchs, "Educational Sciences, Morality and Politics: International Educational Congresses in the Early Twentieth Century," *Paedagogica Historica* 40 (October 2004): 757–84; Daniel Laqua, "Transnational Intellectual Cooperation, the League of Nations, and the Problem of Order," *Journal of Global History*, 6 (2011): 223–47; Proposals of Professor Stanislaw Loria in 1923 for an Institute of International Institute of Intellectual Leaders [sic], December 31, 1923, box 3, folder: CAME, UNECO and the Origins of UNESCO, CR, corr; Liping Bu, *Making the World Like Us: Education, Cultural Expansion and the American Century* (Westport, CT: Praeger, 2003), 34–36, 51–60, 95–104; Teresa Brawner Bevis and Christopher J. Lucas, *International Students in American Colleges and Universities: A History* (New York: Palgrave Macmillan, 2007), 6, 97–98, 85; Madeline Hsu, *The Good Immigrants: How the Yellow Peril Became the Model Minority* (Princeton, NJ: Princeton University Press, 2015), 63–64.

30. Proposals for the Programme of UNESCO, submitted by the Chinese Delegation, February 6, 1946, UNESCO/Prep.Com/42 UNESCO PC, Vol. 1; Alexander Kirk to Secretary of State, October 17, 1945, decimal file 800.42/10–1745, box 4131, Madeline Coury Dinu to Franklin Delano Roosevelt, June 12, 1943, decimal file

800.42/243, box 3247, Fred Esch to Franklin Delano Roosevelt, May 22, 1943, decimal file 800.42/238, box 3247, Felix Vali to Charles Thompson December 18, 1943, decimal file 800.42/357, box 324, H. A. Henderson to Ralph Turner, July 28, 1944, decimal file 800.42/7–2844, box 3252, Roger Domercq to Truman, November 22, 1945, decimal file 800.42/11–2245, box 4131, all in RG 59.

31. John Temple Graves, "This Morning," *Birmingham*, January 28, 1946, box 58, file 13, JFW.

32. "Charter Day Address," College of William and Mary, February 8, 1946, 2, box 4, file 6, JFW.

33. "Student Exchange Enlists 22 Nations," *NYT*, October 10, 1947, 27; "Current Information Regarding the Fulbright Educational Program of Interest to University Professors and Scholars," December 20, 1949, 1, box 94, file 2, CIES; Johnson, "The Making of the Fulbright Program, 1946–1961," 154, 175; Pietsch and Chou, "The Politics of Scholarly Exchange," 38; "Table 1: Awards Made in 1948," *Report on the Operations of the Department of State under Section 32 (B) (2) of Public Law 584*, H.R. Doc. No. 130, 81st Cong., 1st Sess., March 10, 1949, 6; "Table 1: Awards Made in 1949," *Report on the Operations of the Department of State under Public Law 584*, 81st Cong., 2d Sess., H.R. Doc. No. 527, March 14, 1950, 3; "Table 1: Awards Made in 1950," *Report on the Operations of the Department of State (under Public Law 584)*, 82d Cong., 1st Sess., H.R. Doc. No. 86, March 19, 1951, 5; *Report on the Operations of the Department of State under Public Law 584*, H.R. Doc. No. 3764, 84th Cong., 2d Sess. (Washington, DC: U.S. Government Printing Office, 1956), 6–7; Johnson and Gwertzman, *Fulbright: The Dissenter*, 108.

34. *HFSD*, Vol. 2, Part 2, 3, 191–94; *HFSD*, Vol. 2, Part 3, 1–2; "Study under the Fulbright Act," *Christian Science Monitor*, May 24, 1952; *IND*, 20019. Only 16,000 South African dollars were set aside for exchange each year; by 1955, only twenty exchanges had taken place. "South Africa Pays 50,000,000 to U.S," *NYT*, March 22, 1947, 30; "Pact on Surplus Signed," *NYT*, April 2, 1947, 2; *Report on the Operations of the Department of State under Public Law 584*, H.R. Doc. No. 3764, 84th Cong., 2d Sess. (Washington, DC: U.S. Government Printing Office, 1956), 29; "Educational Exchange Agreement with South Africa," *Department of State Bulletin* 26, no. 235 (April 21, 1952): 630.

35. "Netherlands, Norway Granted Credit to Buy U.S. Surpluses," *Wall Street Journal*, September 4, 1946, 3.

36. Sales ranked using the sales price of the major bulk sales, see *Report to Congress on Foreign Surplus Disposal*, July 1949, US State Department Publication 3559 (Washington, DC: Government Printing Office, 1949), 19. On the geographic distribution of early grants, see "Appendix 3: Recipients of Awards During Calendar Year 1948," *Report on the Operations of the Department of State under Section 32 (B) (2) of Public Law 584*, H.R. Doc. No. 130, 81st Cong., 1st Sess., March 10 1949; "Appendix 3: Recipients of Awards during Calendar Year 1949," *Report on the Operations of the Department of State under Public Law 584*, 81st Cong., 2d Sess., H.R. Doc. No. 527, March 14 1950; "Appendix 3: Recipients of Awards during Calendar Year 1950,"

Report on the Operations of the Department of State (under Public Law 584), 82d Cong., 1st Sess., H.R. Doc. No. 86, March 19, 1951.

37. "Professor Leaves for Foreign Study," *New York Amsterdam News*, January 28, 1950, 10; "WE Howard gets Fulbright Award," *Afro-American,* July 23, 1949, 1; "Georgian Receives Fulbright Fellowship for British Study," *Atlanta Daily World* July 14 1949, 1.

38. Bevis and Lucas, *International Students*, 61; Daniel Rodgers, *Atlantic Crossings: Social Politics in a Progressive Age* (Cambridge, MA: Belknap Press of Harvard University Press, 1998), 84–92; Guillaume Tronchet, "The Defeat of University Autonomy: French Academic Diplomacy, Mobility Scholarships and Exchange Programs (1880s to 1930s)," in Tournes and Scott-Smith, *Global Exchanges*, 50, 53, 57; Su-Lin Lewis, *Cities in Motion: Urban Life and Cosmopolitanism in Southeast Asia, 1920–1940* (Cambridge, UK: Cambridge University Press, 2016), chap. 5.

39. Paul Kramer, *Blood of Government: Race, Empire, the United States and the Philippines* (Chapel Hill: University of North Carolina Press, 2006), 204–5; Bevis and Lucas, *International Students*, 45–49, 75–76; Paul Kramer, "Is the World Our Campus? International Students and U.S. Global Power in the Long Twentieth Century," *Diplomatic History* 33(5) (2009): 783–84, 789; "Statement of the United States Senator J. W. Fulbright," September 27 1945, box 8, file 6, JWF; Benjamin Fine, "Education in Review," *NYT*, September 23, 1945, 77; Jeffrey, "Legislative Origins of the Fulbright Program," 40; Justin Hart, *Empire of Ideas: The Origins of Public Diplomacy and the Transformation of U.S. Foreign Policy* (New York: Oxford University Press, 2013), 17; Bu, *Making the World Like Us*, 146–48; Ninkovich, *Diplomacy of Ideas*, 39.

40. Ninkovich, *Diplomacy of Ideas*, 139; Kramer, "Is the World Our Campus?" 792.

41. Minutes of First Meeting, February 11, 1948, box 6, file 1, CIES; Ninkovich, *Diplomacy of Ideas*, 141–43; Greece got two votes to America's five, the Philippines, four. "General Report of the Executive Secretary," March 20 1948, box 107, file 36, Bureau of Educational and Cultural Affairs Historical Collection, Special Collections of University of Arkansas Libraries, Fayetteville, AR [hereafter CU collection]; "Italy and US Sign Pact on Student Exchanges," *NYT*, December 19, 1948; "Anglo-U.S. Unit Named on Student Exchange," *NYT*, September 23, 1948; "Proposed Agenda for October 8–9 Meeting," 9, box 12, file 13, JWF; Walter Johnson and Francis J. Colligan, *The Fulbright Program: A History* (Chicago: University of Chicago Press, 1965), 113–14; Tillman Durdin, "Educational Aid to China Mapped," *NYT*, December 18, 1947, 16; Tillman Durdin, "U.S., China at Odds on Cultural Fund," *NYT*, July 10, 1947, 11; Wilma Fairbank, *America's Cultural Experiment in China, 1942–1949* (Washington, DC: Bureau of Educational and Cultural Affairs, Department of State, 1976), 155–56; "Student Exchange Pact Is Concluded with China," *NYT*, November 10, 1947, 16.

42. "Report Submitted by the Conference Board of Associated Research Councils," October 14, 1948, box 3, file 9, CIES; Minutes of the Eighth Meeting, January 11, 1949, 3–4, box 6, file 2, CIES; Minutes of the Eighth Meeting, BFS, January 21–22, 1949, 7, box 12, file 13, JWF; Giles Scott-Smith, "The Fulbright Program in the Netherlands: An Example of Science and Diplomacy," in *Cold War Science and the*

Transatlantic Circulation of Knowledge, ed. Jeroen van Dongen (Leiden, Netherlands: Brill, 2015); Francis J. Colligan to Gordon T. Bowles, March 9, 1949, box 6, file 2, CIES.

43. Gilman G. Udell (Compiler), *Surplus Property Act of 1944 and Amendments* (Washington, DC: Government Printing Office, 1976), 36; "Table 2—Geographical Distribution," *State Department Report on Public Law 584*, 1950, 4; Fulbright to George V. Allen, October 4, 1948, box 4, file 5, JWF; Woods, *Fulbright*, 19.

44. Official program reports did not break grantees down by gender for these years, so I have, as best as possible, determined gender of grantees based on their names. See "Appendix 3: Recipients of Awards during Calendar Year 1948," *Report on the Operations of the Department of State under Section 32 (B) (2) of Public Law 584*, H.R. Doc. No. 130, 81st Cong., 1st Sess., March 10, 1949; "Appendix 3: Recipients of Awards during Calendar Year 1949," *Report on the Operations of the Department of State under Public Law 584*, 81st Cong., 2d Sess., H.R. Doc. No. 527, March 14, 1950; "Appendix 3: Recipients of Awards during Calendar Year 1950," *Report on the Operations of the Department of State (under Public Law 584)*, 82d Cong., 1st Sess., H.R. Doc. No. 86, March 19, 1951.

45. Thomas J. Hamilton, "Plan to Sell War Stocks for Foreign Scholarships," *NYT*, December 20, 1945, 1; "Veterans Ask Aid to Study Abroad," *NYT*, December 21, 1945, 19; "A Good Swap," *NYT*, September 14, 1946, 4; "Student Exchange," *WP*, February 19, 1946, 6; Molly Bettie, "Fulbright Women in the Global Intellectual Elite," in *The Legacy of J. William Fulbright: Policy, Power, and Ideology*, ed. Alessandro Brogi, Giles Scott-Smith, and David J. Snyder (Lexington: University of Kentucky Press, 2019), 183–86; "Summary of Proceedings," BFS Meeting, October 8–9, 1947, 4, box 108, file 35, CU Collection.

46. Jeffrey, "Legislative Origins of the Fulbright Program," 44; Woods, *Fulbright*, 334–39; Neal Allen, "The Power of the One-Party South in National Politics: Segregation in the Career of J. William Fulbright," in *The Legacy of J. William Fulbright: Policy, Power, and Ideology*, ed. Alessandro Brogi, Giles Scott-Smith, and David J. Snyder (Lexington: University of Kentucky Press, 2019), 32–45.

47. "Seek Assurance for Foreign Scholarships," *Atlanta Daily World*, September 29, 1946, 2; "Fisk Head Named to Foreign Study Board," *Afro-American*, August 2, 1947, 7; Fulbright to George V. Allen, August 4, 1948, Proposed Agenda for October 8–9 Meeting, 11, both in box 12, file 13, JWF; "Blacks Remain a Small Fraction of Fulbright Scholars," *Journal of Blacks in Higher Education* (Summer 2005): 32–33; "Ten Colored Students Have Fulbright Awards," *Pittsburgh Courier*, June 10, 1950, 6; "College Graduation Rate, by Sex, Nativity and Race, 1940–1997," table bc798–805, *Historical Statistics of the United States*, Millennial Online Edition, 2006.

48. Leonard R. Sussman, *The Culture of Freedom: The Small World of Fulbright Scholars* (Lanham, MD: Rowman and Littlefield, 1992), 57; Malvina Lindsay, "One World Campuses," *WP*, December 28,1946, 4; *Mutual Educational and Cultural Exchange Act, Hearings before the Committee on Foreign Relations*, 87th Cong. 20–22, 48–49 (1961); J. William Fulbright, "The International Exchange Program: A Progress Report," August 13, 1962, box 21, folder 37, JWF.

49. Kramer, "Is the World Our Campus?" 796.

50. Bu, *Making the World Like Us*, 159–62; Johnson, "The Making of the Fulbright Program," 160.

51. Benjamin Fine, "Big Foreign Quota of Students Urged," *NYT*, December 12, 1947, 17; "Summary of Proceedings," BFS Meeting, October 8–9, 1947, 3, box 108, file 35, CU Collection; Fulbright, "Role of Education in Foreign Affairs," November 5, 1948, 8, box 7, file, 3, JWF.

52. Bess Furman, "Scholarship Unit Named by Truman," *NYT*, July 18, 1947, 22; Martin R. P. McGuire to Fulbright, September 5, 1947, box 12, file 13.

53. J. William Fulbright, "A Report on the Political Aspects of the London Conference," CBS Broadcast, May 6, 1944, box 3, folder 3, JWF; J. William Fulbright, "Open Doors, Not Iron Curtains," *NYT*, August 5, 1951, 140; Tristram Coffin, *Senator Fulbright: Portrait of a Public Philosopher* (New York: Dutton, 1966), 84–88.

54. Fulbright, "Role of Education in Foreign Affairs."

55. Bettie, "Fulbright Women in the Global Intellectual Elite," 185; Alice Garner and Diane Kirkby, "Tactful Visitor, Scientific Observer, or 100 Percent Patriot? Ambassadorship in the Australia-US Fulbright Program," in Alessandro Brogi, Giles Scott-Smith, and David J. Snyder (eds.), *The Legacy of J. William Fulbright: Policy, Power, and Ideology* (Lexington: University of Kentucky Press, 2019), 200; Bu, *Making The World Like Us*, 184.

56. Craig Robertson, *The Passport in America: The History of a Document* (New York: Oxford University Press, 2010), 153–54; Jane C. Loeffler, *The Architecture of Diplomacy: Building America's Embassies* (New York: Princeton Architectural Press, 1998), 12–36, 47, 130; Ron Theodore Robin, *Enclaves of America: The Rhetoric of American Political Architecture Abroad, 1900–1965* (Princeton, NJ: Princeton University Press, 1996), 65.

57. Loeffler, *The Architecture of Diplomacy*, 32, 47, 50, 117; Robin, *Enclaves of America*, 138–41; *HFSD*, Vol. 1, 41, 121–22.

58. *HFSD*, Vol. 2, Part 1, Unit 1, 25–27, *IND*, 20149; Loeffler, *The Architecture of Diplomacy*, 45–46, 50, 171, 198–99; *HFSD*, Vol. 2, Part 2, 78; *Special Committee Investigating National Defense: Executive Session Overseas Subcommittee with State Department*, January 31, 1945, 45; History of the Office of the Central Field Foreign Liquidation Commissioner: Africa Middle East Theater, March 1946, Appendix II, box 75, folder: AMET History, March 1946, Entry A1 400, RG 59; *HFSD*, Vol. 2, Part 6, 84.

59. Loeffler, *The Architecture of Diplomacy*, 62, 66–67, 93.

60. In Latin America, the United States preferred a Spanish colonial style over a North American one. Loeffler, *The Architecture of Diplomacy*, 24–25, 56, 130; Robin, *Enclaves of America*, 75–82, 94, 99.

61. Loeffler, *The Architecture of Diplomacy*, 59–68, 213–16.

62. Loeffler, *The Architecture of Diplomacy*, 62–63, 95, 178; Andrew Friedman, *Covert Capital Landscapes of Denial and the Making of U.S. Empire in the Suburbs of Northern Virginia* (Berkeley: University of California Press, 2016), 59.

63. Loeffler, *The Architecture of Diplomacy*, 8; Hugh Wilford, *The Mighty Wurlitzer: How the CIA Played America* (Cambridge, MA: Harvard University Press, 2008), 101;

Ninkovich, *Diplomacy of Ideas*, 123–24; Michael Krenn, *The History of US Cultural Diplomacy: 1770 to the Present Day* (London: Bloomsbury, 2017), 71–75; Richard H. Pells, *Not Like Us: How Europeans Have Loved, Hated, and Transformed American Culture since World War II* (New York: Basic Books, 1997), 74–78.

64. Loeffler, *The Architecture of Diplomacy*, 62; "Uncle Sam's Bookstack in Cairo," *Christian Science Monitor* August 5, 1950, WM16; Dan Lacy, "The Overseas Book Program of the United States Government," *Library Quarterly* 24, no. 2 (1954): 178; Henry James, "The Role of the Information Library in the United States International Information Program," *Library Quarterly* 23 (April 1953): 75–86; Richard T. Arndt, *The First Resort of Kings: American Cultural Diplomacy in the Twentieth Century* (Washington, DC: Potomac Books, 2005), 150–60.

65. Graham, *Culture and Propaganda*, 151; White and Leigh, *Peoples Speaking to Peoples* (Chicago: University of Chicago Press, 1972 ed.), 75; Frederick Melcher to Charles Thomson, May 3, 1944, decimal file 800.42/571, box 3251, RG 59; Ninkovich, *Diplomacy of Ideas*, 90–91; John B Hench, *Books as Weapons: Propaganda, Publishing, and the Battle for Global Markets in the Era of World War II* (Ithaca, NY: Cornell University Press, 2010); Greg Barnhisel, *Cold War Modernists: Art, Literature, and American Cultural Diplomacy* (New York: Columbia University Press, 2015), 103, 107–8; Miriam Intrator, "UNESCO in France, France in UNESCO, and the Role of Libraries and Books in Postwar Cultural Reconstruction, 1945–1951," *Journal of the Western Society for French History* 40 (2012), cited from http://hdl.handle.net/2027/spo.0642292.0040.011; Sarah Brouillette, *UNESCO and the Fate of the Literary* (Redwood City, CA: Stanford University Press, 2019), 23–25, chap. 2, 87; James P. Sewell, *UNESCO and World Politics: Engaging in International Relations* (Princeton, NJ: Princeton University Press, 1975), 124–26; Walter H. C. Laves and Charles A. Thomson, *UNESCO: Purpose, Progress, Prospects* (Bloomington, Indiana University Press, 1957), 77–78; Jacob Zuckerman, "UNESCO Book Coupon Scheme," *Notes* 6 (March 1949): 236–38; *Overseas Information Programs of the United States, Hearings before a Subcommittee of the Senate Committee on Foreign Relations, Part 2*, 83d Cong. 909 (1953).

66. Friedman, *Covert Capital*, 58–59; Loeffler, *The Architecture of Diplomacy*, 56; "Diplomatic Titles Often Used to Protect Intelligence Aides," *WP*, December 5, 1979.

67. Jenifer Van Vleck, *Empire of the Air: Aviation and the American Ascendancy* (Cambridge, MA: Harvard University Press, 2013), chaps. 1–2; Alan Dobson, *A History of International Civil Aviation: From Its Origins through Transformative Evolution* (London: Routledge, 2017), 19–20; Anthony Sampson, *Empires of the Sky: The Politics, Contests and Cartels of World Airlines* (London: Cornet, 1985), 27–70.

68. Van Vleck, *Empire of the Air*, 82–84, 91, 106, chap. 4; Jeffrey A. Engel, *Cold War at 30,000 Feet: The Anglo-American Fight for Aviation Supremacy* (Cambridge, MA: Harvard University Press, 2007), 20, chap. 1; Dobson, *History of International Civil Aviation*, 38; Richardson Dougall, "The Office of Transport and Communications Policy," November 1947, 12–14, box 27, Entry A1 715: Drafts of Histories of State Department Organizational Unites and Functions during World War II, RG 59.

69. Elizabeth Borgwardt, *New Deal for the World: America's Vision for Human Rights* (Cambridge, MA: Belknap Press of Harvard University Press, 2005), 157; Woods, *Fulbright: A Biography*, 80; Van Vleck, *Empire of the Air*, 107, 109–10, 117; Samuel Zipp, "Dilemmas of World-Wide Thinking: Popular Geographies and the Problem of Empire in Wendell Willkie's Search for *One World*," *Modern American History* 1 (2018): 295–319.

70. Van Vleck, *Empire of the Air*, 171–72; Dobson, *History of International Civil Aviation*, 8–12.

71. Van Vleck, *Empire of the Air*, 69, 167–68.

72. "Postwar Civil and Military Air Rights Abroad Other than at Destroyer Bases—Determination of Rights Desired," May 17, 1945, "Disposition of War-Time Air Bases and Routes—State Dept Policy toward Abandonment of Airports," April 16, 1945, both in folder: ACC: Air Bases and Rights Part 1, box 2, P47.

73. Van Vleck, *Empire of the Air*, 173–74.

74. Van Vleck, *Empire of the Air*, 10; Dobson, *Peaceful Air Warfare*, 144.

75. Henry A. Wallace, "Freedom of the Air—A Momentous Issue," *NYT*, June 27, 1943, SM3; Clare Booth Luce, "America in the Post-War Air World," *Vital Speeches of the Day*, March 15, 1943, 331–36; Woods, *Fulbright*, 78–79.

76. Sampson, *Empires of the Sky*, 100; Henry Ladd Smith, *Airways Abroad: The Story of American World Air Routes* (Madison: University of Wisconsin Press, 1950), 204–24; Dobson, *Peaceful Air Warfare*, 156; Garrison Norton to Kennan, September 10, 1948, folder: Aviation, box 5, Entry A1 558B: Policy Planning Staff Subject files, 1947–1962, RG 59; "Organization and Procedure–Continuity between the Old ACC and the New ACC," September 24, 1946, folder: ACC: Air Bases and Rights Part 1, box 2, P47; S. Gruneck, to Air Coordinating Committee, February 5, 1946, folder: Foreign Aviation Fields, box 205, Entry P26: Air Coordinating Committee Subject files, 1945–1960, Record Group 220: Records of Temporary Committees, Commissions and Boards, NARA II, MD; Henry L. Stimson, "Policy of the War Department in Regard to Post-War Civil Aviation," April 20, 1944, box 26, RG 197.

77. Dobson, *History of International Civil Aviation*, 44–46; Engel, *Cold War at 30,000 Feet*, 41.

78. Proposals for Consideration by the Principal Committee, June 19, 1943, box 26, folder: International Aviation Policy Reports, RG 197; Van Vleck, *Empire of the Air*, 185–91; Dobson, *History of International Civil Aviation*, 59–60.

79. Sampson, *Empires of the Sky*, 84; Van Vleck, *Empire of the Air*, 191.

80. David Mackenzie, "The Bermuda Conference and Anglo-American Aviation Relations at the End of the Second World War," *Journal of Transport History* 12 (March 1991): 63; Dobson, *Peaceful Air Warfare*, 148; Dobson, *History of International Civil Aviation*, 41; Van Vleck, *Empire of the Air*, 180–81.

81. Smith, *Airways Abroad*, 164, 179; Dobson, *Peaceful Air Warfare*, 164–68; Van Vleck, *Empire of the Air*, 187–90. A further two states ratified it with important reservations. Dobson, *History of International Civil Aviation*, 52.

82. Van Vleck, *Empire of the Air*, 192–93; Proposals for Consideration by the Principal Committee, June 19, 1943, box 26, folder: International Aviation Policy Reports, RG

197; *HFSD*, Vol. 1, 138; "Postwar Civil and Military Air Rights Abroad Other than at Destroyer Bases—Determination of Rights Desired," May 17, 1945, folder: ACC: Air Bases and Rights Part 1, box 2, P47.

83. Dobson, *Peaceful Air Warfare*, 187; Dobson, *History of International Civil Aviation*, 54; Mackenzie, "The Bermuda Conference," 66–67; Van Vleck, *Empire of the Air*, 193–94; James L. Gormly, "Opening and Closing Doors: US Postwar Aviation Policy: 1943–1963," *Journal of Transatlantic Studies* 13 (July 2015): 260.

84. *Civil Aviation Agreements, Hearings before the Committee on Commerce on S.1814*, 79th Cong. 42, 51–52, 59, 76 (1946); Smith, *Airways Abroad*, 247–64.

85. *IND*, 20107–11; "Egypt Holding Up Operations of TWA," *NYT*, October 22, 1945, 2; *HFSD*, Vol. 2, Part 2, 62–64, 125; "Excerpt from ACC Minutes of Meeting of June 23 1945," folder: ACC: Air Bases and Rights Part 1, box 2, P47; "Egypt and Britain in Joint Air Deal," *NYT*, April 24, 1946, 15; "Foreign Lines Bidding for Egypt Airfields," *NYT*, April 4, 1945, 10; "U.S. and Egypt Sign Supplies-Air Pact," *NYT*, June 16, 1946, 20; Gene Currivan, "Airfield Is Given to Egypt by U.S," *NYT*, December 16, 1946, 10.

86. Gormly, "Opening and Closing Doors," 252; *HFSD*, Vol. 2, Part 1, 30, 275–83; "U.S., France in Pact on Air Transport," *NYT*, March 28, 1946, 16; Leo C. Cyr, "Facilities for International Civil Aviation," *Department of State Bulletin*, July 27, 1947, 169–71.

87. Van Vleck, *Empire of the Air*, 194; "US China Air Pact Ready for Signing," *NYT*, December 1, 1946, 36.

88. "US China Air Pact Ready for Signing," *NYT*, December 1, 1946, 36; Giles Scott-Smith and David J. Snyder, "A Test of Sentiments: Civil Aviation Politics and the KLM Challenge in Dutch-American Relations," *Diplomatic History* 37 (2013): 917–45.

89. Department of State Office of the Foreign Liquidation Commissioner, *Report to Congress on Foreign Surplus Disposal*, October 1946, US State Department Publication 2655, 6.

CHAPTER THREE

1. "World Travel: A New Era of United Nations Friendship," *Free World*, September 1945, 49–51.

2. Minutes of International Conference of International Tourist Organisations, First Session, 7–11, ECEFP CFT 21/46, box 65, folder: Documents 21/46, CFT; Second Plenary Meeting Minutes, April 15, 1947, ECONF/PASS/PC/SR/2, box 1, folder: Meeting of Govt Experts Docs 2 of 3, RCEPFF; Executive Committee on Economic Foreign Policy, "Comments on ECOSOC Item 9," July 23, 1947, box 183, folder: Passports and Frontier Formalities, OIC.

3. "Ten Bound for Palestine Barred from Sailing, Passports Seized," *NYT*, June 12, 1948, 1.

4. This chapter explores what Ronen Shamir has called the "Mobility Regime"—the conjoined tendency of globalization to promote travel and movement on the one hand, and to suspiciously police, monitor, and screen travelers on the other. These

processes have been intertwined for decades, well before late-twentieth-century globalization. Ronen Shamir, "Without Borders? Notes on Globalization as a Mobility Regime," *Sociological Theory* 23 (2005): 197–217.

5. George A. Mooney, "Organized Campaign Undertaken to Fight for Single World Passport," *NYT*, June 2, 1946, D1; Donald C. Belarus, "Memorandum of the Air Transport Association: International Air Commerce in the Western Hemisphere," June 27, 1946, CFT D-15/46, box 65, folder: Documents 11/46–20/46, CFT.

6. Preparatory Memorandum, E/CONF/PASS/PC/2, December 5, 1946, box 1, folder: Meeting of Experts to Prepare for World Conference on Passports and Frontier Formalities, RCEPFF; Adam Mckeown, "Global Migration, 1846–1940," *Journal of World History* 15(2004): 155–89; Dirk Hoerder, *Migrations and Belongings, 1870–1945* (Cambridge, MA: Harvard University Press, 2016); Andreas Fahrmeir, "Passports and the Status of Aliens," in *The Mechanics of Internationalism: Culture, Society and Politics from the 1840s to the First World War*, ed. Martin H. Geyer and Johannes Paulmann (Oxford: Oxford University Press, 2001), 93–120; Tara Zahra, "Travel Agents on Trial: Policing Mobility in East Central Europe, 1889–1989," *Past and Present* 223 (2014): 161–93.

7. John Torpey, *The Invention of the Passport: Surveillance, Citizenship, and the State* (New York: Cambridge University Press, 2000); Craig Robertson, *The Passport in America: The History of a Document* (New York: Oxford University Press, 2010); Alan Dowty, *Closed Borders: The Contemporary Assault on Freedom of Movement* (New Haven, CT: Yale University Press, 1987); Aristide Zolberg, *A Nation by Design: Immigration Policy in the Fashioning of America* (Cambridge, MA: Harvard University Press, 2006), 240–41; Alison Bashford, "Immigration Restriction: Rethinking Period and Place from Settler Colonies to Postcolonial Nations," *Journal of Global History* 9 (2014): 26–48; Brooke Blower, *Becoming Americans in Paris: Transatlantic Politics and Culture between the World Wars* (Oxford: Oxford University Press, 2011), 22.

8. Milton Bracker, "Political Barriers," *NYT*, December 12, 1948, x17; "An American Traveler Reports on Travel Restrictions as They Exist Today in the Central American Republics," CFT D/11/46, June 4, 1946, box 65, folder: Documents 11/46–20/46, CFT.

9. Preparatory Memorandum, December 5, 1946, E/CONF/PASS/PC/2 box 184, folder: Passports and Frontier Formalities Conference, 1947, 2 of 2, OIC; Cole, American Legation, Addis Ababa, to Secretary of State, May 13, 1947, box 184, folder: Passports and Frontier Formalities Conference, 1947, 1 of 2, OIC; Belarus, "Memorandum of the Air Transport Association."

10. Glenda Sluga, *Internationalism in the Age of Nationalism* (Philadelphia: University of Pennsylvania Press, 2013), 86; Dowty, *Closed Borders*, 222.

11. "Formalities Hampering International Travel: Report of the Committee of Experts for the Simplification of Formalities in International Transport," March 6, 1947, "Preliminary Memoranda," E/CONF/PASS/PC/2/Add.2, March 12, 1947, both in box 184, folder: Passports and Frontier Formalities Conference, 1947, 2 of 2, OIC. L. Welch Pogue, President, Committee for World Travel Inc., "Proposed Program," January 8, 1947, box 126A, folder: TLC Miscellaneous, TPC; George A. Mooney,

"Organized Campaign Undertaken to Fight for Single World Passport," *NYT*, June 2, 1946, D1.

12. Minutes of International Conference of International Tourist Organisations, First Session, n.d., 14–21, ECEFP CFT 21/46, box 65, folder: Documents 21/46, CFT.

13. Minutes of International Conference of International Tourist Organisations, October 1, 1946, Afternoon Session, October 3, 1946 (Afternoon Session), October 4, 1946 all in box 65, folder: Documents 21/46, CFT.

14. George Tait and Herbert Wilkinson, Confidential Report on International Conference of National Tourist Organizations, November 22, 1946, ECEFP CFT 21/46, box 65, folder: Documents 21/46, CFT; Minutes of International Conference of International Tourist Organisations, October 1, 25–26, 1946, Afternoon Session, ECEFP CFT 21/46, box 65, folder: Documents 21/46, CFT.

15. Preparatory Memorandum, E/CONF/PASS/PC/2, December 5, 1946, box 1, folder: Meeting of Experts to Prepare for World Conference on Passports and Frontier Formalities, RCEPFF; Elizabeth Fagg, "New Travel Goals," *NYT*, October 5, 1941, xx1; "Conference Material Submitted by Passport Division Relative to Item 1 of the Agenda," n.d., box 184, folder: Passports and Frontier Formalities Conference, 1947, 2 of 2, OIC.

16. Preparatory Memorandum, December 5 1946, E/CONF/PASS/PC/2; "Draft Agenda for Meeting of Experts to Prepare for a World Conference on Passports and Frontier Formalities," December 4 1946, UN Doc E/CONF/PASS, PC/1, both in box 184, folder: Passports and Frontier Formalities Conference, 1947, 2 of 2, OIC. George Tait, "Report of the US Delegation," April 25, 1947, box 184, folder: Passports and Frontier Formalities Conference, 1947, 1 of 2, OIC.

17. W. A. Harriman to Winthrop W. Aldrich, December 8, 1946, Harriman to James Byrnes, December 11, 1946, both in box 184, folder: Passports and Frontier Formalities Conference, 1947, 2 of 2, OIC; Victor Sebestyen, *1946: The Making of the Modern World* (New York: Vintage, 2016), 90.

18. Maurice E. Gilmore, "Latin American Aspects of Postwar Tourism," *Foreign Commerce Weekly*, January 12, 1946, box 65, folder: Documents 1/46–10/46, CFT; W. A. Harriman to Winthrop W. Aldrich, December 8, 1946, box 184, folder: Passports and Frontier Formalities Conference, 1947, 2 of 2, OIC.

19. "Conference Material Submitted by Dept of Commerce: Background Material on Importance of Travel in Foreign Trade," addendum to W. L. Clayton to George Tait and Wilkinson, September 24, 1946, Herbert Wilkinson, to Members of Interdepartmental Committee on Foreign Travel Policy, November 8, 1946, CFT D-20/46, both in box 65, folder: Documents 11/46–20/46, CFT; "Introductory Statement Submitted by Department of State for the Guidance of EE Schnellbacher and Eugene M Braderman," n.d., ECAFE/6(f), box 68, folder: CFT Working Papers, CFTWP.

20. Gilmore, "Latin American Aspects of Postwar Tourism"; Minutes of March 20, 1947, Meeting of Committee on Foreign Travel, box 68, folder: CFT Minutes, 1946–1947, ECEFP; "Conference Material Submitted by Dept of Commerce: Background

Material on Importance of Travel in Foreign Trade," September 24, 1946, box 65, folder: Documents 11/46–20/46, CFT.

21. "Recommendations to Be Considered at ECAFE Travel Meeting," CFT D-15/49, September 13, 1949, box 67, folder, CFT Documents, CFT; Anthony J. Stanonis, *Faith in Bikinis: Politics and Leisure in the Coastal South since the Civil War* (Athens: University of Georgia Press, 2014), 51; Jennifer Van Vleck, *Empire of the Air: Aviation and the American Ascendancy* (Cambridge, MA: Harvard University Press, 2013), 211; "Freedom of Movement," *Editorial Research Reports*, August 20, 1948; Marcy to Degolia, "S. Res.111," May 13, 1947, box 126A, folder: TLC Correspondence, TPC; Alan Dobson, *A History of International Civil Aviation: From Its Origins through Transformative Evolution* (London: Routledge, 2017), 23; "Pan Am's Dole a Personal Thing," *WP*, July 24, 1955, E5.

22. "Introductory Statement Submitted by Department of State for the Guidance of EE Schnellbacher"; Gilmore, "Latin American Aspects of Postwar Tourism"; "Freedom of Movement," *Editorial Research Reports*, August 20, 1948.

23. Oliver McKee, "Good Will Spread: Uncle Sam Tells Latin-Americans of the Many Advantages of Making Trips Here," *NYT*, October 22, 1939, 141; "Mrs. Rohde Named to $1-a-Year Post," *NYT*, March 26, 1939, 58.

24. "Statements of Proposed Policies Respecting Int'l Tourist Travel," February 7, 1947, box 126A, folder: TLC Correspondence, TPC; Carr to Wilcox, September 24, 1946, box 65, folder: CFT Membership, ECEFP corr.

25. The CFT had first been formed in October 1945, but due to lackluster leadership, poorly attended meetings, and a too-narrow focus on technical matters, it accomplished almost nothing in its first year. It was therefore reconstituted in November 1946. Executive Committee on Economic Foreign Policy, "Reconstitution of Committee on Foreign Travel," September 7, 1946, ECEFP D-73/46, box 68, folder: CFT Working Papers, CFTWP; Minutes of November 19, 1946 Meeting of Committee on Foreign Travel, box 68, folder: CFT Minutes, 1946–1947, ECEFP.

26. "Ex-official Dead at 49," *WP*, April 11, 1957, B2; Jay Walz, "Research on Travel," *NYT*, November 19, 1950, x26.

27. "Recommendations of the Interdepartmental Committee on Foreign Travel Concerning the US Position on Passports and Border Formalities," February 14, 1947, TLC D-4, box 126, folder: TLC Documents, TPC; H. A. Wilkinson "Suggested US Position on Passports," December 11, 1946, CFT D-25/46, box 65, folder: Documents 22/46–27/46, CFT; W. L. Clayton to George Tait and Wilkinson, September 24, 1946, box 65, folder: Documents 11/46–20/46, CFT; "Conference Material Submitted by Passport Division Relative to Item 1 of the Agenda," n.d., box 184, folder: Passports and Frontier Formalities Conference, 1947, 2 of 2, OIC; "Memorandum for Committee on Foreign Travel," December 18, 1946, CFT D-26/46, box 65, folder: Documents 22/46–27/46, CFT; "Draft Outline of Proposals for the Expansion of World Travel," CFT D-2/47, January 23, 1947, box 66, folder: Documents 1/47–7/47, CFT.

28. Wilkinson, "Foreign Travel Policy Statement," December 23, 1946, CFT D-27/46, box 65, folder: Documents 22/46–27/46, CFT.

29. Clair Wilcox to Frank Waring, n.d.; Clair Wilcox, "Memorandum: American Tourist Trade," August 22, 1945, box 65, folder: CFT General, CFT; Carr to Schaetzel, September 4, 1946, box 65, folder: Documents: CFT General, CFT; Nitze to Carr, October 10, 1946, box 65, folder: CFT Membership, ECEFP Corr.; Canty to Stevens, "Intradepartmental Committee on Foreign Travel," January 10, 1947, box 65, folder: CFT General, CFT; Travel Policy Committee Minutes, February 5, 1947, box 126A, folder: TLC Minutes, TPC.

30. Travel Policy Committee Minutes, February 25, 1947, box 126A, folder: TLC Minutes, TPC.

31. *Control of Travel from and into the United States, Hearings before the Committee on Foreign Affairs*, 65th Cong., 2d Sess. 6, 26, 29, 31 (February 13, 1918); "Senate Accepts Sedition Bill," *NYT*, May 5, 1918, 7; "Proceedings of Congress and Committees in Brief," *WP*, May 14, 1918, 6; Woodrow Wilson, "Proclamation 1473—Issuance of Passports and Granting of Permits to Depart from and Enter the United States," August 8, 1918, APP.

32. *Control of Travel from and into the United States, Hearings before the Committee on Foreign Affairs*, 65th Cong., 2d Sess. 38 (February 13, 1918); "Refuses to Extend Wartime Passport," *NYT*, May 18, 1920, 20; "An Act Making Appropriations for the Diplomatic and Consular Service for the Fiscal Year Ending June 30, 1922," March 2, 1921, Pub. L. No. 357 66th Cong., 1217; "Need Passports No Longer," *NYT*, April 5, 1921, 15.

33. "Strachey Barred under Visa Law," *NYT*, October 16, 1938, 77; Abba P. Schwartz, "The Role of the State Department in the Administration and Enforcement of the New Immigration Law," *Annals of American Academy of Political and Social Science* 367 (September 1966): 97; Calvin Coolidge, Exec. Order No. 4382A: Rules Governing the Granting and Issuing of Passports in the US, February 12, 1926; Calvin Coolidge, Exec. Order No. 4800: Rules Governing the Granting and Issuing of Passports in the US, January 31, 1928; Herbert Hoover, Exec. Order No. 5860: Rules Governing the Granting and Issuing of Passports in the United States, June 22, 1932; Franklin Delano Roosevelt, Exec. Order No. 7856: Rules Governing the Granting and Issuing of Passports in the US, March 31, 1938; Daniel A. Farber, "National Security, the Right to Travel, and the Court," *Supreme Court Review* 1981 (1981): 266.

34. Julia Rose Kraut, "Global Anti-Anarchism: The Origins of Ideological Deportation and the Suppression of Expression," *Indiana Journal of Global Legal Studies* 19 (Winter 2012): 169–93; United States Commission on Government Security, *Report of the Commission on Government Security*, S. Doc. 64 (1957), 527–30; Beverly Gage, *The Day Wall Street Exploded: A Story of America in Its First Age of Terror* (Oxford: Oxford University Press, 2009), 119–22; An Act to Amend the Act Entitled "An Act to Exclude and Expel from the US Aliens Who Are Members of the Anarchistic and Similar Classes," June 5, 1920, 51 Stat. 1008; Eliot B. Coulter, "Visa Work of the Department of State and Foreign Service," US State Department Publication 3649, October 1949, 2; Robert A. Divine, *American Immigration Policy, 1924–1952* (New Haven, CT: Yale University Press, 1957), 104–7; "Distinction between Social Democrats and Communists," Foreign Service Serial No. 252, September 30, 1944, box 1, folder:

Communists 1947–1950, Entry: A1 1505: Bureau of Security and Consular Affairs Records Relating to Passports, 1940–1953, RG 59; J. A. Zumoff, " 'Is America Afraid of the Truth?' The Aborted North American Trip of Shapuriji Saklatvala, MP," *Indian Economic and Social History Review* 53 (July 2016): 405–47; Woods, *Fulbright: A Biography*, 31.

35. G. Howland Shaw to Norman H. Davies, December 9, 1920, Adee to Shaw, December 11, 1920, R. W. Flournoy to Joseph R. Baker, June 2, 1921, Henry Stimson, "Memo: Issue of Passports to Communists," May 5, 1931, all in *The Right to Travel: Hearing before the Subcommittee on Constitutional Rights Pursuant to S. Res. 49*, 85th Cong. 334, 345, 352–56 (1957).

36. Ashley J. Nicholas, Chief Passport Legal Division, "Geographic Limitations on Validity of Passports during the Past 40 Years and Their Application to the Cases of Journalists," *The Right to Travel: Hearing before the Subcommittee on Constitutional Rights Pursuant to S. Res. 49*, 85th Cong., 1st Sess. 190 (April 4, 1957); David Riesman Jr., "Legislative Restrictions on Foreign Enlistment and Travel," *Columbia Law Review* (1940): 807, 828; Maxine Davis, "Mrs Shipley Says No," *Saturday Evening Post*, May 11, 1940, 31–125; Peter N. Carroll, *The Odyssey of the Abraham Lincoln Brigade: Americans in the Spanish Civil War* (Stanford, CA: Stanford University Press, 1994); Franklin Delano Roosevelt, Exec. Order No. 7856: Rules Governing the Granting and Issuing of Passports in the US, March 31,1938.

37. Edward P. Hutchinson, *Legislative History of American Immigration Policy, 1798–1965* (Philadelphia: University of Pennsylvania Press, 1981), 258; Richard Breitman and Allan J. Lichtman, *FDR and the Jews* (Cambridge, MA: Belknap Press of Harvard University Press, 2013), 162–80; "Sharp Limit Is Set on Entry of Aliens," *NYT*, June 15, 1940, 9; Paul A. Kramer, "The Geopolitics of Mobility: Immigration Policy and American Global Power in the Long Twentieth Century," *American Historical Review* 123 (April 2018): 394.

38. *To Amend the Act of May 22, 1918: Unpublished Hearings re. H.R. 4973, House Committee on Foreign Affairs, Executive Session*, 77th Cong. n.p. (June 6, 1941); "An Act to Authorize the Refusal of Visas to Aliens Whose Admission into the US Would Endanger the Public Safety," June 20, 1941, 55 Stat. 252; "An Act to Amend the Act of May 22, 1918," 55 Stat. 252; "Text of the President's Address Depicting Emergency Confronting the Nation," *NYT*, May 28, 1941, 1; "Congress Sets up Checks on Aliens," *NYT*, June 21, 1941, 1.

39. Harold B. Hinton, "Guardian of American Passports," *NYT*, April 27, 1941, SM 21; United States Commission on Government Security, *Report of the Commission on Government Security*, S. Doc. 64 (1957), 447; Jeffrey Kahn, *Mrs. Shipley's Ghost: The Right to Travel and Terrorist Watchlists* (Ann Arbor: University of Michigan Press, 2013), 107; "Worldwide Check on American Passports," *NYT*, January 1, 1940, 1; Graham H. Stuart, "Safeguarding the State through Passport Control," *Department of State Bulletin*, June 10, 1945, p. 1066–70.

40. Graham H. Stuart, "Visa Division," June 1944, folder: Visa Division, box 27, "Memo from Visa Division to Mr. Long, March 5, 1941, Appendix 3B," folder: Visa Division, box 28, "Work of the Visa Division in Eliminating the Influence

and Activities of the Axis in American Republics," May 4, 1942, Appendix folder: Visa Division, box 28, all in Entry A1 715: Drafts of Histories of State Department Organizational Units and Functions during World War II, RG 59; Divine, *American Immigration Policy*,104–7; "Visa Rules Set Up as a Defense Move," *NYT*, June 25, 1941, 22; "New Visa Rules May Be Enacted," *NYT*, September 30, 1941, 10.

41. "Mexican Painter Barred," *NYT*, March 24, 1949, 3; "Communist Visitors to US Hit by Visas," *Christian Science Monitor*, January 26, 1948, 10; Edward T. Folliard, "Canterbury Red Dean, Denied Visa, Waits Wallace's Election," *WP*, August 24, 1948, 1; Mary Ann Glendon, *A World Made New: Eleanor Roosevelt and the Universal Declaration of Rights* (New York: Random House, 2001), 111; Louis L. Jaffe, "The Right to Travel: The Passport Problem," *Foreign Affairs* 35 (October 1956): 24; "Leo Isacson, 86, Upset Winner of a Bronx Congressional Seat," *NYT*, September 25, 1996; Farber, "National Security, the Right to Travel and the Court," 275–76.

42. United States Commission on Government Security, *Report of the Commission on Government Security*, S. Doc. 64 (1957), 544; *Fees Charged for Passports and for Visiting Foreign Passports, Hearings before Committee on Foreign Affairs*, 66th Cong. 20 (February 3, 4, 7, 1926).

43. Comment, "Passport Refusals for Political Reasons: Constitutional Issues and Judicial Review," *Yale Law Journal* 61 (1952): 173; Jaffe, "The Right to Travel: The Passport Problem," 23; Robert Konikow, "Machine Records Installation for Passport Division," February 8, 1946, untitled folder, box 2, Entry A1 1505: Bureau of Security and Consular Affairs Records Relating to Passports, 1940–1953, RG 59; Dorothy Fosdick, "The Passport—and the Right to Travel," *NYT*, July 17, 1955, SM8; United States Commission on Government Security, *Report of the Commission on Government Security*, S. Doc. 64 (1957), 462–63. G. Howland Shaw to Norman H Davies, December 9, 1920 and State Dept. press release, June 18, 1952, cited in *The Right to Travel: Hearing before the Subcommittee on Constitutional Rights pursuant to S. Res. 49*, 85th Cong. 181, 249–51, 356 (1957); Andre Visson, "Ruth Shipley—The State Department's Watchdog," *Readers Digest*, October 1951, 74; *Security and Constitutional Rights: Hearings before the Subcommittee on Constitutional rights pursuant to S. Res. 94*, 84th Cong. 168 (1955); *Passport Legislation: Hearings before the Committee on Foreign Relations*, 85th Cong. 41 (1958); Maxine Davis, "Mrs Shipley Says No," *Saturday Evening Post*, May 11, 1940, 31–125.

44. "Woman's Place Also in the Office, Finds Chief of the Nation's Passport Division," *NYT*, December 24, 1939, 22; "No Final Action Taken," *NYT*, January 6, 1948, 14; Maxine Davis, "Mrs Shipley Says No," *Saturday Evening Post*, May 11, 1940, 31–125; Harold B. Hinton, "Guardian of American Passports," *NYT*, April 27, 1941, SM 21; Helen Worden Erskine, "You Don't Go If She Says No," *Colliers*, July 11, 1953, 62–65; Visson, "Ruth Shipley," 73–76; Kahn, *Mrs. Shipley's Ghost*, 110.

45. Stuart, "Visa Division," "Statement of Duties and Responsibilities of Positions in the Visa Division," n.d., Appendix 5, folder: Visa Division, box 28, Entry A1 715: Drafts of Histories of State Department Organizational Units and Functions during World War II, RG 59.

46. Erskine, "You Don't Go If She Says No," *Colliers*, 63.

47. "Work of the Visa Division in Eliminating the Influence and Activities of the Axis"; Stuart, "Visa Division"; American Embassy in Panama to Secretary of State, August 17, 1948, folder: Administration, 1947–1951, box 1, BSC; Christopher Simpson, *Blowback: The First Full Account of America's Recruitment of Nazis, and Its Disastrous Effect on Our Domestic and Foreign Policy* (New York: Weidenfeld and Nicolson, 1988), 109.

48. "He Can't See Red," *CT*, July 24, 1948, 6; "Report of Spies in UN Disputed by Marshall," *CT*, July 22, 1948, 4; "Scrutiny Dims Report of Spies in UN Employ," *Christian Science Monitor*, July 24, 1948, 17; "Those UN Communists," *NYT*, July 24, 1948, 14; "Text of the Report," press release no. 699, September 1, 1948, folder: General, 1946–1948, box 1, BSC; "State Dept Aid Put on Spot for Attack on Reds," *CT*, September 16, 1948, 3; "Alexander Is Reprimanded for Charging Subversives Entered Country through UN," *NYT*, October 22, 1948, 17; "Marshall Starts UN 'Spy' Inquiry," *NYT*, July 29, 1948, 1; "Evidence of Spies Seen Nil in UN Agents Admitted to U.S.," *Christian Science Monitor*, September 1, 1948, 3.

49. Travel Policy Committee Minutes, February 25, 1947, box 126A, folder: TLC Minutes, TPC; Shipley to James Reber, February 5, 1947, James Reber to Walter Chapman, "Travel Policy Committee," September 8, 1947, both in box 126A, folder: TLC Correspondence, TPC.

50. Travel Policy Committee Minutes, February 26, 1947, box 126A, folder: TLC Minutes, TPC; ECEFP Committee on Foreign Travel, "Recommended US Policy Respecting Passport, Visa and Frontier Formalities for Non-immigrant International Travel," March 12, 1947, ECEFP D-41/47, box 126A, folder: TLC Miscellaneous, TPC.

51. First Plenary Meeting Minutes, April 14, 1947, ECONF/PASS/PC/SR/1, Second Plenary Meeting Minutes, April 15, 1947, ECONF/PASS/PC/SR/2 both in box 1, folder: Meeting of Govt Experts Docs 2 of 3, RCEPFF; Report to Economic and Social Council, April 25, 1947, ECONF/PASS/PC/13 rev.2, box 1, folder: Meeting of Experts to Prepare for World Conference on Passports and Frontier Formalities, RCEPFF.

52. "Proposals by the Govt of the UK," ECONF/PASS/PC/9, April 15, 1947, box 1, folder: Meeting of Experts to Prepare for World Conference on Passports and Frontier Formalities, RCEPFF; "Recommended US Policy Respecting Passport, Visa and Frontier Formalities for Non-immigrant International Travel," as approved by ECEFP on March 28, 1947, ECEFP d-56/47, June 27, 1947, box 66, folder: Documents 1/47–7/47, CFT; "Preparatory Papers by PD and VD Relative to the Geneva Meeting of Experts on Passports and Border Formalities," February 20,1947, TLC D-5, box 126, folder: TLC Documents, TPC; Fourth Plenary Meeting Minutes, April 16, 1947, ECONF/PASS/PC/SR/4, box 1, folder: Meeting of Govt Experts Docs 2 of 3, RCEPFF; Van Courtland Short, Memorandum, April 25, 1946, CFT d-6/46, box 65, folder: Documents 1/46–10/46, CFT; "Passport Service Is Self-Supporting," *NYT*, April 23, 1922, 39; "Woman to Head Passport Bureau," *NYT*, May 20, 1928, 111; Robertson, *The Passport in America*, 223; John Hanna, "Passports—For Revenue Only," *Atlantic Monthly*, February 1929, 264–68; *Departments of State, Justice, Commerce, and the Judiciary Appropriations for 1953: Department of State, Part 1, Hearings before the Subcommittee of the Committee on Appropriations, House of Representatives*, 82d Cong.

1129–33 (1952); Response of US Govt to Secretary-General re. US Practices, to US Representative ECOSOC, July 18, 1947, box 184, folder: Passports and Frontier Formalities Conference, 1947, 1 of 2, OIC.

53. Second Plenary Meeting Minutes, April 15, 1947, ECONF/PASS/PC/SR/2, box 1, folder: Meeting of Govt Experts Docs 2 of 3, RCEPFF; Minutes of International Conference of International Tourist Organisations, October 1, Afternoon Session, 15, ECEFP CFT 21/46, box 65, folder: Documents 21/46, CFT; "Conference Material Submitted by Passport Division Relative to Item 1 of the Agenda," n.d., box 184, folder: Passports and Frontier Formalities Conference, 1947, 2 of 2, OIC; Preparatory Memorandum, December 5, 1946, E/CONF/PASS/PC/2 box 184, folder: Passports and Frontier Formalities Conference, 1947, 2 of 2, OIC.

54. Travel Policy Committee Minutes, September 19, 1947, box 126A, folder: TLC Minutes, TPC; Acheson to US Delegation, April 17, 1947, box 184, folder: Passports and Frontier Formalities Conference, 1947, 1 of 2, OIC; G. J. Haering, to Clayton, October 15, 1946, box 65, folder: CFT General, CFT; ECEFP Committee on Foreign Travel, "Recommended US Policy Respecting Passport, Visa and Frontier Formalities for Non-immigrant International Travel," March 12, 1947, ECEFP D-41/47, box 126A, folder: TLC Miscellaneous, TPC.

55. "Suggestions by the US as to Recommendations by the Meeting of Experts at Geneva," ECONF.PASS/PC.7, April 14, 1947, box 1, folder: Meeting of Experts to Prepare for World Conference on Passports and Frontier Formalities, RCEPFF; Response of US Govt to Secretary-General re. US Practices, To US Representative ECOSOC, July 18, 1947, box 184, folder: Passports and Frontier Formalities Conference, 1947, 1 of 2, OIC; Fifth Plenary Meeting Minutes, April 17, 1947, ECONF/PASS/PC/SR/5, box 1, folder: Meeting of Govt Experts Docs 2 of 3, RCEPFF.

56. "Report of Meeting of Experts to Prepare for a World Conference on Passports and Frontier Formalities," July 16, 1947, ECEFP D-104/47, box 66, folder: Documents 9/47–20/47, CFT; George Tait, "Report of the US Delegation to the Meeting of Experts to Prepare for a World Conference on Passports and Frontier Formalities," April 25, 1947, box 184, folder: Passports and Frontier Formalities Conference, 1947, 1 of 2, OIC; Minutes of October 17, 1947, Meeting of Committee on Foreign Travel, box 68, folder: CFT Minutes, 1946–1947, ECEFP.

57. "US Position re Inter-American Tourist Cards," August 27, 1947, TLC D-10/2, box 126, folder: TLC Documents, TPC; Milton Bracker, "US Against Easing Travel Restraints," *NYT*, February 21, 1949, 5; Milton Bracker, "Hemisphere Touring," *NYT*, February 27, 1949, X15; Travel Policy Committee Minutes, October 6, 1948, box 126A, folder: TLC Minutes, TPC.

58. Travel Policy Committee Minutes, August 22, 1947, box 126A, folder: TLC Minutes, TPC.

59. G. J. Haering, to Clayton, October 15, 1946, box 65, folder: CFT General, CFT; Boykin to Gerald Smith, July 13, 1948, folder: General, 1946–1948, box 1, BSC; H. H. Kelly, "The Place of the Department of State in the Travel Field: Draft," November 1948, box 126A, folder: TLC Correspondence, TPC.

60. Alexander to Owen, December 22, 1947, box 126A, folder: TLC Correspondence, TPC.

61. Alexander to Owen, December 22, 1947, box 126A, folder: TLC Correspondence, TPC.

62. Milton Bracker, "Hemisphere Touring," *NYT*, February 27, 1949, X15; George A. Mooney, "Organized Campaign Undertaken to Fight for Single World Passport," *NYT*, June 2, 1946, D1; Travel Policy Committee Minutes, August 22, 1947, box 126A, folder: TLC Minutes, TPC.

63. W. A. Harriman to Winthrop W. Aldrich, December 8, 1946, and "Conference Material Submitted by Passport Division Relative to Item 1 of the Agenda," n.d., both in box 184, folder: Passports and Frontier Formalities Conference, 1947, 2 of 2, OIC; W. L. Clayton to George Tait and Wilkinson, September 24, 1946, box 65, folder: Documents 11/46–20/46, CFT.

64. Untitled Minutes, n.d., box 68, folder: CFT Working Papers, CFTWP; ECEFP Subcommittee on Foreign Travel, "U.S. Position on Second International Conference of National Travel Organizations," September 12, 1947, CFT D-26/47, box 66, folder: Documents 21/47–33/47, CFT.

65. Travel Policy Committee Minutes, September 19, 1947, box 126A, folder: TLC Minutes, TPC; Minutes of September 12, 1947, Meeting of Committee on Foreign Travel, box 68, folder: CFT Minutes, 1946–1947, ECEFP; Untitled Minutes, n.d., box 68, folder: CFT Working Papers, CFTWP; ECEFP Subcommittee on Foreign Travel, "US Position on Development of a World Travel Organization," CFT D-25/47, box 66, folder: Documents 21/47–33/47, CFT; Subcommittee on Foreign Travel of ECEFP, "Preliminary Draft Paper on Governmental Organization in Field of Foreign Travel," December 18, 1947, CFT D-33/47, box 126, folder: TLC Documents, TPC; Travel Policy Committee Minutes, January 7, 1948, box 126A, folder: TLC Minutes, TPC; Travel Policy Committee Minutes, January 21, 1948, box 126A, folder: TLC Minutes, TPC.

This organization, focused on international travel, would have been distinct from the US Travel Bureau, later known as the Travel Division, that had been created within the Department of the Interior in 1937 to promote travel within the United States.

66. Untitled Minutes, n.d., box 68, folder: CFT Working Papers, CFTWP.

67. Minutes of October 17,1947 Meeting of Committee on Foreign Travel, box 68, folder: CFT Minutes, 1946–1947, ECEFP; Tait and Wilkinson, "Report of the U.S. Representatives to the Second International Conference of National Travel Organizations," October 1–4, 1947, ECEFP CFT D-2/48, box 67, folder: Documents 1/48–10/48, CFT; Kenneth Campbell, "UN For Traveler," *NYT*, October 19, 1947, x15; Bertram M. Gordon, "Touring the Field: The Infrastructure of Tourism History Scholarship," *Journal of Tourism History* 7 (2015): 138.

68. Excerpt from memo by Mr. Farley, September 10, 1947, box 183, folder: Passports and Frontier Formalities, OIC; Farley to Allison, "UN Conference on Passport and Frontier Formalities," November 13, 1947, box 183, folder: Passports and Frontier

Formalities, OIC; Alexander to Kelly, August 3, 1950, box 1, folder: Meeting of Govt Experts Docs 1 of 3, RCEPFF.

69. Harry Fox, "UN and Tourism," *NYT*, March 5, 1950, 110; "U.N. Traffic Convention," *NYT*, April 6, 1952, X19.

70. Minutes of Meeting of Subcommittee on Foreign Travel, CFT M-6/48, August 9, 1948, box 68, folder: CFT Minutes, 1948–1952, ECEFP; Jay Walz, "Research on Travel," *NYT*, November 19, 1950, x26; "Travel Union Optimistic," *NYT*, January 28, 1951, x17; Paul Hofmann, "Europe in 1953: International Travel Officials Look for Another Record Travel Season," *NYT*, October 19, 1952, X17; Gordon, "Touring the Field," 138–39.

71. Minutes of Meeting of Subcommittee on Foreign Travel, CFT M-6/48, August 9, 1948, Minutes of Meeting of Subcommittee on Foreign Travel, CFT M-6/49, November 15, 1949, Minutes of Meeting of Subcommittee on Foreign Travel, CFT M-1/49, January 7, 1949, Minutes of Meeting of Subcommittee on Foreign Travel, CFT M-6/49, November 15, 1949, Minutes of Meeting of Subcommittee on Foreign Travel, CFT M-1/50, February 14, 1950, all in box 68, folder: CFT Minutes, 1948–1952, ECEFP; Charles Sawyer, "International Travel Program Initiated by the United States," *Foreign Commerce Weekly*, November 8, 1948, TLC D-22, box 126A, folder: TLC Documents, TPC; Christopher Endy, *Cold War Holidays: American Tourism in France* (Chapel Hill: University of North Carolina Press, 2004), esp. chap. 2; "Freedom of Movement," *Editorial Research Reports*, August 20, 1948; Torpey, *Invention of the Passport*, 143–57.

72. Theodore Pozzy in Minutes of Meeting of Subcommittee on Foreign Travel, CFT M-1/49, January 7, 1949, box 68, folder: CFT Minutes, 1948–1952, ECEFP; Van Vleck, *Empire of the Air*, 212; Endy, *Cold War Holidays*, 45, 54, 73.

73. Minutes of a Meeting between the U.S. Delegation to the Third Inter-American Travel Congress and Representatives of the Committee on Facilitation of Inter-American Transport, February 10, 1949, box 68, folder: CFT Working Papers, CFTWP; "End to Latin American Curbs on Travel Is Urged," *NYT*, October 28, 1948, 59; Minutes of Meeting of Subcommittee on Foreign Travel, CFT M-1/50, February 14, 1950, box 68, folder: CFT Minutes, 1948–1952, ECEFP; Fox, "UN and Tourism."

74. Olive Brooks, "All the Americas," *NYT*, June 27, 1954, x15; "Uniform Passport Pushed against Firm U.S. Rejection," *Christian Science Monitor*, July 9, 1954, 7.

75. A. L. Simmons, "Red Tape Barrier," *NYT*, June 29, 1952, x23.

76. Minutes of Meeting of Subcommittee on Foreign Travel, CFT M-5/50, September 25, 1950, Minutes of Meeting of Subcommittee on Foreign Travel, CFT M-5a/50, September 29, 1950, Minutes of Meeting of Subcommittee on Foreign Travel, CFT M-6/50, October 9, 1950, all in box 68, folder: CFT Minutes, 1948–1952, ECEFP. "Cuban Free Entry Is Revoked by US," *NYT*, August 25, 1950, 5; "Cuba Set to Retaliate by Requiring U.S. Visas," *NYT*, August 26, 1950, 6; "Cuba to Continue No Visa Policy," *NYT*, December 1, 1950, 16.

77. Mario Daniels, "Controlling Knowledge, Controlling People: Travel Restrictions of U.S. Scientists and National Security," *Diplomatic History* 43 (January 2019): 5; Thomas Ehrlich, "Passports," *Stanford Law Review* 19 (1966): 143; Steffen Mau et al.,

"The Global Mobility Divide: How Visa Policies Have Evolved over Time," *Journal of Ethnic and Migration Studies* 41, no. 8 (July 3, 2015): 1192–213; Mathias Czaika, Hein de Haas, and María Villares-Varela, "The Global Evolution of Travel Visa Regimes," *Population and Development Review* 44 (September 2018): 589–622; Brendan Whyte, "Visa-Free Travel Privileges: An Exploratory Geographical Analysis," *Tourism Geographies* 10, no. 2 (April 28, 2008): 127–49.

78. "Two-Way Tourism," *Editorial Research Reports*, April 19, 1961.

CHAPTER FOUR

1. Raymond Clapper, "World Will Be a 'City Beat Desk' after the War, Clapper Predicts," *EP*, May 23, 1942, 6; Walter E. Schneider, "Enlightened Role for US Press in World Outlined by Sulzberger," *EP*, August 14, 1943, 5.

2. "Cooper Regrets Delay in UNO Press Action," *EP*, February 16, 1946, 18; "Congress Adopts World Free News Resolution," *EP*, September 23, 1944, 12; "Links Peace to Free Press," *Baltimore Sun*, September 9, 1944, 4; Full Report of ASNE Committee on Freedom of Information, 5, reprinted as supplement to *Editor and Publisher*, June 18, 1945; Margaret A. Blanchard, *Exporting the First Amendment: The Press-Government Crusade of 1945–1952* (New York: Longman, 1986), 24–25.

3. Arthur Robb, "Shop Talk at 30," *EP*, May 1, 1943, 48; Full Report of ASNE Committee on Freedom of Information, 5; "World Press Conference," *EP*, April 27, 1946, 78; Kenneth Cmiel, "Human Rights, Freedom of Information, and the Origins of Third-World Solidarity," in *Truth Claims: Representation and Human Rights*, ed. Mark Philip Bradley and Patrice Petro (New Brunswick, NJ: Rutgers University Press, 2002), 111.

4. "Freedom of Information," editorial, *EP*, May 4, 1946, 34.

5. Kent Cooper, *Barriers Down: The Story of the News Agency Epoch* (New York: Farrar and Rinehart, 1942), 90–91, 106–7; Blanchard, *Exporting the First Amendment*, 9–15; William Reed, "50 Years of Resolutions Form Stage for UN Talks," *EP*, April 12, 1947, 13.

6. Cooper, *Barriers Down*, 7. On the history of the news agencies, see Terhi Rantanen, "Foreign Dependence and Domestic Monopoly: The European News Cartel and U.S. Associated Presses, 1861–1932," *Media History* 12, no. 1 (2006): 19–35; Oliver Boyd-Barrett, *The International News Agencies* (Beverly Hills, CA: SAGE, 1990); Jonathan Fenby, *The International News Services* (New York: Schocken Books, 1986); Heidi Tworek, *News from Germany: The Competition to Control World Communications, 1900–1945* (Cambridge, MA: Harvard University Press, 2019); James R. Brennan, "International News in the Age of Empire," in *Making News: The Political Economy of Journalism in Britain and American from the Glorious Revolution to the Internet*, ed. Richard R. John and Jonathan Silberstein-Loeb (Oxford: Oxford University Press, 2015).

7. Cooper, *Barriers Down*, 11–13; Jill Hills, *The Struggle for Control of Global Communication: The Formative Century* (Champaign: University of Illinois Press, 2002), 136–44; Emily Rosenberg, *Spreading the American Dream: American Economic and*

Cultural Expansion (New York: Hill and Wang, 1982), 88–89; Daniel R. Headrick, *The Invisible Weapon: Telecommunications and International Politics, 1851–1945* (New York: Oxford University Press, 1991), 101.

8. Llewellyn White and Robert D. Leigh, *Peoples Speaking to Peoples* (Chicago: University of Chicago Press, 1972 ed.), 60; Rantanen, "Foreign Dependence and Domestic Monopoly," 27; Dwayne Roy Winseck and Robert M. Pike, *Communication and Empire: Media, Markets, and Globalization, 1860–1930* (Durham, NC: Duke University Press, 2007), 202, 274; Cooper, *Barriers Down*, 98–99, 119–25.

9. Headrick, *Invisible Weapon*, 28, 195–98; Rosenberg, *Spreading the American Dream*, 91; Hills, *Struggle for Control of Global Communication*, 169–71.

10. Cooper, *Barriers Down*; Rosenberg, *Spreading the American Dream*, 97–99; Boyd-Barrett, *International News Agencies*; Fenby, *International News Services*.

11. David Wilson to William Benton, February 1, 1946, box 7, folder: AP #1, Entry A1 568D: Records of Assistant Secretary of State for Public Affairs, RG 59; "Note on Sources–Report on International Mass Communication," May 31, 1945, 5, box 2, folder 11, HC; White and Leigh, *Peoples Speaking to Peoples*, 19, 44–45; Jill Hills, *Telecommunications and Empire* (Champaign: University of Illinois Press, 2007), 35; Daniel Immerwahr, *How to Hide an Empire: A History of the Greater United States* (New York: Farrar, Straus and Giroux, 2019), 288–90.

12. "Acute Shortage of Journalists Exists Abroad," *EP*, December 27, 1947, 22.

13. "$1,000,000 a Year Voted for Cooper's Global AP Aim," *EP*, April 21, 1945, 15; "UP and AP Expand Foreign Feature Sales," *EP*, August 11, 1945, 46.

14. Herbert I. Schiller, *Communication and Cultural Domination* (White Plains, NY: M.E. Sharpe, 1976), 29.

15. "U.S. to Launch Free World News Talks," *EP*, November 25, 1944, 21; "United Nations Call Invites Freedom of Information Plan," *EP*, February 17, 1945, 7; "Cooper Regrets Delay in UNO Press Action," *EP*, February 16, 1946, 18; Blanchard, *Exporting the First Amendment*, 55.

16. White and Leigh, *Peoples Speaking to Peoples*, 79; Thomas H. Guback, "Hollywood's International Market," in *The American Film Industry*, ed. Tino Balio (Madison: University of Wisconsin, 1985), 465–67; Emily Rosenberg, "Transnational Currents in a Shrinking World," in *A World Connecting: 1870–1945*, ed. Emily Rosenberg (Cambridge, MA: Belknap Press of Harvard University Press, 2012), 977; Richard H. Pells, *Not Like Us : How Europeans Have Loved, Hated, and Transformed American Culture since World War II* (New York: Basic Books, 1997), 205–29; Anne L. Foster, *Projections of Power: The United States and Europe in Colonial Southeast Asia, 1919–1941* (Durham, NC: Duke University Press, 2010), chap. 3; Victoria De Grazia, *Irresistible Empire: America's Advance through Twentieth-Century Europe* (Cambridge, MA: Belknap Press of Harvard University Press, 2005), chap. 6; Robert Sklar, *Movie-Made America: A Cultural History of American Movies* (New York: Vintage Books, 1994), 47; Brooke Blower, *Becoming Americans in Paris: Transatlantic Politics and Culture between the World Wars* (Oxford: Oxford University Press, 2011), 78–79.

17. Ian Jarvie, "The Postwar Economic Foreign Policy of the American Film Industry," *Film History* 4 (1990): 277–88; Diana Lemberg, *Barriers Down: How American Power and*

Free-Flow Policies Shaped Global Media (New York: Columbia University Press, 2019), 20–21, 55–56; Thomas Zeiler, *Free Trade, Free World: The Advent of GATT* (Chapel Hill: University of North Carolina Press, 1999), 130–34; Toby Miller and Richard Maxwell, "Film and Globalization," in *Communications Media, Globalization and Empire*, ed. Oliver Boyd-Barrett (Bloomington: Indiana University Press, 2007), 33–52; Guback, "Hollywood's International Market," 481; Pells, *Not Like Us*, 212–29.

18. Henry Luce, "The American Century," *Diplomatic History* 23 (1999): 159–71.

19. "Hoyt Calls on Editors to Spur Freedom Fight," *EP*, May 11, 1946, 10; "Atom Bomb Makes New Freedom Essential to Civilization—Hoyt," *EP*, August 11, 1945, 59; "Sees Obligation to Extend Free Press around World," *EP*, May 22, 1943, 9.

20. Lloyd Free, Progress Report to Benton, March 7, 1947, box 5, folder: Lloyd Free, UNFOI; Lemberg, *Barriers Down*, 55–56.

21. UNESCO Constitution, art. 1.2(a), cited from http://portal.unesco.org/en/ev.php-URL_ID=15244&URL_DO=DO_TOPIC&URL_SECTION=201.html.

22. Those "technical" organizations had their own politics, as Sarah Nelson's forthcoming dissertation explicates brilliantly; see "Networking Empire: International Organizations, American Power, and the Struggle over Global Communications in the 20th Century" (PhD diss., Vanderbilt University, 2021). See also, Hills, *Telecommunications and Empire*, 48–51; Frank Beyersdorf, "Freedom of Communication: Visions and Realities of Postwar Telecommunication Orders in the 1940s," *Journal of Policy History* 27, no. 3 (2015): 492–520.

23. MacLeish to Acheson, December 30, 1945, MacLeish to Acheson, January 29, 1946, both in box 1, folder: Dean Acheson, AM; MacLeish to Benton, January 5, 1946, box 1, folder: William Benton, AM; Agreement for Facilitating the International Circulation of Visual and Auditory Materials of an Educational, Scientific and Cultural Character, December 10, 1948, cited from http://portal.unesco.org/en/ev.php-URL_ID=12064&URL_DO=DO_TOPIC&URL_SECTION=201.html.

24. "Special Group to Study Press," *EP*, June 15, 1946, 72; "UN Group on Press Freedom Set to Function in April," *EP*, February 15, 1947, 10; "Step by Step Progress in UN," *EP*, April 12, 1947, 13.

25. Dina Fainberg, "Unmasking the Wolf in Sheep's Clothing: Soviet and American Campaigns against the Enemy's Journalists, 1946–1953," *Cold War History* 15 (2015): 155–78; "Binder Held by Russians Then Freed," *EP*, September 28, 1946, 20; "Eastern Europe Nations Expel US Writers," *EP*, November 8, 1947, 10; "Stalin Tells Stassen: People Distrust Press," *EP*, April 19, 1947, 24; "Polish News Ban Endangers Loan," *EP*, May 18, 1946, 7; "Poles Suppress News So U.S. Suspends Loan," *CT*, May 11, 1946, 4.

26. "US Fights to Kill Soviet Press Proposal," *EP*, October 25, 1947, 68; Gannet, "Winchell Reply to Vishinsky," *EP*, October 4, 1947, 13.

27. William Reed, "Soviet Loses in UN on Censorship Vote," *EP*, October 11, 1947, 8; William Reed, "UN Change from 'Peace' to 'War' Ends Row," *EP*, November 1, 1947, 8; Blanchard, *Exporting the First Amendment*, 135.

28. Blanchard, *Exporting the First Amendment*, 162; "Instrument of Policy," editorial, *EP*, October 18, 1947, 42; "World Press Conference," editorial, *EP*, August 9, 1947, 40; "UN Press Agenda," *EP*, June 7, 1947, 54.

29. Lloyd Free to Howland Sargeant, Memo: Benton's Conference with the President, October 23, 1947, box 5, folder: Freedom of Information, UNFOI; Memo from Lovett to Sargeant, February 13, 1948, Sargeant to Lovett, December 23, 1947, Benton to Hugh S. Baillie, February 13, 1948, all in box 1, folder: US Delegation 1, UNFOI; William Benton, Memo to Mr. Lovett, January 19, 1948, box 250, folder: 2, William Benton Papers, University of Chicago Special Collections, Chicago.

30. Conference on Freedom of Information Annotated Agenda, March 4, 1948, 8, box 2, folder: Delegate's file, UNFOI.

31. William Reed, "Censorship, Propaganda on Freedom Parley Agenda," *EP*, May 31, 1947, 7; "Clash of Ideas Faces Freedom Commission," *EP*, May 25, 1946, 57.

32. Blanchard, *Exporting the First Amendment*, 160; Summary Record of the Second Meeting of Committee I, UN Doc e/conf.6/c.1/sr2, box 3, UNFOI.

33. Conference on Freedom of Information Annotated Agenda, March 4, 1948, 9, box 2, folder: Delegate's file, UNFOI; Press Release of Benton's Address at Geneva, March 25, 1948, box 2, folder: US Delegate Documents, UNFOI.

34. William Reed, "French Submit Plans for Press Freedom," *EP*, March 22, 1947, 11; Summary Record of the Eleventh Meeting of Committee I, e/conf.6/c.1/sr/11, box 3, UNFOI; *Miami Herald Publishing Co. v. Tornillo*, 418 U.S. 241 (1974); Cmiel, "Human Rights, Freedom of Information," 121.

35. Conference on Freedom of Information Annotated Agenda, March 4, 1948, 1, box 2, folder: Delegate's file, UNFOI; Blanchard, *Exporting the First Amendment*, 188–89.

36. "UN Debate Bares Dissent on American Freedom Ideals," *EP*, May 18, 1946, 21; Cmiel, "Human Rights, Freedom of Information," 114.

37. Conference on Freedom of Information Annotated Agenda, March 4, 1948, 32, box 2, folder: Delegate's file, UNFOI; Blanchard, *Exporting the First Amendment*, 189; Erwin Canham, "International Freedom of Information," *Law and Contemporary Problems* 14 (Autumn 1949): 595; Dawson to Delegation, Attitude toward French Convention, April 3, 1948, Minutes of US Delegation Meeting, March 15, 1948, William Benton, Address on Convention on the Gathering and Transmission of News, April 19, 1948, Convention on the Gathering and International Transmission of News, n.d., all in box 2, folder: US Delegation files, UNFOI.

38. Draft Convention on the Gathering and International Transmission of News, Annex A in Final Act of the UN Conference on Freedom of Information, April 22, 1948, E/CONF.6/79, box 2, folder: Final Act, UNFOI.

39. Conference on Freedom of Information Annotated Agenda, March 4, 1948, 11–12, box 2, folder: Delegate's file, UNFOI; Fainberg, "Wolf in Sheep's Clothing," 166–68; Personal correspondence with Fainberg; "US Invoked 1918 Law to Limit Red Writers," *EP*, October 4, 1947, 8.

40. *Headquarters Agreement between the UN and USA Signed at Lake Success*, June 26, 1947, cited from *International Organization* 2 (February 1948), 164–72; Mrs. Shipley to Boykin, Re.: Operation of the Headquarters Agreement, January 14, 1952, box 2, folder: PD UN 1952, Entry A1 1505: Bureau of Security and Consular Affairs Records Relating to Passports, 1940–1953, RG 59; "Austin Denies U.S. Broke UN Accord by

Seizing Newsmen," *Boston Globe*, January 1, 1948, 10; "UN Writer Calls Arrest an Insult," *NYT*, January 10, 1948, 4; "Mixup on UN Reporters Laid to Lack of Liaison," *EP*, December 27, 1947, 52; "Lie Reminds U.S. of Pact as 2nd UN Writer Is Held," *NYT*, December 23, 1947, 1; "U.S. Demands Change of UN Regulations on Correspondents," *Boston Globe*, December 25, 1947, 5; "United Nations Headquarters Agreement," *American Journal of International Law* 42 (April 1948): 447; Neal Stanford, "UN Has Last Word on Visas for Its Reporters," *Christian Science Monitor*, January 13, 1948, 10; Neal Stanford, "US and UN Seek to Settle Clash on Alien Newsmen," *Christian Science Monitor* January 24, 1948, 3; "US Again Objects to UN Reporter," *NYT*, June 20, 1950, 21; "UN Press Unit Protests," June 3, 1950, 4; "Secretariat," *International Organization*, 4, no. 2 (May 1950): 307–9.

41. Mr. Hendrick to Mr. Bohlen, Confidential Memo on UN Conference on Freedom of Information, March 22. 1948, box 5, folder: Freedom of Information, UNFOI; Conference on Freedom of Information Annotated Agenda, March 4, 1948, 27, box 2, folder: Delegate's file, UNFOI; Summary Record of the Fifth Meeting of Committee II, UN Doc e/conf.6/c.2/sr/5, box 4, UNFOI; Blanchard, *Exporting the First Amendment*, 177.

42. Peter J. Humphreys, *Media and Media Policy in Germany: The Press and Broadcasting since 1945* (New York: Berg, 1990), 24–40; Victor Sebestyen, *1946: The Making of the Modern World* (New York: Vintage, 2016), 359–60; John Dower, *Embracing Defeat*, 405–40.

43. Ian M. Rose, "Barring Foreigners from Our Airwaves: An Anachronistic Pothole on the Global Information Highway," *Columbia Law Review* 95 (June 1995): 1195–96; Note, "Government Exclusion of Foreign Political Propaganda," *Harvard Law Review* 68 (June 1955): 1399–403; Burt Neuborne and Steven R. Shapiro, "The Nylon Curtain: America's National Border and the Free Flow of Ideas," *William & Mary Law Review* 26 (1985): 735–36; Brett Gary, *The Nervous Liberals: Propaganda Anxieties from World War I to the Cold War* (New York: Columbia University Press, 1999), 195–216; Murray L. Schwartz and James C. N. Paul, "Foreign Communist Propaganda in the Mails: A Report on Some Problems of Federal Censorship," *University of Pennsylvania Law Review* 107 (March 1959): 621–26; *Dennis v. United States*, 341 U.S. 494 (1951); Claudius O. Johnson, "The Status of Freedom of Expression under the Smith Act," *Western Political Quarterly* 11 (1958): 469–80; Geoffrey R. Stone, *Perilous Times: Free Speech in Wartime, From the Sedition Act of 1798 to the War on Terrorism* (New York: Norton, 2004), 312–426.

44. Minutes of US Delegation Meeting, April 6, 1948; US Delegation Position on Covenant Article Concerning Freedom of Information, n.d., both in box 2, folder: US Delegates Documents, UNFOI; Summary Record of the Fifth Meeting of Committee IV, UN Doc e/conf.6/c.4/sr/5, box 4, RG 43.

45. Memorandum of Conversation, March 27, 1948, box 1, folder: Memorandum of Conversation 1 through 8, UNFOI; Summary Record of the Thirteenth Meeting of Committee 1, UN Doc e/conf.6/c.1/sr13, box 3, UNFOI; "UN Debate Revives Responsibility Issue," *EP*, February 1, 1947, 76; Summary Record of the Sixteenth Meeting of Committee 2, UN Doc e/conf.6/c.2/sr/16, box 4, UNFOI. On Chang, see Lydia H. Liu, "Shadows of Universalism: The Untold Story of Human Rights around

1948," *Critical Inquiry* 40, no. 4 (June 2014): 385–417. On Mehta, see Mary Ann Glendon, *A World Made New: Eleanor Roosevelt and the Universal Declaration of Rights* (New York: Random House, 2001), 38, 90, 111.

46. Blanchard, *Exporting the First Amendment*, 181; Summary Record of the Fifth Meeting of Committee I, UN Doc e/conf.6/c.1/sr/5, box 3, UNFOI.

47. Keith Roberts, "Antitrust Problems in the Newspaper Industry," *Harvard Law Review* 82 (1968), 342–44; Michael Stamm, *Dead Tree Media: Manufacturing the Newspaper in Twentieth-Century North America* (Baltimore: Johns Hopkins University Press, 2018), 5–6; "Economic Barriers to Truth Emphasized," *EP*, December 21, 1946, 30; Summary Record of the Tenth Meeting of Committee III, UN Doc e/conf.6/c.3/sr/10, box 4, UNFOI; Report of the US Delegates, May 7, 1948, box 2, folder: US Delegates Report, UNFOI; Intelligence Unit of The Economist, UNESCO, and the FAO, *Paper for Printing—Today and Tomorrow* (Paris: UNESCO, 1952); Intelligence Unit of the Economist, *The Problem of Newsprint and Other Printing Paper* (Paris: UNESCO, 1949), 53–54; Lemberg, *Barriers Down*, 52–63.

48. Anne Applebaum, *Iron Curtain: The Crushing of Eastern Europe, 1944–1956* (New York: Doubleday, 2012), 184; Blanchard, *Exporting the First Amendment*, 160, 322; Dower, *Embracing Defeat*, 436; Hugh Wilford, *The Mighty Wurlitzer: How the CIA Played America* (Cambridge, MA: Harvard University Press, 2008), 24.

49. "Newsprint and Information," editorial, *EP*, December 7, 1946, 44; Summary Record of the Ninth Meeting of Committee IV, UN Doc e/conf.6/c.4/sr/9, Summary Record of the Fifth Meeting of Committee IV, UN Doc e/conf.6/c.4/sr/5, Summary Record of the Tenth Meeting of Committee IV, UN Doc e/conf.6/c.4/sr10, all in box 4, UNFOI No author, Telegram, April 7, 1948, box 5, folder: Freedom of Information, RG 43.

50. Blanchard, *Exporting the First Amendment*, 192; William Benton, Confidential Report, n.d., box 2, folder: FOI Reports; Report of the US Delegates, May 7, 1948, box 2, folder: US delegates report, UNFOI.

51. William Benton, Confidential Report, n.d., Appendix 1: Memo from Chafee, box 2, folder: FOI Reports, UNFOI.

52. Summary Record of the Tenth Meeting of Committee IV, UN Doc e/conf.6/c.4/sr/10, box 4, UNFOI; Minutes of US Delegation Meeting, April 15, 1948, box 2, folder: US Delegates Documents, UNFOI; US Delegates Report, May 7, 1948, box 2, folder: FOI Reports, UNFOI.

53. See Sam Lebovic, *Free Speech and Unfree News: The Paradox of Press Freedom in America* (Cambridge, MA: Harvard University Press, 2016).

54. Report of the US Delegates, May 7, 1948, box 2, folder: US Delegates Report, UNFOI; William Benton, Confidential Report, n.d., Appendix 1: Memo from Chafee, box 2, folder: FOI Reports, UNFOI; William Benton, Confidential Report, n.d., Appendix 2: Memo from Harry Martin, box 2, folder: FOI Reports, UNFOI; Canham, Report, April 16, 1948, box 4, folder: FOI file, UNFOI.

55. Erwin Canham, "International Freedom of Information," *Law and Contemporary Problems* 14 (Autumn 1949): 594–97; Blanchard, *Exporting the First Amendment*, 208, 217, 227–37; Cmiel, "Human Rights, Freedom of Information."

56. Blanchard, *Exporting the First Amendment,* 268–70, 287, 294; Chafee to Free, December 14, 1948, box 1, folder: US Delegation (2), UNFOI.

57. See https://treaties.un.org/Pages/showDetails.aspx?objid=0800000280033202&clang=_en.

58. UNESCO, *News Agencies: Their Structure and Operation* (Paris: UNESCO, 1953), 47, 60; Fenby, *International News Services,* 65; "Text of Report by Directors of the Associated Press," *NYT,* April 26, 1955, 19.

59. UNESCO, *News Agencies,* 10, 193–97; Fenby, *International News Services,* 60, 67; James R. Brennan, "The Cold War Battle over Global News in East Africa: Decolonization, the Free Flow of Information, and the Media Business, 1960–1980," *Journal of Global History* 10, no. 2 (July 2015): 347–49.

60. International Press Institute, *The Flow of the News* (New York: Arno, 1972 repr.), 16; Jeremy Tunstall, *The Media Were American: U.S. Mass Media in Decline* (New York: Oxford University Press, 2008), 77.

61. Brennan, "The Cold War Battle over Global News in East Africa," 341; International Press Institute, *The Flow of the News,* 23, 50.

62. Laura Belmonte, *Selling the American Way: U.S. Propaganda and the Cold War* (Philadelphia: University of Pennsylvania Press, 2008); Nicholas Cull, *The Cold War and the United States Information Agency: American Propaganda and Public Diplomacy, 1945–1989* (Cambridge: Cambridge University Press, 2008), 22–62; Walter L. Hixson, *Parting the Curtain: Propaganda, Culture, and the Cold War, 1945–1961* (New York: St. Martin's, 1997), 1–14; Frank A. Ninkovich, *The Diplomacy of Ideas: U.S. Foreign Policy and Cultural Relations, 1938–1950* (Cambridge: Cambridge University Press, 1981); Justin Hart, *Empire of Ideas: The Origins of Public Diplomacy and the Transformation of U.S. Foreign Policy* (New York: Oxford University Press, 2013).

63. "Permanent News Set Up Created by Byrnes," *EP,* September 22, 1945, 60; "AP Stops Service of News for State Department Use," *EP,* January 19, 1946, 11; "UP Stops Service to US on February 16," *EP,* February 2, 1946, 10.

64. "McGill Says," *EP,* January 26, 1946, 63; "US Newscast Plans Are Termed Essential," *EP,* May 18, 1946, 13; "Foreign News Plan Offered by Forrest," *EP,* February 2, 1946, 13; Arthur W. MacMahon, *Memorandum on the Postwar International Information Program of the United States,* US State Department Publication 2438 (Washington, DC: Government Printing Office, 1945); Blanchard, *Exporting the First Amendment,* 109; "AP Board to Hear Benton, UP Studies His Arguments," *EP,* January 26, 1946, 7; "Government News Service Justified, ASNE Unit Says," *EP,* December 14, 1946, 11.

65. Canham Report, April 16, 1948, box 4, folder: FOI file, UNFOI; "Problems of Journalism: Proceedings of the 1948 Convention American Society of Newspaper Editors," (Washington, DC, April 15–18, 1948), 260; Robert U. Brown, "ASNE Urges AP, UP Service for Government Newscasts," *EP,* April 24, 1948, 17.

66. Cull, *The Cold War and the United States Information Agency,* 53–54; "Martin's Work with ECA Wins Praise from Acheson," *Guild Reporter,* July 14, 1950, 3; Robert U. Brown, "ASNE Urges AP, UP Service for Government Newscasts," *EP,* April 24, 1948, 17; "Erwin Canham, Long Time Editor of Christian Science Monitor, Dies," *NYT,* January 4, 1982, B10.

67. Elizabeth Hodges to Harry Truman, April 21, 1950, J. Scott Pike to Harry Truman, April 20, 1950, J. H. Bowers to Harry Truman, April 21, 1950, all in box 332, file 200: ASNE 4/20/50 Address, Pro, President's Personal files, Harry S. Truman Library, Independence, MO; Wilford, *The Mighty Wurlitzer*, 33–34, 46.

68. Belmonte, *Selling the American Way*, 32, 44; Fred Turner, *Democratic Surround: Multimedia and American Liberalism from World War II to the Psychedelic Sixties* (Chicago: University of Chicago Press, 2013), 215; Kenneth Osgood, *Total Cold War: Eisenhower's Secret Propaganda Battle at Home and Abroad* (Lawrence: University of Kansas, 2006), 110–12, 118–21, 139.

69. Osgood, *Total Cold War*, chap. 5.

CHAPTER FIVE

1. Ken Lawless, "Continental Imprisonment: Rockwell Kent and the Passport Controversy," *Antioch Review* 38 (Summer, 1980): 304–10; "Artist Rockwell Kent Dies at 88," *WP*, March 14, 1971, B6; "A Vivid as Well as Graphic Artist," *NYT*, October 31, 1982, BR13; Alden Whitman, "Man of Multiple Skills," *NYT*, March 14, 1971, 1; Jeffrey A. Engel, *Cold War at 30,000 Feet: The Anglo-American Fight for Aviation Supremacy* (Cambridge, MA: Harvard University Press, 2007), 39; Patrick O'Brian, *Picasso: A Biography* (New York: Norton, 1976), 436–39; Eleonory Gilburd, *To See Paris and Die: The Soviet Lives of Western Culture* (Cambridge, MA: Belknap Press of Harvard University Press, 2018), 216–67.

2. "Art Surmounts Curbs on Artists," *NYT*, May 10, 1957, 28.

3. Benjamin A. Coates, "The Secret Life of Statutes: A Century of the Trading with the Enemy Act," *Modern American History* 1 (July 2018): 151–72.

4. Murray L. Schwartz and James C. N. Paul, "Foreign Communist Propaganda in the Mails: A Report on Some Problems of Federal Censorship," *University of Pennsylvania Law Review* 107 (March 1959): 634–44; Note, "Government Exclusion of Foreign Political Propaganda," *Harvard Law Review* 68 (June 1955): 1393–409.

5. As part of the reorganization, both divisions became offices in 1952—for the ease of the reader, I refer to them consistently as "divisions" throughout this chapter. *Security and Constitutional Rights: Hearings before the Subcommittee on Constitutional Rights Pursuant to S. Res. 94*, 84th Cong., 2d Sess. 156–57 (November 1955).

6. Edward Alwood, *Dark Days in the Newsroom: McCarthyism Aimed at the Press* (Philadelphia: Temple University Press, 2007), 82–97; "Miss Knight Given Rebuke for Action Sought by FBI," *NYT*, March 23, 1966, 1; "State Dept to Sift FBI Bids," *NYT*, March 25, 1966, 1; "Rusk Tightens Rules on FBI Requests," *NYT*, April 6, 1966, 1.

7. "Congress Passes Bill to Curb Reds by Heavy Margins," *NYT*, September 21, 1950, 1; Internal Security Act, September 23, 1950, Section 22, 64 Stat. 1006–9; Immigration and Nationality Act, Section 215a, Pub. L. No. 414, 66. Stat. 190; Emanuel Celler, "Your Right to a Passport," *Bar Bulletin* 16 (1959): 179; Harry S. Truman, Proclamation No. 3004: Control of Persons Leaving or Entering the U.S., January 17, 1953, cited from https://www.trumanlibrary.gov/library/proclamations/3004/control-persons-leaving-or-entering-united-states.

8. Felix S. Cohen, "Enacting Entry Bans," *NYT*, July 6, 1952, E8; Helen Worden Erskine, "You Don't Go If She Says No," *Colliers*, July 11, 1953, 63; "Truman Paves Way for Veto of New Alien Bill," *CT*, June 3, 1952, 12.

9. Eliot B. Coulter, "Visa Work of the Department of State and Foreign Service," US State Department Publication 3649, October 1949, 4–5; Edward P. Hutchinson, *Legislative History of American Immigration Policy, 1798–1965* (Philadelphia: University of Pennsylvania Press, 1981), 261; Melvin Cohen and David McGowan, "The Semi-Open Door: Ideology, Aliens and the Law," *Revue française d'études américaines* 45 (July 1990): 177; Harry S. Truman, "Veto of the Internal Security Bill," September 22, 1950, APP; *Aptheker v. Secretary of State*, 378 U.S. 500 (1964); David Caute, *The Great Fear: The Anti-Communist Purge under Truman and Eisenhower* (New York: Simon and Schuster, 1978), 245.

10. Meeting Visa Security Clearance Requirements Consistent with the Spirit of the Internal Security Act: A Report of Progress by the Department of State, n.d., folder: Internal Security 1952, box 2, BSC; New York State Bar Association, *Freedom to Travel: Report of the Special Committee to Study Passport Procedures of the Association of the Bar of the City of New York* (New York: Dodd, Mead, 1958), 14–17; Jeffrey Kahn, *Mrs. Shipley's Ghost: The Right to Travel and Terrorist Watchlists* (Ann Arbor: University of Michigan Press, 2013), 115; *The Right to Travel: Hearing before the Subcommittee on Constitutional Rights Pursuant to S. Res. 49*, 85th Cong. 62, 192 (1957); "Freedom to Travel," *Editorial Research Reports*, February 18, 1966; *Zemel v. Rusk*, 381 U.S. 1 (1965) at 3; Anne E. Kershaw, "Constitutional Law–International Travel–Restrictions on Travel-Related Transactions under the Cuban Embargo–*Regan v. Wald*," *NYU Law School Law Review* 31 (1986): 185–86; Joseph L. Rauh Jr. and Daniel H. Pollitt, "Restrictions on the Right to Travel," *Western Reserve Law Review* 13, no. 1 (December 1961): 133.

11. Fisher to Boykin, February 5, 1951, State Department Press Release, December 18, 1951, both in *The Right to Travel: Hearing before the Subcommittee on Constitutional Rights Pursuant to S. Res. 49*, 85th Cong. 244–46 (1957); *Departments of State, Justice, Commerce and the Judiciary Appropriations for 1953: Department of State, Part 1, Hearings before the Subcommittee of the Committee on Appropriations, House of Representatives*, 82d Cong. 118 (1952); Leonard B. Boudin, "The Constitutional Right to Travel," *Columbia Law Review* 56 (1956): 63.

12. "Visa Law Changes to Be Sought in '52," *NYT*, December 9, 1951, 1; "Silent Curtain Seen Erected by Visa Men," *Christian Science Monitor*, July 17, 1952, 6; *Security and Constitutional Rights: Hearings before the Subcommittee on Constitutional Rights Pursuant to S. Res. 94*, 84th Cong. 96, 165 (1955); *Passport Legislation: Hearings before the Committee on Foreign Relations*, 85th Cong. 21 (1958); Caute, *Great Fear*, 245–47, 254; Landon R. Y. Storrs, *The Second Red Scare and the Unmaking of the New Deal Left* (Princeton, NJ: Princeton University Press, 2013), 218, 238–39.

13. *Security and Constitutional Rights: Hearings before the Subcommittee on Constitutional rights pursuant to S. Res. 94*, 84th Cong. 115–40 (1955); Linus Pauling, "My Efforts to Obtain a Passport," *Bulletin of the Atomic Scientists* 8 (October 1952): 253–56.

14. The literatures on Black internationalism and scientific internationalism are vast. Apart from the work cited below, my thinking on Black internationalism is indebted particularly to Penny Von Eschen, *Race against Empire: Black Americans and Anticolonialism, 1937–1957* (Ithaca, NY: Cornell University Press, 1997); Nikhil Pal Singh, *Black Is a Country: Race and the Unfinished Struggle for Democracy* (Cambridge, MA: Harvard University Press, 2004); and Sean L. Malloy, *Out of Oakland: Black Panther Party Internationalism during the Cold War* (Ithaca, NY: Cornell University Press, 2018), chap. 1. On scientific internationalism, see Mark Mazower, *Governing the World: The History of an Idea* (New York: Penguin, 2012), 94–115; Joseph Manzione, " 'Amusing and Amazing and Practical and Military': The Legacy of Scientific Internationalism in American Foreign Policy, 1945–1963," *Diplomatic History* 24, no. 1 (January 2000): 21–55.

15. *Hearings before the President's Commission on Immigration and Naturalization*, 82d Cong. 406–10 (1952); Caute, *Great Fear*, 256–59; "Hungarian Nobel Prize Winner Fails to Get Visa to Visit U.S.," *WP*, January 17, 1947: 10; Anonymous Memo of Off-the-Record Talk with Joseph B. Keopfli, Science Adviser to the Secretary of State, n.d., folder: Internal Security 1952, box 2, BSC; Cohen and McGowan, "The Semi-Open Door"; "15 Scientists May Face Bar," *The Sun*, September 8, 1951, 7; "Visa Barrier," *WP*, October 13, 1952, 9; Jessica Wang, *American Science in an Age of Anxiety: Scientists, Anticommunism, and the Cold War* (Chapel Hill: University of North Carolina Press, 1999), 275–78; Ronald E. Doel, Dieter Hoffmann, and Nikolai Krementsov, "National States and International Science: A Comparative History of International Science Congresses in Hitler's Germany, Stalin's Russia, and Cold War United States," *Osiris* 20 (January 2005): 68; "McCarran Act Called Bar to West Research," *Christian Science Monitor*, May 19, 1952, 14.

16. *Security and Constitutional Rights: Hearings before the Subcommittee on Constitutional rights pursuant to S. Res. 94*, 84th Cong. 86–88 (1955); Wang, *American Science in an Age of Anxiety*, 37–38, 63–64; Comment, "Passport Refusals for Political Reasons: Constitutional Issues and Judicial Review," *Yale Law Journal* 61 (1952): 174–75; Mario Daniels, "Controlling Knowledge, Controlling People: Travel Restrictions of U.S. Scientists and National Security," *Diplomatic History* 43 (January 2019): 5, 20; Travel Policy Committee, Minutes, February 6, 1947, box 184, folder: Passports and Frontier Formalities Conference, 1947, 2 of 2, OIC.

17. Martin Duberman, *Paul Robeson* (New York: Knopf, 1988), 399–402, 435; Jordan Goodman, *Paul Robeson: A Watched Man* (London: Verso, 2013), 187–256; Gerald Horne, *Black and Red: W.E.B. Du Bois and the Afro-American Response to the Cold War, 1944–1963* (Albany: State University of New York Press, 1986), 201–22; Robeson Taj Frazier, *The East Is Black: Cold War China in the Black Radical Imagination* (Durham, NC: Duke University Press, 2015), 41–43; Carol Anderson, *Eyes off the Prize: The United Nations and the African American Struggle for Human Rights, 1944–1955* (Cambridge: Cambridge University Press, 2003), 171–74; Adam Green, *Selling the Race: Culture, Community and Black Chicago, 1940–1955* (Chicago: University of Chicago Press, 2009), 192; William J. Maxwell, *F.B. Eyes: How J. Edgar Hoover's Ghostreaders Framed African American Literature* (Princeton, NJ: Princeton University Press, 2015) 203; "Seek to Deport Woman Author as an Alien Red," *Chicago Tribune*,

January 21, 1948, 30; Kevin Gaines, "Locating the Transnational in Postwar African American History," *Small Axe: A Caribbean Journal of Criticism* 13, no. 1 (January 1, 2009): 193–202; Carole Boyce Davies, *Left of Karl Marx: The Political Life of Black Communist Claudia Jones* (Durham, NC: Duke University Press, 2007), 150–57; Vincent J. Cannato, *American Passage: The History of Ellis Island* (New York: Harper, 2009), 369–71; Charisse Burden-Stelly, "Constructing Deportable Subjectivity: Antiforeignness, Antiradicalism, and Antiblackness during the McCarthyist Structure of Feeling," *Souls* 19 (2017): 342–58.

18. Maxwell, *F.B. Eyes*, 176, 243.

19. Tim Weiner, *Legacy of Ashes: The History of the CIA* (New York: Doubleday, 2007), 41; Christopher Simpson, *Blowback: The First Full Account of America's Recruitment of Nazis, and its Disastrous Effect on Our Domestic and Foreign Policy* (New York: Weidenfeld and Nicolson, 1988), 167; Harry S. Truman, Veto of the Internal Security Bill, September 22, 1950, APP; "Nazis, Fascists and Falangists to be Eligible to Enter U.S.," *WP*, November 12, 1952, 1; Israel Goldstein, letter to *NYT*, January 29, 1953, 26; Caute, *Great Fear*, 254; Peyton Ford to Dean Acheson, April 6 1951, folder: Internal Security 1951, BSC; "Public Attitudes in the US Relative to the Enforcement of the Internal Security Act 1950," November 7, 1950, "Draft Department Position on the Internal Security Act of 1950," November 22, 1950, both in folder: Internal Security 1950, box 2, BSC; *Departments of State, Justice, Commerce and the Judiciary Appropriations for 1953, Hearings before a Subcommittee of the Senate Committee on Appropriations*, 82d Cong. 1132 (1952).

20. Von Eschen, *Race against Empire*; 124; Duberman, *Paul Robeson*, 407; Rogers, "Passports and Politics," 499.

21. Justin Hart has shown how the State Department's cultural programs reflected a similar discovery of the importance of "image" in an enlarged conception of foreign relations. See Justin Hart, *Empire of Ideas: The Origins of Public Diplomacy and the Transformation of U.S. Foreign Policy* (New York: Oxford University Press, 2013); Kahn, *Mrs. Shipley's Ghost*, 35, 112; Singh, *Black Is a Country*, 175–78; Penny M. Von Eschen, *Satchmo Blows up the World: Jazz Ambassadors Play the Cold War* (Cambridge, MA: Harvard University Press, 2006).

22. Lawless, "Continental Imprisonment," 310; Hart, *Empire of Ideas*, 192–94; David Oshinsky, *A Conspiracy So Immense: The World of Joe McCarthy* (New York: Free Press, 1983), 276–79; Greg Barnhisel, *Cold War Modernists: Art, Literature, and American Cultural Diplomacy* (New York: Columbia University Press, 2015), 112–14; New Republic Staff, "The Horrible, Oppressive History of Book Burning in America," *New Republic*, June 29, 1953; "Some Books Literally Burned after Inquiry, Dulles Reports," *NYT*, June 16, 1953, 1; Horne, *Black and Red*, 205; Alice Garner and Diane Kirkby, "Tactful Visitor, Scientific Observer or 100 Percent Patriot? Ambassadorship in the Australia-US Fulbright Program," in *The Legacy of J. William Fulbright: Policy, Power, and Ideology*, ed. Alessandro Brogi, Giles Scott-Smith, and David J. Snyder (Lexington: University of Kentucky Press, 2019), 210.

23. Comment, "Passport Refusals for Political Reasons: Constitutional Issues and Judicial Review," *Yale Law Journal* 61 (1952): 178; Robeson, *East Is Black*, 107.

24. Campbell Gibson and Kay Jung, *Historical Census Statistics on the Foreign Born Population of the United States: 1850–2000*, (working paper no. 81, Population Division, February 2006), tables 1 and 2, cited from https://www.census.gov/content/dam/Census/library/working-papers/2006/demo/POP-twps0081.pdf; "Tourist Rise Seen to South America: Increase in U.S. Travelers Is Predicted," *NYT*, February 13, 1958, 58; Juan de Onis, Catching up with Tourism, *NYT*, November 20, 1960, xx1.

25. Pekka Gronow and Ilpo Saunio, *An International History of the Recording Industry* (London: Cassell, 1998), 95; Kerry Segrave, *Foreign Films in America: A History* (Jefferson, NC: McFarland, 2004), 140; Vanessa R. Schwartz, *It's So French! Hollywood, Paris, and the Making of Cosmopolitan Film Culture* (Chicago: University of Chicago Press, 2007), chap. 3; Gilburd, *To See Paris and Die*, 163; Thomas H. Guback, "Hollywood's International Market," in *The American Film Industry*, ed. Tino Balio (Madison: University of Wisconsin Press, 1985), 481; Thomas Doherty, *Hollywood's Censor: Joseph I. Breen and the Production Code Administration* (New York: Columbia University Press, 2009), chap. 12.

26. "TV Abroad," *Wall Street Journal*, October 20, 1960, 1; "Overseas Viewers Join Market for U.S. Telefilms," *Christian Science Monitor*, July 18, 1957, 5; "Televisionitis Grips the World," *Baltimore Sun*, July 21, 1963, a7; Jeremy Tunstall, *The Media Were American: U.S. Mass Media in Decline* (New York: Oxford University Press, 2008), 74; Kaarle Nordenstreng and Tapio Varis, *Television Traffic: A One-Way Street? A Survey and Analysis of the International Flow of Television Programme Material*, Reports and Papers on Mass Communication 70 (Paris: UNESCO, 1974), 13–15.

27. George A. Van Horn, "Analysis of AP News on Trunk and Wisconsin State Wires," *Journalism Quarterly* 29, no. 4 (September 1952): 426–32; Scott M. Cutlip, "Content and Flow of AP News—From Trunk to TTS to Reader," *Journalism Quarterly* 31, no. 4 (December 1954): 434–46; International Press Institute, *The Flow of the News* (New York: Arno, 1972 repr.), 57, 62; Charles E. Swanson, "What They Read in 30 Daily Newspapers," *Journalism Quarterly* 32, no. 4 (December 1955): 411–21; Jim A. Hart, "The Flow of International News into Ohio," *Journalism Quarterly* 38, no. 4 (December 1961): 541–43.

28. Jim A. Hart, "Foreign News in U. S. and English Daily Newspapers: A Comparison," *Journalism Quarterly* 43, no. 3 (September 1966): 443–48; Summary of discussions, June 5–6, 1945, Document 66, box 3, folder 3, 42–43, "Draft Report–Commission on Freedom of the Press–first revision," Commission doc. #34, 11 box 2, folder 2, both in HC.

29. These figures include stringers as well as full-time correspondents. John Wilhelm, "The Re-Appearing Foreign Correspondent: A World Survey," *Journalism Quarterly* 40, no. 2 (June 1963): 147–68.

30. Leo Bogart, "The Overseas Newsman: A 1967 Profile Study," *Journalism Quarterly* 45, no. 2 (June 1968): 293–306; William Maxwell, "U.S. Correspondents Abroad: A Study of Backgrounds," *Journalism Quarterly* 33, no. 3 (September 1956): 346–48; International Press Institute, *The Flow of the News*, 21.

31. Christina Klein, *Cold War Orientalism Asia in the Middlebrow Imagination, 1945–1961* (Berkeley: University of California Press, 2003).

32. Sam Lebovic, *Free Speech and Unfree News: The Paradox of Press Freedom in America* (Cambridge, MA: Harvard University Press, 2016), 180; Judy Tzu-Chun Wu, *Radicals on the Road: Internationalism, Orientalism, and Feminism During the Vietnam Era* (Ithaca, NY: Cornell University Press, 2013), 66; Seth Jacobs, *America's Miracle Man in Vietnam: Ngo Dinh Diem, Religion, Race, and U.S. Intervention in Southeast Asia, 1950–1957* (Durham, NC: Duke University Press, 2004), 127–63; Hugh Wilford, *The Mighty Wurlitzer: How the CIA Played America* (Cambridge MA: Harvard University Press, 2008), 166–82; Klein, *Cold War Orientalism*, 89–99; Christian G. Appy, *American Reckoning: Our Vietnam War and Our National Identity* (New York: Penguin, 2015), 3–32.

33. Wu, *Radicals on the Road*, 15–103; Susan Zeiger, *Entangling Alliances: Foreign War Brides and American Soldiers in the Twentieth Century* (New York: New York University Press, 2010), esp. chap. 5.

34. Duberman, *Robeson*, 435.

35. Glendon, *World Made New*, 193, 205; Anderson, *Eyes off the Prize*, 216–26, 235.

36. Michelle Brattain, "Race, Racism, and Antiracism: UNESCO and the Politics of Presenting Science to the Postwar Public," *American Historical Review* 112 (2007); Sebastián Gil-Riaño, "Relocating Anti-Racist Science: The 1950 UNESCO Statement on Race and Economic Development in the Global South," *British Journal for the History of Science* 51 (June 2018): 281–303; Todd Shepard, "Algeria, France, Mexico, UNESCO: A Transnational History of Anti-Racism and Decolonization, 1932–1962," *Journal of Global History* 6 (July 2011): 276; Elizabeth Gillespie McRae, *Mothers of Massive Resistance: White Women and the Politics of White Supremacy* (New York: Oxford University Press), 147–49; Anderson, *Eyes off the Prize*, 216–17; "Los Angeles Schools Ban UNESCO Book," *CT*, August 30, 1952, a5; "UNESCO Held Menace to LA Schools," *LA Times*, April 11, 1952, a1; "LA Bans UNESCO Program," *NYT*, January 21, 1953, 3; Glenda Sluga, *Internationalism in the Age of Nationalism* (Philadelphia: University of Pennsylvania Press, 2013), 114.

37. Oshinsky, *A Conspiracy So Immense*, 207; Anderson, *Eyes off the Prize*, 258–59; "Senate Pressure in UN Case Urged," *NYT*, December 27, 1952, 1; "2 Senators Bid UN Oust 'Spies' or Go," *NYT*, November 12, 1952, 1; "Secretary General Says Aide Sought Justice for Those Accused of Subversion," *NYT*, November 14 1952, 1; "A. H. Feller, Ill 2 weeks, Eludes Wife's Effort to Prevent Suicide," *NYT*, November 14 1952, 1; K. G., "International Officials: A Question of Loyalties," *World Today*, November 1954, 488–95; William Preston Jr., "The History of U.S.-UNESCO Relations," in *Hope and Folly: The United States and UNESCO, 1945–1985*, ed. William Preston, Edward S. Herman, and Herbert I. Schiller (Minneapolis: University of Minnesota Press, 1989), 63; Pamela Hanlon, *A Worldly Affair: New York, the United Nations, and the Story behind Their Unlikely Bond* (New York: Fordham University Press, 2017), 88–94; "Loyalty Sessions Wind up in Europe," *NYT*, July 26, 1954, 17; James P. Sewell, *UNESCO and World Politics: Engaging in International Relations* (Princeton, NJ: Princeton University Press, 1975), 157–59, 165; *Scope of Soviet Activity in the United States: Hearing before*

the Subcommittee to Investigate the Administration of the Internal Security Act and Other Internal Security Laws of the Committee on the Judiciary, 84th Cong. 2120, 2137, 2157 (December 17, 1956); "A Tender Spot for Security Risks," *CT*, May 4, 1955, 16.

38. 93 Cong. Rec. 6566, 6965, 6967, 6748–49 (1947).

39. Randall Bennett Woods, *Fulbright: A Biography* (Cambridge: Cambridge University Press, 1995), 102, 180–83; Walter Johnson and Francis J. Colligan, *The Fulbright Program: A History* (Chicago: University of Chicago Press, 1965), 96–104; "McCarthy, Hitting Informational Program, Reveals His Relations with Fellow Senators," *WP*, July 25, 1953, 7; "Teacher Plan under Attack," *Baltimore Sun*, June 11, 1953, 8.

40. Peter Simons, "Grassroots Diplomacy: Fighting the Cold War on the Family Farm with the International Farm Youth Exchange," in *Global Exchanges: Scholarships and Transnational Circulations in the Modern World*, ed. Ludovic Tournes and Giles Scott-Smith (New York: Berghahn, 2018), 188–201; Liping Bu, *Making the World Like Us: Education, Cultural Expansion, and the American Century* (Westport, CT: Praeger, 2003), 182–83; Wilford, *The Mighty Wurlitzer*, 122–26; Jenifer Van Vleck, *Empire of the Air: Aviation and the American Ascendancy* (Cambridge, MA: Harvard University Press, 2013), 266; Hannah Higgin, "The Limits of Liberal Internationalism: The Fulbright Program in Africa," in *The Legacy of J. William Fulbright: Policy, Power, and Ideology*, ed. Alessandro Brogi, Giles Scott-Smith, and David J. Snyder (Lexington: University of Kentucky Press, 2019), 231; Maurice A Sterns, "Educational Exchange in Latin America," *Annals of American Academy of Political and Social Science* 491 (May 1987): 107–8; *Mutual Educational and Cultural Exchange Act, Hearings before the Committee on Foreign Relations*, 87th Cong. 20–22, 48–49, 113 (March 29 and April 27, 1961); Johnson and Colligan, *The Fulbright Program*, 300; Lonnie Johnson, "The Making of the Fulbright Program, 1946–1961," in *The Legacy of J. William Fulbright: Policy, Power, and Ideology*, ed. Alessandro Brogi, Giles Scott-Smith, and David J. Snyder (Lexington: University of Kentucky Press, 2019), 171; Ralph H. Vogel, "The Making of the Fulbright Program," *Annals of American Academy of Political and Social Science*, 491 (May 1987): 19.

41. United States Commission on Government Security, *Report of the Commission on Government Security*, S. Doc. 64 (1957), 465, 592–600, 611; Woods, *Fulbright: A Biography*, 181; Victor Rosenberg, *Soviet-American Relations, 1953–1960: Diplomacy and Cultural Exchange during the Eisenhower Presidency* (Jefferson, NC: McFarland and Co., 2005), 126–30; see also https://blogs.loc.gov/maps/2017/08/restricting-soviet-travel-in-the-u-s-during-the-cold-war/.

42. 104 Cong. Rec. 13,772–73 (July 15, 1958); "Freedom of Movement," *Editorial Research Reports*, August 20, 1948; Tony Judt, *Reappraisals: Reflections on the Forgotten Twentieth Century* (New York: Penguin, 2008), 306.

43. Truman, Veto of the Internal Security Bill, APP; "Watch on Aliens Hit as 'Russian Method,'" *NYT*, February 2, 1948, 13; "McCarran Act Called Bar to West Research," *Christian Science Monitor*, May 19, 1952, 14; Reginald Parker, "The Right to Go Abroad: To Have and to Hold a Passport," *Virginia Law Review* 40 (November 1954): 854–55; "McCarran Restrictions Come Under New Attack," *NYT*, October 19,

1952, E5; *Hearings before the President's Commission on Immigration and Naturalization*, 82d Cong. 406, 408–10 (1952).

44. "Tourism before U.N.," *NYT*, May 16, 1954, X21; "UN Treaties Help Travelers," *NYT*, June 13, 1954, xx45.

45. H. Timothy Lovelace, "William Worthy's Passport: Travel Restrictions and the Cold War Struggle for Civil and Human Rights," *Journal of American History* 103 (June 2016): 114, 120, 123–25; Frazier, *East Is Black*, 72–108; Jinx Coleman Broussard and Skye Chance Cooley, "William Worthy (Jr): The Man and the Mission," *Journalism Studies* 10, no. 3 (June 2009): 386–400; Teishan A. Latner, *Cuban Revolution in America: Havana and the Making of a United States Left, 1968–1992* (Chapel Hill: University of North Carolina Press, 2018), 80; Van Gosse, *Where the Boys Are: Cuba, Cold War America and the Making of a New Left* (London: Verso, 1993).

46. Frazier, *East Is Black*, 96–97; William W. Alfeld, "Newsgathering and the Right to Travel Abroad," *Journalism Quarterly* 36, no. 4 (December 1959): 423–30; *The Right to Travel: Hearing before the Subcommittee on Constitutional Rights Pursuant to S. Res. 49*, 85th Cong. (April 4, 1957); "ASNE Board Asks Dulles to Rescind Ban," *EP*, February 16, 1957, 9; "ASNE and Guild Ask End of China Barrier," *EP*, February 23 1957, 13; "Reporters' Travel Ban Illegal, Ernst Argues," *EP*, January 26 1957, 60; "Editorial," *EP*, April 6 1957, 6; "Bill Assures Newsmen's Passport Bid," *EP*, July 26, 1958, 42.

47. "U.S. Gives Consent for 24 Newsmen to Go to Red China," *NYT*, August 23, 1957, 1; John Spencer Nichols, "Testing the Constitutionality of U.S. Licensing of News Gatherers and Researchers Traveling to Cuba," *Journal of Government Information* 25, no. 3 (1998): 236; "Passport Renewals Set," *NYT*, October 18, 1958, 6; "Freedom to Travel," *ERR*, February 18, 1966; Kenneth L. Penegar, "Constitutional Law–Right to Travel and Area Restrictions–Foreign Relations Power," *North Carolina Law Review* 38 (1960): 260–70.

48. There were minor exceptions before this—Edgar Snow, for instance, was allowed to return to cover a regime that he had done so much to legitimize in the 1940s. "Peiping Said to Bar U.S. Reporters Again," *NYT*, February 26, 1960, 13; "China News Pact Urged," *NYT*, April 20, 1960, 11; "U.S. Answers Red China," *NYT*, May 17, 1960, 5; "Red China Spurns Overture by U.S.," *NYT*, March 9, 1961, 1; "U.S. Says It Still Wishes to Get Newsmen into China," *NYT*, May 13, 1964, 47; "3 U.S. Newsmen Enter Red China for Week's Visit," *NYT*, April 11, 1971, 1. On Snow, see Julia Lovell, *Maoism: A Global History* (New York: Knopf, 2019), 60–87; and Giovanna Dell'Orto, *American Journalism and International Relations: Foreign Correspondence from the Early Republic to the Digital Era* (Cambridge: Cambridge University Press, 2013),135–36.

49. *Security and Constitutional Rights: Hearings before the Subcommittee on Constitutional Rights Pursuant to S. Res. 94*, 84th Cong. 98 (1955); Parker, "The Right to Go Abroad," 869–70; Boudin, "The Constitutional Right to Travel," 48–49.

50. Comment, "Passport Refusals for Political Reasons: Constitutional Issues and Judicial Review" *Yale Law Journal* 61 (1952): 191; "The Passport Puzzle," *University of Chicago Law Review* 23 (Winter 1956): 267–68; John Torpey, *The Invention of the Passport: Surveillance, Citizenship and the State* (New York: Cambridge University Press,

2000), 131; Parker, "The Right to Go Abroad," 869–70; Boudin, "The Constitutional Right to Travel," 48–49; LRS, *Passports and the Right to Travel*, 7; Kahn, *Mrs. Shipley's Ghost*, 60–74; NY Bar Association, *Freedom to Travel*, 2–3.

51. Goodman, *Paul Robeson*, 199–204; Whelan, "Passports and Freedom of Travel," 81–85; "Curb on Robeson Stands," *NYT*, August 8, 1952, 5.

52. *Bauer v. Acheson*, 106 F. Supp. 445 (D.D.C. 1952); Gressman, "The Undue Process of Passports," 13–15; Kahn, *Mrs. Shipley's Ghost*, 19–21; "State Department Upset," *NYT*, July 10, 1952, 14; Boudin, "The Constitutional Right to Travel," 56.

53. 22 C.F.R. s51.135, cited at *The Right to Travel: Hearing before the Subcommittee on Constitutional Rights Pursuant to S. Res. 49*, 85th Cong. 66, 229 (1957); Boudin, "The Constitutional Right to Travel," 68; Kahn, *Mrs. Shipley's Ghost*, 117–18; Caute, *Great Fear*, 245–46; Erskine, "You Don't Go If She Says No," *Colliers*, 63.

54. Boudin, "The Constitutional Right to Travel," 56; Alan Rogers, "Passports and Politics: The Courts and the Cold War," *The Historian* 47 (August 1985): 504; Kahn, *Mrs. Shipley's Ghost*, 121–22; *Boudin v. Dulles*, 136 F. Supp. 218 (D.D.C. 1955); *Boudin v. Dulles*, 235 F.2d 532 (D.C. Cir. 1956); LRS, *Passports and the Right to Travel*, 1966, 29; Nicholas Doman, "A Comparative Analysis: Do Citizens Have the Right to Travel?" *ABA Journal* 43 (1957): 309; Leonard Boudin, "The Right to Travel: A Significant Victory," *The Nation*, July 30, 1955, 95; Ashley J. Nicholas, "Refusal of Passports to Communists," May 29, 1956, in *The Right to Travel: Hearing before the Subcommittee on Constitutional Rights Pursuant to S. Res. 49*, 85th Cong. 268 (1957); *Briehl v. Dulles*, 248 F.2d 561 (D.C. Cir. 1957); Comment, "Authority of the Secretary of State to Deny Passports," *University of Pennsylvania Law Review* 106 (1958): 456–57; Luther A. Huston, "Court Backs Dulles in Refusing 2 Visas," *NYT*, June 28, 1957, 1.

55. Julia Rose Kraut, "The Devil's Advocate: Leonard B. Boudin, Civil Liberties and the Legal Defense of Whistleblowing," in *The Whistleblowing Nation: The History of National Security Disclosures and the Cult of State Secrecy*, ed. Kaeten Mistry and Hannah Gurman (New York: Columbia University Press, 2020), 69–94; Anthony Lewis, "Court Further Limits Travel Restrictions," *NYT*, June 22, 1958, e7; "The Passport Puzzle," 263.

56. Lewis, "Court Further Limits Travel Restrictions," e7; "The Passport Puzzle," 263; *Kent v. Dulles*, 357 U.S. 116 (1958).

57. Anthony Lewis, "Red Query Dropped for U.S. Passports," *NYT*, June 25, 1958, 1; Paul P. Kennedy, "Passport Ruling Sifted in Mexico," *NYT*, June 29, 1958, 26; Alfeld, "Newsgathering and the Right to Travel Abroad," 426; "Kent to Visit Soviet," *NYT*, July 19, 1958, 8; Lawless, "Continental Imprisonment," 311; Frazier, *East Is Black*, 43–44.

58. *Worthy v. Herter*, 270 F.2d 905 (D.C. Cir. 1959); Mary L. Sinderson, "Executive Restriction on Travel: The Passport Cases," *Houston Law Review* 5, no. 3 (January 1968): 499–513.

59. Rauh and Pollitt, "Restrictions on the Right to Travel," 132; Anthony Lewis, "China Travel Ban Stays in Effect," *NYT*, December 8, 1959; "High Court Backs Cuba Travel Ban," *NYT*, May 4 1965, 1; "Cuba Travel Ban by U.S. Is Upheld," *WP*, February 22,

1964, A6; *Zemel v. Rusk*, 381 U.S. 1 (1965), at 16–17; Sinderson, "Executive Restriction on Travel," 499–513.

60. Lovelace, "William Worthy's Passport," 131; *United States v. Laub*, 384 U.S. 984 (1966).

61. *Staughton Lynd v. Dean Rusk, Secretary of State, Jane Wittman v. Secretary of State*, 389 F.2d 940 (D.C. Cir. 1967); Mary Hershberger, *Traveling to Vietnam: American Peace Activists and the War* (Syracuse, NY: Syracuse University Press, 1998), chap. 2, 97; Carl F. Salans and Richard A. Frank, "Passports and Area Restrictions," *Stanford Law Review* 20 (1968): 840–43.

62. Passports issued through 1971, which would be valid until 1976, had a note that said: "Unless otherwise specifically endorsed, this passport is not valid for travel into or through countries or areas to which travel has been restricted by public notice issued by the Secretary of State." In 1971, the note changed to: "United States courts have interpreted United States law in effect on the date this passport is issued as not restricting the travel of a United States citizen to any foreign country or area. However, the use of a United States passport for travel into or through any of the following areas is authorized only when specifically validated for such travel by the Department of State." Harriette Treloar and Susan Benjamin, "Area Restrictions and the Right to Travel Abroad," *University of California Davis Law Review* 8 (1975), 406–9; Lawrence R. Velvel, "Geographical Restrictions on Travel: The Real World and the First Amendment," *Kansas Law Review* 15 (1966): 51, 66; "President Seeks Travel-Curb Law," *NYT*, December 12, 1967, 15; Hershberger, *Traveling to Vietnam*, 97–98.

63. Sanford J. Ungar, "J. Edgar Hoover Leaves the State Dept," *Foreign Policy* 28 (1977): 110–16; Caute, *Great Fear*, 246; "Schwartz Is Forced from Security Post," *CT*, March 7, 1966, c11; "Johnson Defends U.S. Travel Policy," *NYT*, March 11, 1966, 12; Hershberger, *Traveling to Vietnam*, 52; "Bureau Chief Reorganized Out of a Job," *CT*, March 20, 1966, 10; "Heavy Feuding Seen in State Dept Shuffle Plan," *LA Times*, March 14, 1966, 7; Robert Sherrill, "First Lady of the Passport Office—Efficiency Expert or 'Ogress'?" *NYT*, March 4, 1971, XX1.

64. Julia Rose Kraut, "Global Anti-Anarchism: The Origins of Ideological Deportation and the Suppression of Expression," *Indiana Journal of Global Legal Studies* 19 (Winter 2012): 185.

65. *Mandel et al. v. John M. Mitchell and William P. Rogers*, 325 F. Supp. 620, at 624 (E.D.N.Y. 1971); *Kleindienst, Attorney General, et al. v. Mandel et al.*, 408 U.S. 753 (1972); Julia Rose Kraut, *Threat of Dissent: A History of Ideological Exclusion and Deportation in the United States* (Cambridge, MA: Harvard University Press, 2020), chap. 6.

66. *Kleindienst v. Mandel*, 408 U.S. at 759–60; *Mandel et al. v. Mitchell*, 325 F. Supp. at 633; *Lamont v. Postmaster General*, 381 U.S. 301 (1965).

67. *Kleindienst v. Mandel*, 408 U.S. at 770, 776–78, 780; Philip J. Cooper, "The Supreme Court, the First Amendment, and Freedom of Information," *Public Administration Review* 46 (November–December 1986): 626.

68. Richard J. Evans, *Eric Hobsbawm: A Life in History* (New York: Oxford University Press, 2019), 445–57; Eric Hobsbawm, *Interesting Times: A Twentieth Century Life* (New

York: Pantheon, 2002), 389–90; "Do Not Enter," *Boston Globe Magazine*, February 17, 1985, 12; "Would William Shakespeare Get a Visa?" *Christian Science Monitor* May 30, 1984, 17; Susan Mann, "Monopoly in the Marketplace: The Ideological Denial of Visas," *Law and Policy* 9 (October 1987): 418; Cohen and McGowan, "The Semi-Open Door," 192.

69. *Kleindienst v. Mandel*, 408 U.S. at 772, 784–85.

70. "Ballad of William Worthy Lyrics," Genius, https://genius.com/Phil-ochs-ballad-of-william-worthy-lyrics.

71. Fabio Chisari, "When Football Went Global: Televising the 1966 World Cup," *Historical Social Research/Historische Sozialforschung* 31 (2006): 42–54; "Cup Soccer, at $10 to $20, Upsets TV Viewers Here," *NYT*, July 17, 1974, 9; "Fans in Millions to Lose Sleep Viewing World Cup Soccer TV," *NYT*, June 3, 1970, 42; "5 Million Saw Super Bowl TV," *LA Times*, February 7, 1967, C4; "Packers Blast Chiefs," *Chicago Daily Defender*, January 16, 1967, 28.

CONCLUSION

1. "U.S. Foreign Born Population Trends," Pew Research Center, September 28, 2015, https://www.pewresearch.org/hispanic/2015/09/28/chapter-5-u-s-foreign-born-population-trends/.

2. Sam Lebovic, " 'Here, There, and Everywhere': The Beatles, America, and Cultural Globalization, 1964–1968," *Journal of American Studies*, 51, no. 1 (2017): 43–65; Daryl Joji Maeda, "Nomad of the Transpacific: Bruce Lee as Method," *American Quarterly* 69, no. 3 (2017): 741–61; Andrew C. McKevitt, "You Are Not Alone! Anime and the Globalizing of America," *Diplomatic History* 34, no. 5 (2010): 893–921; "World Lite: What Is Global Literature?" *N+1*, Fall 2013; Veit Erlmann, "The Aesthetics of the Global Imagination: Reflections on World Music in the 1990s," *Public Culture* 8 (1996): 467–87.

3. Van Gosse, *Where the Boys Are: Cuba, Cold War America and the Making of a New Left* (London: Verso, 1993); Todd F. Tietchen, "The Cubalogues (and After): On the Beat Literary Movement and the Early Cuban Revolution," *Arizona Quarterly: A Journal of American Literature, Culture, and Theory* 63, no. 4 (2007): 119–52; Judy Tzu-Chun Wu, *Radicals on the Road: Internationalism, Orientalism, and Feminism During the Vietnam Era* (Ithaca, NY: Cornell University Press, 2013), chaps. 4–6, 137; Sean L. Malloy, *Out of Oakland: Black Panther Party Internationalism during the Cold War* (Ithaca, NY: Cornell University Press, 2018), chap. 6, 152; Hershberger, *Traveling to Vietnam: American Peace Activists and the War* (Syracuse, NY: Syracuse University Press, 1998); Cynthia Ann Young, *Soul Power: Culture, Radicalism, and the Making of a U.S. Third World Left* (Durham, NC: Duke University Press, 2006), chap. 1; Sohail Daulatzai, *Black Star, Crescent Moon: The Muslim International and Black Freedom beyond America* (Minneapolis: University of Minnesota Press, 2012); Max Elbaum, *Revolution in the Air: Sixties Radicals Turn to Lenin, Mao and Che* (London: Verso, 2002).

4. Frazier, *East Is Black: Cold War China in the Black Radical Imagination* (Durham, NC: Duke University Press, 2015), chap. 3; Malloy, *Out of Oakland*, 18, 30; Young,

Soul Power, chap. 1, 176–79; Teishan A. Latner, *Cuban Revolution in America: Havana and the Making of a United States Left, 1968–1992* (Chapel Hill: University of North Carolina Press, 2018), chap. 1; Vanessa Freije, "The 'Emancipation of Media': Latin American Advocacy for a New International Information Order in the 1970s," *Journal of Global History* 14, no. 2 (July 2019): 308.

5. Hershberger, *Traveling to Vietnam*, 95; Tim Weiner, *Legacy of Ashes: The History of the CIA* (New York: Doubleday, 2007), 286–87; Malloy, *Out of Oakland*, chap. 6; Frazier, *East Is Black*, 141–43, 195.

6. Hershberger, *Traveling to Vietnam*, 53; Wen-chu Torrey Sun, "Regulation of the Foreign Travel of US Citizens" (PhD diss., Claremont Graduate University, 1993), 49–53; Harriette Treloar and Susan Benjamin, "Area Restrictions and the Right to Travel Abroad," *University of California Davis Law Review* 8 (1975): 426.

7. UNESCO's regional categories lumped the United States with Bermuda, Canada, Greenland, St. Pierre, and Miquelon as Northern American nations. *Many Voices, One World*, report by the International Commission for the Study of Communication Problems (Paris: UNESCO, 1980), 125, 127, 146; Kaarle Nordenstreng and Tapio Varis, *Television Traffic: A One-Way Street? A Survey and Analysis of the International Flow of Television Programme Material*, Reports and Papers on Mass Communication, 70 (Paris: UNESCO, 1974); Jeremy Tunstall, *The Media Are American: Anglo-American Media in the World* (New York: Columbia University Press, 1979).

8. UNESCO, "A Documentary History of a NWICO Seen as an Evolving and Continuous Process, 1975–1986," *Communication and Society* 19:x–xi.

9. "UNESCO to Weigh Press-Radio Plan," *NYT*, November 13, 1960, 22; Ulla Carlsson, "The Rise and Fall of NWICO," *Nordicom Review* 24, no. 2 (November 1, 2003): 35; James P. Sewell, *UNESCO and World Politics: Engaging in International Relations* (Princeton, NJ: Princeton University Press, 1975), 259; Emile McAnany, *Saving the World: A Brief History of Communication for Development and Social Change* (Urbana: University of Illinois Press, 2012), 15–16, chap. 2; Jonas Brendebach, "Towards a New International Communication Order? UNESCO, Development and National Communication Policies in the 1960s and 1970s," in *International Organizations and the Media in the Nineteenth and Twentieth Centuries: Exorbitant Expectations*, ed. Jonas Brendebach, Martin Herzer, and Heidi Tworek (London: Routledge, 2018), 160–61; Cees Hamelink, "MacBride with Hindsight," in *Beyond Cultural Imperialism: Globalisation, Communication, and the New International Order*, ed. Peter Golding and Phil Harris (London: SAGE, 1997), 72; Walter H. C. Laves and Charles A. Thomson, *UNESCO: Purpose, Progress, Prospects* (Bloomington: Indiana University Press, 1957), 59–61.

10. Vijay Prashad, *The Darker Nations: A People's History of the Third World* (New York: New Press, 2007), 45; Final Communiqué of the Conference of Bandung, April 24, 1955, cited from https://www.cvce.eu/en/obj/final_communique_of_the_asian_african_conference_of_bandung_24_april_1955-en-676237bd-72f7–471f-949a-88b6ae513585.html; James R. Brennan, "Radio Cairo and the Decolonization of East Africa, 1953–1964," in *Making a World after Empire: The Bandung Moment and Its Political Afterlives*, ed. Christopher J. Lee (Athens: Ohio University Press,

2010), 173–78; Freije, "The 'Emancipation of Media,'" 301–20; Renata Keller, "The Revolution Will Be Teletyped: Cuba's Prensa Latina News Agency and the Cold War Contest over Information," *Journal of Cold War Studies* 21, no. 3 (2019): 88–113.

11. Brendebach, "Towards a New International Communication Order?" 165; Hamelink, "MacBride with Hindsight," 70; Michelle Fawcett, "The Market for Ethics: Culture and the Neoliberal Turn at UNESCO" (PhD diss., New York University, 2009), 119; Mustapha Masmoudi, "The New World Information Order," *Journal of Communication* 29, no. 2 (Spring 1979): 172–85; McAnany, *Saving the World*, 75–85; Freije, "The 'Emancipation of Media,' " 306; Herbert I. Schiller, *Communication and Cultural Domination* (White Plains, NY: M.E. Sharpe, 1976), Ariel Dorfman and Armand Mattelart *How to Read Donald Duck: Imperialist Ideology in the Disney Comic* (New York: OR Books, 2018).

12. Freije, "The 'Emancipation of Media,' " 309; Sarah Brouillette, *UNESCO and the Fate of the Literary* (Redwood City, CA: Stanford University Press, 2019), 91; Carlsson, "The Rise and Fall of NWICO," 40; UNESCO, "A Documentary History of a NWICO Seen as an Evolving and Continuous Process, 1975–1986," 5; "Meeting of Experts on a Draft Declaration Concerning the Role of the Mass Media," UNESCO Document no. COM-74/Conf.616/5, 24–26, cited from http://unesdoc.unesco.org/images/0004/000476/047669eo.pdf; "Amendments to Draft Declaration of Fundamental Principles on the Role of Mass Media in Strengthening Peace and International Understanding and Combating War Propaganda, Racism and Apartheid," Document no. 18 c/35, 43–45, cited from http://unesdoc.unesco.org/images/0004/000476/047669eo.pdf; Michael Kaufman, "Free Press and Issue at UNESCO Meeting," *NYT*, October 28, 1976, 10.

13. "UNESCO—Tool of News Censorship," *Christian Science Monitor*, July 7, 1976, 27; "UNESCO Rejects Soviet Declaration on 'Using' Press," *CT*, November 7, 1976, 22; Brendebach, "Towards a New International Communication Order?" 165–71; Freije, "The 'Emancipation of Media,' " 314.

14. UNESCO, "A Documentary History of a NWICO," 2, 32–39; *Many Voices, One World*, 85; Freije, "The 'Emancipation of Media,' " 310; James R. Brennan, "The Cold War Battle over Global News in East Africa: Decolonization, the Free Flow of Information, and the Media Business, 1960–1980," *Journal of Global History* 10, no. 2 (July 2015): 353.

15. "East-West Battle over Media Dominates UNESCO Meeting," *WP*, October 31, 1976, 20.

16. Philip H. Power and Elie Abel, "Third World vs. the Media," *NYT*, September 21, 1980, SM29; "UNESCO Panel Shelves Plan Concerning Press," *NYT*, November 7, 1976, 16; *Many Voices, One World*, xii–xx; William Preston Jr., "The History of U.S.-UNESCO Relations," in *Hope and Folly: The United States and UNESCO, 1945–1985*, ed. William Preston, Edward S. Herman, and Herbert I. Schiller (Minneapolis: University of Minnesota Press, 1989), 120–47; Altaf Gauhar and Amadou Mahtar M'Bow, "Amadou Mahtar M'Bow," *Third World Quarterly* 6 (April 1984): 265–71; Hamelink, "MacBride with Hindsight," 74–75; Rosemary Righter, "Who Won?" *Journal of Communication* 29 (1979): 192–94.

17. William Fitzmaurice, "The New World Information and Communication Order: Is the International Program for the Development of Communication the Answer?" *NYU Journal of International Law and Politics* 15 (1983): 960–62, 989–93.

18. Edward S. Herman, "U.S, Mass Media Coverage of the U.S. Withdrawal from UNESCO," in *Hope and Folly: The United States and UNESCO, 1945–1985*, ed. William Preston, Edward S. Herman, and Herbert I. Schiller (Minneapolis: University of Minnesota Press, 1989), 258, 266; Preston, "The History of U.S.-UNESCO Relations," 126–37, 156–58; "Keep the Pressure on UNESCO," *NYT*, December 6, 1984, A30; "GAO Is Critical of UNESCO Policies," *NYT*, December 9, 1984, 9; "Study by Congress Faults UNESCO and Places Blame on Its Director," *NYT*, September 21, 1984, A4; "US Move Praised by Conservatives," *NYT*, December 20, 1984, A10; "Text of Declaration by Independent News Organizations on Freedom of the Press," *NYT*, May 18, 1981, 14; "West's News Organizations Vow to Fight UNESCO on Press Curbs," *NYT*, May 18, 1981, 1; "Reporter Licensing Weighed by UNESCO," *NYT*, February 15, 1981, 11; "House Threatens a UNESCO Cutoff," *NYT*, September 18, 1981, A3; "State Department Authority," *CQ Almanac 1981 Online Edition*, available at https://library.cqpress.com/cqalmanac/document.php?id=cqal81-1172058.

19. "Press Freedom Advocates Are Gaining, Not Losing, at UNESCO," *NYT*, January 31, 1984, A22; "Defogging UNESCO," *NYT*, February 25, 1984, 22; "US to Withdraw from UNESCO at End of Year," *NYT*, December 20, 1984, A1; Preston, "The History of U.S.-UNESCO Relations," 177, 195; Christopher C. Joyner and Scott A. Lawson, "The United States and UNESCO: Rethinking the Decision to Withdraw," *International Journal* 41 (1986): 47; Joseph Mehan, "U.S. Decision to Withdraw from UNESCO: Responses," *Journal of Communication* 34, no. 4 (Autumn 1984): 123; *Assessment of U.S.-UNESCO Relations: Report of a Study Mission to Paris-UNESCO to the Committee on Foreign Affairs, House of Representatives* (Washington, DC: Government Printing Office, 1985): 5, 48–52; "US Considers Withdrawing from UNESCO," *Christian Science Monitor*, December 23, 1983, 1.

20. James Traub, "U.S., Stay in UNESCO," *NYT*, November 28, 1984, A27.

21. Helsinki Final Act, cited from https://www.osce.org/helsinki-final-act?download=true.

22. That is not to say that the Helsinki accords were the primary, let alone the sole, cause of the collapse of communism. Michael Cotey Morgan, *The Final Act: The Helsinki Accords and the Transformation of the Cold War* (Princeton, NJ: Princeton University Press, 2018); Sarah B. Snyder, *Human Rights Activism and the End of the Cold War: A Transnational History of the Helsinki Network* (New York: Cambridge University Press, 2011).

23. Victor Sebestyen, *Revolution 1989: The Fall of the Soviet Empire* (New York: Vintage, 2009), 69; Morgan, *The Final Act*, 8, 67, 71, 117, chap. 6; Daniel J. Sargent, *A Superpower Transformed: The Remaking of American Foreign Relations in the 1970s* (Oxford: Oxford University Press, 2014), 216; Mark Mazower, *Governing the World: The History of an Idea* (New York: Penguin, 2012), 307–10; David Milne, *Worldmaking: The Art and Science of American Diplomacy* (New York: Farrar, Straus and Giroux, 2015), chap. 7.

24. Morgan, *The Final Act*, 200, 213, 223–24; Sarah B. Snyder, " 'Jerry, Don't Go': Domestic Opposition to the 1975 Helsinki Final Act," *Journal of American Studies* 44 no. 1 (February 2010): 67–81; Snyder, *Human Rights Activism and the End of the Cold War*, chap. 2, 83.

25. Snyder, *Human Rights Activism and the End of the Cold War*, chap. 4, 85–86; Morgan, *The Final Act*, 227.

26. "Last Travel Curbs Removed by Carter," *NYT*, March 10, 1977, 11; Daniel A. Farber, "National Security, the Right to Travel and the Court," *Supreme Court Review* 1981 (1981): 282–84.

27. Eugene Clark Lutz, "President Carter's Attempt to Halt Travel to Iran and the Constitutional Right to Travel," *Syracuse Journal of International Law and Commerce* 9 (1982): 115–36; John Spencer Nichols, "Testing the Constitutionality of U.S. Licensing of News Gatherers and Researchers Traveling to Cuba," *Journal of Government Information* 25, no. 3 (1998): 228, 232; Jinx Coleman Broussard and Skye Chance Cooley, "William Worthy (Jr): The Man and the Mission," *Journalism Studies* 10, no. 3 (June 2009): 386–400; "High Court Restores Curbs on Tourist Travel to Cuba," *NYT*, June 29, 1984, A1; Anne E. Kershaw, "Constitutional Law–International Travel–Restrictions on Travel-Related Transactions under the Cuban Embargo–*Regan v. Wald*," *NYU Law School Law Review* 31 (1986): 213; "Qaddafi 'a Pariah,' " *NYT*, January 8, 1986, A1; "U.S. Lifts Travel Ban on Libya," Treasury Department Press Release, February 26, 2004, https://www.treasury.gov/press-center/press-releases/Pages/js1197.aspx; Michael J. Bustamante, "The Cuban Revolution," in *Oxford Research Encyclopedia of American History* (Oxford: Oxford University Press, 2019); Farber, "National Security, the Right to Travel and the Court," 264; Kaeten Mistry, "A Transnational Protest against the National Security State: Whistle-Blowing, Philip Agee, and Networks of Dissent," *Journal of American History* 106, no. 2 (September 2019): 362–89.

28. "Plan to Ease Visa Policy for Communists Facing Tough Foe," *WP*, April 18, 1977, A9; Susan Mann, "Monopoly in the Marketplace: The Ideological Denial of Visas," *Law and Policy* 9 (October 1987): 421–27; "Reprise on McCarran Act," *NYT*, June 4, 1982, B1; "Why Are Some Excluded?" *WP*, March 15, 1986, A22; Burt Neuborne and Steven R. Shapiro, "The Nylon Curtain: America's National Border and the Free Flow of Ideas," *William & Mary Law Review* 26, no. 5 (1985): 725–27; "The Unwelcome Mat Is Out for Ideological Undesirables," *NYT*, July 15, 1984, 166; "Do Not Enter," *Boston Globe Magazine*, February 17, 1985, 12; Steven R. Shapiro, "Ideological Exclusions: Closing the Border to Political Dissidents," *Harvard Law Review* 100, no. 4 (February 1987): 930–45; Julia Rose Kraut, *Threat of Dissent: A History of Ideological Exclusion and Deportation in the United States* (Cambridge, MA: Harvard University Press, 2020), chap. 7.

29. David Rothkopf, "In Praise of Cultural Imperialism?" *Foreign Policy* (Summer 1997): 38–53; Josef Joffe, "America the Inescapable," *NYT, Magazine*, June 8, 1997, 39; "Full Text of Clinton's Speech on China Trade Bill," *NYT*, March 9, 2000, cited from https://movies2.nytimes.com/library/world/asia/030900clinton-china-text.html.

30. Kahn, *Mrs. Shipley's Ghost*.

31. Although the majority opinion cited *Mandel* to support the proposition that it could uphold any "facially legitimate and bona fide" order, it nevertheless went a little beyond this extremely deferential standard by also applying a "rational basis review" of the order—which it comfortably passed. *Trump v. Hawaii,* 585 U.S. (2018); "Trump's Travel Ban: How It Works and Who Is Affected," *NYT,* July 1, 2018, 8; Paul A. Kramer, "Enemies of the State," *Slate*, June 29, 2018, https://slate.com/news-and-politics/2018/06/trump-travel-ban-the-supreme-court-has-long-enabled-executive-power-to-discriminate.html; Vahid Niayesh, "Statistics Show That Trump's "Travel Ban" Was Always a Muslim Ban," *Quartz*, October 28, 2019, https://qz.com/1736809/statistics-show-that-trumps-travel-ban-was-always-a-muslim-ban/.

32. "A Harvard Freshman Says He Was Denied Entry to the U.S. over Social Media Posts Made by His Friends," *WP*, August 27, 2019; "ICE Restrictions on International Students a 'Self-Inflicted Wound,'" *Foreign Policy*, July 10, 2020; "U.S. Travel Ban Disrupts the World's Largest Brain Science Meeting," *NPR*, October 24, 2019; "U.S. Broadcasting Agency Will Not Extend Visas for Its Foreign Journalists," *NPR*, July 9, 2020; "ICE Agrees to Rescind Policy Barring Foreign Students from Online Study in the U.S," *NPR*, July 14, 2020; "U.S. to Expel Chinese Graduate Students with Ties to China's Military Schools," *NYT*, May 28, 2020; "Trump Administration Orders Four Chinese News Outlets in U.S. to Reduce Staffs," *NYT*, March 2, 2020; "The Trump Administration Is Moving to Restrict International Students. Why That's a Bad Idea," *WP*, June 18, 2020; "U.S. Hits Back at China with New Visa Restrictions on Journalists," *NYT*, May 9, 2020.

33. Phillip W. Jones and David Coleman, *The United Nations and Education: Multilateralism, Development, and Globalisation* (London: Routledge, 2005), 72; "UNESCO Accepts Palestinians as Full Members," *NYT*, October 31, 2011, 8; "U.S. Will Withdraw from UNESCO, Citing Its 'Anti-Israel Bias,'" *NYT*, October 12, 2017, 6; Zack Beauchamp, "Here's What UNESCO Is—and Why the Trump Administration Just Quit It," *Vox*, October 12, 2017, https://www.vox.com/world/2017/10/12/16464778/unesco-us-withdrawal-trump.

34. "What Americans Need to Know About Europe's Travel Ban," *NYT*, July 7, 2020, https://www.nytimes.com/article/eu-travel-ban-explained-usa.html; Indi Samarajiva, "American Passports Are Worthless Now," *Medium*, July 9, 2020, https://medium.com/indica/the-plague-states-of-america-53b20678a80e.

INDEX